The Standard Handbook of Business Communication

The Standard Handbook of Business Communication

David E. Gootnick and Margaret Mary Gootnick
Editors

THE FREE PRESS
A Division of Macmillan, Inc.
NEW YORK

Collier Macmillan Publishers
LONDON

The Free Press
A Division of Macmillan, Inc.
866 Third Avenue, New York, N.Y. 10022

Collier Macmillan Canada, Inc.

Printed in the United States of America

printing number

1 2 3 4 5 6 7 8 9 10

Library of Congress Cataloging in Publication Data

Main entry under title:

The Standard handbook of business communication.

Includes index.
1. Communication in management—Addresses, essays, lectures. I. Gootnick, David E. II. Gootnick, Margaret Mary.
HF5718.S69 1984 658.4'5 83-48527
ISBN 0-02-912660-6

Contents

Section III Interactional Communication

Section IV Organizational Communication

Section V Foundations and Frontiers

About the Handbook

The Standard Handbook of Business Communication is a comprehensive and authoritative source of instructional concepts, strategies, methods, and materials for students of education and for seasoned educators teaching business communication subjects. This new resource was conceived to fill a need deeply felt by active leaders in the business communication profession for a respected professional handbook which would help assure quality instruction.

More than at any other time, business communication skills are critical to the success of individuals in business and industry. Because of this, countless courses in business communication are being offered. They are delivered in four-year colleges and universities, graduate programs, community colleges, secondary schools, vocational-technical schools, adult education centers, and business schools.

Professionals concerned with business communication instruction come from many disciplines: business communication, business and office education, English, speech, technical writing, vocational and technical education, adult education, and mass communication. In addition, because of its interdisciplinary nature, business communication is important to professionals in many other fields as well.

The Handbook is the result of the combined talent and experience of twenty-seven contributing authors—all of whom are active professionals, speakers, and writers in the business communication field. Within these chapters, the contributing authors share highly effective techniques for transforming important communication training needs into quality learning experiences.

The Handbook provides comprehensive coverage of the dynamic field of business communication, with subjects ranging from the job search, report writing, and nonverbal communication to communication theory, effective speaking, and organizational communication. Its twenty-one chapters are organized into five major sections:

I. Career Planning and Development
II. Written Communication
III. Interactional Communication
IV. Organizational Communication
V. Foundations and Frontiers

With an ever-growing demand for quality programs, business communication instruction requires excellence in instructional strategies and training methods. *The Standard Handbook of Business Communication* is a new and effective tool to help professionals meet the challenge.

Special appreciation goes to Burton C. Gabriel, Senior Editor, The Free Press, and all the authors for their excellent contributions and commitment to this important professional resource.

David E. Gootnick
Margaret Mary Gootnick

About the Authors

VANESSA DEAN ARNOLD teaches business communication at the University of Mississippi. An Associate Professor, Dr. Arnold has had teaching experience at the secondary, junior college, and university levels, and with the American Institute of Banking. She has had articles published in the *ABCA Bulletin, NBEA Forum, Journal of Business Education, Mississippi's Business,* and the *NABTE Review.* Additionally, Dr. Arnold has presented papers at both regional and national conferences of the American Business Communication Association. Her degrees were earned at the University of Alabama and the University of Florida.

LELAND BROWN is Professor Emeritus of Business Communication at Eastern Michigan University and has taught at Tulane University and the University of Illinois. He has obtained his B.A. and M.A. degrees from Indiana State University, and he has done advanced graduate work at the University of Illinois.

His books include *Communicating Facts and Ideas in Business,* 3d edition, 1982, and *Effective Business Report Writing,* 4th edition, in progress. He is a Fellow, Past President, and Sustaining Member of the American Business Communication Association. He is also an active member of the Midwest Business Administration Association, Delta Sigma Pi, Beta Gamma Sigma, Phi Kappa Phi, and of church, community, and university organizations.

A recipient of Eastern Michigan University's Distinguished Faculty Award, Leland Brown is listed in numerous directories as well as in Marquis's *Who's Who in America* and *Who's Who in the Midwest.*

E. RENNIE CHARLES majored in English language and literature at the University of Toronto, and he began his career in communication as a technical officer in the Canadian Army Signal Corps. He later received master's degrees in library science and education.

During his thirty-five years as teacher, professor, and administrator at the Ryerson Polytechnical Institute in Toronto, he also held senior posts in the

English Department and School of Journalism and became founding Chairman of the Business and Technical Communication Department. As a consultant, he has served many business and professional organizations.

A Past President and Fellow of the American Business Communication Association, Rennie Charles is also an Associate Fellow of the Society for Technical Communication. He is an active writer, editor, and critic and a contributing author of the book *International Business Communication: Theory, Practice, Teaching Throughout the World* by Herbert W. Hildebrandt et al. (University of Michigan and American Business Communication Association, 1981).

PETER B. CLARKE took his baccalaureate degree at DePaul University and graduate degree at Purdue University. Having more than twenty years experience in advertising, he has been a copywriter, account supervisor, and advertising director, and he has also worked with trade magazines. He is the author of *Modern Business Correspondence* (McGraw-Hill) and *Communicating Through Letters and Reports* (Richard D. Irwin, Inc.) and has published numerous articles in the field of business communication. He is a senior member of both the American Business Communication Association and the Society for Technical Communication. He presently is President of Arcus Company, a business communication consulting firm in Chicago.

NANCY A. DITTMAN, Associate Professor at Bloomsburg State University in Pennsylvania, has taught business communication at most levels throughout the country. After Dr. Dittman obtained her Ed.D. degree from the University of Colorado, her special interest in nonlecture instruction led her to experiment and write on individualized instruction, group work, contracts, and the use of nonverbal techniques by teachers. In addition, job-search techniques, especially resumes, have been the subject of several funded projects she has directed.

GEORGE H. DOUGLAS is the Editor of Special Publications of the American Business Communication Association. For twelve years he served as Editor of the *Journal of Business Communication*. He is also a Professor of Business and Technical Writing in the Department of English at the University of Illinois. He is the author of many articles and books and has a keen interest in technical and business history. His most recent book is *Rail City: Chicago U.S.A.*, an informal pictorial history of Chicago as a railroad town. He has recently completed two other books, one of which is a social history of radio broadcasting in the 1920s.

DORIS D. ENGERRAND is Professor and Chairperson of the Business Education and Office Administration Department at Georgia College. Dr. Engerrand has twenty years of teaching experience, including elementary grades, high school, and college. She also has sixteen years business experience. She is a member of the Board of Directors of the American Business Communication Association and a member of numerous other professional organizations. In addition, she is a consultant to business and industry in the middle-Georgia area.

RAYMOND L. FALCIONE is Associate Professor in the Department of Communication, University of Maryland. He is Director of the Speech Communication Division at the University of Maryland and is the chairperson of the Organizational Communication Division of the International Communication Association. His selected publications have appeared in *Human Communication Research, ICA Communication Yearbook I, Personnel Journal, Journal of Business Communication, Journal of Applied Communications Research,* and *Nursing Research.* He is also coauthor, with Howard H. Greenbaum, of *Organizational Communication Abstracts,* Volumes 1 through 7, and has a forthcoming book entitled *Communication in Government Service.* Dr. Falcione has conducted communication audits in various organizational settings and has consulted for numerous government agencies, private corporations, and service organizations.

GERALD M. GOLDHABER is Associate Professor and Chairman of the Department of Communication at the State University of New York at Buffalo. He also serves as President of Goldhaber Research Associates, a polling and market research firm with offices in Las Vegas, Buffalo, and London. As the author of eleven books, numerous articles, and hundreds of presentations, he is acknowledged as one of the nation's leading experts on communication.

DAVID E. GOOTNICK is Director of David Gootnick Associates, a New York-based management consulting firm. He is a nationally recognized authority in management, communication, and career planning and the author or editor of numerous books, journals, and articles, including the popular books *Even You Can Give a Talk* (David Gootnick Associates) and *Getting A Better Job* (McGraw-Hill).

Dr. Gootnick served as Chairman of the Teaching Methodology and Concepts Committee of the American Business Communication Association and is the founder of the *Virginia Business Education Journal.*

He is an active consultant, trainer, and lecturer and has offered many seminars, workshops, and courses to thousands of managers and executives representing a cross-section of the corporate and government communities. In addition, he has been a professor of business at a major urban university for several years.

Dr. Gootnick is involved in many professional organizations, including the American Business Communication Association, the American Management Associations, the American Society for Training and Development, and the National Business Education Association.

MARGARET MARY GOOTNICK is Associate Director of David Gootnick Associates, a New York–based management consulting firm. She is an active trainer and consultant and has assisted thousands of executives and professionals from major corporations through her seminars, professional courses, and career counseling.

She presents top-rated programs in leadership, communication, management, presentation skills, and marketing. She has served on the faculties of such institutions as New York University's Business Management Institute, National Association of Accountants, American Management Associations, Marymount Manhattan College, and Triton College Employee Development Institute.

Margaret Mary Gootnick achieved distinction in various business positions and has served as editor of several business publications. In addition, she is the management columnist for a leading industrial newspaper.

LARRY D. HARTMAN is currently Manager of Documentation and Manual Development for Zenith Data Systems, Zenith Corporation, Chicago, Illinois. He directs the development and documentation of software for microcomputers. He also supervises technical writers and assists with training programs.

Until January 1982 he directed the graduate study program in Business Education and Administrative Services at Northern Illinois University, DeKalb, Illinois. He served as the coordinator of the Business Communication Studies area for the College of Business. He also served as a doctoral program director and taught communication theory, principles of business communication, report writing, business fundamentals of communication, and graduate principles and pedagogy courses.

He has served as an officer and director of the American Business Communication Association since 1977. Currently he is serving as President of the Association.

Dr. Hartman has published regularly in both business and communication periodicals. Additionally, he consults for businesses and universities. Wurlitizer Corporation; Kemper Insurance; Scouts of America; Zenith Corporation; University of Wisconsin; University of North Carolina; Tribhuvan University, Nepal; and University of Northern Iowa are included.

RICHARD A. HATCH teaches in the Information Systems Department at San Diego University. He is author of several textbooks on business communication and information systems, including *Business Communication: Theory and Technique* and *Business Writing,* both published by Science Research Associates.

William C. Himstreet is the author of seven books on communication in business, as well as numerous articles and monographs. Dr. Himstreet's major interest is educational delivery systems resulting in an improved classroom learning environment. He is a Fellow of the American Business Communication Association, a corporate director, a university trustee, and Professor Emeritus of Business Communication at the University of Southern California.

Debra Jones is manager of CHAMPUS Claims of Blue Cross/Blue Shield of South Carolina. She was manager of word processing at Blue Cross/Blue Shield for four years.

Ms. Jones conducted summer workshops for teachers of word processing in South Carolina. She was also a part-time instructor of word processing at Lexington County High School, evening division.

She is a member of International Word Processing and has served as the Secretary and President-Elect of its Columbia, South Carolina, chapter.

James M. Lahiff is an Associate Professor of Management in the College of Business Administration at the University of Georgia. He received his Ph.D. from The Pennsylvania State University, a master's degree from the University of Wisconsin–Milwaukee, and an undergraduate degree from St. Norbert College. His teaching specialties include communication, personnel interviewing, compensation administration, and small-group processes. Dr. Lahiff's articles on these subjects have appeared in various scholarly and practioner-oriented journals and magazines. He is the coauthor of several textbooks on management and communication. He has conducted many training programs for a wide variety of private and governmental organizations.

Phillip V. Lewis is a Professor of Management in the College of Business Administration at Abilene Christian University. Prior to joining the Abilene Christian University faculty, he was affiliated with Oklahoma State University and with Northern Arizona University. He has also worked in retail sales and banking. Dr. Lewis has authored five textbooks, ten chapters or monographs, over thirty articles, eight structured experiences, five training manuals, and one video tape. He also has presented over twenty papers to learned associations. In addition to his academic duties, Dr. Lewis is president of a Texas-based consulting group, Creative Management Associates. He has conducted numerous seminars for business and industry, education, and government.

CHERYL M. LUKE is an Associate Professor in the Management Program, College of Business Administration, University of South Carolina, Columbia. She currently teaches administrative systems and business communication courses at the University. She earned a Ph.D. in business education at Indiana University.

Dr. Luke has been a speaker at state, regional, and national business education conferences and workshops. She also frequently conducts seminars for office workers. She is very active in numerous professional organizations and is coauthor of *Office Systems and Procedures,* published by Houghton Mifflin Company.

LORRAINE MISSLING is a Professor of Business in the Department of Business Education and Information Management at the University of Wisconsin–Eau Claire. Dr. Missling has coached parliamentary procedure teams for the past twenty-five years. Her Phi Beta Lambda parliamentary procedure teams have placed in the top ten in the nation for seventeen years, and several groups have ranked first in the nation. She is a member of the National Association of Parliamentarians and has conducted numerous workshops on parliamentary procedure.

HERMAN F. PATTERSON is Chairman of the Office Administration Department at Memphis State University. He has served as a member of the Institute for Certifying Secretaries and was Dean of the Institute from 1974 to 1976. He is an international honorary member of Professional Secretaries International.

An active and participating member of many professional organizations, Dr. Patterson was the 1983 President of the Southern Business Education Association and a member of the Executive Board of the National Business Education Association. He is also a charter member of Office Systems Research Association.

DONALD P. ROGERS is Associate Professor of Management and Organizational Behavior in the School of Business at the State University of New York at Geneseo. He also serves as the Director of the college's Survey Information Research Center. Dr. Rogers is the author of more than two dozen books and articles on organizational communication, corporate strategy, and industrial development.

TIKA NATH SHARMA is currently a Professor of Business at the College of the Bahamas, Nassau, Bahamas. He serves as department chairman and assists Nassau's business and professional organizations.

He is on leave from the Institute of Technical Education, Tribhuvan University, Nepal, where he is a tenured lecturer. His teaching specialties include business communication and information management.

Dr. Sharma received his doctorate from Northern Illinois University. He received his master's of business degree from Brigham Young University, Provo, Utah. He also possesses bachelor's and master's degrees from Tri Chondra College, Katmandu, Nepal.

He is an editor of business education periodicals in Nepal. Additionally, he contributes regularly to *The Rising Star,* the Kingdom of Nepal's major newspaper.

NORMAN B. SIGBAND is Professor of Management Communication in the Graduate School of Business of the University of Southern California.

His recent books, *Communication for Management and Business,* 3d edition, 1982; *Communicating in Business* (with D. Bateman), 1981; and *Successful Business English,* 1983 (all published by Scott Foresman) are used in over five-hundred colleges and universities. He has also authored over seventy-five journal articles in the field of business and communication.

Dr. Sigband has received the USC's prestigious Excellence in Teaching Award and is listed in *Who's Who in America.* He is also a widely recognized consultant and has worked with dozens of America's blue chip corporations, such as Hughes Aircraft, AT&T, Santa Fe, Lockheed Aircraft, Illinois Bell Telephone, and the Edison companies; and with the cities of Chicago and Los Angeles.

BOBBYE D. SORRELS teaches in the College of Business Administration at the University of Oregon. She is also a former Chairperson of the Department of General Business at Central (Oklahoma) State University and has served as a Professor of Business for twenty-three years, teaching courses on business communication, business research methods, business statistics, and women in management.

Dr. Sorrels has written the following books: *Business Communication Dynamics,* published by Charles E. Merrill, 1981; *Business Communication Fundamentals,* published by Charles E. Merrill, 1984; and *The Nonsexist Communicator,* published by Prentice-Hall, 1983.

She is active in professional organizations and as a speaker and leader of seminars and workshops on communication.

DOROTHY L. TRAVIS is Special Consultant in Business Education, Grand Forks School District, Grand Forks, North Dakota. She has been the coauthor of business textbooks, editor of yearbooks, and author of numerous articles on business education. She has lectured widely on business education in the United States and Canada.

Ms. Travis has been President of the National Business Education Association and Chairman of the FBLA–PBL (Future Business Leaders of America–Phi Beta Lambda) Parliamentary Procedure events since 1957. The Dorothy L. Travis Parliamentary Procedure Award, presented to winning teams in the FBLA–PBL national competition, is named in her honor. Ms. Travis has conducted numerous workshops on parliamentary procedure and is the current Vice-Chairman of the National Association of Parliamentarians in North Dakota.

MALRA TREECE is a Professor of Business Communication in the Fogelman College of Business and Economics, Memphis State University.

She earned a B.S. degree from Arkansas State University, an M.A. from Memphis State University, and a Ph.D. from the University of Mississippi.

She wrote *Communication for Business and the Professions,* Revised Edition, Allyn and Bacon, Boston, 1983. Other books include *Successful Business Writing,* 1980, and *Effective Reports,* 1982, both from Allyn and Bacon.

She serves on the Board of Directors of the American Business Communication Association and was formerly Vice President, Southeast Region.

ALFRED B. WILLAMS is an Associate Professor in the Department of Office Administration, College of Business Administration at the University of Southwestern Louisiana in Lafayette, Louisiana. He holds a Ph.D. in business education from George State University in Atlanta.

Dr. Williams has been actively involved in numerous professional organizations and is under contract with John Wiley & Sons. He has been teaching business communication courses at USL for eight years.

Section I

Career Planning and Development

Chapter 1

Career Planning and Job-Search Communication

David E. Gootnick

Margaret Mary Gootnick

THE BUSINESS COMMUNICATION COURSE is often the only place in the curriculum where students are required to seriously consider the subject of employment. For the first time, students must come to grips with the problems that lie beyond graduation, namely, their jobs and careers. Business communication teachers are, therefore, in a unique position to make a major impact on the lives of their students.

In this chapter, instructional concepts, strategies, and exercises are provided to help you make your employment unit an interesting and relevant learning segment and an educational experience that will be useful to your students long after graduation. In addition, you may use the contents of this chapter to help you develop and deliver a full or short course on career planning and job-search communication.

Five employment modules are presented here:

1. Career planning
2. Job campaigning
3. Resumes
4. Job letters
5. Job interviews

1. Career Planning

The standard teaching objective for the business communication unit on employment is the development of job-search skills and knowledge, including the writing of resumes and letters, as well as the handling of job interviews. While such an objective is, without question, central to our concern, we can do more to enhance the value of the employment unit.

Career planning can be integrated easily and naturally into the introductory lessons on employment with some excellent instructional payoffs: increased student enthusiasm, greater student commitment, and better-quality student projects.

Most college students—even juniors and graduating seniors committed to professional degree programs—have only vague notions about their careers. They lack any real understanding of short- and long-range career opportunities, job requirements, and demands, and of the essential knowledge, skills, and personal sacrifices for career success.

Even amidst all the talk about career education, college students are still haphazardly channeled into careers based on family expectations, popular fads, economic concerns, and romanticized versions of occupations conjured up from television and movies. Through our instruction in the area of career planning, we can play an important role in the lives of our students while enhancing our instructional effectiveness in related areas of the course.

Begin the employment unit by informing your students that they will be required to write a resume and job letters and even take a simulated job interview for the jobs they plan to obtain upon graduation. Explain that it is important to prepare realistic job communications that may have immediate and practical application upon graduation.

This practical approach to the employment unit is usually met with great approval by students but, at the same time, is a source of concern for many who have never seriously considered their own career plans. Help to alleviate such concern at this point by informing students of your intention in the career planning area.

These four learning-activity areas constitute solid coverage of the career planning module:

1. Introductory career exercises
2. Self-analysis
3. Job-market analysis
4. The career planning report

Let us now examine the various learning activities that you may provide to satisfy the career planning needs of your students within the business communication course.

Introductory Career Exercises

The Career Visualization Exercise and The Career Awareness Exercise are two excellent initial experiences that serve to make students aware of the need for career planning.

The Career Visualization Exercise

This is an in-class student activity in which you have your students look into their futures. Give your students the following directions:

> Close your eyes and visualize yourself five years from now. What are you doing and where are you working? Do you work alone or with others?

Allow a couple of minutes for this silent and thoughtful visualization activity. Ask students to refrain from responding aloud until you've completed the activity. Then, continue:

> What did you do to get to this position? What were some of your accomplishments and some of the obstacles? How do you feel about yourself and your progress?

Allow another few minutes for silent visualization, and then solicit open feedback from the students, having them report about their visualization experience. Some students may be able to see clear career paths to practical five-year career goals, while others will find the experience more difficult.

In general, this initial experience in career visualization allows you the opportunity to define a career as "a progression of related job responsibilities over time." Furthermore, you can point out that people who do not attempt to plan their careers are at a distinct disadvantage in the job market.

The Career Awareness Exercise

This activity can be performed in class or as a take-home assignment. Ask your students to provide the following information about their tentative career plans:

1. The titles of two possible positions that could be obtained upon graduation, in two years, five years, and ten years
2. A brief paragraph below each job title describing the basic job requirements

Insist that students complete this assignment without consulting others or referring to published sources on careers. In your follow-up discussion to this assignment, have students share their impressions about the value of the exercise and the problems encountered in doing it.

The results of this discussion will poignantly demonstrate the need for preparing a career plan.

Self-Analysis

Self-analysis helps students to discover themselves by identifying their strengths, interests, preferences, and aptitudes, along with their weaknesses, limitations, and dislikes. Students who know themselves can make more intelligent career decisions, matching their strengths and interests with available jobs in the job market.

Several excellent self-analysis exercises are presented here. Select those student exercises which you believe will provide sufficient basis for student self-discovery, or use all the exercises together in a comprehensive battery. In each exercise, students perform the necessary self-analysis independently.

You can incorporate the results of these individual learning experiences within your class discussion by having students share information from their self-analyses with their classmates.

NEWSPAPER JOB-INTEREST EXERCISE

1. Purchase a Sunday edition of your local newspaper, a Sunday *New York Times,* or the daily *Wall Street Journal.*
2. Examine the classified section for job advertisements. As you identify jobs that you would be interested in upon graduation, in two years, five years, or even ten years, clip them out.
3. Paste the ads within the same period on the same page. For example, all jobs of interest to you upon graduation would be pasted on the same page; all jobs of interest to you in two years would be pasted on the same page, etc.
4. Now, identify the key personal qualities and job requirements desired for each job.
5. Prepare a summary of key personal qualities and job requirements for each group of job ads that you collected.

INTERVIEW FEEDBACK EXERCISE

1. Interview ten individuals who know you well. They may include such individuals as personal friends, teachers, parents, advisers, co-workers, and bosses.
2. Within each interview, find out what each person believes your strengths, abilities, and talents are. Also, find out what type of career each person believes you would be successful in and why. Finally, ask for ways you can improve yourself.
3. Write up a summary of each interview.

4. *Caution:* When asking others for critical and honest feedback about you as a person, you must be able to accept any information you receive in the constructive vein in which it is being offered. Remember, you may hear things you like, as well as things you don't. Any defensiveness or anger on your part will only serve to stop further communication between you and the person you're interviewing. Therefore be open-minded and listen.

Personal Trait Checklist

Directions: Read each word or phrase below and decide whether it describes you. Check the items that do describe you. Upon completing this checklist, write a summary statement, describing both your positive and negative attributes.

_____ Alert
_____ Honest
_____ Insecure
_____ Logical
_____ Results-oriented
_____ Discourteous
_____ Evasive
_____ Energetic
_____ Trustworthy
_____ Optimistic
_____ Condescending
_____ Creative
_____ Steady
_____ Naïve
_____ Contradictory
_____ Abrupt
_____ Accurate
_____ Dishonest
_____ Sincere
_____ Courageous
_____ Long-winded
_____ Grateful
_____ Tactful
_____ Sloppy
_____ Indifferent
_____ Humorous
_____ Analytical
_____ Motivated
_____ Conceited
_____ Timid
_____ Intuitive
_____ Poor listener
_____ Good appearance
_____ Likable
_____ Unambitious
_____ Witty
_____ Imaginative
_____ Persuasive
_____ Cold and distant
_____ Fearful
_____ Negative
_____ Decisive
_____ Gentle
_____ Enterprising
_____ Private
_____ Able
_____ Sensitive
_____ Risk-taker
_____ Giving
_____ Outgoing
_____ Good listener
_____ Independent
_____ Resourceful
_____ Passive
_____ Sophisticated
_____ Energetic
_____ Patient
_____ Conscientious
_____ Businesslike
_____ Intelligent

Summary Statement

Self-Evaluation Work Sheet

One important aspect of choosing a position is understanding yourself. Self-evaluation can help you analyze what is important to you in the kind of work you will do and the kind of organization in which you will work.

The following are some of the things you should consider in your own self-evaluation. Your answers should be honest. They are meant to help you and should not represent a "good" or "bad" value judgment.

1. What are the things you do best? Are they related to people, data, things?
   ______ related to ______
   ______ related to ______
   ______ related to ______

2. Do you express yourself well and easily?
   Orally: Yes ____ No ____ In writing: Yes ____ No ____

3. Do you see yourself as a leader of a group or team? Yes ____ No ____
   Do you see yourself as an active participant of a group or team? Yes ____ No ____
   Do you prefer to work on your own? Yes ____ No ____
   Do you like supervision? Yes ____ No ____

4. Do you work well under pressure? Yes ____ No ____
   Does pressure cause you anxiety; in fact, is it difficult for you to work well under pressure? Yes ____ No ____

5. Do you seek responsibility? Yes ____ No ____
   Do you prefer to follow directions? Yes ____ No ____

6. Do you enjoy new ideas and situations? Yes ____ No ____
   Are you more comfortable with known routines? Yes ____ No ____

7. In your future, which of the following things are most important to you:
   a. Working for a regular salary ____ b. Working for a commission ____
   c. Working for a combination of both ____

8. Do you want to work a regular schedule (e.g., 9 A.M. to 5 P.M.)? Yes ____ No ____

9. Are you willing to travel more than 50 percent of your working time?
   Yes ____ No ____

10. What kind of environment is important to you?
    a. Do you prefer to work indoors? Yes ____ No ____
    b. Do you prefer to work outdoors? Yes ____ No ____
    c. Do you prefer an urban environment (population over a million)?
       Yes ____ No ____
       Population between 100,000 to 900,000? Yes ____ No ____
    d. Do you prefer a rural setting? Yes ____ No ____

11. Do you prefer to work for a large organization? Yes ____ No ____

12. Are you free to move? Yes ____ No ____
    Are there important "others" to be considered? Yes ____ No ____

Self-Analysis Questionnaire

Directions: Answer each question as honestly and completely as possible.

1. What natural abilities do you have?

2. What do you like most about yourself?

3. What do you like least about yourself?

4. What are some of your greatest accomplishments?

5. What things give you the greatest satisfaction?

6. What things get you frustrated and angry?

7. What are your weakest personal traits?

8. What are your strongest personal traits?

9. How can you improve yourself?

10. How have you grown in the last year?

Directions: Fill out the Personal Inventory Form as completely as possible. The information you collect here will help you to better understand yourself and will constitute your data base for preparing resumes and job letters.

If necessary, photocopy different sections of the Personal Inventory Form. For example, if you've attended two colleges, you would fill out two Education sheets; or if you've held four part-time jobs, you would fill out four copies of the form entitled Part-Time, Paid Employment.

Do not fill out the sections entitled "Job Objective" and "References" during the self-analysis. These should, however, be filled out later before preparing your resume and job letters.

Personal Inventory Form

(name)

JOB OBJECTIVE

(Indicate various positions for which you qualify and business, industry, or profession which is of prime interest)

REFERENCES

(Indicate that references will be furnished upon request, or list names, positions, addresses, and telephone numbers of references which would be approved)

PERSONAL STATISTICS

NAME ____________________

CURRENT ADDRESS ____________________
(Building Number and Street)

____
(City) (State) (Zip Code)

TELEPHONE (Home) ( ) ____________________
Area Code

(Office) ( ) ____________________
Area Code

HEIGHT ____________ WEIGHT ____________

HEALTH ____________ BIRTH DATE ____________

MARITAL STATUS ____________ NO. OF CHILDREN ____________

MOBILITY ____________________

MILITARY STATISTICS

BRANCH OF SERVICE ____________ ATTAINED RANK ____________

TIME SPENT IN SERVICE ____________

MAJOR TRAINING RECEIVED ____________________

____

____

MAJOR JOB RESPONSIBILITIES ____________________

____

____

MAJOR ACCOMPLISHMENTS, ACHIEVEMENTS, CONTRIBUTIONS ____________

____

____

JOB EXPERIENCE

Full-time, Paid Jobs
(List jobs held, beginning with latest one first)

JOB TITLE ____________________

COMPANY NAME ____________________

NATURE OF BUSINESS ____________________
(if not clear from name)

COMPANY DIVISION OR DEPT. ____________________

COMPANY LOCATION ____________________

DATES OF EMPLOYMENT ____________________
(beginning) (ending)

MAJOR JOB RESPONSIBILITIES ____________________

____

____

____

____

____

____

MAJOR ACCOMPLISHMENTS, ACHIEVEMENTS, CONTRIBUTIONS ____________________

____

____

____

____

____

____

NUMBER OF PEOPLE SUPERVISED____________________

POSITION TO WHICH REPORTED ____________________

PART-TIME, PAID EMPLOYMENT

(During summers, vacations, second jobs, means of educ. support)

JOB TITLE ____________________

COMPANY NAME ____________________

NATURE OF BUSINESS ____________________
(if not clear from name)

COMPANY DIVISION OR DEPT. ____________________

COMPANY LOCATION ____________________

DATES OF EMPLOYMENT ____________________
(beginning) (ending)

REGULARITY OF WORK ____________________
(no. of hrs. per week/month)

MAJOR JOB RESPONSIBILITIES ____________________

____

____

____

____

____

MAJOR ACCOMPLISHMENTS, ACHIEVEMENTS, CONTRIBUTIONS ____________________

____

____

____

____

____

NUMBER OF PEOPLE SUPERVISED ____________________

POSITION TO WHICH REPORTED ____________________

UNPAID JOB EXPERIENCE

(Volunteer work, student teaching, internships, coop. educ.)

SCHOOL FIELD PROJECTS

(Course-based research projects, working with real business or community problems, using techniques of surveying, observation, consultation, interviewing, etc.)

EDUCATION

(List all degree and certificate programs, special courses, seminars, workshops taken at educational institutions or in company-sponsored training programs. Begin with most recent first.)

TYPE DEGREE OR CERTIFICATE ____________________

EDUCATIONAL SUBJECTS OR EMPHASIS (major) ____________________

(minor) ____________________

SCHOOL OR FIRM NAME ____________________

PROGRAM LOCATION ____________________

DATES SPENT IN PROGRAM ____________________
(beginning) (ending)

IMPORTANT AND RELEVANT COURSES OR SUBJECT AREAS STUDIED (Add grades if high or desirable)

____________________ ____________________

____________________ ____________________

____________________ ____________________

____________________ ____________________

____________________ ____________________

RANK IN CLASS OR OVERALL GRADE ____________________

SPECIAL REPORTS, PROJECTS, OR PRESENTATIONS ____________________

____

____

____

____

ANYTHING APPLICABLE FROM THIS EDUCATIONAL EXPERIENCE TO YOUR CURRENT JOB GOAL? ____________________

____

____

ORGANIZATION AND ASSOCIATION AFFILIATIONS

(List student, job-related, professional, civic, and social/fraternal groups, committees, associations, task forces, etc., that you belonged to or worked with)

NAME GROUP ______________________________

TYPE OF GROUP ______________________________
(civic, professional, etc.)

YOUR POSITION OR MEMBERSHIP TYPE ______________________________
(pres., treas., sec., full member, etc.)

SPECIAL RESPONSIBILITIES AND ACCOMPLISHMENTS ______________________________

____

____

SPECIAL MEETINGS HELD OR CONVENTIONS ATTENDED ______________________________

____

____

____

NAME OF GROUP ______________________________

TYPE OF GROUP ______________________________
(civic, professional, etc.)

YOUR POSITION OR MEMBERSHIP TYPE ______________________________
(pres., treas., sec., full member, etc.)

SPECIAL RESPONSIBILITIES AND ACCOMPLISHMENTS ______________________________

____

____

SPECIAL MEETINGS HELD OR CONVENTIONS ATTENDED ______________________________

____

____

____

HONORS, AWARDS, AND OTHER SPECIAL RECOGNITION

(List any special recognition, whether it be money, plaque, certificate, gift, award dinner, party, honorary listing, program of study, scholarship, fellowship, assistantship, bonus, promotion, etc. Include all business, educational, social, athletic, and professional distinctions; i.e., Million-Dollar Club of Insurance, Who's Who in American Students, Dean's List in school, American Management Association $500 Tuition Scholarship.)

SPECIAL TALENTS AND SKILLS

(List any talents and skills which have provided personal or social pleasure or have served you in school or at work; i.e., ability in foreign languages, public-speaking ability, report-writing ability, typing skills, shorthand skills, athletic skills, pilot, chess and bridge player, pianist and organist.)

ADDITIONAL RESUME ACHIEVEMENTS

You may still have other important achievements which have not yet been considered. An excellent procedure for recalling them is by doing this thought-association exercise in which you allow your thoughts to freely associate with key "action verbs." Complete each action verb with a full sentence. Here is a sample list of key action verbs:

planned	directed	led	coached	prepared	edited
developed	implemented	trained	judged	spoke	presented
organized	coordinated	supervised	evaluated	wrote	published

Here are a few examples of thought associations:

I planned the main campaign for the 1975 Cancer Society Fund-Raising Drive.
I coached the Summerville Little League Baseball Team to the 1974 championship.
I trained the 16 young insurance-agent trainees during the 1973 season. All of them passed their licensing exams.
I organized the banquet for the 1973 York College Alumni Day.

Personal Values Inventory

Directions: People are complex beings and have many human needs and desires. Below is a list of human needs and desires. How important is each item to you? Place the appropriate number next to each item, using the following rating scale:

3 = Very important
2 = Somewhat important
1 = Not important
0 = Not sure

Upon completing the rating, write a summary statement, describing what you have learned about yourself.

Rating	*Need/Desire*
_____	Creativity
_____	Money
_____	Control over others
_____	Independence and freedom
_____	Recognition by others
_____	Intellectual stimulation
_____	Security and peace of mind
_____	Achievement
_____	Responsibility
_____	Companionship
_____	Self-respect
_____	Opportunities for growth and development
_____	Family
_____	Variety
_____	Aesthetics
_____	Interesting things to do
_____	Caring about others
_____	Self-expression
	Other Needs/Desires:
_____	
_____	

Summary Statement

Job-Market Analysis

Now that your students better understand their personal interests, desires, and aptitudes and know their limitations and dislikes, they are ready to explore the job market and the various career alternatives that may be suited to them.

While some of your students may have already made initial career decisions through their enrollment in professional degree programs, the following job-market analysis activities will further help them clarify their choices and deepen their understanding of the nature of their careers and the job marketplace.

Throughout the learning activities described in this section, students should be seeking the following information about possible career fields:

1. Job skills and traits required
2. Formal education and certification requirements
3. Employment projections
4. Various entry-level positions and salary ranges
5. Various higher-level positions and salary ranges
6. Employment opportunities in geographic areas of interest to them

Students should also seek to understand the variety of specialty positions one can acquire within a chosen profession or career field. For example, in the accounting profession, there are accountants involved in tax work, payroll work, inventory-control work, budgeting, general accounting, and cost accounting, as well as other specialty areas.

In addition, students should understand the various work settings in which individuals do their jobs. Three work-setting variables include: (1) organization size, (2) work sector, and (3) industry. An individual may, for example, choose to work within a large, medium-size, or small organization or to become a self-employed professional. An individual may also select a particular work sector, such as business, government, or the nonprofit sector. Further delineation can be made according to industry, such as financial services, pharmaceuticals, electronics, petrochemicals, or computers.

The Placement Office Connection

Your college or university office of career planning and placement is a key resource to your students and can be extremely beneficial in job-market analysis. Since the role of this student service is to assist students in planning and implementing career and educational objectives, you and your students will find its staff to be well-versed about job-market facts and trends. In addition, the office will probably have excellent, up-to-date handbooks, directories, job listings, and other professional resources which can be of great value to your students.

There are three ways you can introduce the placement office to your students:

1. Require that each student visit the office and prepare a brief report overviewing the publications available and employment services offered.
2. Take the entire class on a scheduled visit to the placement office and have the staff give an orientation to the goals, procedures, and services offered.
3. Invite the director of the placement office to speak to your class about the placement office, its value to students, and the job-market information available there.

Library Employment Resource Audit

Your college and university library is another key employment resource on job-market information. Have each student visit the library and prepare a brief report listing and describing publications that provide job-market data. Make sure that students review the following types of publications:

1. Directories of companies
   a. Dun and Bradstreet's, *Million Dollar Directory*
   b. *Thomas Register of American Manufacturers*
   c. *Standard & Poor's Register of Corporations, Directors, and Executives*
2. U.S. Labor Department employment publications
   a. *Dictionary of Occupational Titles*
   b. *The Occupational Outlook Handbook*
3. Trade magazines pertaining to various trades and professions
4. Business magazines
   a. *Forbes*
   b. *Fortune*

The Employment Expert Connection

Invite professional employment specialists from the business community to speak to your class about the job market. Company personnel managers, state employment service specialists, personnel agency managers, and executive recruiters should be considered as possible guest speakers.

The Field Practitioner Connection

Have each student interview three successful practitioners within a field of interest. Then have each student prepare a brief report about the types of jobs and job-markets within that field.

The Career Planning Report

As a result of the introductory career exercises, self-analysis, and job-market analysis, your students should be well prepared to make some tentative and perhaps some serious career decisions.

The objective of this assignment is to have students prepare a well-thought-out career plan based on thorough research. In introducing this assignment, elicit the possible resources that could be used to gather the necessary information, such as the placement office, library, field practitioners, employment experts, and classified sections of newspapers.

After your students have personally prepared their own career plans, their business communication studies will have that much more meaning and relevance.

The career planning report should include the following information:

1. The titles of two positions that could be realistically obtained upon graduation, in two years, five years, and ten years
2. A brief paragraph for each position mentioned, describing job requirements and responsibilities
3. The methods or experiences needed for promotion up the career ladder, such as special degrees, certificates, courses, seminars, significant job-related accomplishments, or even company changing
4. The anticipated salaries and employee benefits, based on current salary scales for all positions mentioned
5. The occupational outlook or forecast for employees in this field
6. A listing of sources of information for this report
7. A brief paragraph explaining any problems encountered in preparing the report
8. A brief paragraph noting the benefits of the project

2. Job Campaigning

Equipped with a career plan, your students should be prepared to enthusiastically learn the skills and strategies of job campaigning. Right from the beginning of this module, be sure to emphasize that good jobs do not magically appear upon command, but must be skillfully and rigorously sought out or hunted for with the approach and magnitude of a campaign—thus are born the common expressions job search, job hunt, and job campaign.

The Sales Approach to Job Campaigning

The goal of any decent job-search effort is to receive solid job offers and land a top-notch job. Because of the tight job market—even for well-educated graduates—those students who land the best jobs are those who have made major efforts in their job campaigns.

Job campaigning is selling—no "buts" about it! Your students simply must be able to launch a quality sales effort and succeed in convincing employment representatives that they are just the right people for the jobs. Selling not only requires self-confidence and personal conviction about one's own strengths and credentials but also communication skills—both written and oral—to present those credentials effectively and persuade employment representatives about the desirability of employment.

The Buying Approach to Company Hiring

Before you introduce the approaches to campaign planning, resume writing, or job interviewing, help your students understand that they are the sellers in the job market and that companies—including government agencies and non-profit institutions—are the buyers.

Make it clear that in selling their products—which are themselves, their skills, and their knowledge—your students will be in keen competition with others, some equally qualified and perhaps even more qualified. Knowledge of the company buying procedure will place them at a real advantage. Therefore, display and describe the company job-screening funnel presented in Figure 1-1.

Explain that most applicants for announced positions are screened out by companies solely on the basis of written communications, such as resumes and job letters. Thus the great importance of written communication skills becomes evident. Those who do succeed at this first screening stage must then meet the challenge of the job interviews and be able to demonstrate superior oral communication skills.

The Job Campaign

A *job campaign* is a preplanned procedure of written and oral communications for selling oneself effectively to company representatives. It is both active and organized, and its goal is to land a job. This definition must be absolutely clear in each student's mind. Therefore, show the diagram of a model job campaign in Figure 1-2.

Note that the campaign model shows the step-by-step sequence of job-getting communications needed for obtaining an announced position. Explain that each step is, in effect, a sales presentation in which the job seeker communicates his or her most favorable image to a prospective employer.

Indicate that this model can serve as the procedure for following up many announced job leads. Also indicate that the model can be revised depending upon the type of job lead being considered.

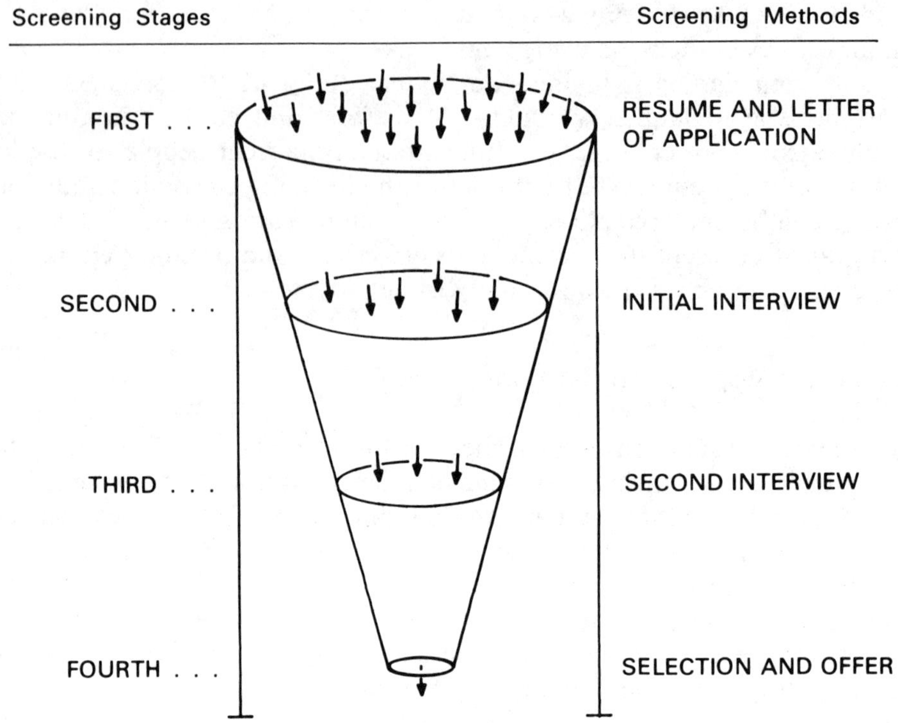

FIGURE 1–1 Company Job-Screening Funnel

Point out that the model job campaign provides each student with a well-planned and organized selling procedure for following up one or one hundred different job leads. In addition, the campaign model is fully compatible with the buyer's job-screening funnel.

The Job-Search Master Plan

A successful job seeker understands the value of "numbers" in sales leveraging within the job market and conducts several different campaigns simultaneously. For example, in one campaign, an individual could follow up thirty-five leads found in the classified section of a major city newspaper. In another campaign waged at the same time, one-hundred direct mail pieces could be sent out to specific types of employers. In yet another campaign, fifty personnel agencies could be sent resumes and job letters.

Since there are many ways in which job leads can be developed—in addition to locating them in the classified section of newspapers—point out the importance of master planning. A *master plan* is a set of carefully selected and

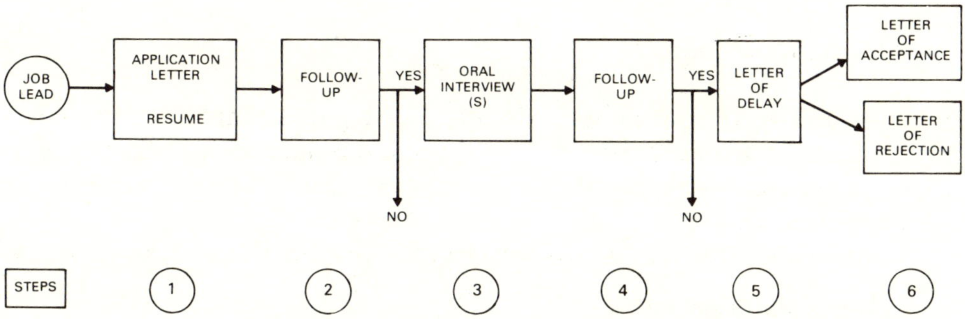

FIGURE 1-2 Model Job Campaign

prepared job campaigns created to maximize a job seeker's efforts in reaching a large number of job leads. Here is a list of eleven job campaigns from which students can build their master plans:

1. Company-announced job campaign
2. Walk-in sales campaign
3. Walk-in exploratory campaign
4. Call-in sales campaign
5. Prospecting campaign
6. Unsolicited sales campaign
7. Direct mail job campaign
8. Advertising campaign
9. Third-party campaign
10. Conference and convention campaign
11. Word-of-mouth campaign[1]

The Successful Attitude

Students must understand that a systematic campaign approach in following up many different leads is a necessary and effective strategy for landing good jobs in a tight job market. Because of keen competition, however, they must expect to receive many rejections. Some of the rejections may even be for jobs they really wanted.

Such rejections must be considered a natural phenomenon as companies may screen out twenty-five, fifty, one-hundred, or more individuals for every position filled. The intelligent job campaigner understands the rules of the game and does not feel dejected. In addition, he or she does not sit around wasting valuable time and energy worrying about one or two companies. Instead, the campaigner continues to rigorously follow up new job leads.

Controlling the Job Search

Effective control of operations is a definite element in the success of any enterprise. This is particularly true of the job search. Solid records of a job campaigner's contacts with prospective employers can definitely enhance the quality of a job search.

A simple but effective recordkeeping system includes these four elements:

1. Job-search journal
2. File folder of active correspondence
3. File folder of inactive correspondence
4. File folder of job documents

The *job-search journal* should be used to record (1) the date a prospect is sent a resume and letter, (2) the name of the company and location, (3) the job title of the position, and (4) the job lead followed up. In addition, there should be designation of any subsequent contacts with the company.

The *file folder of active correspondence* should contain carbon or photostatic copies of all correspondence with active prospects. As letters are received back from the field, they should be attached to the job seeker's correspondence.

Any contacts by telephone should be recorded on a sheet of paper and also attached to the original correspondence. Finally, letters for each job should be filed in chronological order based on the dates each prospect was first contacted.

Whenever a rejection is received, the correspondence with that organization should be pulled from the active file and placed into the *file folder of inactive correspondence.*

Extra copies of resumes, job letters, transcripts and any other documents that may be useful should be kept in the *file folder of job documents.*

Learning Activities

The activities in this module can help you reinforce the philosophy and methods of the job campaign approach. Furthermore, students can be helped to overcome negative self-images and begin viewing themselves as marketable talent capable of operating successfully in a tight job market.

Educational Assets Analysis

Have students completely fill out the PIF (Personal Inventory Form) presented on pages 10–20 if they have not already done so. Then provide them

Student Achievement Inventory

	Achievement	Check If Recorded in PIF
1.	Degree and school	_____
2.	Major and minor areas of study	_____
3.	Rank or standing in class, if high	_____
4.	Overall grade point average, if high	_____
5.	Honor listings, such as dean's list or student of the year	_____
6.	Scholarships or other awards for excellence	_____
7.	Courses relevant to job choice	_____
8.	Course grades, if high	_____
9.	Written and oral class reports and presentations, if relevant to job	_____
10.	Course-related field projects, field visitations, company studies and internships	_____
11.	Memberships on school committees, in school associations, and in professional clubs	_____
12.	Leadership positions in school-related groups	_____
13.	Special skills, competencies, certifications, or licenses	_____
14.	Paid or unpaid work experiences (after school, during summers, or on vacations)	_____

with copies of the sample Student Achievement Inventory and instruct them to make sure that these important achievements have been recorded in the PIF.

Functional-Selling-Point Analysis

It is important that your students see themselves as salable job candidates and present their achievements and abilities to buyers in convincing ways. This exercise has each student taking the recorded PIF data and, through the classification system described here, transforming that data into a number of focused sales presentations called functional selling points. A *functional selling point* is a collection of accomplishments that proves a candidate's job worthiness to perform a key job requirement.

In functional-selling-point analysis, each student first identifies the key job requirements (or functions) and then builds a case around each function to prove that he or she "has what it takes." Have students perform the following analysis:

1. List five key job requirements (or job functions) for the job you will seek upon graduation. You can obtain this information from job ads, position descriptions, job publications, or through interviews with field practitioners.

2. Write down each function as a heading at the top of a blank sheet of paper. Each sheet is now called a functional-selling-point worksheet.
3. Now, take your completed PIF and transfer that data selectively to each of the functional-selling-point worksheets. You can easily transfer PIF data to the proper worksheet by answering this question: "Which PIF item can prove (or support the argument) that I can perform this function effectively?"
4. Continue to transfer information from the PIF to the functional-selling-point worksheets until each worksheet has several items that prove your job worthiness in that function.

Your students' newly developed functional selling points can be used throughout their job searches—in resumes, letters, and interviews—to prove that they have valuable experience and accomplishments in each of the critical job requirement areas.

The Marketing Instructor Talk

Invite a marketing instructor to give a talk to your class on developing a product or service marketing plan. Ask the speaker to introduce the hows and whys of target marketing and market-mix planning. Finally, ask the speaker to respond to questions from your students on how marketing techniques can apply to job hunting.

The Salesperson Interview

Have each student go out and interview three successful salespeople. Ask the students to find out "the secrets of successful selling" from each interview and write up summary reports of their findings.

Provide in-class time for discussion of the interview findings and apply the information obtained to the job-search process. Be sure to draw conclusions about the following:

1. The importance of a positive attitude
2. The value of "numbers" and consistency in campaigning
3. The need for solid preparation concerning product knowledge and product selling points

Review of Job-Search Books

Instruct each student to review one or more job-search books. At the end of this chapter is a list of books that deal with the techniques of waging successful job campaigns. These books should be available in most bookstores or libraries.

3. Resumes

Through the various learning activities in this module, students should become familiar with the most effective writing techniques for developing winning resumes. In addition, students should be able to prepare a high-quality job-search document that would achieve a favorable impression within an actual campaign situation.

Functions of the Winning Resume

Introduce the resume as the most important written communication in the student's job search. Explain that it is not a dull standard data sheet but rather a unique, interesting, and clear statement of the job seeker's value to the firm. Moreover, it is a specially prepared sales piece which features and highlights the student's job-worthy credentials.

Review the various uses of the resume within the student's job search. Point out that the resume can be:

1. Used in combination with a letter of application to seek the interview
2. Offered to an interviewer during an unscheduled walk-in interview
3. Carried to the scheduled interview
4. Filed with placement offices, personnel agencies, and recruiters

Stress here that many individuals with top credentials but dull or unclear resumes fail to win job offers. Recall the job-screening funnel described earlier and emphasize that most contacts with firms in response to announced positions are done in writing via the resume. Most of these individuals are "knocked out" of the running at this first screening stage because of ineffective resumes. Only a few winning resumes are retained and their writers invited in for the important job interviews.

Techniques of Resume Writing

As you proceed through the recommended learning activities in this module, make certain that students learn how to skillfully apply the following techniques to the preparation of their own resume:

1. Resume organization
   a. Order of importance
   b. Chronological order
   c. Functional resume
   d. Centered versus block layout

2. Resume captions
   a. Resume title
   b. Resume section headings
3. Job objective
4. Nutshell summary
5. Job experience section
6. Education section
7. Personal data section
8. Other pertinent sections
9. Reference section
10. Resume packaging
    a. Length
    b. Printing
    c. Paper

Resume Transparency Analysis

An excellent method for teaching resume writing techniques is the large-group discussion of winning resumes that are projected onto a screen with the overhead projector.

On the following pages, you have been provided with four winning resumes drawn from the folio of twenty-one sample resumes in the book *Getting A Better Job.* Each document is accompanied by a "Background and Analysis" statement providing background information on the job seeker and analysis of the writing techniques used.

Create your own transparencies from these four resumes. As you review each one, be sure to discuss the important writing techniques used.

Position: Coordinator
Setting: Mental Health
Length: 1 page

KENNETH N. KEANEN

Background and Analysis

1. Kenneth is a 28-year-old man with a master's degree in the field of community mental health and a good background of professional experience. He seeks upward movement in his current or a related field.
2. This resume is a guaranteed winner for the following reasons: (a) his credentials are excellent, (b) there is heavy demand for such a specialist, and (c) his credentials are effectively presented and packaged in this short and powerful one-page resume.
3. The nutshell summary succinctly states his three big offerings: (a) current position, (b) state-wide plan for which he was partially responsible, and (c) published article. This combination leads readers to the conclusion that Kenneth is definitely a young professional who can offer substantial capability.
4. Since the nutshell summary clearly presents important accomplishments of his current position, Kenneth decides to avoid repeating them in the job-experience section. Instead, he presents a skeleton job-experience listing. This technique is a space saver and prevents the need for a second page.

KENNETH N. KEANEN, M.S.

PROGRAM COORDINATION CREDENTIALS

3300 Brookland Avenue   Apt. 3C   Boston, MA 02155   (617) 244-0067

Qualifications for planning or coordination in community mental health and drug-abuse-prevention functions

Significant Professional Accomplishments

As Assistant Treatment and Rehabilitation Director of the Massachusetts Division of Drug Abuse Control, I and the director jointly prepared a four-volume Comprehensive Plan for Drug Abuse Control and submitted it to the U.S. Department of HEW in 1973. After due consideration, the Plan was approved for implementation by the State of Massachusetts in 1974. In addition, my article entitled "New Dimensions for Drug Prevention in Urban Areas" was submitted to the British Journal of Addictions and published in Volume 63, pp 71–89, on January 1, 1974.

Comprehensive Working Responsibilities

Assistant Treatment and Rehabilitation Director, Massachusetts Division of Drug Abuse Control, Office of the Governor, Boston, Massachusetts, 1972–present.

Social Worker, Division of Vocational Rehabilitation, Atlanta, Georgia, 1970. Primary responsibilities involved field contact with families of clients involved in training, evaluation, and social adjustment programs.

Correctional Counselor, Florida Department of Corrections, Division of Youth, Melville Correctional Center, 1969. Responsibilities included counseling, testing using basic standardized psychological tests, and family contact.

Assistant to Dean of Students, the University of Florida, 1967–69. Actively assisted in the functions of student housing, activities, associations, counseling, finances, and job placement.

Professional Training and Education

Postgraduate Training in Drug Addiction, NIMH-funded program at Georgia State University's Warwick Center for Drug Addiction Rehabilitation, Atlanta, Georgia, 1971–72.

Master of Science Degree, Community Mental Health, Georgia State University, internship and field work accomplished in four states, 1971.

Bachelor of Arts Degree, Major in Psychology, University of Florida, 1968.

Associate of Arts Degree, Roosevelt Junior College, Tampa, Florida, 1967.

Affiliations and Professional Memberships

American Society of Group Psychotherapy
Society for the Study of Drug Addiction
American Psychological Association
National Addiction Counseling Society

REFERENCES & REPRINTS
WILL BE SENT UPON REQUEST

Traits and Interests

Date of Birth: 7/7/47
Height: 6′2″
Weight: 190 lb
Enjoy music, travel, and work. Interested in community development programs

Position: Management Trainee
Setting: Retailing
Length: 1 page

MAXWELL T. MEEKS

Background and Analysis

1. Maxwell is a 22-year-old soon-to-graduate college student with a major in business administration and management. He wants to begin working for Macy's as a management trainee. As yet, his career management direction in retailing is not clearly defined. This is acceptable, however, for the company management training program will in a short time help him to make that decision.
2. In this one-page resume, many impressive qualities are noticeable: (a) an appropriate college degree and major, (b) fine grades and honors, (c) experience in selling, even though only part-time, (d) ability to get along well with others and to assume leadership positions, and (e) interesting and positive section headings.
3. The section headings in this resume speak with confidence as they attempt to show that Maxwell will be successful on the job.

MAXWELL T. MEEKS'S QUALIFICATIONS
FOR AN EFFECTIVE CAREER IN MANAGEMENT
WITH MACY'S

535 North Hollywood Drive, Richmond, VA 23246
(804) 355-0049

FIRM BUSINESS FOUNDATION

Bachelor of Business Administration Degree, special emphasis on Managing Retail Organizations, Metropolitan University, Richmond, Virginia, to be awarded June 1976. Honor student.
Associate of Arts Degree, majoring in Business, Ferrum Junior College, Ferrum, Virginia, awarded June 1972.
Academic Degree, John Dale High School, Chester, Virginia, awarded June 1970.

Course Title	Grade	Course Title	Grade
Financial Management	A	Retailing Strategies	A
Principles of Retailing	A	Group Psychology	B
Accounting Systems	B	Business Writing	A
Business Environment	A	Business Law	B

JOB EXPERIENCE THAT COUNTS

Commission Salesman, wholesaling auto parts for Reasonable Automotive Parts, Richmond, Virginia, part-time, approximately 25 hours per week, 1972–74.
Commission Salesman, retailing auto parts for King's Discount, Ferrum, Virginia, part-time, approximately 25 hours per week, 1970–72.
Senior Lifeguard, supervising two other lifeguards for the Department of Parks and Recreation, Ferrum, Virginia, full-time, summers of 1970 and 1971.

ACTIVELY INVOLVED WITH PEOPLE

Chairman of Membership Committee of Phi Beta Lambda, 2 years during college.
Member of Budget Committee of Society for Advancement of Management, 2 years during college.
Member of Football Team, 15 hours per week, 4 years during high school.
Regular participant in golf, football, and swimming.

PERSONALLY FIT AND READY

Marital Status: Single	Health: Perfect
Very Willing to Relocate	Height: 5′ 10″
Mobility: Owns Car and Likes to Travel	Weight: 175 pounds
Date of Birth: September 7, 1953	Father's Business: Auto Dealership

ENDORSED BY EXPERTS

Mr. Bernard Lansing, Owner	Dr. Harold Hornblow	Mr. Scott Herring, Mgr.
Reasonable Automotive Parts	Professor of Retailing	King's Discount
3333 Franklin Street	Metropolitan University	546 North Avenue
Richmond, VA 23215	Richmond, VA 23275	Ferrum, VA 23247

Position: Junior Accountant
Setting: CPA Firm
Length: 1 page

LYNWOOD R. LEVINE

Background and Analysis

1. Lynwood is a 22-year-old new college graduate with an accounting degree who is seeking an entry-level accounting position with a certified public accounting firm. This goal is clearly stated in the title and in the following combination job objective/nutshell summary.
2. Lacking any paid job experience, Lynwood decides to highlight his capabilities for public accounting by presenting several well-supported qualities in a functional resume pattern.
3. This resume is designed to look and read like a report—an important medium of the accounting profession. Note the appropriate language used within the title: "Statement of Employment Assets." Patsy P. Publiski is another new college graduate who impresses her readers by creatively applying language and medium in her resume.

LYNWOOD R. LEVINE
STATEMENT OF EMPLOYMENT ASSETS
FOR A CAREER IN PUBLIC ACCOUNTING

to become associated with a progressive accounting firm initially as a junior accountant, with the goal of advancement to partner. with a bachelor of science degree in accounting and a major in public accounting, I offer substantial capability to fully support my serious professional interests.

CAPABILITY	Bachelor of Science in Accounting, major in public accounting, minors in data processing and management, Chicago State University, 1975.
Technical Accounting	• Auditing Methods • Cost Accounting • Managerial Accounting • Advanced Accounting • Financial Accounting • Governmental Accounting • Tax Accounting • Cases in Federal Income Tax
Calculation and Computer Systems	• EDP Systems & Methods • Computer Program Languages • Information Systems • Decision Mathematics • Office Machines with proficiency in: • Ten-Key Adding Machine • Full-Key Adding Machine • Electronic Calculator • Printing Calculator • Rotary Calculator • Programable Calculator
Communications	• Business Communications • English Composition • Conducted regular meetings of the CSU Accounting Club • Kept regular minutes of Data Processing Mgt. Assoc. meetings • Prepared various reports on the financial conditions of a number of companies for accounting courses
Business	• Business Environment • Business Finance • Theory of the Firm • Subscribes to <u>The Wall Street Journal</u> • Business Law • Subscribes to <u>Business Week</u>
Management and Leadership	• Office Management • Personnel Management • Behavioral Management • Marketing Management • Secretary of Data Processing Mgt. Assoc., 1 year • Vice-president of the CSU Accounting Club, 1 year
Dealing with People	• Student tutor in accounting, 1 year, approx. 15 hrs./wk. • Active member of Society for Advancement of Mgt., 2 years • Active member of Accounting Club, 3 years • Active member of Data Processing Mgt. Assoc., 2 years • Active member of Chess Club • Sold advertising space in Student Directory to Businesses • Psychology • Sociology
Personal	• 2322 Riverdale Road, Chicago, IL 60607 • Telephone No. (312) 345-6709 • Height is 6′ 1″ • Weight is 185 pounds • References will be sent upon request

Position: Business Teacher
Setting: High School
Length: 2 pages

LAURIE M. LEMON

Background and Analysis

1. Laurie is a 25-year-old college graduate seeking a job as high-school teacher of business. She worked various full-time and part-time jobs after graduating from high school, was married, and then returned to attend college.
2. Her job goal follows the resume "contact information" and states the name of the organization to which she is applying.
3. She has no paid teaching experience but uses the resume nutshell summary, which is entitled "Academic and Career Experiences," to effectively sell the credentials she does possess.
4. Her business experience is listed in reverse time order with greater development and coverage given to her most recent job as school assistant. This job, although part-time, shows Laurie's familiarity with the operation of an educational program.

LAURIE M. LEMON

BUSINESS EDUCATION QUALIFICATIONS

9001 Riverdale Drive   Meanlake, New Mexico 87154   (505) 333-0097

A position teaching high-school business with the
County of Tulane

Academic and Career Experiences

While student teaching at Hermit High School, I worked with students in the areas of office machines, office procedures, bookkeeping/accounting, and data processing. These classroom experiences were supplemented by a broader participation in student counseling, course evaluation, course selection and planning, and program development. Actively involved in a number of school organizations, I was the primary figure behind the launching of the new Junior Achievement student company.

For a relatively young woman who is happily married, my varied experiences in business have given me a sophistication and maturity which I consider vital for successful business teaching. In fact, it was because of my business connections that I was able to arrange for a large number of student field trips in the business community.

Business Employment Profile

School Assistant, Department of Business Education, the University of San Luis, San Luis, New Mexico, provided secretarial support to the departmental secretary in all office activities, assisted in the scheduling of student-teaching assignments and cooperative office experiences, and maintained the department's student resource room, part-time, 1974–76.

Bookkeeper, General Waterworks, Inc., Ronald, New Mexico, part-time, 1972–74.

Accounts Payable Research/Key Puncher, County Medical Group, Ronald, New Mexico, 1971.

Accounts Payable Clerk/Petty Cash Cashier, County Medical Group, 1970.

Theater Hostess, Saga Dinner Theater, Nomad, New Mexico, part-time, 1970.

Salesclerk, Pupils Dept. Store, Nomad, New Mexico, responsible for cosmetics counter, 1969.

Salesclerk, Pupils Dept. Store, responsible for women's clothing section, 1968.

Academic Support

Bachelor of Science in Business Education, the University of San Luis, state certification to teach typing, shorthand, office machines and procedures, accounting/bookkeeping, and data processing, minor taken in English, 1976.

Major Area Course Work

Accounting	12 hours
Data Processing	15 hours
Education	9 hours
Business Math	6 hours
Office Procedures	12 hours
Communications	3 hours
Shorthand	6 hours
Typing	6 hours

Extracurricular Activities

Member of Phi Beta Lambda
Member of Accounting Club
Secretary of Data Processing Society
Student Delegate to Faculty Senate
Organizer of PBL's Fund-raising Drives for 1974 and 1975

Academic Degree, Lansing High School, Lansing, Texas, very active in school team sports, the orchestral society (my instrument is piano), and the Latin Club, also student assistant in the Dean's Office, 1968.

Special Interests

Professional Enrichment
Challenging Work
Working with People
Community Participation

Performing Arts
Swimming and Volleyball
Ceramics and Painting
Music and Sculpture

Personal Attributes

Date of Birth Is July 1, 1950
Marital Status Is Married
Height Is 5′4″/Weight Is 120 lb

My husband is a graduate of the Wharton School of Business and is currently Assistant Controller of the C & L Processing Company, based in Landow, New Mexico. He has given me his full support in my aspirations to become a top-notch business education teacher. This is important because we respect each other's profession.

People Who Know Me Well

Dr. James L. Ball
Professor of Business Education
School of Business
The University of San Luis
San Luis, NM 87156

Mr. Samuel P. Pupils
Pupils Department Store
355 Westerly Drive
Nomad, NM 87177

Mrs. Salley N. Norton
Supervising Teacher
Hermit High School
Goodland, NM 87154

Mr. Carl C. Pitman
Controller
C & L Processing Company
Landow, NM 87167

Individual Resume Analysis

Ask each student to obtain a copy of an actual job resume from a relative, friend, or business acquaintance. Have the students then analyze the documents for strengths and weaknesses based on your class discussion.

Resume Preparation Trial Run

Develop a fictitious job seeker who needs a winning resume for a planned job search. This can be done by filling out a copy of the Personal Inventory Form presented earlier with fictitious but realistic job credentials. Then hand out copies of the PIF to all students, and instruct them to prepare the needed resume.

Actual Resume Preparation

Assign each student the preparation—for grading—of his or her own job resume. Require that a PIF be filled out and submitted along with the completed resume. Emphasize that these resumes must be tailored to jobs which may be sought upon graduation.

4. Job Letters

The letter of application is one of the most important letters an individual can write. And if sent out on a large scale—as prescribed in the campaign approach to job hunting—this letter is also probably one of the most frequently prepared letters.

Make it clear to students that while the goal of the entire job search is to land a good job, the goal of the letter of application is to persuade employers to grant job interviews.

Sales Approach in the Letter of Application

The letter of application is a sales letter with the resume serving as the promotional enclosure. Teach your students the three major parts of the application letter, using the highly effective A-I-D-A sales formula.

Parts of the Letter of Application

Letter Part	A-I-D-A	Function
Opening	Attention Interest	To capture an employer's attention and build interest in you as a serious candidate
Middle	Desire	To create desire by proving you have what it takes. The resume enclosure can be referred to here
Ending	Action	To stimulate the action of granting you the interview

Techniques for Preparing the Letter of Application

The students should be made aware of thirteen important techniques for preparing the letter of application. Review the following list with your students. When writing the letter of application, the job seeker should:

1. Be positive and confident, but not presumptuous or arrogant.
2. Talk of key credentials to fulfill the job requirements.
3. Show interest in working for the company.
4. Show knowledge of the company.
5. Show knowledge of the job requirements.
6. Prove that specific, individual capabilities and experience fulfill key requirements.
7. Be forthright in seeking the interview, but still respectful.
8. Compliment the firm's work or reputation but avoid obvious or insincere flattery.
9. Refer to the resume for evidence of your qualifications.
10. Avoid being self-critical or negative about others, including the company.
11. Use the letter opening to excite the reader and to express a keen interest in the job by capturing attention and building interest. The applicant should mention such things as:
    a. the job-ad source
    b. a person well known to the reader
    c. a person of fame
    d. a comment that assures reader agreement
    e. a significant accomplishment of the firm
    f. an accomplishment of the reader
    g. an award or honor of the reader
    h. a significant change in the field
    i. an important and felt need of the firm
    j. a personal qualification currently in need by the firm

12. Use the letter middle to create desire. The writer should prove, in this part, that he or she has what it takes to excel in the job, whet the reader's interest by highlighting key capabilities, and refer to the enclosed resume as a reservoir of key accomplishments to prove strengths. If there is a nutshell summary in the resume, this part of the letter should be phrased or slanted somewhat differently.
13. Use the letter ending to request the interview and stimulate action.

The Interview Follow-up Letter

Another important job letter which should be taught in this module is the interview follow-up letter. The goal of this letter is to continue building goodwill and achieve a lasting favorable impression following the interview.

Review these five techniques used by the applicant for preparing the interview follow-up letter:

1. Convey appreciation for the interview
2. Make a positive comment about some points discussed during the interview
3. Express greater interest in the job as a result of the interview
4. Briefly reiterate your key credentials
5. Seek to know the current status of your job candidacy

Job-Letter Transparency Analysis

As you have already successfully used the overhead projector to teach resumes in module 3, again use this projector to display and discuss winning examples of job letters. On the following pages, you have been provided with four winning job letters from the job-letter folio of *Getting A Better Job*. Each letter is accompanied by a letter analysis section which provides a sentence-by-sentence breakdown.

Create your own transparencies from these four letters. Be certain to discuss the important techniques used in each.

Individual Application-Letter Analysis

Have each student obtain a copy of an actual letter of application from a relative, friend, or business acquaintance. Have the students then analyze the documents for strengths and weaknesses based on your class discussion.

Letter of Application: Response to Company Announcement

22 Center Street
Tutorville, MD 21345
May 1, 19–

Mr. George L. Wrenwrite
Public Relations Director
Holyoke Insurance Company
Canton, IL 61520

Dear Mr. Wrenwrite:

Communications ability is essential for the person filling the new public relations position which you advertised in the Sunday Times Tribune. I can offer you facility in both written and spoken English, as well as other key capabilities required for successful public relations work.

Majoring in English at college, I have applied techniques of speech writing and presentation, proofreading, and correspondence-writing on numerous occasions. Some of my other skills of communication include article-writing and the ability to work effectively with others on joint projects. These, as well as my other capabilities, are shown in the enclosed resume.

Accompanying my education is a good understanding of the public relations field and a knowledge of preparing press releases, newsletters, and advertising and promotional brochures.

About to graduate from Pennsylvania State University, I would like to begin my professional public relations career with a firm that is respected throughout the insurance industry.

Please contact me soon to discuss this position.

Sincerely,

Patsy P. Publiski

Enclosure: Resume

Letter of Application: Response to Company Announcement

Paragraph	Sentence	Planned Ideas
1	1	Statement of key job requirements Mention of job opening Job-lead source
	2	Confident statement of two specific job qualifications Confident statement of general job qualifications
2	1	Mention college major Mention several impressive communications skills
	2	Mention other impressive communications skills
	3	Refer to enclosed resume
3	1	Confident statement of public relations knowledge Mention several public relations media
4	1	Indicate college graduation and name of school Express desire to become career-oriented in field Compliment company
5	1	Request interview

Letter of Application: Unsolicited Letter

Dear Mr. Samuals:

Can you use a person with solid credentials in retail-store management and a genuine desire to work for Centerville's number-one downtown family department store? After two years of happy shopping at Regency, I am now very interested in joining your ranks in a sales management or buyer capacity.

I have successfully managed all operations of a Centerville retail business doing approximately $500,000 in sales per year. This won me two bonuses and moved store earnings up to an all-time high. In addition, I can deal with people under all conditions, including customers, employees, vendors, and corporate management. Under the pressures of fast-paced retail operations, I was able to earn the full respect and cooperation of all employees, while at times having to administer necessary discipline.

My educational background and personal flexibility, as shown in the enclosed resume, will allow me to quickly adapt to any new and different situation which may be encountered at Regency. Because I am young, interested in growing in retailing and particularly with Regency, and willing to work where the sales or buying needs exist, you will find me a sound addition to your personnel.

May I have an opportunity to interview with you soon with regard to a position? Please call me at home at 224-1133 or at 771-6645 where a message can be taken.

Sincerely,

Mrs. Salley N. Norton

Letter of Application: Unsolicited Letter

Paragraph	Sentence	Planned Ideas
1	1	Ask lead-off question to engage reader Suggest two important store needs Indicate possession of needed attributes
	2	Compliment store Show experience with store Express interest in a position with store
2	1	Give key accomplishment plus impressive figure
	2	Show resulting benefits: personal and store
	3	State important capability
	4	Point out difficult working conditions of current job Show how these were successfully handled
3	1	Mention two valuable traits Refer to resume enclosure Show beneficial results of two traits
	2	State three valuable traits Express interest in working for store Show beneficial results of three traits
4	1	Request job interview
	2	Give two telephone numbers for contact purposes

Letter of Application: Direct Mail Letter

22 Center Street
Tutorville, MD 21345
May 5, 19–

ENTERING THE JOB MARKET THESE DAYS
IS NOT EASY. THE MORE AGGRESSIVE,
CREATIVE, AND ARTICULATE GET THE JOBS. . . .

The same thing applies to staying and growing with a firm—aggressiveness, creativity, and solid communications skills are vital. I want to work for your organization as a public relations worker and can offer these qualities and more.

My enclosed resume is not traditional, but then, the job I seek is not either. Please note the extensive mind-building experiences during college which have given me the capabilities that count in effective public relations work.

While I do eventually seek management responsibility in public relations, now is the time to begin where the work must be done. Therefore, please give me the opportunity to talk with you about utilizing my abilities and interests in your department.

PATSY P. PUBLISKI

Enclosure: Public Relations Credentials

Letter of Application: Direct Mail Letter

Paragraph	Sentence	Planned Ideas
OPENS WITH ATTENTION-GETTING HEADLINE INSTEAD OF INSIDE ADDRESS AND SALUTATION		
Headline		Make interesting comment about job-seeking Seek agreement from reader about qualities needed
1	1	Indicate qualities needed to grow in a company
	2	Express interest in a position Offer the above qualities
2	1	Refer to resume Point out novel approach to resume Point out similar novelty needed in type of job
	2	Emphasize experience gained during college Indicate positive benefits of these experiences
3	1	Talk of future management goals in field Indicate serious desire to begin job doing any needed work
	2	Request job interview to discuss credentials

9001 Riverdale Drive
Meanlake, NM 87154
June 24, 19–

Mr. Barry B. Baretta
Supervisor of Instruction
Tulane County Public Schools
Tulane County, NM 87145

Dear Mr. Baretta:

Thank you very much for the interesting time you spent with me this past Wednesday. As you know, this business teaching position with Tulane County is very important to me, and your complimentary remarks about my credentials and personality were music to my ears.

You mentioned that two teaching positions in business were up for consideration at this time and that six candidates were being given serious consideration. I'm very glad to be one of these people.

As I mentioned, I am certified to teach all the business education courses offered within the high schools. This versatility should provide for the most effective planning of my teaching program. In addition, my substantial work experience would provide for interesting and relevant classroom discussion.

My determination to become a top-notch business teacher in Tulane County is greater than ever. Your plans to develop business education within the Tulane high schools sound great and confirm my desire to work with you.

Sincerely,

Laurie M. Lemon

Interview Follow-up Letter

Paragraph	Sentence	Planned Ideas
1	1	Express appreciation for interview Compliment reader
	2	Express interest in job Remind of compliments reader gave to writer during the interview
2	1	Recall discussion of two vacant positions Recall discussion of six candidates
	2	Express pleasure to be considered a candidate
3	1	Remind of general certification
	2	Show resulting benefit to school programs
	3	Indicate extensive work experience Show resulting benefit to school programs
4	1	Express even greater interest following the interview
	2	Compliment reader's plan Indicate that reader is a reason for greater interest

Application-Letter Trial Run

Take the fictitious job seeker you developed in Module Three and hand out copies of the PIF you created for that individual. Then instruct your students to prepare one of the following types of application letter using the PIF:

1. Response to a company announcement
2. Unsolicited letter to a company
3. Direct mail letter

Actual Application-Letter Preparation

As an assignment for grading, ask the students to prepare their own application letters. Have each student prepare two out of the three types listed above.

Instruct the students to write the letters for the kinds of jobs they might seek upon graduation. For realism, you may want to require that each letter be accompanied by a student's resume and be inserted and sealed in an envelope addressed to you.

If a student chooses to write a letter in response to a company announcement, require that the announcement be included in the submitted envelope. If an actual job ad or posting cannot be obtained, the student should enclose a simulated announcement.

Actual Follow-up–Letter Preparation

Have each student prepare—for grading—an interview follow-up letter. In carrying out this assignment, a student should assume that one of the two application letters was successful in obtaining a job interview and that this letter is being written a few days after the job interview.

5. Job Interviews

The job interview is the critical stage in any job campaign and certainly one of the most important face-to-face selling opportunities in most people's lives. It is the result of hard campaigning and the reward for a well-prepared resume and letter of application. Therefore, it is absolutely imperative for instructors of business communication to help prepare students to successfully handle this important event.

In this module, you are provided with (1) descriptions of six valuable job-interviewing techniques, (2) important job-interviewing concepts, and

(3) several excellent learning activities for delivering an effective educational experience to the class.

Valuable Job-Interviewing Techniques

Acquaint yourself with the following interviewing techniques so that you may introduce them during your lecture/discussion and learning activities.

1. *Self-Knowledge.* The interviewee is completely familiar with, and can talk with facility about, all the facts and figures contained in the job resume. The interviewee can also talk with full knowledge and conviction about his or her carefully prepared career plan.
2. *Functional Selling Points.* The interviewee can identify key job functions and can prove individual capability in each function by mentioning several supporting accomplishments.
3. *Personal Success Stories.* The interviewee can describe several job-related situations in which he or she successfully solved problems. Well-told stories help to prove a job seeker's job worthiness.
4. *Company Knowledge.* The interviewee impresses an employer by demonstrating knowledge of the company, its major problems, programs, needs and plans.
5. *Intelligent Responses.* The interviewee responds intelligently and positively to the most frequently asked interviewing questions.
6. *Insightful Questions.* The interviewee asks important and relevant questions to learn more about the job and company, but never asks fundamental questions which suggest lack of basic research and interest in the job.

Important Job-Interviewing Concepts

Students must see the job interview as a sales meeting which must be carefully planned, skillfully executed, and promptly followed up. Your discussion of the following material is essential for clarifying the job-interviewing process and establishing realistic student expectations.

Job-Interviewing Process

The intelligent job seeker views job interviewing as a logical process consisting of five stages: (1) Pre-Interview, (2) Interview Opening, (3) Interview Development, (4) Interview Closing, and (5) Post-Interview. To progress successfully through the job interview process, the job seeker must demonstrate various skills at each stage.

STAGE I: PRE–INTERVIEW

While an invitation to interview is a well-earned accomplishment, it is not the signal to start celebrating and stop campaigning.

Arriving at the right location at the designated time is essential. Plan to arrive about five to ten minutes early so that you may relax for a few moments in the outer office, collect your thoughts, and be refreshed when you are called in to interview.

Arriving late for the job interview is one of the worst things you can do. If for any reason you must be delayed, call the interviewer and explain the problem and ask for permission to arrive a little later or on another day. If you fail to call and explain and simply show up late, you may not be seriously considered further. Reliability is a critical trait that is first demonstrated by your punctuality on the job interview.

Look businesslike when you arrive at the office and carry an attache case or briefcase that includes your job-getting documents, paper, and pen. Introduce yourself courteously to the secretary and state the purpose of your business. If you are not absolutely certain of the pronunciation of the interviewer's name, ask the secretary.

STAGE 2: INTERVIEW OPENING

In your greeting, use the interviewer's name and apply a firm handshake. A favorable first impression can help a great deal in the interview. On the other hand, an unfavorable first impression can hurt. Do not smoke in the interview, even if asked.

Show the interviewer that you recognize and respect his or her authority and position by allowing him or her to open the conversation. The interviewer may attempt to put you at ease with "small talk" about your trip, some news events, or the weather. Respectfully react with agreement or appropriate thoughts of your own on the subject. Or, the interviewer may directly launch into business with a question about you. The interviewer may start telling you about conditions, needs, or problems around the company. Listen closely to this valuable information for a few minutes. Then, as soon as the opportunity allows, begin to inject your thoughts into the conversation.

STAGE 3: INTERVIEW DEVELOPMENT

After a few minutes of opening remarks, you should begin to develop your sales presentation and score points. You have limited interviewing time in which to present your case. Therefore, find an appropriate opportunity to begin talking about those things you want the interviewer to hear.

Throughout this stage of the interview, maintain a positive frame of mind and demonstrate your grasp of job-getting interview techniques.

STAGE 4: INTERVIEW CLOSING

As soon as you sense the interview coming to a conclusion, start to close out the session on a "high note." Use these last few minutes to (a) summarize a few key credentials in a final statement, (b) express enthusiasm about working for the company, and (c) express appreciation to the interviewer for an interesting time.

The interviewer will probably tell you the next step in the procedure. If nothing is mentioned by the interviewer, however, you may raise the subject by saying, "What is the next step?" or "I would like to continue our discussion again soon if you feel there is a basis for another meeting!" Such closing comments encourage commitment.

The interviewer may offer you a brief take-home project. If offered such a project, willingly and graciously accept it, for this is a sign that the interviewer is interested in you and your thoughts.

Before you leave the meeting, be certain that you have all the correct information concerning the next step in the selection procedure: Where, when, and with whom is the next interview? When can you expect to hear any word? Or, when is your brief project needed, if one is requested?

STAGE 5: POST-INTERVIEW

Immediately following an interview, record the key points of the discussion—important and interesting remarks made by both you and the interviewer. Note the names and key comments of all other people you talked with while you visited the company.

On another sheet of paper, evaluate the success of your interview. Note your strengths and weaknesses. What things said by you interested the interviewer, and what things bored, irritated, or disappointed him? How could you improve your next interview presentation based on this session? Keep this evaluation sheet.

Five to seven days following the interview, send a "thank-you" letter to the interviewer. In it express appreciation, comment on key points of the discussion, allude to others you met in a complimentary manner, reiterate key credentials, and if new events have occurred during the intervening period, provide a brief update on these accomplishments. Such a follow-up letter shows thoughtfulness, perseverance, and motivation.

Desirable and Undesirable Traits

During the job interview, the interviewer makes a series of judgments or evaluations about your ability to do the job. All these judgments go toward forming the overall impression that plays a crucial role in the selection procedure.

Three factors are particularly important in the forming of the overall impression: appearance, oral communications skill, and social skill.

Another factor that is seriously considered in the job interview is "personality." This factor, however, is more complex, less evident, and more subjectively judged by interviewers than the three factors just mentioned. The employment representative wants to know your attitude toward, and feelings about, yourself, your past, the company, the job, and the profession so that a prediction about your future performance with the company can be made.

Whereas a candidate's underlying motivations, attitudes, and feelings may not be clearly revealed in resumes and letters, these personality traits are sought out and frequently discovered within the face-to-face exchanges of the interview. A technique for exploring one's personality is referred to as depth interviewing. Broad, open-ended questions are put to the interviewee, and the resulting responses are followed up by probing questions that elicit more details, revealing feelings and attitudes. Probing questions often deal with reasons behind an act and the feelings associated with the act. Here is such a depth-interviewing exchange:

Broad, Open-Ended Question

"Tell me about yourself at Murphy's Store."

Probe 1:

"How did you go about getting your promotion to assistant section supervisor?"

Probe 2:

"Why did you handle it that way?"

Probe 3:

"How did you feel when you received the promotion over Judy Stickler, who had been there three years longer than you?"

Depth-interviewing techniques have the appearance of casual conversation but actually reveal much information to the skilled interviewer about the inner workings of one's personality. In any such conversation, be careful to reveal attitudes, feelings, and motivations that are desirable.

Do not be deceived by the cordiality of an interested and curious interviewer; such behavior is essential to place you at ease, get you to talk, and make you reveal *everything* about yourself. Be as honest and frank as possible in revealing positive personality traits that will help on the job. But before uttering a negative, cynical, pessimistic, resentful, or antagonistic remark, think twice. The fact is that the prospective buyer will decide to buy your talents for your positive qualities and will decide to reject your talents for your negative qualities.

The following list contains many desirable traits:

Professional appearance
Good speaking skills
Good listening skills
Adaptability
Enthusiasm and determination
Self-confidence
Practical and realistic approach
Courtesy, appreciativeness, and consideration
Believability and persuasiveness
Willingness to work hard and assume responsibility
Imaginativeness, creativity, and resourcefulness
Good sense of humor
Conscientiousness and dedication
Insightful, thoughtful, and analytical
Alert and attentive

Honest and truthful
Logical and well organized

The following list contains many undesirable traits:

Poor appearance
Inability to express oneself
Poor listening skills
Lack of common courtesy
Lack of preparation for interview
Lack of confidence, interest, and enthusiasm
Passiveness and indifference
Conceit and overconfidence
Negative, apologetic, and insecure
Evasive, deceitful, and dishonest
Contradictory
High-pressure selling
Long-winded or abrupt

The likelihood is that you now possess many of the positive traits needed to make that favorable personal impression. Try not to be shy, meek, overly modest, or embarrassed in expressing your desire for the job and your reasons for qualifying. Only you can state your case.

Fifteen Important Questions

Much of what you say in job interviews is in the form of direct replies to important interviewer questions. This section deals with 15 of the most frequently asked questions.

In addition to answering these important questions, you may be asked to verify and clarify parts of your resume, letter of application, or application blank. The interviewer's attention will especially be drawn to "delay statements," such as "To be discussed during interview," written on the application blank. Therefore, have a thorough knowledge of all facts and figures submitted before the interview.

Key Question 1

"Tell me about yourself!"

Reply Hints

A common opener, this broad question throws many unprepared interviewees. It is, in fact, a "sell-me" invitation. Impress the interviewer by expressing your interest in and desire to work for the company. Offer to discuss a number of your qualifications. Then present a few of your functional selling points and ask the interviewer to choose the ones he or she is interested in hearing about. You can also mention how you learned about the position and company.

Key Question 2

"Why are you interested in working for this company?"

Reply Hints

Emphasize that you are very interested in working for the company, that you've considered joining the company for a while, and that your decision to seek employment here is based on sound reasons. Then produce those reasons, supported by facts and figures from your Company Data Sheet.

Key Question 3

"Why do you want to leave your job?"

Reply Hints

One of two conditions prevail: you're either employed or unemployed. Obviously, being employed is the preferred condition, especially if you're happily employed and are merely investigating possibilities for even greater achievement. Being unemployed detracts from your bargaining position, especially if you were fired for incompetency, negligence, or other serious reasons.

If you have already left or plan to leave a position due to poor working relationships, one of the worst interviewing errors you can make is to respond to this question by ventilating your negative feelings, accusing superiors, claiming unfair treatment, or condemning people with whom you've worked. By leveling personal charges against others in your self-defense, you make the interviewer conclude that you were unable to handle an interpersonal job situation to the point of separation, that you may have been the cause of the trouble, and that, after some period of invested time with your employer, you are displaying disloyalty and could be as disloyal to your new employer.

You can sell yourself more effectively when you associate with successful people, programs, and companies. Build the image of your employer and you will be building your own.

Respond to this question as positively as possible by stating new job objectives rather than old job failures.

Key Question 4

"Why have you chosen this particular field?"

Reply Hints

Here is a perfect opportunity for impressing the interviewer with your interest, knowledge of the field, and ability to perform successfully on the job. Explain that this type of work gives you a strong sense of purpose, identity, and accomplishment, a feeling that you could not derive from other types of work. Avoid discussion of fringe benefits. Emphasize your feelings for and knowledge of the work itself. Mention key functions of the job and claim that you are interested in and possess competency in them. Develop this claim and support your beliefs by presenting functional selling points.

Key Question 5

"Why should we hire you?"

Reply Hints

This question is the most important question any interviewer can ask. Whether it is asked directly or indirectly, be certain that it is uppermost in the interviewer's mind throughout the interview. It is a direct invitation from the interviewer to you to "sell me" and requires extra attention.

Key Question 6

"What are your long-range goals?"

Reply Hints

This question is very popular in interviewing because it gathers a lot of useful information: (1) maturity, foresight, and realistic outlook; (2) degree of preparation in career planning; (3) knowledge of yourself, the occupation, and the company; and (4) commitment to the company and profession.

In your reply, reveal a career plan. In your research, determine what position you could reasonably expect to reach in five years and in ten years. Read about and speak to others who have successfully advanced themselves in your field and with this company, if possible. In your answer note that you have the potential and capability, possess the knowledge and desire, and will acquire the necessary skills for growth within the organization.

Key Question 7

"What is your greatest strength?"

Reply Hints

This is a direct "sell-me" question. Select one key quality you possess that you know to be in great demand on this job. State the quality, then support your claim with past achievements.

Key Question 8

"What is your greatest weakness?"

Reply Hints

This is a "suicide question" that has probably caused the downfall of many qualified but thoughtless interviewees. Interviewers pose this question to you in a fair-play manner, implying, "Well, everyone has weaknesses as well as strengths; it's only human!" You will be coaxed and prompted to answer this question. But before you volunteer anything negative, remember this important rule:"You are screened in because of your strengths and screened out because of your weaknesses."

In stating your reply to this question, emanate self-confidence, express a desire to further improve the good credentials you now possess, and possibly point to a relatively unimportant, non-job-related area that needs some improvement.

Key Question 9

"What salary do you require?"

Reply Hints

There is a wrong time and a right time to discuss salary matters. The wrong time is before you've had the opportunity to sell yourself in person during the interview. The right time is after the interviewer tells you that a specific job is available and that he or she wants you for the opening.

Who should initiate the first figure in discussing salary, you or the interviewer? It is generally to your advantage to get the interviewer to throw out the first figure.

Key Question 10

"What is important to you in a job?"

Reply Hints

The interviewer wants to hear that the things that satisfy you personally are the same things that contribute to the organization's programs and objectives. One effective reply is, "What really motivates me at work is the personal pleasure and feeling of accomplishment I can derive from doing a good job in an organization where my opinions and contributions really count!"

Play down the importance of salary and fringe benefits in response to this question. First, impress the interviewer with your desire to do a good job; then, after you receive the job offer, you can negotiate for fair compensation.

Key Question 11

"What do you do in your spare time?"

Reply Hints

From your reply, you want the interviewer to realize that:

1. You use your time wisely;
2. You are well rounded and have diverse interests and involvements in cultural, recreational, and civic affairs;
3. You would get along well with others in the company;
4. You are a participant and not just a spectator; a leader and not just a follower; a doer and not just a sitter.

To make a favorable impression here, find out the preferences of successful people in your field as to sports, magazines, and books. If you are involved in these activities, emphasize them in your reply. Also, if you have a unique or special talent, hobby, or skill, mention it. This will make you more memorable and add to the uniqueness of your image.

Key Question 12

"Which feature of the job interests you least?"

Reply Hints

This is another "suicide question," as was Key Question 8. It can, however, be converted into a positive selling opportunity.

Tell the interviewer that all aspects of the job interest you, which is the reason you have chosen this line of work. Do not admit that anything about the job bothers you, no matter how much you are coaxed to do so. If the interviewer mentions that the work is difficult and could require frequent overtime, unpredictable work schedules, or hard-to-handle customers, reply in a positive manner.

Key Question 13

"How do others describe you?"

Reply Hints

Tell the interviewer that you get along well with your co-workers, have the respect of your subordinates, and are respected by your boss. Your ability to work well with other people is extremely important to the interviewer; therefore, paint a positive picture of your social relationships on the job.

Key Question 14

"What are your plans for continued study?"

Reply Hints

Convey your desire for continued growth and self-improvement. Indicate that your studies will help you stay current and be better prepared to cope with the new and changing techniques of your profession.

Key Question 15

"Tell me about your schooling!"

Reply Hints

The key to this question is to keep your reply positive. Speak well of your alma mater, for you are, in part, a product of your school's educational programs. If you praise the programs, you indirectly praise yourself; and if you condemn its programs, you indirectly condemn yourself.

If you are asked to explain some low grade, avoid being defensive or blaming others. Follow up with a reasonable explanation of your priorities, indicating that you had to work 30 hours a week to help support yourself and family, if this was the case. Then add that whatever grade you earned, you learned a great deal from that course, much of which you still use today.

Dramatization of a Poor Job Interview

The following skit of a poor job interview helps you to dramatize how a lack of preparation and interviewing skill can hurt a person's chances in obtaining employment.

Have two students volunteer to perform the skit in front of the class. Give both students copies of the skit and ask them to play their roles of interviewer and interviewee as realistically as possible. After the student dramatization, have your class identify the problems involved in this interview and the likely outcome of this meeting.

Setting: Mr. Bill Johnson comes in ten minutes late to the interview. The interviewer, Mr. Paderewski, is looking disturbed at his watch. Mr. Johnson is messy looking, is carrying no pad, no resume, and no pen. He pulls out a cigarette and starts smoking while sitting back on his chair, tipping the chair so it stands on the rear two legs.

Mr. P.: Well, Mr. Johnson, you finally made it?

Mr. J.: I got lost getting here, Mr. Pidesky!

Mr. P.: So, you're interested in working for Booz, Booz, and Cracker?

Mr. J.: Yeah, I figured on checking you guys out! After all, a firm with a name like yours can't be all bad. And anyway, I'll be graduating this June.

Mr. P.: What about our firm interests you?

Mr. J.: Well, it's a pretty big accounting firm, isn't it? And, besides, you've got an office here in Richmond. I'm not too keen on movin'. Ya know, family and all that stuff.

Mr. P.: What type of work do you see yourself doing here with Booz, Booz, and Cracker?

Mr. J.: Accounting work! Isn't that what the job's for?

Mr. P.: Yes, of course, but I mean, in what capacity do you see yourself specializing in—auditing, tax, financial, consulting?

Mr. J.: Yeah, they're all interesting.

Mr. P.: Well, why don't you tell me about yourself.

Mr. J.: What do you want to know?

Mr. P.: Well, for example, what do you feel your special capabilities are?

Mr. J.: As you saw from my resume, I'm an all-around honor student. Learning comes easy to me. So, I guess you might say just about everything!

Mr. P.: That's nice! Oh yes, since you obviously excel in your work, what do you consider to be a reasonable salary for, say, three years in the future?

Mr. J.: Well, considering that inflation is knocking the hell out of the dollar, I'm shooting for at least 75 Gs a year.

Mr. P.: How did you enjoy your four years at MPI? I've heard it has a top-notch accounting department!

Mr. J.: Well, the school's all right. I personally feel the textbooks could have been a little more up-to-date. But ya know how schools are.
Mr. P.: Did you like your professors?
Mr. J.: Yeah, they were all OK, except for that joker Professor Bell. He taught me business communication. He gave me my only D.
Mr. P.: And why was that?
Mr. J.: Well, I knew the stuff in his course inside out and so I didn't attend class very much.
Mr. P.: But aren't there attendance rules at MPI?
Mr. J.: Sure, but those kinds of rules are made to be broken. Ya know!
Mr. P.: Yeah, I know!

Handling the Stress Interview

In stress interviewing, the interviewer deliberately and continuously subjects the job seeker to stressful conditions. This is done to test an individual's behavior and emotional control under pressure.

Fortunately, most job interviewers recognize the existing stress that accompanies the normal job-interview situation and see no need for imposing additional stressors. In the event, however, a person does encounter stress conditions—intended or not by the interviewer—he or she must be prepared to tactfully deal with the situation.

Some of the techniques used by the interviewer in stress interviewing include:

1. Criticizing the interviewee's statements
2. Not responding to the interviewee's remarks
3. Interrupting the interviewee in the middle of comments
4. Asking irritating questions and placing the interviewee on the defensive
5. Questioning the interviewee in rapid-fire fashion

As Rogers points out, "Aside from keeping your wits about you and trying to foresee such traps, about all you can do is to live through this trial; ride it out in the hope that it will get you to a later, normal interview."[2] The key to effectively handling stress conditions is to remain calm, understanding, and gracious, as difficult as it may be.

The following stress dialogue helps to dramatize what could occur during a job interview. Have two students volunteer to perform the skit in front of the class. Give both students copies of the skit and ask them to dramatize the situation realistically.

Following this activity, have the class share their feelings about stress interviews, identify some stress techniques, and recommend effective approaches for dealing with stress conditions in the job interview situation.

E.R.: What made you decide to go to college?
E.E.: My parents never had the opportunity and wanted their children to go.
E.R.: Weren't you able to make that decision on your own?
E.E.: Yes, I think so, but there were family finances to consider.
E.R.: Well, then, why didn't you go to work instead?
E.E.: My parents and I decided that in the long run a college education would qualify me to make more money.
E.R.: In other words, college was just a way of making more money?
E.E.: No, that wasn't all we had in mind.
E.R.: Well, then, just why did you decide to go to college, which, if you recall, was my first question? (Asked with heavy sarcasm.)[3]

Cold-Turkey Question/Answer Practice

Tell your students that to make a favorable impression, they must be able to respond intelligently to certain important questions that are likely to be asked during an interview. Then start calling volunteers to the front of the class. Playing the role of a job interviewer, ask each volunteer a question on your list of fifteen important questions.

When a student has finished responding, ask the class to comment on the quality of the response. Following the student comments, give some helpful hints on the type of response that evokes a favorable reaction within the interview.

Functional-Selling-Point Analysis

In the job campaigning module, you were given the procedure for functional-selling-point analysis. As you recall, a functional selling point is the statement of a key job function followed by several supporting accomplishments. The purpose of using functional selling points is to prove that the job seeker has sufficient credentials to perform well in each of the key job areas.

If you have not done so yet, have each student prepare five functional selling points. Require that the students "memorize" their functional selling points, which can then be retrieved from memory when needed during an interview.

Personal Success Story Analysis

Another skill that impresses interviewers is the ability to draw upon personal success stories that demonstrate problem-solving ability in relationship to the job at hand.

Ask students to write up five personal success stories that prove they have experience and capability to solve problems that will exist on the job. A personal success story contains four essential steps:

1. Identify the situation and problem.
2. Describe what you thought, said, and did.
3. Point out the solution.
4. Explain the positive results in terms of increases in sales, profits, and production or in terms of savings in time, money, and materials.

Have students memorize their personal success stories so that this information can be drawn upon to prove job worthiness during the job interview.

Company Information Analysis

Employers are constantly surprised by the ignorance of interviewees concerning the companies for which they are interviewing. Therefore, one of the surest ways of impressing an interviewer is by demonstrating genuine interest through company research.

Have each student select one organization he or she would be interested in working for upon graduation. Then instruct each person to write a brief report on the organization, providing the following information:

1. Company name
2. Major products or services
3. Names of key executives
4. Locations of offices and plants
5. Size of organization by sales, assets, number of executives, and share of the market
6. Financial position
7. Brief history and growth record
8. General reputation in its field and industry
9. Comparison with other companies
10. News reports about the company in the media
11. Company programs, methods, processes, and problems with which you are acquainted

Ask students to memorize these facts so that company knowledge can be demonstrated during the job interview.

Intelligent-Response Analysis

Give your students a list of the fifteen important job interview questions (see pages 58–62) and instruct them to write up an effective response to each one (with the exception of Key Question 3: "Why do you want to leave your job?"). Suggest that they draw upon the analyses performed thus far in this module by appropriately incorporating functional selling points, personal success stories, and company information.

As you have done for other learning activities, ask the students to memorize their responses (only as ideas–not word for word) for use within the job interview. Explain that their ability to respond quickly, naturally, and confidently will help form positive impressions.

Job-Interview Role Plays

Inform your students that they will be participating in job-interview simulations which are to be held in class. This in-class activity is an important learning experience because it allows students to apply and test their new job interviewing skills in a near-real situation.

Request that students follow this procedure in setting up and running their role plays:

1. Break up into groups of three.
2. One individual will play the interviewee, and another the interviewer, while the third will play the observer-reporter. The observer-reporter will quietly observe the action and be prepared to report the observations to the entire class upon completion of the interview.
3. The interviewee will provide the interviewer with copies of his or her resume and application letter, as well as the company analysis prepared earlier. The interviewer will take a minute or two to review these documents and become familiar with the particular case situation to be role played.
4. The interviewee and interviewer will now perform their roles as realistically as possible. The simulation will take approximately fifteen minutes. (Actual interviews run approximately thirty minutes on the average.)
5. Upon completion, the observer-reporter will stand and report on the interview. This may be followed by any thoughts of the role players.

If you want each person in a group to gain experience as an interviewee, then carry through this same procedure, having students switch roles. An alternative to the foregoing procedure is to eliminate the observer-reporter and create groups of two. In this situation, you would have the interviewee and interviewer stand and provide feedback to the entire class about their session.

Videotaped Job Interviews

Should you have the desire, time, and equipment, videotaping student job interviews can be an excellent learning activity. If you do decide to use videotaping, students can follow the dyadic approach (groups of two) just discussed. In addition, be sure to have students dress appropriately for this occasion so they can see the importance of a professional appearance during the playbacks.

Encourage those on the tape, as well as other members of the audience, to make constructive comments following each playback. This form of audiovisual feedback can be a powerful instructional tool when used properly.

Actual Job Interviews

Recommend that your graduating seniors sign up for the on-campus recruiting program of job interviews sponsored by your college or university placement office. While gaining valuable job-interviewing experience, your students will also be exposed to interesting job opportunities.

Big Payoffs for a Winning Employment Unit

Your efforts and enthusiasm in developing and delivering this unit will be quickly recognized by students, colleagues, and others in your organization and community. Without a doubt, the communication skills you help provide here will have relevance throughout the working lives of your students.

During each job change and career shift, your students will look back with gratitude and go forward with confidence.

Acknowledgments

Pages 11–20 from David Gootnick, *Getting A Better Job* (New York: McGraw-Hill Book Co., 1978), pp. 224–253. Reproduced by permission. List on p. 22 from ibid., p. 172. Reproduced by permission. Figure 1–1 from ibid., p. 2; Figure 1–2 from ibid., p. 4. Reprinted by permission. List on p. 27 from ibid. Reproduced by permission. Pages 33–41 from ibid., pp. 178–179, 186–189, and 230–232. Reproduced by permission. List of techniques for preparing a letter of application (pp. 43–44) from ibid., p. 85. Reproduced by permission. Pages 45–52 from ibid., pp. 88, 89, 96, 97, 100, 101, 112, and 113. Reproduced by permission. Description of job interview (pp. 54–62) adapted from ibid., pp. 129–134 and 137–148. Adapted by permission. List on p. 64 from ibid., pp. 127–128. Reproduced by permission.

Notes

1. For further explanation of each type of job campaign, read pp. 7–17 in Gootnick, *Getting A Better Job.*
2. Edward J. Rogers, *Getting Hired* (Englewood Cliffs, N.J.: Prentice-Hall, 1982), p. 110.
3. Adapted from ibid., p. 110.

Bibliography

BOLL, CARL. *Executives Jobs Unlimited.* New York: Macmillan Publishing Co., 1980.

BOLLES, RICHARD N. *The Three Boxes of Life.* Berkeley, Calif.: Ten Speed Press, 1978.

ERICSON, KATHERINE. *The Solar Jobs Book.* Andover, Mass.: Brick House Publishing Co., 1980.

GOOTNICK, DAVID. *Getting A Better Job.* New York: McGraw-Hill Book Co., 1978.

HALDANE, BERNARD. *Career Satisfaction and Success.* New York: AMACOM, 1974.

HART, LOIS BORLAND. *Moving Up!* New York: AMACOM, 1980.

JACKSON, TOM. *The Hidden Job Market.* New York: Quadrangle Books, 1978.

JAMESON, ROBERT. *The Professional Job Changing System.* Verona, N.J.: Performance Dynamics, Inc., 1976.

PAYNE, RICHARD A. *How to Get a Better Job Quicker,* New York: Taplinger Publishing Co., 1979.

ROGERS, EDWARD J. *Getting Hired.* Englewood Cliffs, N.J.: Prentice-Hall, 1982.

Chapter 2

Careers in the Communication Field

Peter B. Clarke

BUSINESS COMMUNICATION has become an essential tool for everyone engaged in business, industry, medical and educational administration, government. . . in short, anyone who is part of an organization of people working toward a common purpose.

American business, industry, and government are continually changing in response to the conditions they find themselves in. People working in these organizations must be informed about those conditions and about how to react to them. In general, this is done by maintaining a constant flow of information between people and between organizations. *Working* or *being in business or government* means, in fact, being part of this flow of information.

Some information about what is going on takes the form of numerical data: engineering and accounting data are examples. But words convey all the rest through writing and speaking. And someone must eventually digest and convert numerical data to written or oral form so that management can use it.

Communication, then, is how business does business. Memos, letters, reports, meetings, manuals, procedures, proposals, sales literature, videotapes, films, magazine articles, speeches, advertising—the forms of communication are as varied as the information they carry and the activities of the people who use them.

Everyone in business and government communicates to some degree or other. It may be as little as the single annual report a supervisor makes on the status of a department in a factory. Or it may be as much as someone can turn out who does nothing but write full time.

In this chapter, I am going to discuss some of the things a communicator can do for an organization, for there are indeed careers in communication in business, industry, and government. The focus of my attention will be on the many and varied careers of writers within organizational settings. In addition, I will discuss how one can learn to become a business communicator and even a business communication educator. Throughout this book, the subject of careers in communication will be thoroughly discussed with numerous references to the careers presented in this chapter. Furthermore, many different types of jobs involving oral, interpersonal, and organizational, as well as technological, communication skills will be addressed.

Business-writing careers can be personally and materially rewarding, and they can lead as far up the ladder as one's ability permits. The activities of a writer often spread over many areas, bringing him or her into contact with more of the operations of an organization than most people usually see early in their careers.

But just as important, perhaps more so, is the personal satisfaction in writing. It is one of the few jobs that must be done alone, and that yields something you can look at and say, "I did that." Despite whatever supervision you receive and despite how many people contribute material to what you write, eventually you alone at your typewriter must do the job. There is an independence in writing that is rarely found today, an opportunity to "be on your own" that is immensely challenging and rewarding.

What follows is hardly a complete description of the opportunities for careers in business communication. The jobs vary widely from organization to organization depending on what each organization does.

Technical Communication

One kind of communication career is technical communication. This might start with turning out manuals, but the job goes well beyond that. Parts manuals that generally show drawings of something and list the parts that go into it are a simple but essential form of technical communication. So are the service manuals that accompany products to show how to operate and maintain them. These are more complex and often present a real challenge to a writer to simply and directly describe complex operations.

There are other kinds of technical communication than manuals, such as special bulletins to customers and to company personnel. There are communications to people in the field, failure analysis reports, and procedure manuals for quality assurance and zero defect programs. Organizations often videotape procedures to show processes in action, and someone has to script these.

Safety is a primary concern to any organization, especially when manufacturing is involved, and there is a constant need for safety procedures and rules, and for audiovisual materials to teach these rules and procedures. Companies also call on communicators for safety contests, awards, displays, and the like.

Writing procedures is a specialized type of technical communication, and some writers find themselves spending all or most of their time preparing them. Gathering the material for writing procedures can give valuable insights into how an organization works and present opportunities to make real contributions to it.

Proposals are another type of technical communication. Usually, they are detailed explanations of why an organization is qualified to handle a project and how it expects to go about it, should it get the job or be given the responsibility. Proposals are extremely important; an organization's well-being may depend on them.

Whatever goes on in an organization must be communicated to its management and customers. This is accomplished through written and oral reports. Depending on what is being reported, and to whom, such reports can range from single-page memos to elaborate multimedia presentations. Some examples are personnel reports, feasibility studies, research reports, progress reports, and corporate quarterly and annual reports. There are many more. Someone has to organize and put all of these into final form.

Technical communication also presents opportunities for writing and editing speeches and articles. Executives may ask people to "ghostwrite" articles and speeches for them. This may mean writing the article or speech from scratch, or it may require just editing and polishing. In either case, it brings the communicator into close contact with management. There are also numerous opportunities to write original articles, and there is a ready market for them in the many magazines published for business and industry. As well as giving the writer recognition in an organization, such articles can be financially rewarding.

Training and Education

Many organizations, especially larger ones, carry on extensive training programs for their employees. These organizations need people to plan courses, to interview consultants and employees, and to write course outlines and descriptions, text materials, audiovisual aids, programmed instruction materials, videotaped courses, and "how-to-teach" materials. There is a constant need for skilled communicators in this area. Often companies describe these training activities as industrial education, training and development, or management development.

Marketing and Public Relations

One of the biggest, but at the same time most amorphous, areas of communication in business and industry deals with marketing, sales promotion, and public relations. Career opportunities abound in both business and government, and in the advertising and public relations agencies that serve them. Such communication is distinguished by one common attribute: it involves selling products and services.

This may mean preparing sales training materials such as films, videotapes, sales letters, manuals, etc. It may also mean creating sales materials, the tools salespeople use. These may be brochures, or they may be audiovisual materials: sound-slide presentations, motion pictures, videotapes, or the familiar flip charts. Such communication is often called *sales promotion,* and it is an essential part of any company's sales effort. People in an organization may write its sales literature and sales presentations, or an advertising agency or outside company that specializes in such work may do them.

Another type of communication to support sales is advertising. For industrial products this usually takes the form of advertisements in trade and business magazines. For consumer products, advertising makes use of newspapers, magazines, radio, television, and usually represents a much bigger outlay of money. Advertising is generally prepared by advertising agencies, and advertising copywriters do the writing. Anyone can practice this specialized kind of writing, provided they have the creativity and talent to do it. It's a hard field to break into, but it can pay very, very well for those who are successful. There are also companies who do all their own advertising and need copywriters in the same way advertising agencies do.

Advertisements, especially printed ones, often circulate inside and outside a company separately from their appearance in magazines and newspapers. This is called *merchandising* advertising, making sure customers and company personnel see the ads. Someone has to write the supporting material that accompanies this kind of advertising.

Whether industrial- or consumer-oriented, most companies support their products and services with direct mail, basically letters and literature sent directly to customers and prospects. You've received direct mail: subscription offers from magazines, offers to sell you insurance, books, and just about anything else you might be persuaded to buy. For some companies, direct mail may be their only way of selling. Whether it is or not, it is nevertheless an important form of promoting sales, and all of it must be written. Like advertising copy, direct mail is a pretty specialized kind of writing. However, for those who have a knack for it, and who have gained the experience needed to do it, direct mail writing is a needed and well-paid job.

Advertising and public relations overlap and blend into each other, partly because their functions differ from organization to organization. This is especially true of public relations, a line of work no one has ever been able to define satisfactorily.

In its most familiar form, public relations can be preparing press releases, the announcements sent to news media about developments in a company or its products or services. These announcements are designed to provide material for the media to print or broadcast.

Public relations usually, however, calls for a wide range of communicating jobs. Often, management may ask public relations to prepare a speech for someone to give, or to handle special or "problem" correspondence. Frequently, it is the public relations department that fulfills the requests for information that continually come in to any organization.

The annual report is often a public relations function. This is an important publication, since it usually represents a company's major contact with its stockholders and the financial community. Quarterly and annual reports and other similar corporate publications are sometimes prepared internally, sometimes by outside firms specializing in such design and writing, sometimes by an advertising agency. In any publicly held company, stockholder relations is a most important function, and contact with stockholders is made almost exclusively in writing—by the company's regular reports, by special publications, and by correspondence.

Public relations work may involve setting up meetings for different groups of people. This can mean choosing the location and making the physical arrangements, but it also can mean preparing the meeting program or agenda and writing or assisting with the presentations to be made at the meeting. At conventions and trade shows, public relations may assume the responsibility for arranging for the design and construction of an exhibit and for shipping it, erecting it, running it during the show, dismantling and then returning it when the show is over.

Also, public relations may be called on to ghostwrite or edit articles for general, business, and technical magazines.

Employee Communications

In most organizations, the employee communications function comes under industrial relations. Sometimes the task of preparing material for employees is called corporate or organizational communications. Whatever the name, it is a vital part of smoothly running a company, of keeping employees interested and motivated to do a good job.

The most basic kind of employee communications is a company magazine or newspaper. Some of these are quite sophisticated and in large organizations have circulations that are the envy of commercially published magazines. Writing and editing the company magazine is important and respected work, and many successful careers have been built doing this.

Other employee communications are reports to employees, safety and morale campaigns, directives to employees, and employee education and training. All of these require writing, though they may be oral or audiovisual in their final form.

Magazines, Books, Television, and Motion Pictures

There are also the businesses of publishing magazines and books and producing films and television programs. All publishers and producers require writers and editors. If this type of journalism is appealing, there are many opportunities available for those willing to serve their apprenticeships.

Business Communication

You can see that there is a wide range of communication jobs in business, industry, and government: jobs in technical communication, training and education, marketing and public relations, employee communications, magazine and book publishing, and entertainment.

We have only looked briefly at some of the areas of communications that exist, and must admit that we have barely scratched the surface.

For instance, there are communications and management consultants, working either on a free-lance basis or for consulting firms. Writers and teachers who are experienced in business communications frequently find excellent positions as consultants.

Another operation that makes use of communication specialists is a bureau of business research. These are numerous and are usually attached to universities.

Communication jobs exist everywhere in business, industry, government, education—in short, everywhere people communicate with each other.

Learning To Be a Communicator

There are two keys to preparing for a career in communication. The first is practice. The second is education.

No one was ever born knowing how to communicate. Writing and speaking are like golf or tennis in one respect: The more you practice, the better you get at it. You can be taught *about* writing and speaking, but you must teach yourself *to* write and speak. You do this by writing and speaking and by submitting what you do to experts who can critique what you have done.

The other key, education, is essential. The minimum is a bachelor's degree—a master's degree is better. Some universities now offer undergraduate and graduate programs in technical or business communications, and these have proved to be successful and effective.

Learning To Teach Communicators

Should you wish to teach business communication, you will of course need at least a master's degree to teach in a community college. To teach in a university requires an earned doctorate. The usual procedure is to pursue a Ph.D., DBA, or Ed.D., following one of the usual tracks toward the degree, but doing the dissertation in the area of business communication.

What the rest of this chapter recommends is admittedly an ideal. If you are considering working toward an advanced degree or counseling a student who is interested in our field, this is the kind of educational foundation that will prepare a person to teach business communication, do research in it, or both. Naturally, the requirements set by the school granting the degree will be the prime governing factor in determining the program, but many universities are displaying a great deal of flexibility today in meeting their graduate students' needs. These recommendations, then, are a guide.[1]

First, we assume a thorough grounding in the fundamentals of oral and written communication upon completion of undergraduate work—a reasonable assumption for anyone who does not assiduously avoid all courses having to do with writing or speaking.

The Master's Degree

Basically, a master's degree should prepare one for a management position in corporate communications. Thus, we recommend an MBA with a concentration in business communication. Whether the student enters the business world after completing the MBA or goes on to a doctorate, this program will provide a solid background.

Ideally, it would be good if the program allowed eighteen hours in business communication courses and six hours in electives and required coursework. Since this ideal is unlikely to be achieved, we suggest that, within the requirements of the department granting the degree, the student complete the core program, take as many business communication courses as is practical, and complete the requirements with interdisciplinary electives.

CORE PROGRAM

Accounting	Marketing management
Economics	Statistics
Electronic data processing	
Financial management	Electives

BUSINESS COMMUNICATION

Theory of communication
Administrative communication
Organizational communication
Seminar(s) in business communication

INTERDISCIPLINARY ELECTIVES

Economics	Marketing
Education	Mass communication
Journalism	Psychology
Linguistics	Speech and dramatic arts
Management	

The Doctorate

As with the master's degree, the school of business administration appears to be the logical place for a doctoral program in business communication. Such a program should prepare the student for a career in research, teaching, and service to both the academic world and the world of business, industry, and government. Thus, the degree work calls for a blend of theory and practice, with each program tailored specifically for the student following it.

The ABCA Graduate Studies Committee envisioned a total of 60 semester hours coursework for the MBA and DBA combined, and this is both reasonable and in accord with current practice. On the master's level the student should have a solid grounding in:

English	Organization theory
Speech	Information systems
Education	Communication sciences

It would be well to add mass communications to this list, if possible.

The doctoral candidate can major in business communication and minor in a department of the school of business, or major in a department of the school of business and minor in another school or department in the university (English, psychology, speech, mass communication, etc.). Assuming the student has completed an MBA, most of the business school core requirements will be satisfied. For the DBA, he or she will have to fill these out, and demonstrate an understanding of:

Accounting	Marketing
Finance	Statistics
Management	Organizational behavior

Other areas of study may be specified by the school.

For the minimum requirements in communications and interdepartmental work, the following is a suggested guide:

COMMUNICATIONS

Advanced exposition for business communicators
Research methods
Information analysis
Studies in communication research
Seminars
- Written communication in business
- Oral communication in business
- Theories of persuasion and argument
- Organizational communication
- Administrative communication

INTERDEPARTMENTAL

Organizational/industrial psychology
Behavior in organizations
Message analysis
Intercultural communication
Interpersonal and group communication
Elements of persuasion
Discussion and conferences
Society and the mass media
Technical writing
Industrial communication
American English
Linguistics and history of English

The program requirements may also include other useful courses that the resources of the particular university can provide.

The Process

These are the basic steps in earning a DBA or Ph.D. in business, and they are roughly the same everywhere.

1. *Prepare a Program of Study.* The business school and the student's advisory committee must approve the planned program of study, and it may be necessary to get approval as well from other schools and departments where applicable.
2. *General Preliminary Examination.* The student will demonstrate an understanding of the core business courses required for the doctorate, and show how they interrelate when applied to business problems.

3. *Concentration Preliminary Examination.* This will cover the field of business communication and will be taken after all the coursework has been completed. The student will demonstrate an understanding of business communication both in its theory and practice and in its function within various areas of business.
4. *Minor Preliminary Examination.* If the student has a minor in another department or school, he or she will take an examination covering that work.
5. *The Dissertation*
   a. *Prepare a Prospectus.* As the ABCA Graduate Studies Committee points out, the usual format is:
      (1) The problem and its significance to business communications
      (2) Proposed methods of research
      (3) Suggested outline of the dissertation
      (4) Primary and secondary source material
      Generally, the dissertation committee will approve the subject and methodology of the dissertation research.
   b. *Form the Dissertation Committee.* The committee is usually chaired by the candidate's major professor. The other members are drawn from various areas, depending on the candidate's background and the subject of the dissertation. The committee will guide the candidate in writing the dissertation and conduct the succeeding oral examination.
   c. *Take the Final Oral Examination.* The candidate will stand an oral examination of his or her dissertation and defend it.

Acknowledgment

I have based the communications graduate study recommendations freely on the valuable work done by the Graduate Studies Committee of the American Business Communication Association, ably chaired by Dr. H. W. Hildebrandt. I acknowledge my indebtedness.

Chapter 3

Organizations for Business Communicators

George H. Douglas

TEACHERS AND RESEARCHERS in the area of business communication are served by a rich diversity of professional associations and societies. The business communication field is interdisciplinary, and because it cuts across a number of disciplines and subject-matter areas, practitioners have more associations and societies open to them than most of their colleagues in the academic profession. The typical professor of economics, let us say, has only a small number of professional associations open for consideration, and these are mostly large and unwieldy. Professors of business communication come to their profession from a number of different paths and are constantly being brought into contact with colleagues in a variety of disciplines, with the result that they have open to them a heartier selection of professional affiliations than their typical colleague in a business department or an English department.

In this chapter an attempt will be made to describe the major associations and societies that are likely to be of interest to business communicators. Naturally, it is not possible to mention every local organization or group that might be joined by the professional, and in fact some organizations will receive fuller treatment than others. However, the business communication teacher will get a fuller idea of what associations are available, what kinds of services they offer, and where to write for further information. Insofar as possible I have tried to make the information in this chapter useful reference material for teachers interested in knowing names, addresses, functions, and facilities. It hardly needs to be added that professional affiliations as well as association with colleagues will provide additional and more individualized information about some of the groups described below.

The American Business Communication Association

The American Business Communication Association (ABCA) is probably the core association for teachers of business communication. Its membership is composed mainly (although by no means exclusively) of college and university teachers of business communication. However, there are numerous academics from other areas as well as training directors, business executives, consultants, technical writers and editors, and others.

Detailed information about membership and activities may be obtained by writing to: American Business Communication Association, University of Illinois, English Building, 608 South Wright St., Urbana, IL 61801.

History of the Association

ABCA developed out of what was once called the American Business Writing Association (ABWA). The ABWA was formed at an informal meeting in New York City in December 1935. This meeting was attended by E. J. Kilduff, N. W. Barnes, Mrs. Alta Gwinn Saunders, and C. R. Anderson. This group, whose principles and intentions were later concurred with by R. R. Aurner and L. W. McKelvey, decided to divorce its scattered interests from the American Management Associations and concentrate upon developing an association devoted entirely to the interests of business writing teachers.

In April and May of 1936, the first letters were sent out to secure charter members, resulting in thirty-four acceptances. Solicitation was continued in the fall, and membership was increased to fifty-six. The first publication of the association, *The ACTBW Bulletin,* appeared in December 1936. The original unwieldy name of the bulletin and of the association, which was the Association of College Teachers of Business Writing, was changed to the American Business Writing Association when a constitution for the group was prepared and adopted. This constitution was submitted to the members and approved in April 1937. The first *ABWA Bulletin* appeared in June 1937.

ABCA has grown and changed greatly over the years, although it remains essentially an association of academic people interested in business communication. For thirty years the name remained the American Business Writing Association, but in 1967, after a great deal of soul-searching, the name was changed to the American Business Communication Association. In the early 1960s one faction of the membership felt that in this age when there are many important media besides writing, such as audiovisual and statistical presentations, the association could not just be devoted to problems of writing. Others, on the other hand, argued that communication was too broad a term and too nonspecific to identify the nature of the association properly. However, the name was changed, and, in the decade or so since that time, membership has increased considerably.

The name of *The ABWA Bulletin* was changed to *The ABCA Bulletin*. At the same time, the association began a second serial publication to complement the *Bulletin*. This was *The Journal of Business Communication,* which has been published regularly since 1967 on a quarterly basis. Whereas the *Bulletin* devotes itself mainly to practical teaching aids and materials, the *Journal,* in a somewhat different format, is devoted to research and scholarly articles in the field.

ABCA, whose offices are located at the University of Illinois, has been managed by three Executive Directors since its inception. From 1935 to 1957 the Executive Director of the association was C. R. Anderson. From 1957 to 1983 the Executive Director was Francis W. Weeks. Since that time the Executive Director has been Bob Gieselman.

The presidency of the association is an annual rotating office. Presidents are selected from active association members who have achieved some degree of eminence in their field. Among the well-known association presidents since the beginning are: E. J. Kilduff, R. R. Aurner, L. W. McKelvey, C. E. Parkhurst, A. L. Cosgrove, J. H. Menning, C. W. Wilkinson, Erwin M. Keithley, Raymond V. Lesikar, Norman B. Sigband, Robert D. Hay, and Morris P. Wolf. Since 1970 the association has broadened its scope in numerous ways. It held its first International Convention in Toronto in 1975, and it has embarked on a program of special publications in various areas which complement the regular publications of the *Bulletin* and *Journal.* Some of these special publications in book form have been issued in conjunction with other related associations such as the International Communication Association and the Society for Technical Communication.

Organization of the Association

ABCA is governed by its Board of Directors, which meets once a year at the national convention. The day-to-day operation of the association is carried out by its Executive Director. The association has its offices on the campus of the University of Illinois, Urbana, Illinois. In addition to the executive director, the Urbana office also houses the offices for the ABCA *Journal* and *Bulletin*. The editor of the *Journal* is assisted by a secretary who handles subscriptions and membership inquiries. The secretary to the Executive Director also is extremely involved in day-to-day operation of the association and with various production aspects of ABCA publications. Also run from the

Urbana office is the placement or "position referral" service of the association. A director of advertising handles the advertising for the two regular serial publications.

Interests of the Association

The American Business Communication Association and its members are devoted to a good number of areas in the business communication field. A rundown of the major standing committees of the Association will give some idea of the major interests of the association. There is a unit of the association devoted to college and university curricula. Among the various divisions of this unit is the Graduate Studies Committee, which in the last few years has concerned itself with developing curricula for master's and Ph.D. programs in business communication. At the same time there has been an Undergraduate Studies Committee to make further refinements and improvements in the undergraduate studies of business communication in American colleges and universities.

An extremely active part of the association has been the Reports, Letters, and Case Committee. In recent years, this has produced several volumes of case material which has been sold to members and nonmembers. Case material is written by ABCA members, for the most part, and used in their classes for instructional purposes. The Reports, Letters, and Cases material has been one of the most important contributions of ABCA in recent years and continues to be one of the most active interests of the membership.

Another major unit of the ABCA has been its Research and Methodology unit. At present this is divided into two major sections: one dealing with research in communication, usually communication theory, and the other teaching methodology and concepts. All of these committees make regular reports to the Board of Directors at the annual national convention.

Another unit of ABCA at the present time is its Business Practices unit, which has been developed to further explore the relationship between the academic field of business communication and business itself. There is a Practices and Problems Committee and a Business Membership Committee, which has mainly taken on the responsibility of soliciting more members for the association from the business world.

At the present time the association has several ad hoc committees, each of which does one of the following: (1) work on operational guidelines, (2) produce a career booklet, (3) study the quality of higher education in business communication, (4) attend to minority needs, and (5) focus on long-range planning. In addition, there are numerous committees of the association which deal with administration. There are also a membership committee, a publications committee, a nominating committee, a fellow-selection committee, and an international communication committee. In addition to these is a committee on the Council of Communication Societies, of which ABCA is a member. This committee and its official delegate are charged with the responsibility of maintaining a liaison with CCS, which is an umbrella association providing numerous relationships and ties with all associations and societies in the communication area.

Publications

The association's major publication is *The Journal of Business Communication.* It is a 6-by-9-inch quarterly that contains articles, association news, calendars of meetings, and book reviews. Articles deal with research results, empirical studies, and widely applicable techniques in the field of business communication: information systems, communication theory and research, and semantics.

Manuscripts submitted to the publication should not exceed 3,000 words nor be shorter than 1,000 words. A short biographical sketch should accompany the manuscript. An abstract and a synopsis of the manuscript should also be submitted. Manuscripts should be typed double-spaced on good-quality white paper.

The association also publishes *The ABCA Bulletin* in an 8½-by-11-inch format, which includes teaching and training aids and discussion of business communication problems. Manuscripts for both publications should be submitted to the editor, Arnold M. Tibbetts, University of Illinois, 608 So. Wright St., Urbana, IL 61801.

In the last several years the association has also involved itself in a program of special publications, most of these having been book length. It has published *Guidelines for Research in Business Communication, Employee Communication: A Bibliography, Technical Writing: A Bibliography,* and in the last three years has added an additional serial: *Organizational Communication Abstracts,* which is a joint publication of ABCA and ICA. It has also published several volumes of report and letter case material, prepared by the Reports, Letters, and Cases Committee of the association. The editor of books and special publications is George H. Douglas, University of Illinois, 608 So. Wright St., Urbana, IL 61801.

Membership

The association consists primarily of teachers, writers, supervisors, and industrial training personnel. Members from industry and universities specialize in English, business, and technical writing. The membership rates as of Spring 1978, are as follows: Regular, $30; sustaining, $40. There is a special membership fee of $17 for *full-time* students. The library subscription rate is $30 (and includes both quarterly publications). The single-copy rate for the *Journal* is $7.50. The *Bulletin* single-copy rate is $2.50. Information about life membership in the association may be obtained by writing to the association. All active members are entitled to vote, hold office, and receive the regular publications of the association. Members attend national conventions and regional meetings enabling them to talk with leaders of the field and discuss important issues.

Other Services

The association maintains a position referral service whereby universities may be put in touch with candidates seeking teaching positions and candidates in turn may be put in touch with universities looking for applicants in the field of business communication. The association publishes special reports, bibliographies, and lists of doctoral theses, and it maintains a file of case studies. Members are entitled to all of these services and may order from the association offices all books and special publications.

The executive director would try to suggest knowledgeable speakers in the area of business communication for anyone looking for a speaker. He will also suggest consultants and specialists in various areas.

Other Related Organizations

Academy of Management

This association is, of course, not strictly concerned with business communication. However, since a great many of its members are concerned with communication problems of management, its official organ, *The Journal of the Academy of Management,* frequently runs articles dealing with organizational communication. It is more than appropriate in a listing of organizations of interest to the specialists in business communication.

The address for information about membership is: Academy of Management, Mississippi State University, Mississippi State, MS 39762.

American Society for Information Science

This association, formerly known as the American Documentation Institute, was formed in 1937, and the name changed to American Society for Information Science in 1968.

The purpose of the association is to promote the improvement of the information-transfer process through research application, development, and education. There are numerous special areas of interest, including: automated language processing, biological and chemical information systems, classification research, education for information science, information analysis centers, library automation networks, foundations of information science, nonprint media, and user on-line interaction.

The society's major publication is *The Journal of the American Society for Information Science,* published bimonthly in an 8-by-11 inch format. For information about membership, write: American Society for Information Science, 1010 16th St., N.W., Washington, DC 20036.

American Society for Training and Development

While this association is mainly composed of persons involved in the personnel field, it is mentioned here because of the close relationship between training and development and the field of business communication.

The society is composed of people engaged in training and development of business, industrial, and government personnel. It conducts annual institutes for training professionals, operates a position referral service, maintains a fund for research in training and development, and undertakes special research projects.

There is a monthly journal, a biweekly national report, a training resources and consultant directory, and an annual membership directory. It has also, in the past, published a *Training and Development Handbook.*

Write to: American Society for Training and Development, P.O. Box 5307, Madison, WI 53705.

Associated Business Writers of America

Members of this association are mainly full-time, self-employed writers. The association publishes a membership directory, a monthly bulletin, and otherwise attempts to put authors in touch with those who may be interested in their work.

For information write to: Donald E. Bower, Executive Secretary, 1450 So. Havana, Suite 620, Aurora, CO 80012.

The Association of Teachers of Technical Writing

A new and still small, but vigorous, association mainly composed of teachers of technical writing, this association holds an annual meeting and publishes a quarterly journal, *The Technical Writing Teacher.*

For information about the association, write to: John A. Walter, Department of English, 110 Parlin Hall, University of Texas, Austin, TX 78712.

College English Association

A somewhat smaller, academic association of English teachers, the College English Association publishes a monthly journal, conducts national and regional meetings, conducts conferences with business and industry, manages a creative-writing fellowship program, and provides employment information.

The association's major publications are the *CEA Critic* and the *CEA Forum.* For information about activities and membership, write to: College English Association, Inc., Kean College of New Jersey, Union, NJ 07083.

Council of Communication Societies

The Council of Communication Societies was established in 1969 to further applied scientific research into the principles, techniques, and uses of communication, to advance the development of courses, curricula, and other programs of education, to create and promote publications, exhibits, and other educational devices to instruct the public in the importance of communication in human affairs, and to enhance the education of members of professional societies in the communication field, as well as members of the public interested in communication.

The Council publishes directories, leaflets, and folders on various aspects of communication and, most importantly, publishes a *Communications Directory,* which is a comprehensive compilation of information about the world of human communication. It also publishes *Communication Career Sources, Communication Data Sources,* and *Communication Calendar,* which lists national meetings of communication associations.

Since this council in some ways is an umbrella society embracing communication organizations and societies of many diverse sorts, all people interested in business communication will probably wish to receive at least some of the regular publications of this council. For further information, write to: Council of Communication Societies, P.O. Box 1074, Silver Spring, MD 20910.

Direct Mail/Marketing Association

This association is concerned with the creation and production of direct mail advertising. While most of its members are active in the direct mail industry, numerous academic teachers of direct mail are also members. It issues several publications, including the independently published *Direct Marketing*. It also sponsors Direct Mail Institutes and Direct Mail Awards. Write: Direct Mail/ Marketing Association, 6 East 43d Street, New York, NY 10017.

An independent foundation allied to this association is the Direct Mail Educational Foundation. It provides grants-in-aid to university faculty members, awards fellowships for undergraduate students, and encourages an academic concern for writing and advertising for direct mail purposes.

Industrial Communication Council, Inc.

This association is mainly composed of members not from the academic world but from business and industry. However, a number of academic members are also included.

The purpose of this association is to improve cooperation between managers and employees, and between customers, owners, and the public through the sharing and interchange of ideas, experiences, techniques, and research consistent with the responsibilities to member organizations.

The council consists primarily of managers of industrial communication departments in business and government who are engaged in interpersonal and organizational communication as well as occasional writing, teaching, film productions, speech writing, illustrating, and programming.

There is a newsletter. Write to: Industrial Communication Council, Inc., P.O. Box 3970, Grand Central Post Office, New York, NY 10017.

International Association of Business Communicators

This association also is composed mainly of people in business and industry, but its membership is large and it is growing vigorously at the present time. The International Association of Business Communicators was formed in June 1970 by a merger of the International Council of Industrial Editors and the American Association of Industrial Editors.

The purpose of the association is to promote cooperation, understanding, and exchange of ideas, to collect and disseminate information of interest and benefit to members, to encourage effective communication by improving methods of training personnel and developing managerial skills, to improve understanding of the economic system with which members must deal, to assist in the development of college-level curricula in the communication arts, to stimulate general belief in the practical value of effective communication, and to strive for the highest standards in carrying out these purposes.

The association publishes a journal and a newsletter. There is an annual meeting, and there are a great many regional and local chapters. For information write to: International Association of Business Communicators, 870 Market St., Suite 940, San Francisco, CA 94102.

International Communication Association

This association, formerly known as the National Society for the Study of Communication, consists primarily of teachers and researchers in colleges and universities who are interested in the broader field of communication.

The association is administratively divided into five divisions: information systems, interpersonal communication, mass communication, organizational communication, and intercultural communication.

Main concerns of the association are to encourage systematic study of communication theories, practices, and skills, to disseminate current information about information theories, and to encourage the application of research results in the communication field to the development of human understanding and public welfare.

The association's major publication is the *Journal of Communication,* a 6-by-9-inch quarterly journal containing articles, biographical notes, book reviews, and an annual index. Articles deal with recent developments in communication theory, empirical research, and application, relating to information systems and to mass, interpersonal, and organizational communications.

For information about the association, including membership grades and annual dues, write to: International Communication Association, P.O. Box 9589, Austin, TX 78766.

International Society for General Semantics

Since general semantics is highly concerned with the relation of language to human behavior and to improving human communication, many business communicators have been members of this society. The association has a biennial international conference and publishes *ETC: A Review of General Semantics.*

Write to: International Society for General Semantics, P.O. Box 2469, San Francisco, CA 94126.

Modern Language Association of America

Another extremely large academic association, this one occasionally may prove to be of interest to teachers of business communication because of its very large placement service and because of its well-attended meetings in New York, Chicago, or some West Coast city. The association's main publication is the *Proceedings of the Modern Language Association,* a 7½-by-10½ inch, 200-page, bimonthly, containing professional notes and advertising as well as articles on language and literature.

Write to: Modern Language Association of America, 62 Fifth Avenue, New York, NY 10011.

National Business Education Association

This association, founded in 1946, consists mainly of teachers of business subjects in secondary schools and colleges, administrators and research workers in business education, businessmen interested in business education, and teachers in educational institutions training business teachers. The association administers student typewriting tests for measuring proficiency of students and administers business entrance tests for high school and college students preparing for careers in business.

There are two major publications: *Business Education Forum,* which appears eight times a year, and *The National Business Education Yearbook.* This association is a large one, with 20,000 members. Although not all of these members are concerned with business communication, many colleges and universities around the country offer business communication courses that are taught or staffed by those whose background and experience is in the business education area.

For information about the association and membership, write to: National Business Education Association, 1914 Association Drive, Reston, VA 22091.

National Council of Teachers of English

This association may occasionally prove to be of benefit to teachers of business communication, especially those located in English departments and those who regularly teach writing courses of different varieties. The association is a large one, having a membership of over 35,000 members.

Of the association's major publications, the main ones of interest to business communication teachers are: *College English,* the *English Journal,* and *English Education.* NCTE also copublishes *College Composition and Communication* in conjunction with the Conference on College Composition and Communication.

For information about the activities and the publications of the association as well as membership, write to: National Council of Teachers of English, 1111 Kenyon Road, Urbana, IL 61801.

New York Business Communicators

A young, but apparently lively and vigorous, association of communicators in the business field is the association known as the New York Business Communicators.

They publish a newsletter and have regular luncheon meetings in the New York area. Write: New York Business Communicators, P.O. Box 2025, Grand Central Station, New York, NY 10017.

Society for Technical Communication

The Society for Technical Communication consists primarily of writers, editors, and teachers of technical communication; technical librarians; and administrators of technical publications in industrial research and military organizations. The present name of the association was changed in 1971 from the Society of Technical Writers and Publishers, which earlier had been formed by a merger of the Technical Publishing Society and the Society of Technical Writers and Editors. The present society has nearly 3,000 members.

The purpose of the Society for Technical Communication is to advance the theory and practice of technical communication in all areas, to encourage research in technical communication, to develop programs for self-improvement of technical writers and editors, to develop programs for on-the-job training of technical communicators, to provide scholarship aid to students of technical communication, and to develop college curricula in the field of technical communication.

The society's major national publication is *Technical Communication.* It is an 8½-by-11-inch quarterly containing articles, society news, conference data, book reviews, and letters. Articles deal with such subjects as technical publications management, use of computers in publication production and retrieval, use of film, audiotape, and other media to convey technical information, the education of technical writers, editors, and illustrators, the preparation of technical illustrations and oral presentations, and other related topics.

The society holds an annual meeting, but in addition to this there are numerous chapter meetings in cities and regions around the country.

For information about membership in the society and other details, write to: Society for Technical Communication, 815 15th St., N.W., Suite 506, Washington, DC 20005.

Speech Communication Association

This association consists primarily of teachers, researchers, writers, broadcasters, public relations personnel, and persons with careers in the theater, law, and administration. Most of the members are located in colleges and universities or in other educational institutions.

The purpose of the association is to promote study, criticism, research, teaching, and application of artistic, humanistic, and scientific principles of communication, especially as they apply to speech.

The association sponsors several important publications: *Speech Monographs, The Quarterly Journal of Speech,* and *The Speech Teacher.*

For information about these publications and about the activities of the association, write to: Speech Communication Association, 5105 Backlick Road, E., Annandale, VA 22003.

Section II

Written Communication

Chapter 4

Writing Style and Mechanics

Herman F. Patterson

Nancy A. Dittman

For the experienced and the beginning teacher alike, teaching the mechanics of writing and the development of an acceptable writing style presents new problems with each new class. Experienced teachers of business communication do not have to be reminded that students entering their classes have forgotten, did not learn, or failed to see the need for grammar, punctuation, and syntax. Beginning teachers of business communication will discover this fact very early and will, at times, feel that they are fighting a losing battle. As in any other discipline, both the beginning and the experienced teacher must be reminded that it is necessary to begin with the students at their particular levels and attempt to carry them as far as possible in the time allotted.

Experienced teachers know that the majority of students enrolled in business communication classes leave the course at the end of the term with a reasonably good skill in writing, yet teachers in other classes may insist that the students cannot write even reasonably well. It seems very important to point out that students in business communication classes are directed toward a goal or an objective, and they know that in this course "writing counts." However, in other classes the writing is not emphasized, and they tend to forget. This fact bears remembering if the business communication teacher is under fire for poor or ineffective teaching.

Since the mechanics of good writing and the development of an acceptable style are major objectives of any business communication course, it is important for the business communication teacher to use a variety of techniques to assist the learner in attaining these objectives. This chapter is divided into four major sections: The Teaching of Style, The Teaching of the "You" Attitude, The Teaching of Grammar, and Show and Tell.

The Teaching of Style

Although there is a multitude of definitions and examples of style, a universal definition is still elusive, and no true or absolute standard exists. The style that is acceptable for business communication should not be compared to the writing style of a William Shakespeare or a Mark Twain. The teacher who tells the students to "improve your style" or to "work on a better style" is giving them a life sentence with no possibility of parole. Specific instructions, with practice, are necessary if students are to improve their writing style.

Even though no absolute standard of style exists, there is agreement on certain elements that contribute to effective writing style. Most frequently these elements are stated in negative terms or things to be avoided. Therefore, style in writing may become what it is not rather than what it is. What, then, are students to do to write in an acceptable style? They must avoid confusion of terms; they must avoid using words that are already overused; they must not use slang and jargon, or adjectives and adverbs that are meaningless; and they must not use a ten-thousand-dollar word when a one-dollar word will suffice.

Stated positively, style in business communication seems to mean the ability to communicate facts clearly without undue verbiage, to maintain a courteous tone (tone becomes another term without a precise definition), and to present the situation with complete and accurate facts.

The gestalt principle may be employed effectively in teaching the various aspects of style, as it is not easy to teach or learn style as "whole." Rather, it must be broken down into its various components with lectures, discussion, and practice on each of the parts. As each part is mastered, the whole will begin to emerge.

The Oral Approach to Teaching Writing Style

The oral approach to teaching writing takes advantage of the most natural communication medium. Students who do not have severe language handicaps speak more naturally than they write. Nobody ever says, "Enclosed please find," when they hand someone an envelope. Furthermore, studies in English show that individuals with moderate language handicaps speak better than they write. That is, the student who cannot put together a coherent sentence when writing can, and does, speak in sentences.

Cases create more student interest than do isolated sentences. There is some evidence that the skills learned in isolated sentence practice (in which sentences are corrected) do not always transfer to original composition. Students who are bright and only need to have their language skills polished do benefit from such practice, but anyone with a severe problem may not benefit.

When choosing cases for teaching writing style, teachers should be careful to include internal as well as external messages. The writing style within a company may be considerably different from its external style, particularly as represented by sales messages. Internal messages should include cases where subordinates write to their superiors, as well as superiors writing to subordinates. A diversity of cases encourages discussion of style—not merely correctness or accuracy.

Using role play for early cases helps students avoid dictating cliches that they've heard their employers use. Facing a real person also helps students visualize the receiver of their message. Teachers may record the play, play it back to the class while they copy (or provide students with a verbatim copy if enough time intervenes), and ask the class to edit the copy. A good discussion of just what an editor does for a writer—and what an editor doesn't do—can result. Students will usually find that some nonverbal communication was involved in the role play. The communication is, therefore, incomplete and new material must be added.

One aspect of the situation that may arise from this discussion is that the choice of face-to-face communication over written communication or vice versa may be based on the desirability or undesirability of face-to-face nonverbal communication. For instance, a communicator who wishes to tone down his anger will choose to write his message while a communicator who wishes to demonstrate his pleasure may speak to the individual personally. In situations where emotions are important, people can usually control their words more readily than their body language.

The preceding discussion of style and comments on teaching are basic to the understanding of the following discussion on some specifics of style—clarity, conciseness, completeness, correctness, and courtesy.

Teaching for Clarity

Assuming that there has been no previous discussion regarding clarity, the model lesson plan might be used to introduce the importance of clarity, and it will also serve to illustrate the gestalt principle.

MODEL LESSON PLAN

Objective: To teach the importance of clarity in writing and to give students practice in writing simple directions clearly.

1. Teacher begins class with oral directions on how to get to this week's post-football-game dance:

   After leaving the stadium, drive east on Elm Street to the third light, turn right and proceed to green building on the left where you turn right and continue west on Broadway. When you reach Broadway, turn left and again turn left immediately where you will see a large red sign pointing east. Follow the directions on the sign.

2. Immediately following these directions, ask Student A to repeat them to Student B. Both Student A and Student B will be confused and unclear about how to get to the designated building. The stage has been set for a discussion of clarity.
3. Questions by the teacher:
   a. To Student B: "Can you get to the dance by following the directions given by A? If not, why not?"
   b. To Student A: "Why did you not give clear directions?"
      (The answers will be that there were too many turns, too many buildings, too many colors, etc.)
4. Give the class a duplicated copy of the directions and ask them to rewrite for clarity.

   Rewritten, the directions may read as follows:

   Upon leaving the stadium, proceed east on Elm Street, turn right on Summer Avenue, and then right to Broadway. Continue on Broadway to Walnut, turn left, and left again on Henderson where there will be a red sign pointing toward the building in which the dance will be held.

5. Show some of the rewritten directions on the opaque projector, asking the class to criticize. In such instances, the student whose work is being projected will often be the first to point out errors.
   Note: This activity must be prefaced with remarks from the teacher that this is a learning experience and that it should not offend anyone.
6. Have students write one paragraph announcing a meeting of Delta Sigma Pi business fraternity.
7. Again, show some of the written work on the opaque projector.
8. Have students evaluate their paragraph in terms of Who? What? When? Where? Did the sentences or paragraph answer these questions?

   Some typical examples than can be anticipated are:

   Delta Sigma Pi will meet at 4:00 P.M. on March 13.

   Delta Sigma Pi will meet at 4:00 P.M. in Room 18.

   Delta Sigma Pi will meet in Room 18, College of Business Building, on March 13.

These simple illustrations point up the need for clarity and the consequences that will arise when information is not presented clearly, and will lead to the next important and more complex aspect of clarity that answers the question, "How?"

9. *Assignment:* Write detailed instructions on how to smoke a cigarette.
10. *Next class meeting:* Teacher chooses one paper that is poorly written and "hams it up" by attempting to smoke a cigarette according to the directions given. For example, if the directions say, "Put the cigarette in the mouth," the teacher will put the entire cigarette in the mouth rather than just the correct end.

This lesson plan is not intended to be all-inclusive or an outstanding model. It is presented merely as an illustration of the types of activities that may be used in teaching one segment. Note, however, that it does employ a variety of activities: oral instructions, written instructions to be rewritten, the use of visuals, practice writing assignments, and an assignment that carries the student forward to the next class activity.

From this point, the student may be given additional assignments on such topics as

How to change a tire
How to start a power lawn mower
How to hang wallpaper
How to start a charcoal fire
How to plant african violets

The list of topics is as great as the teacher's imagination, but the purpose remains the same for each: Write clearly.

If students continue to have difficulty in writing clearly, the teacher may introduce the idea of flowcharting prior to beginning the writing assignment. By breaking the activities down into steps through the use of flowcharts, a flow of writing will emerge so that writing will become clearer and less labored.

The Meaning of "Conciseness"

Brief and to the point.

The preceding paragraph gives the definition. Or does it? If no further elaboration is given and no examples presented, the reader feels cheated.

Conciseness, then, becomes a matter of judgment. When is elaboration needed and when is it unnecessary? If elaboration is necessary to make the writing have clarity, if elaboration is needed to make the writing more courteous, if additional words make the message more correct or complete, brevity is forsaken.

As an example of conciseness, have the students evaluate the following letter from a college admissions office:

Dear Miss Lord:

You have not been admitted to this college.

Sincerely,

Evaluated only in terms of conciseness, the letter gets a high grade. The students, however, will put themselves in the place of Miss Lord and will point out the lack of completeness and the distinct lack of courtesy.

Now, reverse the situation and have the students evaluate the following letter from the same college admissions office:

Dear Mr. Franklin:

You have been admitted to this college.

Sincerely,

The second letter has one word less than the first but the criticism will not be nearly as severe as it was for the first letter. Evaluation of these types of situations will serve the purpose of showing that, generally speaking, good-news messages can be more concise than bad-news messages.

The balance must be maintained. When students learn that bad-news messages usually are longer, they tend to go overboard in that direction. Witness the following opening paragraph from a student's letter denying credit to a prospective customer:

> Sometimes we experience difficulties in our lifetime but yet we face them and deal with them respectively.

The paragraph is obviously leading up to a ''No,'' but it says nothing. The student was merely making an attempt to soften the blow.

Complete and Correct Communication

Correspondence or reports originating in any office are expected to contain complete and correct information. Incomplete information requires the recipient to ask that additional information be supplied. Not only is additional time required in getting a response, but the cost is increased—to say nothing of the inconvenience that may result.

Illustrated below is a partial lesson plan for introducing and teaching the concepts of completeness and correctness. Note that, once again, the plan proceeds from simple to complex and that the learner is an active participant. The order letter is an excellent choice of project with which to begin. Clarity and completeness are absolutely essential in such a letter and the information may be presented in such a way that the student can readily see omissions such as order or stock number, quantity, size, color, price, description, method of payment, etc.

PARTIAL LESSON PLAN

Objective: To introduce the concept of correctness and completeness in writing and to give students an opportunity to gain writing practice.

1. Teacher leads very brief discussion on necessity of supplying correct information in all writing.
2. Show the following letter on the overhead projector:

   Gentlemen:

   Please send me the dress advertised in yesterday's paper, size 5. Charge it to my account.

   Sincerely,

3. Have students note information that is needed to make it complete.
4. After discussion of information that should be included, assign an order letter to be written using the following information:

   Mary Jones is a teenager who saw a coat in Berman's catalog that her mother, Mrs. Elizabeth Jones, said she could order. Mary wears a size 3 and wants to get a green coat. Her mother's charge card is #806543-M but she is going to send a check for it. The coat costs $39.50 plus 6 percent tax. The catalog order number is 874329X.

5. Collect papers and project some samples on the opaque projector.
6. Some points to be noted from the samples are:
   a. Did they include the order number?
   b. Did they include the quantity?
   c. Did they include the description?
   d. Did they include the size?
   e. Did they include the cost?
   f. Did they add the proper amount of tax?
   g. Was the total amount correct?

h. Did they say that a check was enclosed?
i. Did anyone use the credit card number? It should not be used at all.

More discussion and practice will be needed, but the necessity of completeness and correctness has now been established and the next writing exercises can become increasingly more complex. Students must be encouraged to constantly evaluate their own written work in terms of accuracy and completeness. If the second act of a three-act play is omitted, the audience may know the final outcome but may never know why. The events leading up to the finale are important in understanding the ending. The same is true in any written communication.

When the students have mastered the concepts of correctness and completeness, they should then learn that there are times when it may be proper, even desirable, to give incomplete information and that incomplete information does not always make the writing incorrect. The teacher may present a letter such as the following to illustrate this fact.

Dear Mr. Smith:

Mr. Fatharee regrets that it is necessary to cancel his appointment with you on Monday, July 10.

If you will call us at 487-9611, we will be glad to schedule a new appointment at your convenience.

Sincerely,

The letter just illustrated is intentionally incomplete, but it is not incorrect. No reason is given for canceling the appointment and none is necessary. As indicated earlier, the idea in teaching is to move from simple to complex. As the teacher moves from the simple order letter to the type of writing illustrated in this letter, more judgment is required of the student; therefore, the situation becomes more complex.

More complexity is added as correctness is further defined to include word usage as a part of good writing style. No list of confused words, redundant expressions, meaningless words or phrases, or overused expressions will be exhaustive. However, writing style can be improved through the study of such lists and a concentrated effort to substitute more acceptable words or phrases in students' written communication.

Following is a partial list of words or expressions that can be used more effectively. Many others are readily accessible to communication teachers. Particularly recommended is *A Dictionary of Contemporary American Usage* by Bergen and Cornelia Evans.

REDUNDANT EXPRESSIONS

mutual cooperation	joined together
original source	new innovation
past history	one and the same
refer back	small in size
reiterate again	consensus of opinion

(Using two or more words when one will suffice)

CONFUSED WORDS

ability/capacity	corrode/erode
majority/most	respectfully/respectively
assure/insure	cooperation/corporation
affect/effect	persecute/prosecute
role/roll	cite/site/sight

MEANINGLESS WORDS AND PHRASES

fairly	point in time
significant	considerably
various	utilization
as a matter of fact	relatively
definitely	comparatively

OVERUSED EXPRESSIONS

in a position to	cognizant
this day and age	inform
aforementioned	minimize
earliest convenience	feel free to
appreciate	if and when

Drills promote transfer of learning. Since conciseness, completeness, and correctness are frequently taught by use of examples and by editing, students need help in transferring the material they've learned to original compositions. They not only need to recognize good or bad writing; they need to be able to write well. Automatic transfer does not occur. The teacher can promote transfer by using drill assignments that closely parallel and precede a written assignment. When using this method, teachers must stress that the written assignment should not *copy* any of the sentences used in the drill. Copying can be reduced by not permitting the students to keep corrected drills. Drills may be returned to students for review after the assignment is collected if desired.

Another method is for the teacher to provide an assignment which usually results in a specific type of error. The teacher then constructs a drill using student sentences or paragraphs but not using student names. The drill is then reviewed in class the day that papers are returned to the students.

To take advantage of the psychological principle of spaced practice, drills should be used at intervals during the semester in addition to the day or days when the concepts were originally taught.

In addition, a variety of drills and drill practices should be used to maintain student interest. Since English drills of any kind have negative associations for many students, repetitive use of these drills loses ground rather quickly.

Degrees of Courtesy

Both initial business and repeat business rely on courtesy and respect. The greater portion of business is conducted with unseen individuals. Therefore, courtesy in written communication is important. Again, balance is important. Students of business communication frequently go from one extreme to the other. Good writing style includes balance between the cold, impersonal tone and the overly ingratiating tone.

To illustrate these two extremes, the communication teacher may wish to use examples such as the following:

DISCOURTEOUS AND IMPERSONAL

Dear Mrs. Lincoln:

Your account is 120 days past due and we have no recourse but to begin legal action to collect the $986 that you owe us.

Sincerely,

COURTEOUS BUT INGRATIATING

Dear Mrs. Lincoln:

We have been so happy to have you as a customer for many years. We hope that you have been satisfied with our service and merchandise and that you will continue the wonderful relationship that we have built up over the years.

We are always glad to be of service to you and hope that you will let us know of any dissatisfactions you may have with us.

Your account with us, however, is now 120 days past due; and, even though we regret calling this to your attention, our legal counsel insists that we must do so. Can we work out some arrangement whereby this account can be paid in full?

We want very much to maintain your good will. We know that you are important to us and we hope that we are important to you.

Most sincerely,

The degree of courtesy expected in written business communication should fall someplace between the two extremes illustrated in the previous letters. The following illustration should give the students an idea of what is expected.

THE BALANCE

Dear Mrs. Lincoln:

You have been one of our valued customers for many years and we would like to maintain this relationship.

We feel, however, that something is wrong that has prevented payment of your account which is now 120 days past due. The balance of the account is $986, and we feel there must be some reason that we have not received payment.

We shall appreciate a response from you by October 10. Perhaps we can outline a payment plan that will be agreeable to you and to us.

Sincerely,

The Teaching of the "You" Attitude

The easiest portion of teaching writing that conveys the "you" attitude is the simple requirement that the reader be the subject of most sentences, not the writer. The following letter demonstrates a lack of "you" attitude.

Dear Mrs. Allen:

We appreciate your recent order for two boxes of Christmas cards. Since it is so close to the holiday, we are sending the cards by Air Express. Our company is eager to provide the best service we can.

We're sure that your friends will be pleased to receive handsome cards.

Bama Greeting Card Company wishes you a Merry Christmas!

Sincerely,

The emphasis in this letter is obviously on the sender, not the receiver, even though the message is intended to be friendly and helpful.

The letter modified to make the "you" attitude more obvious would look like this.

Dear Mrs. Allen:

Your recent order for two boxes of Christmas cards was sent by Air Express today. Since the holiday is almost here, we knew you'd want them in a hurry.

As you prepare them for mailing, just think how pleased your friends will be to receive these handsome cards.

Merry Christmas!

The changes are really rather superficial. We, the company, has been removed as the primary actor. Obviously not all communications respond to this treatment. Sometimes the conscious or subconscious attitude of the writer is at fault. The use of imagination and empathy must be encouraged.

Here are two methods by which letters to students can be used to teach concepts involved in conveying a reader-oriented attitude.

Students can be asked to bring in one "junk" mail salesletter which they received. These letters can be used to stimulate a discussion about the assumptions the writer of the letter made about the reader. Once these assumptions are delineated, the next logical step is to decide whether the assumptions are correct. Students are asked to raise their hands if the assumptions the writer made about them were incorrect. The discussion then centers upon the cause of the error. Usually students will indicate stereotyping, inaccurate information, and lack of effort on the part of the writer as reasons for making incorrect assumptions. The teacher should sum up the discussion and indicate that a poor understanding of the reader leads to a letter that lacks a "you" attitude while a good understanding aids the writer.

The letters can be used to demonstrate a variety of aspects of good writing which lead to the "you" attitude. The class should divide into groups of three to five. Each group discusses which of the letters seems to reflect best the reader's way of life. Naturally, the discussion centers around why some letters are better than others. Usually dramatization and the writer's clear understanding of the nature of the reader will be mentioned. Group work has the advantage of involving more people more actively in the learning process. The smaller the group, the harder it is for students to daydream or to permit one student to do all the work.

If a summary of the discussion is required, the discussion is more likely to be pertinent to the subject. Summaries may be written jointly by the group, assigned to one member to report (orally or in writing), or given by the teacher. When students report group activities, the teacher may summarize the group reports, or if necessary points have not been made, the teacher may initiate discussion of the group reports and then summarize the discussion.

This type of activity encourages full coverage of what constitutes a "you" attitude rather than a superficial substitution of "you" for "we." Sentence drills are not very effective for teaching a "you" attitude because the changes of necessity tend to be superficial.

Certain skills needed in reader adaptation and "you" attitude can easily be taught together.

An exercise that can help students to imaginatively visualize the reader uses a set of facts from which students must write a descriptive paragraph about the reader. An example can be used of a mailing list which is purchased. The purchaser knows that the list consists of names of subscribers to *Fortune* magazine. Teachers can help students get started by asking a few leading questions. "Is the reader likely to be male or female?" "What income range is the reader likely to be?" After the class answers the questions, the class is asked to write a paragraph so descriptive that an artist could draw a person based on the description. After the students finish, volunteers are asked to read their descriptions, and the class discusses the accuracy of the portraits. Naturally, the accuracy of the description will be dependent upon the knowledge of the student. This assignment can be used as a basis for another written assignment; that is, students can be asked to write a letter to a person who answers to such a description. Since some of the students will not have written good descriptions, the teacher should select one from these submitted or prepare one to be used.

Another way of helping the students to write with "you" attitude is to have them verbalize their feelings as a receiver of communications and then have them role-play the communicator. For example, the teacher may say, "How do you feel when . . . ." The situations may include being reprimanded, fired, or promoted at work, being graduated from high school, or being admitted to college.

Of course, differences in reactions will occur. The teacher then explains that the communicator must understand the emotional reactions of the average receiver of the message. The writer is, in effect, playing the odds. Role-playing helps the students transfer general understanding to specific application.

The Teaching of Grammar

The evidence that students benefit from the teaching of formal grammar is mixed. Generally, those who already have considerable language skills will benefit from a grammar review and are capable of improving their grammatical constructions in original compositions. However, those who write very badly do not appear to benefit from formal grammar instruction.

At least one university teacher has found that there was a significant difference in the performance of her students on a grammar test when one group of students received grammar instruction and the other group did not. Nothing is known on the effect on original compositions.

As a result of the poor performance of formal grammar instruction and the pressures of the subject matter, many teachers prefer to omit formal grammar instruction. Others, reacting to the concern of their colleagues and the community, feel that it is a necessary part of the course.

Most business communicators, however, debate about how to teach grammar rather than whether grammar should be taught. Grammar drill work is usually avoided.

Using Student Papers to Teach Grammar

When grading a set of student papers, the teacher should mark grammar errors. If a group makes many errors, the teacher may concentrate on a few errors for each assignment and tell the students what is being done. Marking too many errors may discourage the learner, while restricting the number of errors marked helps the learner focus on the corrections noted. Sentences in which students made errors may be placed on a transparency so that they can correct the errors. Student corrections are more easily remembered than are teacher corrections, which are frequently ignored. Generally, the lower the level of the course, the more time should be devoted to teaching grammar.

If a class has severe grammar deficiencies, programmed instruction may be used. Programmed instruction can be assigned as homework (except for testing). Frequent checks need to be made to be sure that students are doing assigned work. This method leads to individualized instruction because usually there is a pretest, which is diagnostic, and a post-test. Students could skip the sections they already know; or they could be permitted to take the post-test on request and then be excused from the rest of the work if they reach a specified level. This helps student morale.

Teaching Transitions

There are two basic methods of teaching how to write so that sentences and paragraphs relate to each other. One is indirect and the other uses the student's previous experience in English. When using the indirect method, the teacher shows the students examples of business documents and requests that the class describe the means by which the author's ideas are connected.

The examples chosen will control students' perceptions of transitions. A sales letter may demonstrate purely mechanical means such as color coding, indentions, or type changes. A better sales letter may demonstrate repetitive use of words, phrases, sentence structure, or paragraphing as a means of connecting the author's ideas. Politically motivated persuasive letters are apt to demonstrate the use of paragraphs which end with a word, phrase, or clause which reflects on the content of the next paragraph and paragraphs which start with a word or phrase or clause which reminds the reader of what went before.

This indirect method may be followed by the direct method. The direct method is a simple review of the principles of transitions as taught by English books. Since most students must study freshman English, they usually have in their possession a good description of what a transition is and how it is used. *Harbrace College Handbook* and *Perrin's Writers Guide and Index to English* are particularly helpful. Using the freshman English handbooks helps to promote good feeling between the English and business communication departments and demonstrates to the student that a commonality exists among disciplines. Students should be asked to reread appropriate sections and to write a paragraph demonstrating the use of one or more of the techniques. Words intended for use as transitions should be underscored. These paragraphs can be projected with the opaque projector for discussion if desired. Publishers of English handbooks are usually willing to provide a free copy to the business communication teacher when the teacher explains how the copy is to be used. Sometimes it's helpful to mention the number of students per year who buy the book at your school.

If the teacher wishes to emphasize transitions without using time for paragraph writing, a choppy letter (one with inadequate transitions) may be assigned for rewriting. The complexity of the letter will control the type of transitions used, but other word changes should be kept to a minimum.

Show and Tell

Although textbook examples are usually good, teachers will want to supplement these. Overuse of the book causes some students to skip their reading assignments. Since reading is a more efficient way of learning than is listening, this is undesirable. In addition, other students are encouraged to copy whole sentences from the examples into their assignments rather than to create their own. Examples chosen by the teacher can be tailored to fit the particular needs of the group or the community where they live. Wise teachers will use models they've written, students' writings, and letters written by businesspeople. Students particularly like letters written locally.

Show Models

Once in a while teachers should write several illustrations of good and bad writing styles to show to classes. Whenever possible, these communications should be on letterhead or memo forms and use correct setup. This puts the emphasis where it is wanted—on the writing—as it reinforces correct letter or memo structure. When using an overhead projector, the teacher should remove bad examples as soon as the discussion is finished. The good example (or examples) should be projected for longer periods of time so that the good image is fixed in the students' minds. More good examples than poor examples should be projected. Transparencies are preferred because they reduce student copying. When handouts are used, the bad examples should not be left in the students' possession.

The following examples demonstrate how the use of letters written by a teacher can be used to teach business writing principles; in this instance, a proper relationship between writer and reader in a goodwill letter.

> J. Jones, southern regional manager, has read in the company magazine about J. Smith's promotion to midwest regional manager. You are Jones. You have met Smith, but are not well acquainted. Write a goodwill letter to Smith. Both reader and writer are of the same sex.

The case is deliberately worded in a nonsexist manner. The student can assume that the reader and the writer are both male or both female.

LETTER 1

Dear M____ Smith:

I wish to congratulate you on your promotion to area manager of the Midwest region.

I am sure that you will be a welcome addition to our group.

Do introduce yourself to me at our next area managers' meeting. I would enjoy talking with you.

Very truly yours,

J. Jones

Letter 1 obviously concentrates on the needs of the writer. The writer is patronizing, like an adult speaking to a promising child; a gatekeeper admitting a newcomer; "big me" being generous to "little you."

LETTER 2

Dear Jerry:

Congratulations! You certainly beat down the competition when you won that big one.

We regional managers will certainly have to watch our stuff now that you're in the competition.

Look me up at the next regional meeting. I'll buy you a drink to celebrate your promotion.

Best wishes,

Jean

Letter 2 is certainly worse. Many students will assume that the writer is male because of the language. If the first letter is patronizing, the false bonhomie of the second is nauseating. The informal writing is over-familiar, but the writer's attitude is still patronizing. This writer, like the first, insists that the reader take the next step while offering nothing in return.

LETTER 3

Dear M____ Smith:

I was pleased to read about your recent appointment as midwest regional manager.

You should be proud of the good work that this promotion represents. If I can help you with any of the SRA forms or in any other way, do call on me.

In any case, let's get together before the evening session at the next regional meeting.

Cordially,

J. Jones

Letter 3 is better. The writer, though still the subject of several sentences, proves a sincere interest in the reader by offering help. The last sentence treats both reader and writer as equals.

The Process of Revision

Revision skills can be taught by having the class edit rough drafts. Letters or memos for display should be volunteered as this method can be quite hard on the ego. Volunteers may be rewarded by being permitted to rewrite the assignment to improve the grade. Teachers should stress that there is no right answer or perfect letter. Each letter must reflect the personality of the writer. When using student work, emphasize the process of writing, not the errors.

Use of Real-Life Business Communications

Letters received in the mail become property of their receivers. Teachers may make transparencies or reproduce letters quite legally. You are legally liable if what you say about the *person* writing the letter is slanderous.

Real letters can be used to teach writing style, writing mechanics, rewriting, use of form paragraphs, letter style, "you" attitude, or any other aspect of business-letter writing. One letter should not be used for too many things, because student interest will lag. Better results are achieved when one or two concepts are emphasized each class period. At this point in the course, the strategy or plan of the letter should not be discussed. However, when the plan is taught, re-use of the letter helps to review the principles previously taught.

Getting the Act Together

"Getting the act together" implies an additional consideration—the mechanics. The finished product must be attractive also. Well-chosen words and a flowing style can be lost through poor typewriting, incorrect placement, or other mechanics that detract from the appearance.

The type of students enrolled in the course will determine how much time is spent on mechanics. Obviously, secretarial and office administration students who are nearing completion of their programs will not need much, if any, review of letter or memorandum mechanics. Others will probably need some review; still others will need to be taught. Teachers can determine the needs of their students through survey or by including such items in the pretest.

As a rule, most students will need a review which stresses what is currently preferred in letter style, salutations, courtesy titles, reference initials, subject lines, and enclosure notations. The full range of acceptable form should not be taught. Nothing is accomplished by teaching archaic usages such as indented letter styles and complimentary closings such as "very truly yours," or by teaching rare usages such as hanging indented letter styles or salutations such as "Reverend Sir."

Since businesspeople are frequently quite conservative, the mechanics that they learn in their communications classes now will be used most of their working lives. Most teachers want to teach for the future, but what is the future is always controversial. For instance, will the simplified letter style ever become the everyday letter style? How widely accepted will nonsexist language become? No certain answer can be given. However, students should be informed of existing movements and their controversial nature. The discussion generated will demonstrate that even within the confines of the class substantial disagreement exists. Although examples used by the teacher may include such salutations as "Gentlepeople," students should not be required to use them. The bulk of class time and student practice should be spent on mechanics which are currently widespread.

Writing style may always be improved upon, and no two individuals will use the same words to express a specific thought. Therefore, the business communication teacher should be primarily concerned with the topics previously presented in this chapter. A major objective of teaching will have been accomplished if the student has become acutely aware of writing clearly, concisely, correctly, completely, and courteously.

Bibliography

ARCHER, ROBERT M., RUTH PEARSON AMES, and LLOYD I. BARBER. *Basic Business Communications*. Englewood Cliffs, N.J.: Prentice-Hall, 1971.

BLUMENTHAL, JOSEPH C. *English 3200: A Programmed Course in Grammar and Usage*. Chicago: Harcourt Brace Jovanovich, 1977.

CORNWELL, ROBERT C., and DARWIN W. MANSHIP. *Applied Business Communication*. Dubuque, Iowa: Wm. C. Brown Co., 1978.

DAGHER, JOSEPH P., *Writing. A Practical Guide*. Boston: Houghton Mifflin Co., 1976.

DEAN, HOWARD H., and KENNETH D. BRYSON. *Effective Communication*. Englewood Cliffs, N.J.: Prentice-Hall, 1961.

FELBER, STANLEY B., and ARTHUR KOCH. *What Did You Say?* Milwaukee: Prentice-Hall, 1978.

FRANCO, LEONARD N., and PAUL M. ZALL. *Practical Writing in Business and Industry,* North Scituate, Mass.: Duxbury Press, 1978.

HODGES, JOHN C., and MARY E. WHITTEN. *Harbrace College Handbook,* 8th ed. Chicago: Harcourt Brace Jovanovich, 1977.

LAIRD, DUGAN. *Writing for Results: Principles and Practice,* Reading, Mass.: Addison Wesley Publishing Co., 1978.

MCINTOSH, DONAL W. *Techniques for Business Communication,* 2nd ed., Boston: Holbrook Press, 1977.

PERRIN, PORTER G. *Reference Handbook of Grammar and Usage,* 4th ed. Chicago: Scott, Foresman and Co., 1972.

REIN, IRVING J. *Rudy's Red Wagon: Communication Strategies in Contemporary Society*. Glenview: Ill.: Scott, Foresman and Co., 1972.

WHALEN, DORIS H. *Handbook of Business English*. Chicago: Harcourt Brace Jovanovich, 1980.

Chapter 5

Effective Letters and Memos

Richard A. Hatch

IN MANY TRADITIONAL BUSINESS COMMUNICATION COURSES, the section on letters and memos has been half or even more of the course. Unquestionably, the first application most students will have for their business writing training will be in writing letters and memos. And most students can improve their writing skills quite significantly through practice with these short messages.

Recently, business communication courses have been designed to deal with ever-broader subjects, including report writing, group dynamics, presentations, and communication theory; and teachers have had to learn to cover the basic material on letters and memos more quickly. This chapter will discuss approaches for teaching letters and memos either as approximately half a semester or as a three- or four-week unit.

Key Concepts

The basic techniques of business writing can be divided into three categories: (1) techniques of readability, (2) techniques of tone, and (3) techniques of organization. Before students begin material on memo and letter writing, they should have completed a study of basic writing style and mechanics applicable to all kinds of business writing. In this discussion, I am assuming that students have already done exercises helping them learn to write clearly and right to the point and they have seen that the "business-ese gobbledegook" style of writing is inefficient and hostile sounding. Thus, they have already studied techniques of readability and tone.

Therefore, the major goals of this part of the course involve learning to use organizational structures appropriate to letters and memos.

In addition, I am assuming that learning to type letters and memos neatly in the accepted formats will not be considered more than one small part of the material to be presented. In my own course, I ask students to submit memos typed in an accepted format, because it is so easy, and I ask them to submit one or two of their practice letters typed in an accepted format. This is sufficient to give them a reasonable feel for letter format, so they can supervise clerical employees who will be typing their letters.

Basic Categories of Analysis

There are several useful ways to subdivide the material on letters and memos for purposes of analysis. Although a division between *letters* and *memos* would be obvious, the two actually aren't very different in organizational patterns or techniques. Some other subdivisions are functionally more important.

The division that is most important in its effects upon writing techniques is the division between situations in which the key goal is to communicate *facts* and situations in which the key goal is to deal effectively with the reader's *emotions*. When the emphasis is on communicating facts, messages are organized in *direct* order, and techniques leading to reading efficiency are important. When the emphasis is on the reader's emotional response, messages are organized in *indirect* order, and techniques of vividness, exaggerated clarity, and tact are important.

When the emphasis is on communicating facts, letters and memos are commonly called *good-news* or *informational* messages, as textbooks refer to them. When the emphasis is on the reader's emotions, textbooks commonly talk about *bad-news* and *persuasive* messages. Organizational structures differ between these three types of messages.

Another kind of division some teachers find useful is between *routine* and *nonroutine* messages. To beginners, all messages are nonroutine, and all need to be crafted with care and plenty of revising. As good habits develop, however, many routine messages are actually written as quickly as possible with no revision. One of the goals of the beginner is to develop habits that serve well when writing must be done quickly. Hard work at the beginning means writing is easier and quicker later on when time counts.

Even though the division between letters and memos isn't the most important for analysis, there are some differences that are worth talking about. Inside the organization, memos are normally less formal and more to the point, written on the assumption that fellow staff members share the basic goals of the organization and the common terminology. Outside the organization, letters are more carefully tactful and clear, and they may involve more highly developed organizational structures.

Finally, it is sometimes useful to distinguish between normal letters and memos on the one hand, and letter-reports and memo-reports on the other. When short reports are typed as letters or memos, writing style and organizational structure should be guided by report practice, which is different in some important ways (see Chapter 6).

Important Sources of Information

Since this is the first textbook on business communication intended for teachers, the best available systematic explanations of the key concepts of letter and memo writing are in the textbooks intended for students themselves. As a teacher, you will want to read business communication textbooks voraciously. As new concepts and approaches appear, they arrive first in the new textbooks.

Of the textbooks, probably the standard complete introduction to widely used terminology in the field is *Communicating Through Letters and Reports* by J. H. Menning, C. W. Wilkinson, and Peter B. Clarke. This is an encyclopedic book covering letter writing as intensively as any source available. Most of the commonly used terminology in the field is reflected in this volume, which is a terrific introduction to the field for the new teacher.

A second source of information is the instructor's guides that textbook authors write. Many of these are simply answer manuals for the problems and exercises in the textbooks, but others are miniature teacher's handbooks, with a great deal of useful information about teaching the course. Although it strongly espouses one particular approach to teaching, the *Teacher's Guide* to Menning, Wilkinson, and Clarke is an especially informative one. Make a practice of checking the instructor's guides you receive with sample textbooks to see what kinds of information they include.

A third source of information about concepts and terminology is the *ABCA Bulletin,* published by the American Business Communication Association, a society of business communication teachers and business communicators. The *Bulletin* is devoted to material specifically on teaching business communication, and most teachers in this field find it very helpful.

Since textbooks are such an important source of information, a fourth source worth looking at is the book review section of the *ABCA Journal.* Most new texts are reviewed in the *Journal* soon after publication, and information is provided to allow you to write for examination copies.

Instructional Objectives

The kinds of instructional objectives that could be used in this part of the course may vary depending upon the time allocated to it and the orientations of the instructor and students. The following suggestions are a sample of the kinds of objectives that could be used.

Minimum Objectives for Brief Coverage

If letters and memos are to be covered briefly, in about six to ten instructional hours, then the following objectives may be appropriate:

1. Students can distinguish between the direct plan and the indirect plan and can describe the organizational structure of each. The most important single concept of this part of the course is the idea of organizational structure—that messages can be organized in certain ways. Many students have no experience at all with the idea that writing can be structured, and it seems to be a hard concept. Once they learn to recognize one or two structures, however, then learning others is much easier. The most important structures for the letter and memo writer are direct and indirect plans.
2. Students understand the efficiency advantages of the direct plan. In the direct plan, we have a structure that is easier to write than the equivalent unstructured message, and it is also more efficient to read. Both writer and reader benefit—an unusual situation. The writer benefits because the hardest part of writing is to get started, and the direct plan provides a quick and reliable way of getting the first sentence down on paper. The reader benefits because the information is easier to understand when the overall idea—the big picture—comes first. And if you have your main point first, then even the skimmer is likely to notice it; anyplace else, it could be missed completely.
3. Students understand the psychological advantages of the indirect plan. When the reader would not understand the meaning of the main point without prior explanation or when there is significant emotional resistance to it, then it is advantageous to explain first and state the main point last. Students should be able to distinguish situations in which this would be useful.
4. Students can identify the main point in direct-plan situations and they remember to put it first. It takes most people some practice to identify the main idea reliably. Sometimes the main point is the thing the reader most wants to know, and sometimes it is the thing the writer most wants to say. In a given situation, most people would agree on one idea as the main point after some practice.

Additional Objectives for Fuller Coverage

If twenty to twenty-five hours of instruction can be devoted to letters and memos, then additional objectives are needed. There are two general approaches beyond the objective listed above. Some teachers believe the best approach is to discuss specific types of letters and memos, such as inquiries, acknowledgments of orders, letters dealing with credit, sales letters, and so forth. Following this approach, Menning, Wilkinson, and Clarke deal with more than forty specific types of letters and memos in detail.

Other teachers believe the best approach is to concentrate on a smaller number of more general types of messages; many use the good-news, bad-news, persuasive typology. These teachers believe that the simpler typology allows students to attain a surer grasp of the organizational techniques they feel are vital. My own textbook, *Communicating In Business,* is one that takes this approach.

Following this second approach, here are some sample instructional objectives for a fuller treatment:

5. Students can distinguish between the writing style appropriate to direct-plan messages and that used in indirect-plan messages. Direct messages are written in a style emphasizing clear and efficient phrasing; conciseness is an important criterion. Indirect messages should be written vividly, which usually means that they aren't particularly concise. They often take quite a few words to say things that are factually pretty simple. Students should be able to analyze these differences.
6. Students can shift among writing styles as situations demand. That is, not only can they explain how different situations call for different styles, but they actually can write in those varying styles.
7. Students can determine when a bad-news message would be appropriate, and they can organize and write effective bad-news messages. The bad-news plan is a highly developed organizational structure for communicating unpleasant information. It is certainly not the only way to do it, but it is one widely applicable way that is easy to remember and use. It's worth learning.
8. Students can determine when a persuasive message would be appropriate, and they can organize and write effective persuasive messages. This is another fairly well-developed structure for dealing with difficult communications. It is somewhat less specific and mechanical than the bad-news plan, and so it is harder to apply, but at the same time students find it more interesting.
9. Students can write vividly when appropriate. The techniques of vividness are central to writing when the reader's emotions are involved, and most students find them challenging to master. The use of very specific detail to convey the feeling of reality is perhaps the most difficult, and if time is available, students should work on this technique. Mastery of it makes all their writing more interesting.
10. Students can differentiate intelligently between routine and nonroutine messages at their level of skill, and they expect to revise all nonroutine messages intensively. Accomplished business writers

consistently are people who spend more time on revising nonroutine messages than they do on writing them. Students who learn the value of revising early save themselves time, because it is quicker to write and revise to achieve high quality than it is to take great pains at the writing stage and thereby avoid revising. This is true partly because it doesn't work; the writing always turns out to need revising anyway, and the extra pains taken in the writing stage are largely wasted. Revising shouldn't be seen as a penalty to be paid by those who lack skill; rather, it should be seen as a normal part of the writing process that makes things easier by breaking up a complicated job into separate, relatively easy steps.

Unit Outlines

Because teaching philosophies, textbooks, prior coursework, and specific case problems vary so much, it is difficult to outline appropriate unit sequences for this part of the course. The following suggestions are based on the approach discussed in this chapter, and should be taken as loose guides rather than as anything more. Much of the classroom activity will center upon making, receiving, and discussing assignments, and these activities are hard to outline very explicitly.

OUTLINE FOR TEN CLASS SESSIONS

1. Present introduction to letters and memos.
   a. Summary of basic writing style
      (1) Simple phrasing
      (2) Friendly tone
      (3) Right-to-the-point message
   b. Direct-plan memos and letters
2. Lead class activity on finding the main point. Assign and discuss first case problem.
3. Collect and discuss first assignment. Assign and discuss second case problem.
4. Collect and discuss second assignment. Cover differences between letters and memos:
   a. Formats
   b. Uses
   c. Writing styles
5. Discuss applications of direct-plan letters.
   a. Three specific types:
      (1) Inquiries
      (2) Orders, acknowledgments
      (3) Goodwill letters
   b. Assignment: letter of inquiry

6. Collect and discuss inquiry assignment
   a. Specific applications of direct plan memos
      (1) Directives
      (2) Requests for specific action
   b. Assignment: directive memo
7. Collect and discuss directive assignment
   a. Letter- and memo-reports
   b. Objective style, based firmly on facts
8. Indirect plan: assign indirect-plan memo-report
9. Collect and discuss memo-report assignment. Review for examination.
10. Hold student examination.

ADDITIONAL MATERIAL FOR SEVEN-WEEK UNIT

To extend the outline above to about seven weeks, my approach would be to spend the first three weeks (nine sessions) just as outlined, and add the following material. Because varied activities and assignment schedules are possible in this longer period, I am specifying only the conceptual content of these weeks.

Week 4: Writing style for emotional situations
   a. Psychologically effective techniques:
      (1) Writing vividly
      (2) Giving extra attention to connotative and implied meanings
   b. Bad-news letter plan

Week 5: Activities and practice: Bad-news letters

Week 6: Psychology of motivation and persuasive-letter plan

Week 7: Activities and practice: Applications of persuasive-letter plan
   a. Sales letters
   b. Applications for jobs

Teaching Philosophy

Teaching students to write is a different kind of task from most college teaching. To the writing student, facts and concepts are less important than skill-building. The major goal of the teacher is not to transfer a large volume of information into students' minds, although there is a certain amount of information to learn. The major goal is to help students develop a skill based on good habits and evaluated by actual performance.

Therefore, the most important teaching activity focuses upon students' writing practice. Making good writing assignments, helping students complete them successfully, and evaluating student papers are of the highest priority for the writing teacher. Preparing other classroom activities must come second.

In allocating your time, this means that you will spend time first on student writing, and only second on preparing lectures and other classroom activities not directly related to student writing practice. To do this, you will have to resist the natural pressure of those three hours a week of class time that you have to fill. First, do a great job of getting the papers graded, then spend the remaining time preparing for class as well as you can. Through most of the term, activities that require relatively little teacher preparation are the best learning activities anyway, and so the need for intensive and time-consuming preparation is reduced in this course.

The Teacher as Coach

The best role model for the college writing teacher is the high school football coach. The coach has one goal—to win football games. It's very clear and simple. And the good coach does what it takes to win football games.

Step one for the coach is to induce the players to want to win football games as much as the coach does. If player's don't feel like working hard, then the coach gets them to work hard anyway, pushing them just short of the point where they'll quit the team. If the coach discovers a six-foot-three-inch, 210-pound sophomore who really doesn't think playing football would be a good idea, then the coach spares no effort to change that student's mind.

If this coach's high school doesn't happen to have the most talented athletes, then the coach doesn't simply give up. On the contrary, the *real* coach redoubles the effort and makes up in motivation for what is lacking in talent. It's a truism of high school athletics that the most talented athletes aren't the ones who win the tournaments; it's the most motivated team who wins.

The essential point is that the good coach is a winning coach, but the coach cannot actually do anything personally that directly contributes to the winning. The players have to do the winning. The role of the coach is to get the players to do what they have to do to win.

The good writing teacher is a coach. The teacher's goal is for the students to write well. If the students come poorly prepared, then the goal doesn't change a bit—the people who will have to read those students' writing won't be making allowances for the fact that they had poor high school backgrounds. And the good writing teacher does what it takes to get the students to write well.

The key factor is motivation. Students who are required to take "another writing course" are hardly in the proper frame of mind to work as hard as necessary, especially if they've felt unsuccessful in earlier writing courses. You will have to spend some time and effort specifically inducing them to believe that hard work will be worthwhile. They need to see (1) that working hard will have an immediate payoff (that improvement will really be rewarded); (2) that they really can learn to write well, in spite of past experience to the contrary; and (3) that writing well is a goal worth striving for.

The coach doesn't have grades to motivate the players. The writing teacher does, but doesn't rely exclusively on them. The coach uses team spirit and praise very heavily. The writing teacher realizes the value of a pleasant group feeling in the classroom. The good teacher also realizes that praise is valuable, especially if it doesn't come too cheaply. To be valuable, praise must reflect genuine accomplishment; it cannot be mechanical or given regardless of real performance. To praise strongly when it is deserved requires tht you really pay attention to individual performance.

Most important of all, coach and players share the main goal of winning. But it's not unusual for writing students to have the feeling that the teacher really doesn't share their goals. After all, it's the teacher who so often chastises them for their shortcomings; it's easy for students to see their roles as opposed to the teacher's role.

The good teacher places his or her role firmly on the side of the student. Instead of student versus teacher, it's student and teacher against the problem of learning to write well. This is a difficult role model to maintain, but it's worth working at.

The most difficult problem with this role model is that you yourself are the one who ultimately decides whether students are succeeding. Football teams play games with clear outcomes of success or failure. Students depend upon you to judge success or failure. It is difficult to be coach and judge at the same time. The checkmark grading system, discussed below, is a step in the right direction.

Classroom Activities

Although a certain amount of material must be covered in class and we cannot dispense with lectures completely, this kind of course should emphasize student activity and de-emphasize lecturing. Given all the well-known limitations of lecturing as a way of communicating information, business communication teachers should practice what they preach.

Avoiding lectures as much as possible need not mean that students will dominate the situation, pooling their collective ignorance, as some teachers seem to fear. The teacher clearly plays a dominant role in the classroom, intentionally or otherwise, and student activities really aren't so likely to get out of hand as the beginning teacher may worry about. In any case, avoiding lectures doesn't just mean turning the course over to the students. It should mean that the instructor guides and directs the students as they actually participate in learning activities. Here are some activities I've found useful.

Discussion of Example Letters

One way to stimulate students to think about letter and memo writing is to look at examples with them. Make transparencies illustrating a variety of situations, flash them on the screen, and invite students to comment on them.

One excellent source of sample letters is business communication textbooks other than the one you're using. Another source is the business mail you yourself receive. Educational administrators are known far and wide, as a group, for their inept communication, and although you will want to be tactful in exposing your administration's messages to students, you may find yourself receiving a good many messages that could be discussed. A third source is the letters students themselves bring in. A good assignment, in fact, is to ask students to obtain samples of various kinds of business letters and memos for classroom analysis and discussion. Finally, on a limited scale you may find you can write example messages illustrating the points you want the class to discuss.

Discussion of Scheduled Assignments

Although teachers vary in their feelings about group discussion in advance of assignments, an activity many teachers find valuable is to invite students to share their first thoughts about an assignment you have just made. You certainly will expect students to sit down individually to do the actual writing of their papers, but you may find that group discussion broadens their thinking about possible approaches and tactics. When the grading system is noncompetitive, students are normally very open about sharing ideas and suggestions. Twenty minutes of discussion in class, perhaps in small groups of five or six, may be just the start students need to do well in their early practice.

Discussion of Student Papers

One very profitable activity, in my experience, is to pick up the stack of papers students are handing in and immediately display them using an opaque projector. If you're experienced in grading business communication papers, or if you're willing to expose your occasional temporary indecision to students, then you may want to comment on the papers, suggesting the kinds of criteria you'll use in evaluating them.

The questions and comments of students as they read others' papers will give you a chance to respond to the immediate concerns of the class. They also allow other students to think about questions that you might not happen to raise. Of course you'll make some arrangements for papers to be displayed anonymously, either by folding down the corner where students put their own names or by asking students to put their names only on the backs of the sheets. Then students who suddenly realize they've made dumb mistakes don't have to share these insights with the rest of the class.

Students can discuss each other's papers profitably if you can help them avoid lacing the discussion with self-justification and attempts to win you over to the approach they have taken in their own papers. If they sense that you are secure in your judgments, once you make them, then they may be less inclined to argue just for the sake of their grades. And you may find that once in a while students will take approaches that you hadn't thought of and that you might have quickly rejected if they hadn't been able to press their points of view.

The check mark grading system (discussed on pages 134–35) fosters an atmosphere in which students feel unusually free to discuss their papers together without becoming frustrated. This is one of the important advantages of the check mark system because comparing notes on their papers as they hand them in gives students important immediate feedback on their work.

One disadvantage of displaying a sampling of student papers on the screen is that it is quite time-consuming. Even to look at six or eight papers may take half a class period or more. A way to give students a feeling for the range of approaches others have taken without spending this much time is to invite them to exchange papers among themselves and read each other's work. In this approach, the students lose the benefit of public discussion and your own comments, but they do get a chance to see each other's solutions.

Discussion of Case Problems Not Assigned

On some points, it may be useful to ask students to work out basic approaches, but not actually write messages, for ten or twelve of the case problems in your textbook. This makes a good small-group activity. For example, in helping students learn to identify main points in the direct plan, you might ask them to form groups of five or six and go through the first dozen or so problems in the appropriate section of the textbook simply identifying main points. Again, when you are introducing bad-news and persuasive structures, you might ask students simply to outline messages in response to three or four textbook problems, identifying good lines of reasoning or reader benefits.

Grading Papers

If you are an experienced teacher and confident about your grading standards, you may want to spend some class time near the end of this unit actually grading student papers in class. You can sit or stand in the classroom and invite students to queue up, while you go through the papers one by one. As you see problems many students are sharing, you can comment to the remaining students on these, thereby avoiding the task of saying (or writing) the same thing to individuals one after the other.

This activity makes more sense if you use a revision-oriented grading system, so you and the students share an interest in getting their papers up to standard. When I do this, I immediately give back papers that will require further revision, and I keep the papers that seem to be ready for evaluation. Then I can go back, in private, and reread the good papers to be sure my pubic assessment was correct; occasionally I find that under pressure to respond immediately I had been overly optimistic about the quality of a paper.

Grading papers in class has the advantage of giving the fastest possible feedback to students, and they like it, even though many of them spend the greater part of the hour just standing in line. If they can talk back and forth with the teacher about the paper, then they're sure they know exactly what needs to be revised and why. Sometimes even the most extensive written comments don't communicate clearly enough.

Writing Practice

The one absolutely essential learning activity in this part of the course is writing practice. The way to learn to write is to write. And you are not likely to assign too much student writing. A typical semester-long business writing course might involve forty to fifty pages of student writing, including fifteen or more letter and memo assignments and one or more longer reports. The lion's share of the shorter papers normally would come in this part of the course.

If you're covering letters and memos briefly in three or four weeks, then you should consider about five writing assignments as minimum. I would assign four direct-plan messages of increasing complexity and one indirect-plan message, probably a memo explaining a point the reader won't understand without prior explanation.

If you're spending a longer time in this area, you might want to assign about twelve to fourteen papers as a minimum. Some of these may be practice in the basic business writing style discussed in Chapter 4. Normally these fourteen papers would include about three bad-news messages, about two or three persuasive messages, perhaps a letter applying for a job (see Chapter 1), two or three letter- and memo-reports, and a number of direct-plan letters and memos.

If you're human, you're already thinking that this will be an enormous grading job; and it will be. That's the price you have to pay to teach the most interesting course (in every other respect) that you'll ever teach. Instead of spending your time preparing lectures, you'll spend your time teaching through paper grading. Few other teachers can spend time on a one-to-one basis with students; you must do so to teach this course effectively.

Assignment Scheduling

The important thing about the writing practice is that it should continue over as long a time as possible. Learning to write is a skill-building activity, and calendar time is important. It is possible to build a skill by intensive practice—doing nothing else twenty-four hours a day—for a fairly short time, the way some people learn languages. But college students can seldom do that. The alternative is to practice regularly and to spread this practice over as long a calendar period as possible.

Students should begin writing almost from the very first day of the course, and they should continue just as long as possible. Even if the course moves on to oral communication or small-group communication, the writing practice should continue. If a business communication course does not drastically improve students' writing, then almost no matter what else it does, it won't be considered effective by most people. Keep those students writing!

Assignment Format

One of the things you'll want to look for as you read textbooks is the structures of the assignments. Teachers' philosophies on assignment structures vary quite a bit, and you'll want to experiment to see what works best for you.

Occasionally you'll see a text that contains assignments like this: Imagine that you're the campaign manager for a mayoral candidate in your city; write a letter persuading citizens to vote for him. Such an assignment might really stimulate some students' imaginations, but even for these the effectiveness of their letters will depend more on successful imagination than upon successful writing.

My own feeling is that assignments should be structured so all the students can understand clearly what the dynamics of the situations are. This is a difficult criterion. Business communication courses commonly include students with varying backgrounds and goals, and situations that would be obvious to some are completely outside the experience of others. For this reason, I believe case problems should include fairly extensive descriptions of the situations students are to deal with, and they should suggest the kinds of difficulties that may be encountered when these are at all subtle. This takes some space, and good case problems do tend to be somewhat lengthy.

Writing Your Own Case Problems

One way of helping students understand the situation dynamics is to build all the case problems around one basic situation. There are a number of staff positions in organizations that involve varied writing tasks, and giving students the continuing role of director of personnel (or staff assistant to the director of personnel, a kind of position some of them will soon have) allows them to develop a feel for the basic situation. Each assignment they do in that same position will increase their knowledge of the situation, just as in real life. You may have to write your own case problems to experiment with this structure; *Communicating In Business* contains two semester-long cases of this kind.

Writing your own case problems is worthy of serious consideration. If your textbook is used by other teachers at your school, probably the best problems in it have been assigned over and over, and some students will no doubt have access to file copies of old papers. More importantly, writing your own problems allows you to structure problems that exactly fit your approach to the course. The most important learning occurs in practice writing, and so everything connected with this activity is your prime responsibility. If nothing else, writing your own problems will provide a ready-made file of good problems to include in your own textbook when you write it.

In-Basket Games and Simulations

One kind of case problem that you will probably have to write yourself applies the idea of putting students in a continuing role, but in a form that is relatively easy to produce. This is the so-called in-basket game. The idea is that you give the student a series of messages taken that morning from the in basket of some imaginary employee, and you ask the student to do what needs to be done in response to each message. You might want to include an introductory description of the role the student is to play and any other information needed. Some in-basket games put the student in the role of a new employee reporting for work the first day, with little or no information about the job or the company. This increases the realism of the game, since inside knowledge is unavailable by definition.

Use your own imagination in developing situations to place in the in basket. It is possible for the in basket to contain a whole series of messages about one situation that the student must assimilate, in addition to other things. Incidentally, there are a few first names to use in such roles that apply equally to female and male students—Pat and Chris are two.

After you have tried an in-basket game, you will no doubt get interested in applying the same idea on a larger scale. Why not set up an interactive in-basket game, in which each student's messages actually go into the in baskets of other students? A terrific idea, but one that gets extremely complicated right away. If you decide to go ahead and try it, good luck! If you want to see an example of a full-scale simulation that has worked for other teachers, take a look at Melrose, *BUCOMCO,* a group simulation exercise for business communication students. Since it is already structured and tested and all the materials are provided, *BUCOMCO* is an easy way to try simulation for the first time.

Analyzing Real Letters and Memos

The more their writing practice connects to the real world, the more they take it seriously. One way of giving students real-world experience is to ask them to write real letters and mail them. Students enjoy this.

To make the experience doubly valuable, you may want to ask students to reply to advertisements for products they're interested in, asking for more information. I sometimes give credit for writing and mailing the inquiries early in this part of the course, then further credit for analyzing the replies later on. As part of the assignment, I ask students to request several pieces of specific information they think won't be covered in the companies' standard brochures; then when replies come in, one part of the analysis concerns whether the companies actually answered all the questions satisfactorily. The analysis also covers the other letter-writing principles we have been discussing in the course.

If you use this idea, ask students to reply to ads in special-purpose hobby magazines or other nonmass consumer magazines. The large, mass consumer advertisers simply cannot afford to reply to individual inquiries. You might also suggest they avoid insurance companies and encyclopedia publishers unless they want salespeople to call.

Interviewing Business Communicators

A further development of this idea, useful when the course covers small-group communication in addition to writing, is to ask students to form small groups and interview an organizational manager about communication problems in the organization. In each interview, students should be directed to request some copies of written messages the manager thinks are particularly good (or bad) examples for discussion. If students offer to blank off any names and keep the examples anonymous, most managers will agree to this. Interview reports center on the manager's perceived communication problems, with the messages as exhibits. You can collect many good examples this way.

In selecting interviewees, students should make use of any personal contacts they may have in their groups. They should try to find a middle-level manager (higher than supervisor, lower than vice-president) in a good-sized company or organization. These people communicate as the most important part of their jobs, and they often are articulate about communication problems.

Advise students to avoid interviewing relatives and close friends of relatives; if the interviewee perceives the interviewers as little kids rather than interested adults, then the interview probably won't be productive.

Interview reports could be written or oral or both. As an exercise in small-group cooperation, I insist that the group work together for a single group grade that every member will receive. If one member refuses to contribute, then it's the responsibility of the others either to get that one working or else to do the work themselves. I sometimes suggest, when students complain about this, that typing the final paper is a heroic task that could be assigned to the miscreant, if they can trust him or her to do it. That often turns the trick.

Evaluating Student Writing

Certainly the most time-consuming part of teaching letters and memos is the paper grading. It is also the most important teaching-learning activity. And it is the greatest source of anxiety for students. Therefore, you method of evaluating student writing should be selected very carefully.

Unfortunately, your evaluations will be largely subjective, and that is unavoidable. There simply aren't formulas for success in business writing. In the final analysis, your evaluations will represent your estimate of the likelihood that a given paper will meet the requirements of a communication situation effectively. If your think a message probably will work, then you will give it a good grade; if you don't, then you won't. And your judgment is shaped by your own perceptions, which are partly (at least) idiosyncratic. Sometimes students will honestly disagree.

Some Evaluative Criteria Are Objective

At the same time, part of your evaluation can be firmly based on objective criteria. Normally these are criteria that will automatically disqualify a student message from a high grade:

1. Grammar should be reasonably correct. Glaring errors in grammar, such as subject-verb disagreement or incomplete sentences, should disqualify a paper from a high grade.
2. Punctuation should be reasonably standard. Glaring errors, such as incorrect punctuation of compound sentences or misuse of the apostrophe, should disqualify a paper.
3. Spelling should be correct. Any misspelling should disqualify a paper from a high grade.
4. Appropriate organizational structures should be used. Inappropriate patterns of organization, such as burying the main idea of a brief informational message in a de-emphasized position, should disqualify a paper.
5. A reasonable level of courtesy should be maintained. An unmistakable insult to the reader, even if unintentional, should disqualify a paper.
6. Sentences should say what the writer intended. A sentence that would be misinterpreted by nearly every reader should disqualify a paper from a high grade.

Beyond criteria like these, however, you are pretty much on your own. And the distinctions between the B's and the A's (and sometimes even the C's) fall almost entirely into the subjective area.

Dealing with the Subjective Criteria

For the new teacher who may not be very secure in these subjective judgments, grading can be very uncomfortable. And since you have to do so much of it, you will want to seek out ways to reduce the discomfort.

One way is simply to be as honest to students about the situation as you can, admitting that the judgments are partly subjective (although not completely), and doing your best to explain your reasoning at least part of the time so students can see that your subjective judgments are at least well-thought-out. This approach works for some teachers and some students, but not all. There's some risk in it, which you may or may not find acceptable.

Another approach, which teachers should use in any case, is to provide students as much information as possible about how the evaluations are determined. Each time a set of assignments is returned the teacher should discuss the three or four major problems students had with it, why those are problems, and how they could be solved. In addition, the teacher should indicate how each of those problems affected the evaluations.

In addition to public discussion, written comments on papers should provide information about standards. You'll need to strike a balance between writing half a textbook on each student's paper and not providing enough information, but as long as your writing hand holds out, you should lean toward giving plenty of feedback.

An intermediate step that may work is to write extensive comments on certain papers that clearly illustrate common problems, then make transparencies (anonymously) and display these on the screen for every student to see. Then you can key other students' papers (using code words) to your in-class discussion.

On early assignments especially, you may want to bring in an opaque projector that can display directly from typed papers and flash every paper on the screen for brief comments. This provides a tremendous amount of feedback to students fairly quickly, and although it will put you on the spot to respond instantly, it has real advantages. When I do this, I qualify my comments by pointing out that I will be reading the papers much more carefully later, and my reactions might change (though I find most of the time my first impressions were fairly accurate).

Letter-Grading Standards

One common way of evaluating student papers is to put a letter grade on each one. This gives students fairly clear feedback about your evaluations of their work, and it also indicates pretty clearly what they can expect in their overall grades.

If you use letter grades, you will need to explain to students what the letter grades mean in terms they can understand. One way is to relate the grades to the reactions of a reasonably enlightened boss in a company that takes pride in the quality of its communications. Here is a way I have explained it:

A—The company would be delighted to send this message. It not only meets the problem goals, but it does so in a particularly ingenious or elegant way. It is substantially better than the ordinary acceptable message.

B—The company would be willing to send this message. It meets the problem goals and communicates adequately in every respect.

C—The company would be unwilling to send this message. Although it is acceptable in many respects, it must be disqualified for one major difficulty or several minor ones. It could probably be turned into an acceptable message with some judicious editing; the writer would not have to start over from scratch.

D—The company would be unwilling to send this message and would be inclined to question the competence of the writer. Although it shows some evidence of an attempt to apply principles discussed in the course, the attempt was not generally successful. Rather than attempting to revise, the writer should throw out this message and begin again from scratch.

F—The company would seriously consider firing this writer. The message shows no evidence of application of the principles discussed in the course and probably would do much more harm than good if it were sent. The writer should study basic principles carefully before beginning this message again from scratch.

Although a letter-grading system is clear and understandable, it does have some important disadvantages. First, it provides a difficult setting in which to ask students to revise their papers. How will you credit revisions? If you allow, say, a maximum of one grade additional credit for revisions, students have limited incentive to revise. If you allow unlimited revision, then you are giving yourself a lot of work, since you will have to re-evaluate and put a new grade on each revision; what if a revision improves a paper, but not as much as one full grade? And so forth.

Second, you will find yourself spending a lot of time telling students why each paper is not an A paper. Even if the paper was pretty good (perhaps a B), students see success as A's, and they are reasonable in expecting to know where they went wrong. Your emphasis in commenting will be drawn toward the defensive side (why it wasn't an A) instead of toward the instructional side (how to improve your writing so it will be worth A's). You can resist this pressure, but you will have to work at it.

Third, a letter-grade system will forcefully and continuously cast you in the role of judge of student work, a role that will interfere with your efforts to be a coach. Everytime you have to make a fine distinction between a high B and a low A, students are reminded that your important role in their lives is your judgmental role. That makes it harder to teach.

Letter-grading systems have real advantages, and that is why they are widely used. But if you use one, you should be aware of the potential problems.

Point-Grading Systems

Some instructors use a point system, in which each assignment, quiz, exam, and so on, is worth a specified number of points. In this system, students accumulate points throughout the semester, and letter-grade equivalents are established (usually on a curve) at the end. This allows the instructor some flexibility in establishing grade equivalents after all the totals are known, and beginning teachers sometimes feel more comfortable with that. The advantage, however, may be more apparent than real, since students will feel, understandably, that if they got, say, 85 percent of all the points during the term, they are entitled at least to a C no matter what the curve looks like. Therefore, you are somewhat limited in establishing grade equivalents.

The point systems have most of the advantages and all the disadvantages of the usual letter-grade systems. There's also a problem that you should be aware of before you start a point system: It is often difficult to discriminate accurately five levels of quality available in the letter-grade system; will it be possible to discriminate ten or twenty different levels of quality available in a point system with that many different possible point levels? If you have to sit and ponder each evaluation separately, grading the papers will take you a long time.

One version of the point system involves taking off fixed numbers of points for each "mistake" students make, deducting two points each for spelling errors and so many points for apostrophe errors and so forth. If the deductive system is limited to errors like these, it could make sense, but how will you specify how many points to deduct for an unclear sentence, and how will you apply it equally to a detail sentence and to a sentence that disrupts the main point of the message? At that level, the value of specific "mistakes" is hard to allocate.

Even worse, such systems give students the impression that their writing would have been perfect (no deductions) if they had just avoided the "mistakes" that you deducted for. It would be a reasonable conclusion, but nothing could be further from the truth. In fact, a piece of writing must be evaluated as a whole in terms of its probable effectiveness with respect to one audience, and that is not a simple matter of adding up pluses and minuses. If simply avoiding mistakes were the answer, writing would be a lot easier than it is.

Check Mark–Grading System

Recently a number of instructors have adopted a system of evaluation which emphasizes revising messages until they are successful. In this system, student papers are rated "successful" (check mark) or "needs revision" (no check mark). The check mark is given for work that normally would be evaluated as B work or better. Students may revise unsuccessful papers, repeatedly if necessary, until they are accepted. Here is one description of a check mark system given to students at the beginning of a term:

> Your homework assignments will receive either a check mark or no check mark. If your work doesn't receive a check mark, you may revise it in accordance with the comments and suggestions made by the instructor and hand it in again. You may continue to revise as many times as necessary. A check mark on a revised paper counts just as much as one on a first try. Your final grade on homework will be determined as follows:
>
> A—15 check marks (on a total of 15 papers)
> B—14 or 13 check marks
> C—12 check marks
> D—11 check marks
> F—10 or fewer check marks

Notice that the grade levels are established to provide incentives. Students who manage to get up to D level can raise that grade to a C by doing just one more paper. Those who get to B level may be willing to work pretty hard to raise the grade to A; they have to do two more. And there's no payoff whatsoever for C work on papers. Students who do fifteen C papers will not receive check marks on any of them. After they graduate, students will need to communicate better than at C level, and this system encourages them to start now.

The most important advantage of the check mark system is that it puts the teacher in the role of coach rather than judge. Although some judgment is involved in discriminating between check mark work and non-check mark work, the accompanying comments are directed entirely to how students can make the writing better—they will have a chance to do it. Instead of seeing themselves as opposed to you in their efforts to get good grades, they soon come to see that you share their interest in having the work done well; after all, if they get that check mark, then you won't have to look at another revision.

At first glance, it might seem that students would object to all this revision—it is more work for them. But in fact, students welcome the opportunity to keep working until their writing is good if they know they will be rewarded for it. Students' reactions to the check mark system are almost unanimously positive.

It may also seem that you will be looking at a lot more papers, and you will. There are, however, such compensations as the pleasure of seeing students improve. Moreover, you will find that the second and third times you look at a paper, you are only looking to see whether specified problems have been fixed. Sometimes that involves reviewing the entire paper, but other times it involves looking only at some small section. It's more work for the teacher, but not as much more as it first appears, and it goes quickly.

The other potential problem with the check mark system is that grades can be pretty high. If you tell students exactly what they have to do to get A's, then an amazing number of them will do it. In some schools, a high proportion of A's would not be acceptable, so you may have to find ways to temper this effect. One solution is to count the check mark grade as only a small part of the overall course grade. The benefits are still there with the check marks counting as little as one-fourth of the final grade, in my experience. Another way is to provide periodic deadlines for work assigned in any period; every three or four weeks, say, there could be a final deadline, after which no further revisions would be accepted. This rewards timeliness rather than quality of work, but you may find that acceptable.

In my own teaching, I have found the check mark system to be invaluable. In changing the relationship between teacher and student, it changes the whole orientation of the course for the better. I recommend it.

Final Evaluation

At the end of the semester or unit, two tasks remain: measuring students' learning and assigning final grades.

Final Examinations

Based upon the approach to teaching letters and memos discussed in this chapter, it would be reasonable to focus a final examination on three areas. First, a final examination should measure students' abilities to produce good writing. The most direct approach is to give them one or more writing problems to do in class during the examination. Unless the problems are very easy or the exam lasts longer than an hour, one problem will keep most students plenty busy, especially if there are any other questions on the exam. My own approach is to assign a problem that should be a routine piece of writing for students at the expected skill level; the pressure of the time limit and the classroom setting provide a good test of their abilities to produce a routine piece of writing quickly.

Second, a final examination can measure students' abilities to organize messages. In response to two or three case problems, students could be asked to sketch out the substance of messages without necessarily phrasing them completely. This should be in addition to, not instead of, some actual writing.

Third, a final examination can measure the students' understanding of the concepts used in this part of the course. Although this unit has not been heavy on concepts, the few major ones are worth learning. An examination could test on organizational structures and on the differences among the various appropriate writing styles used.

Of these three factors, the most important certainly is to test writing performance. Test conditions are analogous to the writing conditions most students will soon face, and asking them to complete a case problem during the exam period is therefore quite reasonable. In addition, since most of their work has been done out of class through the semester, completing at least one case problem in class provides some assurance that the work you have been grading is actually theirs. In fact, it is not a bad idea to schedule several in-class writing assignments for this reason.

Final Grades

In a business communication course, grades play so many roles that it can be difficult to sort out how to make a final evaluation. Grades are used as immediate feedback, as motivators, as rewards, as indicators to future instructors and employers, and finally as evaluations of the students' overall work. However, in the end, a single overall grade must be given.

Three factors are commonly considered in assigning final grades: (1) concept learning, (2) quality of writing at the end, and (3) improvement in writing quality during the course. The following comments are my own views about these factors; teachers do honestly disagree on these points, and you should develop your own point of view thoughtfully.

In my opinion, evaluation in a business communication course should emphasize quality of performance over concept learning. Although a good communicator ideally can articulate the reasons behind his or her choices, it's really the performance that makes the difference. Therefore, I weigh the quality of students' actual writing more heavily than their work on question-and-answer exams.

Some teachers feel that question-and-answer exams help equalize the opportunity for students who are not inherently very talented in writing. But I would respond that grading, by its very nature, is not a democratic thing; every student does not really have an equal opportunity for a high grade. Some students are more talented in communication than others, just as some are more talented at football than others, and I believe grades in writing courses should reflect students' abilities to write.

For the same reason, I believe improvement is not a good basis for grading. The student who begins the course as a good writer really does have an advantage over another who begins at a lower level. On the job, nobody will equalize these people's skill levels, and in the classroom, I think, we should not mislead the poor writer who has worked hard and improved to average level. To be successful, that person will still have a long way to go.

Few, if any, students will enter this course able to produce high-quality letters and memos. Not many will have ever written letters or memos before, and the stylistic and organizational patterns of letters and memos are quite different from those of essays and term papers. Therefore, even the most talented will have plenty to learn in the course. Often enough, the most talented aren't the ones who perform best by the end of the term, just as in football.

Bibliography

Bibliographies on Business Writing

BALACHANDRAN, SAROJINI. "Journal of Business Communication Index to Vols. 1–10." *Journal of Business Communication,* vol. 13 (Summer 1976), pp. 65–103.

BOWMAN, MARY ANN. "Books on Business Writing and Technical Writing in the University of Illinois Library." *Journal of Business Communication,* vol. 12 (Winter 1975), pp. 33–67.

FALCIONE, RAYMOND L., and HOWARD H. GREENBAUM. *Organizational Communication Abstracts, 1975.* Urbana, Ill.: American Business Communication Association, 1976.

GREENBAUM, HOWARD H., and RAYMOND L. FALCIONE. *Organizational Communi-*

cation Abstracts, 1974. Urbana, Ill.: American Business Communication Association, 1975.

WALSH, RUTH M., et al. "Business Communications: A Selected, Annotated Bibliography." *Journal of Business Communication,* vol. 11 (Fall 1973), pp. 65–112.

Textbooks and Guides About Letters and Memos

HATCH, RICHARD A. *Communicating In Business.* Chicago: Science Research Associates, 1977. See also *Instructor's Guide.*

MELROSE, JOHN. *BUCOMCO.* Chicago: Science Research Associates, 1977.

MENNING, J. H., C. W. WILKINSON, and PETER B. CLARKE. *Communicating Through Letters and Reports.* 6th ed., Homewood, Ill.: Richard D. Irwin, 1976. See also *Teacher's Guide.*

POE, ROY W., and ROSEMARY T. FRUEHLING. *Business Communication: A Problem-Solving Approach.* New York: McGraw-Hill Book Co., Gregg Division, 1973.

Further Discussion on the Check Mark–Grading System

FREEMAN, CARYL P., and RICHARD A. HATCH. "A Behavioral Grading System That Works." *ABCA Bulletin,* Vol. 38 (June 1975), pp. 1–9.

Chapter 6

Successful Report Writing

Vanessa Dean Arnold

Reports are commonplace in modern life. One characteristic of a highly organized society is the emphasis it gives to reports. Civic and church groups, professional people, and governmental agencies, as well as business firms, use reports extensively in order to make decisions that affect their organizations. These reports may range from the extremely formal to the highly informal; from elaborate volumes of hundreds of pages to letters and simple one-page memorandums.

Importance of Business Reports

Many kinds of information are exchanged continually in carrying on a business. Production and distribution analyses, income statements, balance sheets, hours of overtime per worker, employee turnover, evaluation of ongoing projects, sales projections, annual reports to stockholders are all examples of business reports. As firms grow in dimension and diversification, their need for a steady flow of information up, across, and down organizational lines also increases.

Throughout the business world, every moment of the business day, someone is being asked to make a search and write a report on some state of fact, or else to read and analyze a report so that action may be taken. The growth in the use of reports as a tool of management has been parallel with the growth of business and industry. It has been said that reports are the means by which business substitutes knowledge for guesswork. It is also generally believed that more business mistakes are due to faulty facts than to faulty judgment. Consequently, it is the task of the researcher and report writer to provide adequate and correct information clearly and concisely so that management can make knowledgeable decisions that will enable their firm to operate smoothly and meet its objectives.

Need for Report-Writing Skill

Because the report has become an essential part of the system of business organization, many authorities in the field of business communication believe that skill in report writing is an employee's key to business success. Treece, for example, points out that the ability to excel in reporting knowledge and techniques can be an outstanding asset in the progress of an individual's career in business. Furthermore, she observes that "knowledge and skill in reporting will be beneficial in any occupation or profession as well as being an important part of a liberal education."[1]

Brown and Reid advise individuals that skill in writing clear, well-organized, thorough reports may well be a major factor in determining how far they will go in a chosen profession. "Having good ideas and suggestions is not enough," they caution. "The person in business must be able to put these ideas and suggestions in writing so that he or she can communicate them to others in higher positions who can put the ideas and suggestions into action."[2]

Lesikar presents a similar analysis: "The ability to write good reports and other business papers is a requisite for business advancement," he explains, "and employees without this ability are likely to be doomed to mediocre roles in business."[3] Similarly, Himstreet and Baty emphasize that "Whether written or spoken, the report is a key to business success. It should be communication in its finest sense."[4]

In summary, the ability to write good reports is a valuable personal asset that leads to recognition and advancement as well as to personal satisfaction. Consequently, if students are made to recognize the importance of report writing to success in their business careers—and the very near certainty of their having to prepare and present reports—they will be more likely to approach this topic with some enthusiasm, or at least with resignation and determination.

Most people who have not studied how to write reports do them rather poorly. A survey by Graves and Hoffman of more than two-hundred persons professionally concerned with the effectiveness of reports yielded this consensus: "Too many reports are badly organized, too wordy, and too inconsiderate to the reader."[5] Along the same line, an article in *Business Week* points out that the quality of written reports in some companies is so appalling that managers are being sent through writing courses "intended to put some point back into the reports that cross their desks and to eliminate the extraneous material that increasingly obscures that point."[6]

Characteristics of Good Report Writers

What are the significant research and reporting skills that teachers should emphasize when presenting a unit on report writing? According to Graves and Hoffman, good report writers develop the following characteristics:

They can analyze a problem, state it clearly, discover pertinent issues, and define them.
They look for relevant evidence.
They know what to include in a report and what to leave out.
They have the energy, curiosity, and diligence to dig out the information they need.
They can evaluate sources and evidence, distinguish the relevant from the irrelevant, separate the sound from the unsound. They recognize significant relationships and reason logically to a conclusion.
They are objective. Prejudices and preconceptions are kept under control.
They learn to condense and summarize; they can say much in a few words.
They are accurate. They check and recheck their figures, check and recheck their words.[7]

Barzun and Graff emphasize that a good report writer must have both skill as a researcher and a conscious feeling for words and their uses and meanings. "Whoever wants to write and be read," they state, "must develop a habit of attending to words—not just to important words and on occasions of formal writing, but to words at all time." Moreover, they believe that understanding a text and taking notes on it requires the same attention to words and meaning as preparing and polishing a report. "Whoever gains skill at the one and is a good researcher can develop skill at the other and become a good report writer," they explain.[8]

Good report writers, then, are made through their own efforts. One can learn the reporting process only by researching and writing. Therefore, in any report-writing class students should have practice in compiling: (1) a memorandum report, (2) a letter report, (3) a short report, and (4) a long formal report. This means that teachers of report writing must spend countless hours correcting papers (and, when so doing, giving careful attention to spelling, vocabulary, and syntax, as well as to clarity and organization). It is only in this way that they can advance their students' ability to write. This is the process that leads to the development of effective reports.

The Report-Writing Process

Basically, there are two kinds of business reports: (1) the information report and (2) the research report. As its name implies, the information report provides information that will keep the reader up to date with events, developments, and projects. The research report, on the other hand, is the outcome of an investigation of some phenomena. This may be any branch of human activity, ranging from an investigation of the market for electric cars to surveying employee lunchtime eating preferences; from an experiment to determine if workers produce more when allowed to select their own working hours (flexitime) to studying sites to determine the best location for a fast-food restaurant.

In keeping with established principles of learning, that is, having students advance progressively from the simple to the complex, a memorandum-report that involves a small amount of library research might be selected for the first report-writing assignment. The second assignment might be a letter-report, and the third and fourth assignments—a short report and a long formal report—might be investigative in nature. The length of the longer report would depend, of course, on the time allotted for the topic of report writing.

If at all possible, students should have the experience of producing a report that is long enough to require some serious effort at information gathering. However, in a business communication course where the primary emphasis is placed on letter writing, time might not permit the writing of an extremely long report. In this event, the teacher should select an example of a fairly lengthy report and by the use of transparencies, slides, or some other visual medium, spend some time discussing the various parts that make up the formal report. Ideally, this would cover the following: title page, letter of transmittal, table of contents, summary or synopsis, body of the report (purpose, method, findings, conclusions, and recommendations), and addenda (bibliography, appendix material, and index).

An additional purpose in presenting this overview is, of course, to introduce students to the total report-writing process. By showing the development of a report from the selection of a topic to its appearance in final form containing all the preliminary and addenda parts, a "gestalt" of the report-writing process is established.

Numerous business communication textbooks, as well as books dealing exclusively with report writing, contain excellent examples of full-length reports that could be used in the above mentioned overview of the report-writing process. Additional sources for illustrations of this kind are bureaus of business and economic research, and departments of management and marketing. Reports from sources such as these have the added advantage of realism and interest. Permission for their use is usually easy to obtain.

Planning the Report

It is always easier to conduct a successful piece of research if the problem is clearly defined in advance. There should be no doubt about the researcher's goal. One way of making sure that the problem is fully understood is to consider the purpose of the report. When this is done, the kind of answer or solution required can be visualized more readily.

Once students have selected (or have been assigned) a research topic, they should submit to the instructor, in memorandum form, a plan for conducting their study. It should begin with this sentence, "The purpose of this study is . . . ," and then, after stating the purpose, tell of the method or methods to be used in gathering information. The teacher can then evaluate the plan presented by each student and accept it, accept it pending modification, or reject it. On rare occasions, a few plans will have to be rejected because they are too broad or too vague. At other times, students may have selected a method for gathering information that will not suit their purposes. In any event, the memorandums should be returned to students with appropriate written comments. If students are made to understand that these memorandums constitute a quasi-official contract, they will be more likely to stay on track while researching and writing their reports.

Teachers may want to defer the planning process as sketched above until they have spent some class time discussing methods of gathering information. However, students should understand that in actual practice, defining the problem is the first step in the report-writing process. To this end, beginning with a clear view of what the report is supposed to accomplish, who will be using it, and for what purpose, will get the report writer off to a good start.

Methods of Gathering Information

After a problem has been defined, the report writer must plan a method of gathering information. Sources of information are either secondary or primary. Because it deals with materials already published—books, pamphlets, government documents, magazines, encyclopedias, brochures, and almanacs—library research contributes *secondary data.* Original data created as a result of research from observation, surveys, and experiments are known as *primary data.* A report-writing assignment using secondary data and an assignment which involves the gathering of primary data should be planned so that students may understand the data-gathering function of each method.

Library Research

Library research should be the starting point in any data-gathering process. It is a way of discovering what other information on a particular topic has been uncovered by other researchers. Students will understand the function of library research more clearly if they are told it can prevent them from "reinventing the wheel." The facilities of present-day libraries—data banks, joint repositories, microcollections, and the like—have grown in number and variety and have many time-saving features to aid the report writer.

After a discussion of these facilities, the basic reference sources, and the steps to finding needed library information, an appropriate assignment would be as follows: "Select two articles from the *Business Periodicals Index* that apply to some aspect of business, and prepare a memorandum report addressed to the instructor." This is a good time to point out to students that the memorandum is the most-used report format in business, and although it is the least formal of reports, the memorandum may incorporate all the steps in the problem-solving process and all of the writing techniques employed in formal reports. Memorandum form should also be discussed at this time if the topic has not been covered previously.

If at all possible, students should have practice in locating materials in the school library. However, high school teachers might find it beneficial to maintain a vertical file of newspaper clippings and magazine articles on topics that would be suitable for a report-writing assignment. Many students do not have periodicals in the home, and because of part-time jobs, riding an early bus, participating in sports, and the like, are able to spend only enough time in the library to check out books. Furthermore, in many high school libraries, students are not permitted to enter and search for information at their convenience. Sad to say, there are many reasons for rules such as these (some of them good ones) and teachers must abide by them.

Materials in the vertical file will also be useful during class time when specific sections of report writing are discussed. For instance, magazine articles could be handed out at the beginning of a class period and each student asked to read one article and prepare an entry for an annotated bibliography according to a previously discussed form. Then, at the next class meeting each student would summarize his or her article in a memorandum-report addressed to the instructor. A complete bibliographical reference should be included with the report.

Teachers who receive—or have friends who receive—magazines such as *Newsweek, Time, U.S. News and World Report, Business Week, Forbes, Dun's Review,* and *Fortune* can accumulate a multitude of materials on topics appropriate for report-writing assignments. This material can be updated yearly and used for letter- and memorandum-reports, as well as for longer reports.

Persons who conduct workshops or training sessions might also find the above approach useful, particularly if library material is not readily available. An added feature of this plan is that it illustrates to college students that there really are articles published weekly that are of importance to business firms, and that they should acquire the habit of reading business periodicals.

Recently, articles on the previously mentioned publications have dealt with such subjects as the increasing use of robots in business and industry, the business use of lie-detector tests, the market for electric cars, and the newly enacted bankruptcy laws—all of which might be appropriate topics for report-writing assignments.

Survey Research

Survey instruments—questionnaires, checklists, and interviews—are widely used to obtain business information. Whether conducted by mail or by personal or telephone interviews, surveys are used to determine facts not obtainable through library research. The opinion polls reported in newspapers and magazines and on television are familiar to students and are an excellent means of introducing the topic of surveying as a method of obtaining information for a report.

Teachers can easily accumulate a large file of clippings, reporting the results of opinion polls, market surveys, etc., to use as examples when discussing survey research concepts. In addition, students could be asked to submit an example they have found in their reading. This is not a difficult assignment, for practically every day there are numerous examples in both campus and local newspapers. In any given week articles with headings such as the following can be noted:

Americans Favor SALT Pact 3 to 1, Poll Indicates
Study Shows Americans Unsure About Energy Crisis
Extremes Fade In College Poll
Survey Shows Americans Favor Death Penalty
Survey Reveals Students Unhappy With Dorm Visitation Policy

A survey of the reading preferences and buying habits of college students was recently reported in newspapers across the country. Entitled "Who Reads What" it stated:

> *Time* and *Newsweek*—not, as some might guess, the youth-oriented *Rolling Stone* or *Playboy*—are the magazines most read by college students. Of the students surveyed by . . . Marketing and Research Corporation, 39 percent said they read *Time* and 35 percent read *Newsweek*. . . . The survey showed that 84 percent of the students drank alcoholic beverages, 78 percent use headache or pain relievers, 47 percent own stereo speakers, 46 percent use stomach-upset remedies, 29 percent drive foreign cars and 28 percent smoke cigarettes.[9]

The newspaper article noted that the survey, which is to be done annually in the future, cross-tabulated various media with products so that an advertiser could, for instance, find out how many students who buy stereo records read particular publications. The complete findings in this survey are available to clients of the firm which conducted the study for $6,000.

A discussion of the methods by which the data in these surveys were obtained leads naturally into a discussion of (1) random sampling, (2) stratified random sampling, (3) systematic random sampling, and (4) sample size. In the latter category, sample size, students are usually surprised to learn of the relatively small numbers of people included in surveys conducted by nationally known public opinion poll organizations such as Gallup, Roper, and Harris—usually fewer than two-thousand persons. Yet, their findings are considered valid. Why? Because these organizations use accepted sampling techniques.

The main point to be made in any discussion of sampling techniques is that the sampling process is based on the principle that a sufficiently large number drawn at random from a population will be representative of the total population.

Many of the techniques of survey research can be illustrated by distributing a short questionnaire to members of the class. The one shown opposite elicits opinions on issues familiar to most students at the time of this writing. The list of items could be revised from time to time to reflect the current *Zeitgeist*.

After the responses to the questionnaire have been tabulated, (previously prepared transparencies with a listing of the items will facilitate this process), the following questions can be posed:

1. Can we generalize these results to the total population of this city/state/nation?

The answer, of course, is "no" because we have not used sampling techniques.

2. Are the opinions expressed in this class representative of the student body at this campus?

We cannot know the answer to this question until we administer the questionnaire to a random sample of the student body.

By using the previously discussed questionnaire as an example, the terms *validity* and *reliability* can be explained, as can the procedures that would be followed if the survey instrument were used to elicit opinions by mail, by personal interview, or by telephone interview. The advantages and disadvantages inherent in collecting data by each of these processes should be enumerated.

Recently, some controversy has arisen over the wording of questions used in opinion polls. For example, some news organizations have been accused of "poll-rigging" by asking biased questions about a controversial subject and then publicizing the biased results. The questions were worded so that respondents were forced to make certain replies. For example: "Do you think that the United States should or should not negotiate a treaty with the Russians to limit strategic military weapons?"[10] Given the way the question was worded, it is surprising that it did not elicit a 100 percent favorable response.

What's Your Opinion?

Directions: Please respond to the following questions by check marking the appropriate blank.

	Yes	No
1. Do you think the major oil companies should be prevented from taking over other sources of energy such as nuclear, solar, and coal?	____	____
2. Experts have said that to further the use of energy resources such as coal, air pollution standards will have to be relaxed. Are you in favor of such a trade-off?	____	____
3. Do you favor loan guarantees to business for the development of alternative energy resources?	____	____
4. Do you think that billions of dollars should be spent in an effort to develop a synthetic fuel?	____	____
5. Despite possible price increases, do you feel that deregulation of oil and gas wellhead prices is necessary to stimulate domestic production and reduce dependence on imported fuels?	____	____
6. Do you feel that we should depend more on nuclear power plants than present policy allows?	____	____
7. Do you favor tax credits for industries, communities, and individuals who install equipment and devices which will reduce air and water pollution?	____	____
8. Are present efforts to curb pollution of the nation's water and air adequate?	____	____
9. Do you favor drilling and mining in national forests in order to get more fuel?	____	____
10. Do you feel that present standards for air and water are sufficient to provide for a clean environment?	____	____

Anytime a question poses a problem that is recognized as a problem by the respondent and a valid solution is also presented, he or she will be likely to jump at the answer. The results of such a poll are totally meaningless. To be valid, a question should propose alternative solutions which allow respondents to make clear choices of how they would solve the problem.

The subtleties involved in the wording of items on a questionnaire is a complex topic that probably cannot be adequately covered in a written communication class. Even so, because of all the attention given to survey research in our society, some class time should be allotted to the subject of effective questionnaire design. Too, given a choice, students will often select this method for gathering information for their reports. Marketing majors in particular will find knowledge of questionnaire design to be helpful in their profession.

Observational Research

As its name implies, observational research is a method in which a situation is systematically witnessed and the significant facts about it are recorded. Probably the best-known use of observational research was that carried out by Frank and Lillian Gilbreath in the early nineteen-hundreds. In their highly regarded time-and-motion studies, they observed the tasks being performed by workers and they analyzed the workers' body movements. From these studies they formulated the laws of efficient motion. This resulted in much higher production in business and industry and became one of the principles of scientific management. It is doubtful that there are any management textbooks used in college classrooms today that fail to take note of the Gilbreaths' studies.

Another example of observational research can be found in hospital kitchens where dieticians observe and record the amount and type of food left on patient's trays. This helps them plan meals that will be eaten and, consequently, reduce the amount of food that is wasted. Other examples of observational research include: traffic counts on streets and highways, inspections of safety methods in plants, and observations based on watching customers as they select brands of merchandise from store shelves.

There are numerous phenomena in a community or on a college campus that are appropriate subjects for observational research. For instance, on a campus where parking is at a premium, one student researcher observed much wasted space between parked cars. After measuring the maximum amount of space needed for any one car, the student researcher recommended (in a letter report) to the campus traffic manager that the parking lanes be repainted at *x* number of intervals. These recommendations were accepted and, as a result, seven-hundred additional parking spaces were created. This particular research report (and the researcher) rated a story on the front page of the campus newspaper.

On another occasion, students were asked to observe the physical features and ambience of a discount department store and submit a short report to the manager enumerating recommended changes that would, hopefully, increase business. Their recommendations included turning down the sound system used to summon store personnel and the elimination of radios that had been placed at intervals in the store to broadcast music and commercials (the observers found these irritating). Other recommendations included some changes in physical features. The management of this store accepted and utilized almost all of the recommendations and reported increased business and positive comments on the changes from both customers and store personnel. Incidentally, none of the changes called for the expenditure of funds.

Experimental Research

The very mention of experimental research may cause students to conjure up visions of test tubes, laboratory smocks, and white rats. Because of this, concrete examples of business research should be used when this topic is introduced. A classic example, and one well worth discussing because of its findings and their implications for today's business firms, is the Hawthorne experiments made in the late 1920s at the Hawthorne Works of the Western Electric Company.

Carried on jointly with the Harvard Graduate School of Business Administration, this study lasted for a period of twenty-six months. The two major conclusions to emerge from the findings were:

People work better when they feel they are part of a team.

People work better when they feel what they are doing is important.

The Hawthorne experiments have been called the most exciting and important study of factory workers ever made. Teachers who are unfamiliar with this study will find detailed accounts of this on-the-job experimental research study in any management textbook.

Business firms have used, and will continue to use, experimental research to study the effects that noise, lighting, incentive pay, and other variables have on the production of workers. Again, management books, especially those that cover the topic of personnel management, contain many concrete examples of experimental research that has been carried out in offices and factories. It is doubtful that many students in report-writing classes will have either the time or the facilities for engaging in an experimental research project while in school. Nevertheless, enough time should be spent on this topic to enable them to gain a basic understanding of what is meant by "variables," "control groups," "experimental groups," and certain other concepts that are fundamental to an understanding of experimental research.

Organizing the Data

After information for a report has been gathered, report writers must then organize their data in an orderly and understandable fashion in order to produce a clear and effective written report. Outlining will help the writer arrange the basic structure of the report, and illustrative aids will assist in communicating the report story.

Preparing the Report Outline

While not compulsory, outlines serve as a means of organizing material and as a guide for writing the report. Writers are fairly evenly divided into those who find outlines indispensable and those to whom they are a nuisance. In the latter category are authors who simply ignore the topic entirely when discussing the organization of a report. However, most business communication textbooks include a section on outlining, and some go into great detail. In any event, outlining need not be a problem. It is simply a plan that will be used in writing the report. Just as a construction supervisor needs a blueprint for putting up a building, the report writer needs a plan for determining the best sequence for putting together the information that has been gathered for a report. Additionally, in a long report, the outline can be used for the table of contents, and in all reports it can serve as a basis for headings, subheadings, and caption guides.

Probably the best reason for preparing an outline, though, is that it forces the writer to think before writing; and until one becomes an experienced report writer, an outline can aid in perceiving the probable appearance of the final written report. For example, a preliminary outline such as the following might be used as a starting point in organizing the report:

- Introduction
    - The origin, nature, purpose, etc., of the report
- Body
    - Procedures or methods
    - Results and findings
- Conclusions and Recommendations
    - The significance of the findings
    - Recommendations of the researcher

This could be followed by a more comprehensive outline which would precede and guide the final typing of the report. But even in this comprehensive outline, the writer should keep in mind that the main parts will consist of an introduction, a body, and a conclusion although these words may not actually be used.

The choice of outline symbols is a matter of preference. All three—Roman numeral, decimal, alphanumeric—are suitable and provide a logical approach to writing the report. However, there are certain rules in regard to outlining and the use of symbols that should be discussed:

1. A section must have at least two subdivisions or it should have none. A "1" in an outline calls for a "2," and "A" for a "B," and so forth. Failure to abide by this rule when outlining is one of the most common mistakes made by students.
2. No heading should appear twice in the same outline.
3. A consistent numbering scheme must be followed in order to show the relationship between parts.
4. Avoid having only one subhead under a main heading. This may mean combining the subhead with the main heading.
5. Maintain consistency in phrasing topics and subtopics. In other words, use either phrases or complete sentences—but not both.
6. Indentations should be uniform, and end punctuation should either be used or omitted consistently.
7. Parallel construction in headings should be observed.

In summary, to organize their material in a manner that will lead to writing a report, students should:

1. Decide what is to be accomplished (the general purpose in writing the report).
2. Prepare a plan (outline) of their material, indicating the order in which ideas will be presented.
3. Classify the most important ideas into main sections; subordinate the lesser ones into subsections.
4. Build sections carefully, then the paragraphs within sections.
5. Write a few paragraphs experimentally to see how effectively they express meaning. (The main advantage in doing this is to help clarify one's ideas about the report.)

Proceeding through these five steps will help students organize their information. Their next step will be to determine which, if any, of their data should be illustrated by means of tables and graphs.

Tables and Graphic Presentations

How important are visual aids to a good report? Is it true that "a picture is worth a thousand words?" The experimental findings in a study of 448 college students conducted by Gros indicated that written plus graphic communications is a more effective communication technique than either written or graphic communication alone.[11] Thomas has pointed out that the most obvious feature of corporate annual reports is their use of visual aids to attract attention, supplement the narrative, and give order to a maze of facts and figures. Photography, charts, tables, cartoons, drawings, and other visual aids used in these reports help the reader's understanding of the report content.[12]

Lesikar observes that the primary function of graphic aids in a report is to assist the words in communicating the report contents. "Even though it is generally true that the report story is best told in words," he writes, "words alone usually are not adequate. In such instances, some form of graphic aid may be used to help put over the meaning of the words."[13] Treece feels that graphic aids present important trends and relationships more quickly, clearly, and emphatically than can be done in words. However, she cautions that poorly chosen, placed, or designed graphic aids and tables are counterproductive when they are harder to understand than words would be or if they distort the intended meaning.[14]

A general principle for students to keep in mind when using tables and graphs in their reports is that they should have some utilitarian function; that is, they should be purposeful and selected for their relevance and their capacity to clarify or emphasize. Thus, illustrative aids should be used to support the written analysis and help communicate the report story.

Tables

A broad area of information is presented in a convenient and orderly fashion through the use of tables. The arrangement of data into columns and rows to show relationships makes comparisons and analyses easy and gives the reader's mind quicker access to the data. Tables should be numbered consecutively throughout the report, and each should have a title that is complete enough to clarify what is included in the table. Here are some other practices that students may find helpful in table preparation:

Numbers should be clearly separated from each other by adequate space.
Decimal points should be aligned.
Figures without decimals should be aligned on the right.
Signs signifying positive and negative values should be aligned.
Dollar and percent signs should be placed only at the first entry of the column and aligned.

Graphics

Generally, the most-used graphic forms are bar charts, line charts, pie charts (the terms "chart" and "graph" are often used interchangeably), maps, pictograms, and photographs. Graphic methods of presentation are an effective means of conveying information, and students should be encouraged to use these visual devices in both their written and their oral reports when and where they are appropriate. When graphs are well designed, they can be extremely effective in explaining and illustrating information in a report. Business periodicals such as *Fortune, Business Week,* and *Forbes* provide excellent examples of the use of graphic devices to make statistical concepts easy for readers to grasp.

In an oral or written report, tables and graphic aids can bring an extra dimension by adding clarity, force, and interest. Moreover, they are a must for presenting quantitative data. However, students should be cautioned not to use so many tables and charts that they overwhelm the rest of their report. The test to apply in deciding to use illustrative aids is simple: Would the use of the aid assist the reader or listener in understanding the information being presented better or more easily?

There are two areas in regard to the use of visual aids that should be emphasized. One is the proper and effective labeling of tables and graphic material, and the other is lead-in sentences that introduce these aids. Both of these areas can be considered by presenting sets of data (either on transparencies or on handouts) and having students decide the most effective graphic means of representing the data. Then a label and a lead-in sentence could be prepared for each set of data.

Writing the Report

The quality of a report can be judged by answering "yes" to these two questions: Is the material in the report true, reliable, and complete? Is it clear, orderly, and easy to grasp and remember? Often, when the answer to the first question is "yes" the answer to the second is "no." When a written report is lacking in concrete nouns and active verbs, the result is a general haze. The capacity for vivid and precise phrasing is especially important in reports because of their length and the amount of data that is usually included. Just as it is important that the material within a report be accurate and complete, it is important that this material be presented with clarity and coherence. Thus, the quality of a report depends largely on the writer's verbal resources, and teachers of report writing must spend some time on this important phase of communication.

Readability

Along with the use of illustrative aids, the most popular trend in modern business reporting is the move toward using clearly understandable language. The topic of style, clarity, and precision will have already been considered at length if report writing is taught as one unit of a business communication course. However, at least one or two class periods should be devoted to reviewing the characteristics of "readable writing." Books such as *Word*

Watcher's Handbook by Phyllis Martin, *The Dictionary of Do's and Dont's* by Harry Nickles, *Plain Words: Their ABC* by Sir Ernest Gower, and *The Modern Researcher* by Jacques Barzun and Henry F. Graff will be helpful in this review.[15-18] In a class devoted exclusively to report writing, these books should be required reading for all students.

If time allows for only a brief review of word usage, the use of an overhead projector to exhibit examples of words and phrases that are misused in writing and speaking will facilitate the presentation of ideas from these books. In any event, the reasons for writing clear and concise reports should be discussed.

Redundancies often appear in reports. Some of the most common appear below:

adequate enough (adequate)	exact same (same)
consensus of opinion (consensus *or* opinion)	necessary requisite (necessary *or* requisite)
true facts (facts)	merge together (merge)
each and every (each *or* every)	basic fundamentals (fundamentals)
past history (history)	other alternative (alternative)
personal opinion (opinion)	same identical (same *or* identical)
exactly identical (identical)	personally, I think (I think)

The most "popular" redundancies can be heard each evening on network news programs when members of Congress and high governmental officials are being interviewed. These are: "personally, I think," "each and every American," "it is the consensus of opinion of this committee," "the basic fundamentals of this plan are," and "it is my personal opinion." The important point, of course, is that students be warned not to use these phrases when writing their reports and when presenting them orally.

Here is an additional list of phrases that should be avoided when writing and presenting a report. They have been overused.

the beauty of this plan is	all things being equal
at this point in time	by the same token
estimated at about	due to the fact that
in accordance with	for your information

For students who use misspelled words in a report, a heavy penalty should be levied. The reason for taking this approach is obvious. The ability to spell is assumed to be a universal acquisition of educated people. Therefore, the reader of a report that contains misspelled words will assume that the author is either badly educated or, worse, contemptuous of the reader's opinion. Recommend that students buy a good dictionary—and use it.

To sum up, reports should be written in clear, concise, and correct English. Vagueness, grammatical errors, mistakes in spelling and punctuation, and excessive verbiage present barriers to communication and thus hinder an understanding of the message. Persons who request reports have busy schedules to maintain and multitudes of material to read. Therefore, they have neither the time nor the patience to plow through a wordy report that requires extra time to comprehend.

Reports in Final Form

For many reports, the conclusions and recommendations are the writer's most important contribution. Consequently, teachers should spend some time making sure that students understand that conclusions and recommendations are based upon the findings presented earlier in their reports. (Caution students not to present *new* information in these concluding sections.)

In addition, teachers should stress the importance of report writers' being as objective and impartial as possible in presenting information. In order to accomplish this, they should (1) avoid emotional terms, (2) identify assumptions, and (3) keep prejudices and preconceptions under control.

And finally, before reports are turned in, students should make one final check on the accuracy of technical facts, quotations, references, spelling of names, and dates. They should check all statements in general and give particular attention to documentation.

The report-writing process can be an intellectually challenging and satisfying learning experience if teachers will assist students in selecting interesting topics. Moreover, given an adequate amount of time, a readable, lively report can be created that is consistent with the principles of good communication. Therefore, the final word of advice is to begin planning for reports at the beginning of the term in order to allow sufficient time for their proper preparation and presentation.

Notes

1. Malra Treece, *Communication for Business and the Professions* (Boston: Allyn and Bacon, 1978), p. 385.
2. Harry M. Brown and Karen K. Reid, *Business Writing and Communication Stratègies and Applications* (New York: D. Van Nostrand Co., 1979), p. 276.
3. Raymond V. Lesikar, *Report Writing for Business* (Homewood, Ill.: Richard D. Irwin, 1981), p. 4.
4. William C. Himstreet and Wayne M. Baty, *Business Communications* (Belmont, Calif.: Kent Publishing Co., 1981), p. 244.
5. Harold F. Graves and Lynn S. Hoffman, *Report Writing* (Englewood Cliffs, N.J.: Prentice-Hall, 1965), p. vi.
6. "Teaching the Boss to Write," *Business Week,* Oct. 25, 1976, p. 56.

7. Graves and Hoffman, p. 5. Adapted by permission of Prentice-Hall, Inc., Englewood Cliffs, New Jersey.
8. Jacques Barzun and Henry Graff, *The Modern Researcher,* 3d ed. (New York: Harcourt Brace Jovanovich, 1977), p. 229.
9. "Who Reads What," *Daily Mississippian* (University, Miss.), Sept. 18, 1978, p. 1.
10. "Wording of Polls Questioned," *Tupelo (Mississippi) Daily Journal,* June 6, 1979, p. 4.
11. Ridley J. Gros, "Determining the Effectiveness of Selected Techniques Taught in Business Report Writing," *Journal of Business Communications,* Spring 1974, p. 21.
12. Edward G. Thomas, "The Corporate Annual Report: A Basic Resource in the Written Communications Course," *ABCA Bulletin,* June 1978, p. 29.
13. Lesikar, p. 200.
14. Treece, p. 442.
15. Phyllis Martin, *Word Watcher's Handbook* (New York: David McKay Co., 1977).
16. Harry G. Nickles, *The Dictionary of Do's and Don'ts* (New York: McGraw-Hill Book Co., 1974).
17. Sir Ernest Gower, *Plain Words: Their ABC* (New York: Alfred A. Knopf, 1954).
18. See note 8.

Bibliography

BARZUN, JACQUES, and HENRY GRAFF. *The Modern Researcher.* 3d ed. New York: Harcourt Brace Jovanovich, 1977.

BROWN, HARRY M., and KAREN K. REID. *Business Writing and Communication Strategies and Applications.* New York: D. Van Nostrand Co., 1979.

BROWN, LELAND. *Effective Business Report Writing.* Englewood Cliffs, N.J.: Prentice-Hall, 1973.

GOWER, SIR ERNEST. *Plain Words: Their ABC.* New York: Alfred A. Knopf, 1954.

GRAVES, HAROLD F., and LYNN S. HOFFMAN. *Report Writing.* Englewood Cliffs, N.J.: Prentice-Hall, 1965.

HATCH, RICHARD. *Communicating In Business.* Chicago: Science Research Associates, 1977.

HIMSTREET, WILLIAM C., and WAYNE M. BATY. *Business Communications.* Belmont, Calif.: Kent Publishing Co., 1981.

LESIKAR, RAYMOND V. *Report Writing For Business.* Homewood, Ill.: Richard D. Irwin, 1981.

LEWIS, PHILLIP V., and WILLIAM H. BAKER. *Business Report Writing.* Columbus, Ohio: Grid, Inc., 1978.

LINDAUER, JACQUELINE S. *Communicating in Business.* Philadelphia: W. B. Saunders, 1979.

MARTIN, PHYLLIS. *Word Watcher's Handbook.* New York: David McKay Co., Inc., 1977.

NICKLES, HARRY G. *The Dictionary of Do's and Don'ts.* New York: McGraw-Hill Book Co., 1974.

SHURTER, ROBERT L., J. PETER WILLIAMSON, and WAYNE G. BROEHL, JR. *Business Research and Report Writing.* New York: McGraw-Hill Book Co., 1965.

TREECE, MALRA. *Communication for Business and the Professions.* Boston: Allyn and Bacon, 1978.

WELLS, WALTER. *Communications In Business.* Belmont, Calif.: Wadsworth Publishing Co., 1977.

Chapter 7

Skills of Technical Writing

E. Rennie Charles

MANY A TEACHER with qualifications in arts, education, or business administration—perhaps in journalism—has had to face a college or university class in engineering, science, or some other professional discipline. The mandate is to "teach them how to write." Perhaps the task has been a similar one in business, industry, or government.

For those in such a situation—those who have never taught technical writing or have done so for only a short time—this chapter is intended primarily.

Some may have been teaching technical writing for quite some time, but still feel uneasy because of lack of anything but the most elementary background in the students' field of study. As time passes, however, and experience grows, the uncertainty will diminish. At least at the undergraduate level, the strong similarities between business writing and technical writing become apparent. Most instructors in written communication feel more comfortable in that realization. Only terminology and some special characteristics and techniques require mastery.

The versatility and resiliency of most teachers of written communication will enable them to adjust to these conditions quickly. This chapter is designed to provide some suggestions and some reminders.

Definition of Technical Writing

Interpretation of the Term

The instructor should have a clear understanding of what technical writing is. While the term seems elementary in its application at first, a look through a few books on the subject and discussion with a few technical writers in industry will soon reveal that interpretation is not simple at all.

Certainly in North America, the term *technical writing* can be applied in several ways. This fact alone, to say nothing of the effect of personal attitudes, interests, and prejudices on its definition, soon makes it clear that before a course in the subject may be developed, the educator must decide how the term is to be defined.

Types of Technical Writing

1. Written assignments and projects carried out by the technical student in secondary school and by science or engineering students as part of a college writing skills development course or program.
2. Laboratory reports and other assignments prepared by technical, technological, science, or engineering students as part of their technical course work in proceeding to a degree or diploma in their field of specialization.
3. Writing and publishing assignments carried out by professional technical writers in government and industry as part of a product development or marketing program or of an engineering project.
4. Writing and publishing assignments carried out by professional or other skilled writers in government and business but in other than science or engineering fields.
5. Journalism devoted to scientific or technical subjects in highly technical, semitechnical, or popular publications.

Selecting the Appropriate College Course

Course Objectives and Teacher Qualification

It is very important to determine, before a course in technical writing is planned, the precise purpose it is to fulfill. If it is designed simply to provide a series of writing-development exercises for technically oriented students, probably a minimum of technical knowledge or expertise is required of the teacher. If laboratory experience is the *raison d'être* of the writing, a great deal of technical expertise is required.

Professional technical writing also involves a great amount of expertise, unless the job is simply to edit (and sometimes it's not so simple) material that has already been written by scientists, engineers, and technologists.

If the technical writing is in what most engineers and scientists would consider a nontechnical field, essentially the same criteria as those applied to the professional category pertain.

To the journalism types of technical writing, similar yardsticks should be applied as far as technical expertise is concerned. The whole function of journalistic writing, however, makes it essential that other professional criteria as well must be included, aspects which are characteristic of that sort of writing and publishing. This type of technical writing, then, is in quite a separate field.

Criteria for Selecting an Appropriate Course

THE BASIC WRITING COURSE

Student Interests. Basic writing courses on technical subjects can be given at almost any level from secondary school through college and university. Since writing skill is generally acknowledged as a necessary achievement in government, business, and industry, most educators are agreed that as much time as possible should be devoted to its development. Indeed it is very frequently the subject of specially prepared courses in government, business, and industry, courses often administered by professional educators.

Technical writing is a necessary skill for students preparing for vocations or professions in the technical field. It is also generally agreed among experienced educators that the incentive in learning how to write well is much greater among technical students if the subject matter about which they write is technical. This is one very effective way of generating enthusiasm, or at least encouraging willing participation, among students for whom the whole subject of language study and application has been traditionally a distasteful chore, if not anathema.

Those who over many years have taught writing, and who have tried both traditional English literature and business or technical subject matter—the latter as closely related as possible to the interests of the students involved—are agreed that a technical base is without question the more-effective medium for learning writing skills.

Teacher Interests. Naturally, the greater the teacher's knowledge of the subject matter, or the more closely one's interests are related to it, the easier will be the task of teaching related writing. Ideally such courses should be given by the specialists in the related fields. Various circumstances, however, combine to make this practice very difficult if not impossible. Most teachers find that the problem of planning, developing, and testing the knowledge and understanding of classes of students—usually larger than one feels it possible to cope with adequately—is difficult enough to solve in one field of expertise alone. An attempt to teach and develop in them another sort of competence simultaneously would probably result in detriment to both types of study.

Limits on the amount of time that would be allocated in curriculum planning for a course of this sort would also make the practice ineffectual, if for no reason other than that it is traditionally not done. Another reason, however, is that most instructors in technology or science do not consider themselves sufficiently competent in language, whether they are or not, to give instruction in the technicalities of language and its application. Some resent any implication that they should be competent to do so or that they should be required to do so. This situation is not surprising, for most are a product of an educational system that, if it has not fostered this attitude, has at least given it every opportunity to persist. It is unlikely to change in the near future.

Teacher Preparation. The result of these circumstances is that many nontechnical people are required to teach "technical" writing—often as an adjunct to "business" writing. To carry out the assignment, some preparation is obviously required:

1. Examination of as many as possible of the most popular texts devoted to the subject. The majority are readily available from major publishers. Some are listed at the end of this chapter.
2. Familiarity with and as much reading as possible of *Technical Communication,* published by the Society for Technical Communication; *The Journal of Technical Writing and Communication;* and *The Technical Writing Teacher,* published by the Association of Teachers of Technical Writing. To these might be added *The Journal of Business Communication* and *The Bulletin* of the American Business Communication Association, both of which carry, from time to time, articles about the teaching of technical writing or communication. All are published in the United States.
3. Membership in the Society for Technical Communication, the Association of Teachers of Technical Writing, and perhaps the American Business Communication Association. Involvement in the latter can be helpful because such a high percentage of its membership consists of educators who teach business writing and in many cases technical writing as well. The similarities, furthermore, between business writing and technical writing are so great in so many respects that teaching one—at least at junior levels—is an excellent form of preparation for teaching the other.

   Advantages of membership in the Association of Teachers of Technical Writing should be self-evident. The Society for Technical Communication, on the other hand, is oriented toward professional communicators in industry: writers, editors, authors, illustrators, publishers, and other specialists in the industrial communication field—not to be confused with electrical engineers and technologists working in the electrical communications field.

   All of these associations, as well as others of similar interests in other parts of the world, organize seminars, conferences, and conventions for their own members and visitors. Experience has shown that attendance at such conferences is one of the quickest ways to become familiar with current activity and developments, to become acquainted with others of like interests and occupation, to develop awareness and a sense of involvement in a discipline, to increase maturity of judgment, and to prepare for greater responsibility and promotion on a local, national, and international scale.

4. Cultivation of acquaintance with and consultation with teachers of technical subjects. While it may take some time to develop association with technical departments in a secondary school, college, or university, doing so is one of the most effective methods of increasing one's understanding of the elements of the field concerned and the types of projects characteristic of the technical courses of the curriculum.

   An additional advantage is the confidence that will gradually be inspired in the technical faculty by the demonstration of such interest. Cooperation is virtually guaranteed—even to the point where joint projects and assignments can be arranged. In colleges where technical writing is considered a peripheral subject or is included as an option, the eventual result can be—and indeed has often proved to be—the inclusion of technical writing as a mandatory element in the core curriculum.
5. Participation in field trips and plant visits by the teacher of technical writing. The benefit for the teacher is much the same as for the students, and also provides topics and material for technical papers and reports, including trip reports, which are included in many technical writing courses.

College Laboratory Report Writing

Relation to Technical Course Work. Since laboratory reports are an integral part of science, technical, and engineering courses, it is obvious that they deal with laboratory experiments and other projects. Their integration in those assignments limits the scope of their content, and usually dictates an almost rigid pattern of procedure and presentation characteristics of the discipline in which the work is done. The prospect, therefore, of the technical writing teacher's involvement in such exercises is negligible.

Cooperative Projects. Despite this apparent limitation, however, one very encouraging sort of opportunity exists in many programs. If the technical courses include major laboratory projects extending, for example, over several months, it is sometimes possible to carry out a cooperative exercise through the integration of a writing assignment—usually a major report—involving the establishment of a realistic set of circumstances in business or industry, hypothetical or otherwise, in which such a project might be carried out; a search of the literature of the subject; the preparation of appropriate related materials and documents; and the organization, preparation, and presentation of the report itself. Thus the literature search and the laboratory work can form one cohesive unit of study, while the report can perform two functions: (1) the medium of presentation of results of the laboratory work, and (2) the practice in preparation of a realistic technical report.

Other assignments appropriate to the technical writing course can be included: correspondence, short reports of various kinds, and oral and visual presentations. A variety of preliminary and supplementary exercises can be planned around the central project or theme. It can become anything from a fairly elementary but thorough series of related projects to an almost professional sort of business "game" extending over a full term or even longer.

The organization and administration of this type of project requires thorough consultation and cooperation between technical or engineering faculty —if it is not conducted within an engineering school—and the faculty responsible for courses in technical communication. Mutual interest and understanding of the objectives of both groups must be achieved.

Professional Technical Writing and Publishing

The sort of work done by technical writers, editors, and publishers is seldom attempted in a college setting in North America. On this continent, most of the preparation for such a vocation consists of the development of writing, organizational, and presentation skills either in general writing courses or courses like those just described in the subsection on the basic writing course, pages 160–62, and on college laboratory report writing, pages 162–63. Most professionals learn these special skills on the job.

Efforts to improve writing skills alone occupy an appreciable segment of practically every educational program. It is consequently difficult, in the minds of the majority, to justify spending a great deal more time in the sharpening and the application of those skills in a specific field of activity unless that activity in itself is a well-recognized and highly regarded vocation. Outstanding examples are journalism and secretarial work. Despite the fact that thousands earn their living as technical writers, editors, and illustrators, relatively few are prepared in their years of formal education for such specific work.

The reason lies largely in the need to become familiar with one field of technology or science, sometimes very narrow. It lies also in the need to learn techniques of material organization and layout for publication; characteristics, advantages, and disadvantages of various printing materials and processes; advantages and disadvantages of various types of illustration and illustrative techniques; and ways of determining quality, deciding the level of quality required, and determining cost effectiveness. In short, most of the background required is that usually gained from a program in graphic arts management.

Coupled with these requirements is the need for a relatively broad knowledge of the ways of business and industry. Education provided by colleges of business administration is particularly useful in such a vocation. It it thus evident that the professional technical writer—as opposed to the more general writer on technical or semitechnical subjects, or to the nontechnical editor who polishes the material of technical specialists—must be competent in several fields. The college writing course or program can supply, as a rule, only part of the preparation required.

It should be noted here that a few programs providing all or part of the background described above as being necessary for the professional are available in various parts of the world, mostly in polytechnics or similar educational institutions. Some engineering colleges in North America and elsewhere provide selected or occasional courses in some of the elements of the professional technical communicator's special requirements.

Nontechnical Technical Writing

For the purpose of this chapter, medicine, dentistry, forestry, architecture, and other like disciplines are classed as science. Writing in those fields can logically be termed technical. Because many people in business, however, consider their work to be technical writing despite the fact that it has little to do with science or technology—and nothing to do with engineering—that category should be mentioned here. Financial institutions, insurance companies, some social services, and some nontechnological marketing organizations classify some of their positions as "technical writing."

While this nomenclature is bound to cause some confusion, it is at least partly understandable because the only other term broad enough in application is "special writing" or "specialist writing." That certainly does not convey much. And so "technical," in the sense of being specially related to a field of interest or activity, is the term used.

Teaching the types of technical writing required in law, for example, could hardly be done by anyone untrained in the legal profession. On the other hand, the types of writing required in the social services requires of the teacher about the same degree of adaptability as do science and engineering. Chiefly the approach to situations, method of organization, and vocabularly differ.

The same could be said about teaching technical writing in many other disciplines and highly specialized fields. In the majority, adaptation of business writing experience and techniques provides the capability required of an instructor. As with writing about science, technology, and engineering, the fear of the unfamiliar is the main obstacle to be overcome. The best way to overcome that is the same sort of association, cooperation, and coordination with faculty recommended for those who are to teach engineering and science students.

Technical Writing as Journalism

Technical journalism can be divided roughly into two types: (1) the highly technical sort that produces articles of such a very specialized nature that only the professional in the field—a scientist, technologist or engineer—is likely to gain much from reading them and (2) the popular or semipopular sort—such as one might find in *Scientific American*. In either case the technical writing involved is guided by most of the principles of journalistic practice. These are well established by the writer's experience in meeting the needs of the public and of those casually interested in science and technology, or of the specialist interested in keeping abreast of developments in his or her field. This experience and the resulting traditional practices have placed journalistic writing in a class by itself.

Since this chapter is intended for those who wish to teach technical writing rather than journalism, no attempt is made to relate its material to journalistic interests, despite the fact that many college graduates in journalism find their way into technical writing as a career. Almost invariably the job involves composing or editing material provided by scientists or engineers, as opposed to original production of articles on subjects about which they themselves are highly knowledgeable. Only rarely have they previously completed a college program in science or technology which would prepare them to write for a highly specialized readership.

Planning a Technical Writing Course

The Ideal Setting

Since the types of professional writing described in the sections on publishing, page 163, and journalism, above, are beyond the scope of most technical college programs, it is inappropriate here to deal with courses relating to them. The elementary sort described in the basic writing course, page 160, while it may be little different from any other sort of college writing course, may however be developed, if the instructor is familiar enough with the subject matter and its significance in industry, into a fairly substantial writing course with a strong technical base.

Ideally, the technical writing course is a combination of the basic writing course and the laboratory project writing course, i.e., a major exercise in writing, closely related to a major technical laboratory project—experimental or developmental. Essential to its success, in addition to its contribution to the student's progress in achieving language competence, is the cooperation of and, if possible, integration with the science or technology course to which it is related.

Length of the Course

Because of the number of very important elements that can comprise a course in technical writing, and because of the novelty of most of them to the average class of technical students, the first decision to be made concerns the length of the course. Very often the instructor has little to say about this because the curriculum planning is done at a more senior level. It is wise, however, to have a clear idea as to optimum characteristics of the course, including the length.

Minimum length for such a course is one term or semester, twelve to fourteen weeks. In the ten-week quarter, it is manageable, but some topics must then be omitted or abbreviated. The ideal length of a technical writing course is three class hours a week for two terms, or about twenty-six weeks. This much time allows an opportunity to cover all the essentials, although some elements, if the students have had no previous exposure to them, will be brief enough. This is particularly true of correspondence.

Information and Instructions for Students

In presenting a course in technical writing, at least three important documents should be prepared:

1. A statement of prerequisites and course objectives, along with a brief description
2. A course outline and detailed description
3. Instructions for carrying out a major project

Prerequisites, Objectives, and Course Description

For those who must determine whether or not they should take the course, if it is not mandatory, a statement of prerequisites and objectives and a brief course description are necessary.

Prerequisites normally consist of courses that must be successfully completed before admission to the technical writing course is granted. In some cases, particularly in continuing education programs, certain levels or types of experience are required.

Course objectives should be identified in the sort of statement that is usually published in the college catalogue: the course's scope, nature, length, (number of class hours a week), and purpose. One very obvious purpose of the technical writing course is to provide students with an understanding of the role of written communication in an industrial organization and to provide instruction and practice in communicating effectively within that environment.

A brief description of the course should include major characteristics. Since they are all designed to prepare students for writing as part of the responsibilities of management, emphasis should be placed on the management aspect.

Course Outline and Detailed Description

The course outline should list and describe the various segments of the course, as well as explain where emphasis is placed. It should be made clear that, besides the three class hours a week and the major report-writing assignment, many other related assignments, both in and out of class, are required. A statement of scope or content could include all or some of these topics:

1. Basic management writing style
2. Information searching, gathering, and organization techniques
3. Direct and indirect organization of information
4. Information presentation
5. Techniques of persuasion
6. Business and technical correspondence
7. Employment correspondence
8. Short technical reports
9. Graphics
10. Oral presentation

Most of the topics listed here are easy to incorporate and to schedule. Writing style and oral work, however, pose a problem if they need to be included. They are normally the basis of complete courses in themselves, perhaps as prerequisites for this course. While oral presentation is not logically a part of a writing course, if no time is devoted to oral work elsewhere in the curriculum, this is an appropriate place to include it if time is available. It often is not available.

Language Skills Required. The amount of instruction and practice in basic writing style is very flexible and depends on the background of the students. If a great deal of time is required for developing basic language skills, the effectiveness of a technical writing course can be destroyed. It is very important, therefore, to set an appropriate standard for admission to the course, including prerequisites, and to make this quite clear in any course description. Experience has shown that many students who wish to take such a course as an aid to employment will make every effort to circumvent such requirements. If they are successful in doing so the value of the course in its technical application will surely suffer, and students in the class who can cope with the language requirements will suffer and most likely lose their enthusiasm as well.

Rigor of Course Requirements. Some warning should be included in the statement as to the rigor of the course, e.g., the large numbers of assignments required, the scope of the major assignment, consistency of student involvement required, and the amount of out-of-class work necessary. Such a statement will probably deter those who are under the impression that it is primarily a reading course. It can also serve as a supportive document for the instructor if, much later, the course is criticized by those who are faring badly because it is too rigorous. Fair warning is a very important vindicating factor when the pressure becomes too heavy for those who are unprepared for it.

Some emphasis should also be placed on the importance of classroom work, its evaluation and weighting. In times when it has become so easy for the less conscientious to find others to produce assignments for them, it is essential to find means of avoiding the attendant uncertainties, accusations, and other unpleasantness and embarrassment. Heavy emphasis on class work is an effective safeguard.

It can be helpful in this document to list the major blocks of course content and perhaps the amount of time planned for each. If several instructors are teaching the same course and it is important for the sake of course credit that the content be almost identical, such blocking and scheduling is essential. The longer the course, however, the less important the sequence of the parts, except for the major report and the employment correspondence. The report must be scheduled so as to allow time to give related assignments; to permit the instructor to have enough time for reading, criticism, and grading; and perhaps to synchronize with a laboratory project. The correspondence must be scheduled so that students may use their knowledge at once in their applications for employment, often three to five months before term-end.

The greatest challenge in planning and scheduling of the major report assignment can come in the effort to coordinate it with the scheduling of a technical department's project. Such coordination usually involves some flexibility or even some sacrifices on the part of both departments.

Instructions and Schedule for a Major Project

Probably the simplest way to describe the preparation of an assignment sheet for a major technical report-writing project is to demonstrate. Since it is a well-established fact, emphasized in most texts, that report writing consists chiefly of preparing and submitting information for management decisions, every opportunity that presents itself in the conduct of this project should be taken to refer to the decision-making process. In both the report and its related assignments the aim should be clearly that of facilitating results. Consequently, the term *management* should be used as much as, or even more than the term *technical* in the statements and instruction sheets referring to the major report. The preamble could read like this:

> The objective of this project is to enable students to learn how to analyze a problem or situation in technology or industry, locate information, organize it, and present it to the intended reader or readers so that management decisions may be made. Topics may be assigned by the instructor or selected by each student, subject to approval by the instructor. The report must conform with the standards specified by the instructor and must be typed double-spaced.

If the project is one undertaken jointly with a technical department, the requirement could be phrased like this:

> The student is required
>
> 1. to select a subject of current interest and significance in technology, important to the business and industrial community
> 2. to consider the various aspects, ramifications, and applications of that subject sufficiently to define one element which would be suitable for investigation in the literature of the field and in a laboratory setting
> 3. to examine printed sources of information in libraries and elsewhere, to discuss the topic with those in industry willing to help, and to apply the results to a project authorized by both the [name of technical department] and [the name of department conducting the writing course].

Managing the Project

Topic Selection

If the project is carried out in conjunction with a laboratory project in a technical department, the only problem facing the technical writing instructor is the application of the project to a realistic business or industrial management requirement. This should not be difficult if technical faculty are prepared to discuss applications and suggest realistic situations.

If this condition is less than gratifying in its success, students themselves can often suggest applications, particularly if they are in their junior or senior year of studies.

The ideal state of affairs, of course, is that the instructor should become familiar enough with the technical discipline to be able to make sensible and realistic proposals of topics for the writing projects. It may come as a surprise to some how quickly this familiarity can develop, even for a person of very limited technical background.

FORMAT

Experience has shown that the most-effective method of teaching report writing is to use the formal report as a medium. While short reports are easier to manage and can be fitted into a brief period of time, each one usually can include only a limited number of report characteristics. The fact that some important aspects must almost always be omitted makes it necessary to make a number of short report-writing assignments.

The long-form report includes a great number of important characteristics which are thus easier to demonstrate in context and in relation to one another. Furthermore, it is relatively easy to explain and demonstrate how any of the elements of a formal report can be adapted to the short report—even to a relatively simple memorandum report. Every feature of the long form can be shown to have an equivalent part—even if only a sentence or phrase, to use an extreme case—in the short report.

If one has taught report writing to students of business administration or in similar programs, the teaching of the formal report should present no problems, for only the subject matter and terminology, and the number and type of graphics, are likely to differ. Method of organization, layout, and general appearance are quite similar. In fact, it seems sometimes that one of the chief reasons for teaching technical report writing per se is psychological. Most students of science and technology are proud of their field of specialization; they feel that everything involved in their education must be special, or must be presented in a manner special to their interests. Consequently, technical report writing, despite the fact that it is very often almost indistinguishable from business report writing, has a special appeal because of what it is called.

The elements of the formal technical report, as in the formal business report, consist of these parts:

1. Cover with a label bearing at least the title, but sometimes several other identifying or distinguishing items
2. A title page giving the following information: short title or topic; a descriptive title, if necessary; name and position of the author; name and position of the authorizing person or group; place of presentation; and date of presentation. The author's position and reader's position are normally assumed to be imaginary but realistic.
3. A memo or letter authorizing the project
4. A memo or letter covering the submission (transmittal or presentation document) and performing the function of a preface
5. Table of contents
6. List of illustrations, tables, etc.
7. An abstract, summary, or synopsis
8. The text of the report, including an introduction, appropriate chapters or sections, conclusions, and recommendations

9. Footnotes or references, or both, organized and laid out according to a standardized format
10. Appendixes as appropriate, including a glossary if required and if not preceding the text
11. Bibliography, organized and presented according to a standard format

A good deal of flexibility is essential in the content of the reports in order to enable them to appear as realistic as possible. In business and industry, nearly every one of the elements listed above appears in various forms and with various characteristics, according to the policies and preferences of the organization. If this fact is explained to students, despite the normal tendency among them to prefer and practice uniformity, no difficulty should be experienced in persuading them to produce a document whose characteristics meet the special requirements of the situation they have chosen and the person for whom it is intended.

At this stage it is very helpful to be able to show a class samples of real technical and business reports prepared within a company. It is also helpful to have on hand reports prepared by previous students under similar circumstances. The only necessary safeguard in the latter case is the prevention of any attempt to follow slavishly a pattern, topic, or technique demonstrated in such a report. For many a student it is easier to follow what somebody else has done than to take the time or trouble to work out an appropriate system that meets the requirements of this particular project and the topic selected.

Preparatory Projects and Assignments

As is the practice in business and formal report-writing projects, a schedule of the assignments and due dates should be provided. A schedule of the most appropriate assignments is shown on page 172. Items can be much more concise, with the explanatory material provided verbally in class.

Ideally, the whole project, from topic selection to submission of the typed report, should take at least twelve weeks. During this time, the assignments should be spaced at intervals calculated to enable a student to complete each, and the instructor must have time adequately to criticize and to grade the assignments. Some must be returned in very short order so that a student may not be delayed in carrying on with the project. In fact, a twenty-four-hour return schedule sometimes has to be met.

Delay can be very detrimental to morale. In a major project like this, morale seems to reach a high level, probably because of the magnitude and comprehensiveness of the project, as well as because of its close relation to the student's subject of specialization. It is a precious factor to maintain.

While it is not essential to grade each assignment, the more that can be evaluated, the better. Most students today are grade-oriented, and so expect a

Schedule of Report Project Assignments

Assignment Number	*Description*	*Due Date*
1.	Definition of the problem or objective selected	_____
2.	Preliminary outline or series of statements showing the anticipated form of the report	_____
3.	Schedule to be followed in the production of the assignments related to the project	_____
4.	Bibliography cards, set up according to a standarized format and identifying the sources of information examined or to be examined	_____
5.	Sample of notes taken from the sources, recorded according to the specific format or system that is most useful for continuing referral and best suited to the forthcoming report's structure	_____
6.	Draft of the introductory or other section of the report as a basis for checking technique of presentation	_____
7.	Formal, detailed topic outline of the report in standarized format, to be presented before the submission of the report	_____
8.	The formal report, organized, laid out and presented in such a fashion as to influence management to make decisions in a business or industrial situation	_____

number or letter to rank the results of their efforts. Less effort is usually applied to assignments that are returned ungraded, even if comments make the instructor's reaction clear. In this respect the student differs from an individual taking a course within a business organization, where the motivation is holding a job or achieving promotion. There the comments and criticism are paramount; a grade is usually of little or no consequence; improvement is the main concern.

Of the assignments listed above, numbers 1, 2, and 3 could be graded on the quality of the statement made—in terms of language and organization. Number 6 will appear in edited form in the final report, and so may not require grading. The rest should receive grades based on technique, accuracy, and criteria of effectiveness.

Setting and Meeting Deadlines

It is essential for the instructor, as well as for the student, to ensure that deadlines be unequivocally set and met. While it may seem to be unnecessarily harsh or demanding to set the terms firmly, experience has made it clear that the following considerations make such rigor important:

1. Class discussion of all of the related assignments and the elements of the report can be carried out only if precursory and prerequisite work

has been completed. Maintaining sequence and continuity, in this part of the course, is essential to completion of the report on schedule.

2. Allowing some individuals to fall behind or neglect the submission of some assignments or accepting hasty or half-hearted work—even if the weighting of some units is lower than that of others—diminishes the credibility of the exercise and damages the morale of those who take the project very seriously.
3. Technical students, and sometimes technical faculty as well, are inclined—particularly if the latter themselves have not been required in business or industry to produce the kinds of written material the students must do—to consider the project of much lesser importance than purely technical assignments. Thus, if any assignments take precedence, they are sure to be technical ones. An easy excuse is readily available for the lateness of technical writing projects.

   This in itself is a good reason for having as many assignments as possible done in class. Maintaining the integrity of the technical writing course requires the same rigors as those applied to technical subjects. Almost the worst thing that can happen to a technical writing teacher is to be considered a second-class citizen of the educational community; the only thing worse is the instructor's willingness to accept that classification.

   One solution to the problem of status is to manage, when the curriculum is being developed or revised, the inclusion of technical writing as part of the core. It will then most likely be a mandatory subject, with official and professional—technological, that is—acknowledgment of the significance of the subject.
4. In this type of project it is impossible for the culmination to be achieved —an adequate formal technical report, into whose preparation have gone all the training and developmental factors—without rigid adherence to all the deadlines set. If they are not met, some part of the sequence and some part of the training value will be lost.
5. The submission of the report itself on time is of equal but different significance. Some careful judgment on the part of the instructor is required in the first place to ensure that not only can the students be expected to produce the report on the due date, but sufficient time is allowed to complete the criticism and evaluation of the report.

   The average instructor is inclined to be an optimist when scheduling the grading of these major assignments, whose evaluation is an exceedingly time-consuming, as well as arduous, task. To avoid the disturbing, unprofessional, and perhaps embarrassing eventuality of having to rush through the reading, commentary, and grading, it is wise either to allocate about twice as much time as one at first believes is necessary for the process, or—if the instructor is a model of self-discipline and determination—schedule the job in equal portions over the length of time available, and arrange, by requesting early submission, for that time to be as long as possible.

6. Another factor which may necessitate especially careful planning is coordination with technical project schedules. Laboratory projects particularly are subject to a wide variety of unforeseen circumstances. Experiments which do not produce expected or useful results, breakdown of equipment, shortages of equipment or materials, and problems in teamwork if partnership is attempted—all can disrupt schedules or make it difficult to complete projects on time, or even complete them at all.

Awareness of these possibilities and experience in coping with resulting problems indicates the desirability of some safeguards. Three kinds of arrangements can be made at the outset of the project:

1. It can be agreed that if the coordinated laboratory project is unsuccessful or cannot be completed, hypothetical results may be provided for the preparation of a credible report, if justification of that is provided by technical faculty. Thus, the writing project can be completed. The technical department can make its own decisions about credit for the laboratory element.
2. A report can be prepared in such a way as to include the unsuccessful experiment or laboratory project as the basis for recommendations against a process or product—a realistic situation common in industry and government testing facilities.
3. A subject other than that of the laboratory project can be chosen. This, however, is a last resort and should be avoided if possible. Student incentive is usually much lower; in fact, the poorer student is frequently inclined under these circumstances to attempt to use as his or her model a report that has already been evaluated and returned to its owner. The attendant problems for the instructor are readily apparent. Coordination of the technical writing project with a laboratory project greatly reduces the possibility of a student's use of work done by predecessors.

Project Evaluation

Evaluation of writing assignments, always a contentious matter, is no less difficult to perform consistently for major reports than for brief assignments. In the long run judgments will be made subjectively, and they will probably vary somewhat in uniformity from time to time despite every effort to be consistent.

Experience has shown that the most reliable system is to make a basic decision as to whether or not the assignment is acceptable. This decision is based on such criteria as the degree to which the report:

1. conforms with the topic chosen
2. includes the elements required
3. is mature in treatment of the subject
4. demonstrates an acceptable amount of research
5. appears to be the work of the student submitting it
6. demonstrates reasonable competence in language
7. is neat and presentable in appearance

To ensure that each student knows the basis of evaluation, and can see quickly where strengths and weaknesses lie in it, an evaluation sheet should be attached to the report and returned with it after grades are assigned. It is wise, if possible, for the instructor to retain a copy of that sheet as a basis for future discussion or consideration if that becomes necessary. It could follow the form shown here.

While the form recommended saves a great deal of time and discussion, it is wise to include as much comment as possible. The space allotted to this section should be at least a half page.

Author:	Grade:
Title:	Date:
Course and Program:	
✓ = Acceptable	X = Unacceptable or missing
1. General appearance ____	16. Heading display ____
2. Cover and label ____	17. Organization of material ____
3. Title (suitability) ____	18. Introduction ____
4. Title page ____	19. General content ____
5. Page numbering ____	20. Conclusions ____
6. Letter of transmittal ____	21. Recommendations ____
7. Acknowledgments ____	22. Scope ____
8. Table of contents ____	23. Style ____
9. List of illustrations ____	24. Language ____
10. List of tables ____	25. Illustrations and captions ____
11. Abstract or summary ____	26. References ____
12. Glossary ____	27. Appendices ____
13. Section headings ____	28. Bibliography ____
14. Section numbering ____	29. Index ____
15. Section order ____	30. Other (specify) ____

General Comment

(using item numbers listed above)

If the course consists mainly of the report-writing project, no great problem should be encountered in distribution of grades for the assignments given. Since the writing of the report, however, is for most students a long, arduous undertaking, many are inclined to overlook or ignore the relevance and perhaps misunderstand the function of the related assignments, e.g., bibliography cards, note cards, and topic outline. It is thus important to assign enough weight to the related assignments to ensure their recognition as having major consequence. In some courses, under these circumstances, 50 percent of the credit is granted for all the preparatory work.

In longer courses including other forms of written communication, if the whole report-writing project constitutes only 50 percent of the length of the course, that project could generate only 50 percent of the credit for the same reasons as those given above. The report itself would then most likely be worth 25 percent of an academic year's work.

Most instructors in writing can understand the reasons for such weighting. It is difficult, however, for many technical instructors to accept—particularly those who think of technical writing as simply the production of technical reports and nothing else, or those who have never been faced with the responsibility in industry of other forms of communication. This is further reason for the desirability of much discussion and interaction among departments, and for joint projects.

Late Assignments and Penalties Imposed

While an instructor's judgment must be the key factor in deciding on appropriate action when assignments are late, a few criteria have developed through experience.

Obviously, although every effort is made to ensure that the students' major writing assignments meet the deadline, care must be taken in dealing with those that do not. In view of the great amount of work that must be done by the student in completing the project, the effect of refusal to accept it can be shattering. It is wiser therefore to set a moderate penalty—perhaps a third of a letter grade a day. This procedure will usually allow a project to meet course requirements but will reduce the value of what might otherwise be a fine piece of work.

In-class assignments are, however, another matter. They should not be accepted after the time allotted for their completion. It is wise, in order to maintain the integrity of the assignment and to encourage participation in the class work, to either refuse special consideration or, if conditions warrant it, administer a substitute assignment.

While only the first three of the report-related assignments listed in the subsection on preparatory projects and assignments, pages 171–72, are intended to be done in class, other exercises—report-related or not—such as letters and memorandums, will all or almost all be classroom projects. All the second term's work—if the report project is in the first—is of this sort.

Related Assignments: Scheduling the Theory and Practice

As pointed out in the subsection on the course outline and detailed description, pages 167–68, most of an entire term's work can be related to the preparation and presentation of the major report. If the report project must be carried out during the second term of an academic year, the course content discussed in the business correspondence subsection, pages 181–83, should be applied to the first rather than the second term. Of the topics listed in the outline on page 167, only items 1 to 4 are specifically report-related. The rest, including the letter-writing applications of indirect organization of information, should involve classroom work only.

Besides controlling conditions under which the writing is done, this practice helps to limit the grading load to a manageable number of assignments.

Introduction to the Course

Introduction to the technical writing course and the report project may take as long as two weeks (six class hours). During this time, the documents listed in the subsection on information and instructions for students, pages 166–69, as well as book lists, should be distributed and class lists compiled. Lectures and discussion of information theory and the role of communication in an organization provide the groundwork for the course at this stage.

If the report is to be completed by the end of the first term, it is essential that the project be introduced by the beginning of the second week. Since many students will already have heard via the "grapevine" about the project, probably many will be anxious to get started. Beginning early provides an advantage in that generally they have not become too heavily involved in other courses to be deterred, as might later be the case.

Discussion of objectives and the value of using a hypothetical management situation should lead to almost immediate topic selection, and should provide an incentive to get under way with the students' laboratory projects, if the latter are coordinated with the technical report-writing assignment. Each student must determine who needs the information, what information is required, how it is to be used, and when it must be available.

Once these decisions have been made, a classroom assignment can be given, requiring each student to draft the body or content only of a memorandum of request or authorization—from the hypothetical individual requiring the report to the prospective author of the report (the student). This assignment should enable the instructor to decide on acceptance, rejection, or modification of the project proposal, and need not be graded. As soon as the project is authorized, a work or production schedule for the whole project should be produced and checked in the same fashion.

Searching the Literature and Recording Data

It is essential to emphasize the need for a thorough search of the literature—books, periodicals, etc.—for information and to include a warning to avoid the use of textbooks.

Description and discussion of library resources, the organization of them and means of access to them, should precede any search. The amount of time spent on this will depend on the students' previous library orientation in secondary school or college. Time required for this phase of the course could range from zero to three class hours and could involve library visits for instruction.

Frequently, a few days after the project gets under way, one or more students will inform the instructor that no information is available on the subject; the reasons given are endless. Despite the student's conviction that such is the case, and a very convincing presentation of the evidence to support the view, it is *never* true; the information does exist somewhere. Time is the most common limiting factor in the search for it.

The instructor may propose to the student that:

1. much more thorough investigation is in order—with suggestions as to scope, interpretation of topic, sources of data, interviews with individuals, etc.
2. the topic be modified to match the student's capabilities.
3. the topic and circumstances be changed entirely. This is a last resort, and should never be done after the first month has passed.

Techniques in the preparation and use of bibliography cards and note cards should be demonstrated and discussed now. Note-taking techniques and acknowledgment of sources must be emphasized. By the end of the third week (nine hours) a preliminary submission of bibliography cards should be made in order to check techniques and to ensure that each student has made some progress. Grading is optional.

Style and Mechanics

The following two to three weeks, while the search is in progress, should be spent on various applications of style and mechanics of language to technical writing assignments. If, at this stage, the basics of the English language require teaching, the technical writing course is in jeopardy. Little or no time is available, except for very brief review, to discuss fundamentals. Students in need of help should be directed to either the handbook section of a text or to remedial classes. Precursor or prerequisite courses should make the need for these measures minimal.

At least four class sessions should be devoted during this period to discussion and practice of the special characteristics of *defining and describing* an object and a process, *explaining* a process, and *analyzing* a problem. In the latter topic, emphasis should be on the writing techniques associated with analysis rather than on problem solving. Most of the better texts include reliable sections devoted to these subjects, which should be related as closely as possible to the students' chief technical interests.

Organizing and Outlining

At this point, the students should have collected an appreciable amount of data. It is time for the instructor to examine the record of those data (note cards) and conduct a discussion of their organization. Grading the note cards is optional, but the instructor must examine and return them very quickly.

The instructor should then show the students how to organize material for the report and should include techniques in the preparation of outlines. The topic outline is by far the most appropriate, and, for technical students, its topics should be identified by the multidecimal system. At least two weeks before the submission of the completed report, a final topic outline should be submitted and graded. If it seems necessary, the instructor could make a preliminary outline assignment at the time the instruction is given. One or two hours are required for this segment.

Documentation

The function and importance of documentation must be thoroughly discussed and must be quite clear to the students. The method of transfer of information from source to notes to manuscript and the attendant pitfalls are traditional subjects of careful attention in all college programs.

Use of the footnote, list of references, and bibliography, and awareness of the content and location of each, are of prime concern. Format should be determined and based on a standard as demonstrated in a selected style guide, handbook, or text. In some scientific, technical, or engineering disciplines, special styles are well established and should be carefully observed and applied. In such fields as chemistry, biology, bacteriology, and virology, unless the instructor is a specialist in the discipline, great care must be taken to avoid requiring the students to follow a practice applied only in the liberal arts or in some other sciences. Such care will bring a substantial reward in confidence and cooperation from both the students and the faculty of the science or technology involved.

Two hours of class time should suffice for this topic, which can be complicated by the fact that in some technical programs much use is made of ephemeral material: company reports, laboratory reports, departmental reports, product data sheets, brochures, catalogues, and handbooks. Most students require a good deal of instruction in the documentation of these sources, which are mentioned in almost no texts. If one is in doubt about preparing entries for them, the best plan is to follow the sort of procedure used in documenting government publications.

Prefatory Elements

At least two hours' instruction and discussion are required to clarify the functions of all prefatory sections of the report: cover to abstract. During this time, the body of the letter or memo of authorization or request should be submitted.

Text Layout

Three class hours are required to explain page organization and layout, topic and page numbering, coordination of illustrations and text, and text documentation, i.e., the use of footnotes and list of references. Footnotes are used very little in science and technology. When they are used, they appear chiefly as explanatory notes. Even for that, a glossary is more commonly used either immediately before the first page of text or at the beginning of the appendix. A list of references is the almost universal practice in documentation, either at the end of the text or divided and used at the end of each chapter.

Particular attention should be given to the careful and clear statement of conclusions, and to ensuring that each one is separately identified. The same is true of recommendations, which are most useful if numbered and concisely listed. They bring the report to its culmination, should be forcefully expressed, and should lead to a decision by the reader for whom the report is prepared. The instructor should reemphasize that this is the purpose of the report.

Supplementary Material

One hour usually suffices to deal with the end matter of the report. In the technologies, bulky items such as charts, sketches, tables, drawings, maps, and large photographs are often included. The function of the appendix should therefore be made quite clear, particularly in terms of the contrast between the use of that section and of the text proper for illustrative material. Emphasis should also be placed on judicious selection of items, as opposed to inclusion of anything at all that does not seem to fit easily into the report.

Bibliography

One hour is enough to spend on bibliographic organization, as most important points have already been covered in discussions of the entries made on bibliography cards and the list of references.

Since an index is almost never used, a comment about its function is sufficient.

Business Correspondence

Transition to Correspondence

There is very little difference, if any, between business and technical correspondence, except in topic. Perhaps memorandums are used more often. At any rate, because of the similarity, the same teaching techniques are employed for both.

As is customary in the teaching of business correspondence, the basic principles of communication should be reviewed. Not even a whole hour should be required, as the introduction to the course should have covered the basics.

First-Term Introduction to Correspondence

When the report-writing project is nearing completion, two to three weeks, i.e., six to nine hours, of class time are still available. Certainly endless questions will be asked in class about the report project which students are still completing. However, since letter writing is a flexible sort of subject and assignments can easily be worked into class time, the subject can be begun and a good basis laid for another term's work.

If only one term is available for the whole of a technical writing course, a dilemma is virtually unavoidable. In that case, only a brief run through the essentials of the simplest aspects of correspondence is possible. Most of the time is likely to be spent on format and on direct or deductive messages: providing routine information, simple or routine requests, order letters, acknowledgments, etc.

If a three-week period is available, indirect or inductive messages can be considered, and perhaps technical jargon, but litte time will be available for practice. At this point the major assignment, the report, will likely be submitted. The pressures on both students and faculty make it unwise to attempt to do a comprehensive study of even the less complex aspects of correspondence. An introduction is therefore about all that can be achieved with any effectiveness.

It is assumed here that another term is available for the study and practice of technical writing. That means that another thirteen-week period can be used to build on the experience of the first term. If the quarter system is in use, judicious pruning, of course, will be inevitable.

A Full Course in Correspondence

On the assumption that a full academic year is available for a technical writing course, a fairly thorough treatment of business and technical correspondence is possible. The introduction to the subject in the first term makes a good grounding for the second term's work, providing the break between terms is not long. If it is, all the skills of a good teacher are required to ensure the successful carryover.

It should be possible, near the beginning of the second half of the course, to move quickly to inductive (indirect) message organization. The inductive approach particularly requires a good deal of attention, as does the whole technique of persuasion.

Many science and technology students are averse to indirect or persuasive messages. Their disciplines encourage them to be direct (deductive), forthright, and concise in the statement of facts. Many interpret this as a license to be blunt. They are proud of their directness and consider it the most forceful and effective approach to communication. It consequently is often difficult to convince them that there are sometimes better ways. The value of the indirect approach is such that it is well worth while to spend the time necessary to work this out. Successful teaching of inductive communication techniques provides the groundwork for nearly all the second term's activity.

A couple of weeks spent at this stage on the more elementary types of inductive messages can set the scene for more complex situations later. Persuasive requests, mixed responses, negative responses—all using science or engineering situations or cases—are appropriate. This segment of the course provides effective preparation for the employment correspondence to follow.

Employment Correspondence

For students in science and technology the interest in and need for direction in anything that has to do with employment, temporary or permanent, are always intense. It is thus a simple matter to schedule three weeks for the various applications of correspondence to this subject. During that time some of the more tedious detail of letter writing can receive, in this interesting context, attention that it is less likely to receive otherwise.

Solicited applications, in response to advertisements or requests, are a good starting point. Former work done on simple requests or inquiries, handled deductively, is the logical background.

From requests and inquiries the instructor should proceed to the resume, giving that subject careful and detailed attention, for it will most likely be used by the student in a real-life situation very soon, perhaps immediately. It should be pointed out that it is the enclosure of a covering letter, and that the letter does the persuading.

The application letter then is taught as an inductive communication, with this term's introduction to correspondence as a base. Then follow letters of acceptance (deductive), refusal (inductive), and requests for more time to decide (inductive). Students will periodically request personal assistance in relation to these topics for at least the next two months.

Graphics

In planning the graphics element of the course, due consideration must be given to the fact that most students have already studied drafting of one sort or another, that they are already familiar with and can produce circuit diagrams, flowcharts, elevation drawings and sketches, layout drawings, etc., common to their field of specialization. It is therefore unnecessary to spend time on these topics. Graphics useful in management decision making are, however, important to study and produce.

Instruction must be given in the use and preparation of various kinds of tables, charts, and graphs. Since information for management is the aim, emphasis should be placed on the presentation of statistical data and on the ability of the graphic forms to demonstrate trends. They are useful only if they can be quickly and easily interpreted.

Another very important aspect of this phase of the course is the relation of graphic presentation to text in a report. No doubt this point has already been made during the preparation of the major report. However, there probably has not been time to give it anything but very sketchy consideration. The instructor must make sure that students clearly understand the importance of that correlation. Several assignments should be given which include (1) the production of graphic representation of related or comparative data and (2) written copy to introduce the circumstances or conditions. Placing and phrasing of captions must be included.

A number of texts contain an excellent chapter on this subject; some are very helpful to the teacher with little background in the subject. Newspapers, periodicals, and annual reports are excellent sources of tables, charts, and graphs which can provide plenty of classroom material for examination. A collection of company and government annual reports is a worthwhile investment of time and effort.

About three weeks should be spent on this phase of the course.

Memorandums, Short Reports, Further Correspondence

If no oral element is included in the technical writing course, about five weeks should remain for the development of writing skills in preparing short reports, memorandums, and composing more difficult letters.

Correspondence requiring a negative response to a query or request seems to be most difficult for technical students. As mentioned already, many would prefer a direct approach. A considerable amount of practice is required to develop their skill and confidence in an indirect technique.

Cases including all three forms of written communication can extend over a week each. If possible, the memorandums and reports should relate to either the major report already written, the material or situation dealt with in their employment correspondence, or to other subjects with which they have developed some familiarity. Progress reports, trip reports, inspection reports, personnel reports, follow-up reports, and numerous other short documents can provide excellent, realistic media for writing practice. At the same time students have the opportunity to adapt techniques learned during the major project to these other forms of written communication.

Oral Presentation

If oral work is included in the writing course, the five-week segment discussed above must be reduced by about half—perhaps more, depending on class size and the extent of the work intended. Three weeks constitute a worthwhile period.

Use of the major report is almost unavoidable. So much effort is devoted to that project that real or hypothetical circumstances, information, and ideas are all readily available. Conditions are ideal for a brief period of oral instruction and practice.

It may well be that the text used for the technical writing course does not include a section on oral presentation. Perhaps a text is not required; the short duration of this part of the course hardly warrants the expenditure necessary for a separate book.

Student Evaluation

The comments made in the subsection titled "Project Evaluation," pages 174–76, about report appraisal apply to some degree here. Assignments and presentations are marked subjectively, with or without a set of printed criteria. Experience has shown that final examinations are an unnecessary burden. Plenty of opportunities exist during either the one-term or the two-term period for the development of a set of grades which can be averaged, interpreted, or weighted so as to produce a realistic result. Comparison of teaching systems with and without final examinations demonstrates that the result is practically the same.

Text Selection

The attached bibliography lists a number of books which can be used with very satisfactory results for a technical writing course of the type described here. While strong personal preferences are unavoidable, experience has revealed that what pleases one instructor may very well be quite inadequate for another.

The best approach is to examine as many as possible of them, and others not listed here. It could well be that not one seems to meet all the needs of a particular course or situation. That is normal. Never yet has the perfect book in this or any other field been published. A common practice in this field of study, as in others, is to change texts periodically, if for no other reason than to experience a fresh approach. The instructor, to avoid the rut of the dull professor, needs that therapy from time to time.

The Future of Teaching Technical Writing

Some teachers of writing may, from time to time, wonder a little about the future of their profession. They may wonder about the continuing appropriateness of the techniques they are teaching, or about their own credibility in the future. Technology has for some years been introducing changes that, to some, seem to threaten the status of their expertise.

One fact in which they may take comfort is that, while message-handling methods—recording, reproduction, distribution and delivery—may change rapidly, the goals and content of those messages do not. Human nature has changed very little, if at all, in the recorded past. The effect of wise and careful organization and presentation of ideas, therefore, is as important, and will be so, as it ever was.

While teachers of technical communication may experience some relief in that knowledge, they must face the fact that credibility depends also on awareness of current technological developments and their applications in business and industry. It is essential, therefore, to take the time and make the effort—and it shouldn't be an effort—to read about progress in computer-controlled communication facilities, in the full realization that they really are people-controlled. Word processing, text processing, and the various kinds of storage devices that reduce the drudgery of recording, editing, and reproducing information, should be the subject of more than just nodding acquaintance. The technical-writing teacher must—head high—look and move forward.

Bibliography

American National Standard Guidelines for Format and Production of Scientific and Technical Reports. ANSI Z39. 18-1974. Secretariat, Council of National Library Associations, 1973.

ANDERSON, W. STEVE, and DON RICHARD COX. *The Technical Reader: Readings in Technical, Business, and Scientific Communication.* 378 pp. New York: Holt, Rinehart and Winston, 1980.

Three parts, consisting of 15 sections altogether, with a total of 77 articles. Each part and section is preceded by an introduction.

ANDREWS, DEBORAH C., and MARGARET D. BLICKLE. *Technical Writing: Principles and Forms.* 431 pp. New York: Macmillan Publishing Co., 1978.

Includes notes, exercises, selected sources, 39-page handbook section.

BARNETT, MARVA T. *Writing for Technicians.* 2d ed. 358 pp. Albany, N.Y.: Delmar Publishers, 1982.

Revised and expanded. Includes proposals, emphasis on interoffice communication; proofreading guides.

BLICQ, RONALD S. *Technically-Write! Communicating in a Technological Era.* 2d ed. U.S. Edition. 381 pp. Englewood Cliffs, N.J.: Prentice-Hall, 1981.

Canadian Edition. 401 pp. Scarborough, Ont.: Prentice-Hall Canada, 1983.

Primarily for students of engineering and technology.

Includes assignments; writing and illustrating techniques; 6 articles on and 30-page glossary of technical usage, including abbreviations, numbers, prefixes, and symbols; metrics; marking control chart.

BRUNNER, INGRID, J. C. MATHES, and DWIGHT W. STEVENSON, *Preparing Technical Reports.* 232 pp. Indianapolis, Ind.: Bobbs-Merrill Educational Publishing, 1980.

Includes copious examples and illustrations; exercises at end of each chapter.

BRUSAW, CHARLES T., GERALD J. ALRED, and WALTER E. OLIU. *Handbook of Technical Writing.* 2d ed. 697 pp. New York: St. Martin's Press, 1982.

Includes guide to use of handbook; five steps to successful writing; checklist of writing processes; topical key to alphabetical entries; 635 pages of alphabetical entries; bibliography; correction chart.

DAGHER, JOSEPH P. *Technical Communication: a Practical Guide.* 322 pp. Englewood Cliffs, N.J.: Prentice-Hall, 1978.

Includes exercises (applications); 29-page grammar review; teacher's manual.

DAMERST, WILLIAM A. *Clear Technical Reports.* 2d ed. 325 pp. San Diego: HBJ Media Systems Corporation (subsidiary of Harcourt Brace Jovanovich), 1982.

Includes case studies; 31-page handbook section; use of Gunning Fog Index readability formula; subjects and sources of information; subject-area classification of indexes and abstracts.

Effective Communication for Engineers. 216 pp. New York: McGraw-Hill Book-Co., 1974.

Primarily for practicing engineers or engineering students. Consists of a compendium of 51 sections, each by a different author or authors.

Eisenberg, Anne. *Effective Technical Communication.* 355 pp. New York: McGraw-Hill Book Co., 1982

Includes exercises at end of each chapter; method of keeping a laboratory notebook; common grammatical and punctuation faults.

Fear, David E. *Technical Communication,* 2d ed. 385 pp. Glenview, Ill.: Scott, Foresman and Co., 1981.

Includes exercises at end of each chapter; 61-page handbook section; planning worksheet and correction chart on inside front and back covers.

Godfrey, David W. H. *Modern Technical Communication.* 288 pp. Toronto: McGraw-Hill Ryerson Limited, 1983.

Primarily for students of engineering and technology or for special courses.

Includes example of an automated publications department; reading list; proofreader's marks; format requirements for scientific and technical reports prepared for the U.S. Department of Defense; program management systems at SPAR Aerospace Ltd., RMS Division; transmittals; communicating by computer graphics.

Hart, Andrew W., and James A. Reinking. *Writing for Career-Education Students,* 2d ed. 501 pp. New York: St. Martin's Press, 1982.

For students in technical and vocational programs or those in a mixture of vocational and liberal arts studies; for freshman composition courses; for courses in technical communication at freshman or sophomore level.

Includes suggested assignments; sample library research paper; examples of application letters; 112-page handbook of grammar, usage, punctuation, and mechanics; revision symbols for student papers on back endpapers.

Hirschhorn, Howard H. *Writing for Science, Industry, and Technology.* 265 pp. New York: D. Van Nostrand Co., 1980.

Includes copious examples and illustrations; 18-page list of 33 information centers for scientific and technical writers; a personal information retrieval system; the metric system and conversion factors.

Houp, Kenneth W., and Thomas E. Pearsall. *Reporting Technical Information.* 4th ed. 547 pp. Encino, Calif.: Glencoe Publishing Co., 1980.

Includes exercises at end of each chapter; 32-page handbook section; sample student report; technical reference section; history of measurement; metric conversion chart; selected bibliography.

Jordan, Stello, ed., and Joseph M. Kleinman and H. Lee Shimberg, associate eds. *Handbook of Technical Writing Practices,* 2 vols. 1,373 pp. New York: John Wiley & Sons, 1971.

Primarily for practicing technical communicators.

Thirty-two chapters by different authors. Includes handbook evaluation plan; 25-page index, separate for each volume.

KEMP, JEROLD E. *Planning and Producing Audiovisual Materials.* 320 pp. New York: Thomas Y. Crowell, 1975.

Includes background; planning materials; fundamental skills; producing materials; photographic prints, slides, filmstrips, tape recordings, overhead transparencies, motion pictures, television and display materials, multi-image/multimedia; correlated still/motion Super 8-mm films; books, films, pamphlets, and periodicals; sources for equipment and materials; services; glossary.

LANNON, JOHN M. *Technical Writing.* 2d ed. 650 pp. Boston: Little, Brown and Co., 1982.

Includes assignments; examples; exercises; expanded section on preparation of proposals; instructor's manual.

LAY, MARY M. *Strategies for Technical Writing: A Rhetoric with Readings.* 308 pp. New York: Holt, Rinehart and Winston, 1982.

Reading for analysis and discussion. Includes copious exercises and assignments.

LEVENS, A. S., *Graphics, Analysis and Conceptual Design,* 2d ed. 771 pp. New York: John Wiley & Sons, 1968.

Primarily for professional engineers and engineering students.

Includes tables; abbreviations and symbols; useful technical terms.

MACGREGOR, ANETTE JEAN. *Graphics Simplified.* 64 pp. Toronto, Ont.: University of Toronto Press, 1979.

Concise handbook.

MATHES, JOHN C., and DWIGHT W. STEVENSON. *Designing Technical Reports: Writing for Audiences in Organizations.* 400 pp. Indianapolis, Ind.: The Bobbs-Merrill Co., 1976.

Includes 17 pages of guides and checklists; samples of eight different types of reports, including application letter and resume, totalling 160 pages; teacher's manual.

Military Standard Format Requirements for Scientific and Technical Reports Prepared by or for the Department of Defense. MIL-STD-487A. Alexandria, Va.: Defense Technical Information Center of the Defense Logistics Agency, 1980.

Includes instruction for preparation of report documentation page; index to DD Form 1473; transliteration of foreign alphabets.

MILLS, GORDON H., and JOHN A. WALTER. *Technical Writing.* 4th ed. 587 pp. New York: Holt, Rinehart and Winston, 1978.

Includes 57 pages of excerpts and samples; 30 pages of grammar and usage; selected bibliography.

MORRIS, GEORGE E. *Technical Illustration.* 250 pp. Englewood Cliffs, N.J.: Prentice-Hall, 1975.

Out of print, 1982.

NELSON, JOHN A. *Technical Illustration.* 113 pp. New York: Van Nostrand Reinhold Ltd., 1979.

Out of print, 1982.

PAULEY, STEVEN E. *Technical Report Writing Today.* 2d ed. 321 pp. Boston: Houghton Mifflin Co., 1979.

Includes models; exercises and assignments at ends of most chapters; outline of contents on end-papers; 17 pages of common technical writing errors.

PEARSALL, THOMAS E., and DONALD H. CUNNINGHAM. *How to Write for the World of Work.* 2d ed. 397 pp. New York: Holt, Rinehart and Winston, 1982.

Six chapters on technical communication, plus one dealing with oral and visual presentations; suggestions for application at end of each chapter; 40-page writer's guide; metric conversion tables; selected bibliography.

PICKETT, N. A., and A. A. LASTER. *Technical English.* 3d ed. 627 pp. New York: Harper & Row, Publishers, 1980.

Junior level.

Includes forms of communication; selected readings; handbook section.

Pocket Pal: A Graphic Arts Digest for Printers and Advertising Production Managers. 12th ed. New York: International Paper Co., 1979.

ROSEN, HAROLD J. *Construction Specifications Writing: Principles and Procedures.* 2d ed. 235 pp. New York: John Wiley & Sons, 1981.

Professional.

Includes principles, bidding procedures, conditions of contract; example of preliminary specifications; project manual checklist.

SHERMAN, THEODORE A., and SIMON S. JOHNSON, *Modern Technical Writing.* 4th ed. 512 pp. Englewood Cliffs, N.J.: Prentice-Hall, 1983.

Includes handbook of fundamentals; bibliography; teacher's handbook.

SOUTHER, JAMES W., and MYRON L. WHITE. *Technical Report Writing.* 2d ed. 93 pp. New York: John Wiley & Sons, 1977.

Includes exercises and discussion topics; selected bibliography.

STRATTON, CHARLES R. *Technical Writing: Process and Practice.* 448 pp. New York: Holt, Rinehart and Winston, 1983.

For science, engineering and technology majors.

Includes exercises and assignments; instructor's manual.

STRONG, CHARLES W., and DONALD EIDSON. *A Technical Writer's Handbook.* 368 pp. New York: Holt, Rinehart and Winston, 1971.

Includes preparation of technical articles and government publications; evaluation of data; preparation and display of graphic aids; technical editing; advertising and public relations; sample papers; 26-page guide to references; 29-page index.

TURNER, RUFUS P. *Technical Report Writing.* Rev. ed. 210 pp. San Francisco: Rinehart Press, 1971.

Includes exercises; 88 pages of specimens.

ULMAN, JOSEPH N., and JAY R. GOULD. *Technical Reporting.* 3d ed. 419 pp. New York: Holt, Rinehart and Winston, 1972.

Includes 95 pages of style and mechanics; 41 pages of specimens; bibliography.

WEISMAN, HERMAN M. *Basic Technical Writing.* 4th ed. 414 pp. Columbus, Ohio: Charles E. Merrill Publishing Co., 1980.

Includes problems and exercises at end of each chapter; references at end of most chapters; 36-page guide to grammar, punctuation, style, and usage, followed by discussion problems and exercises in grammar and usage; 5 pages of requirements for progress reports; 47 pages of examples of technical writing; 8-page classified bibliography.

Chapter 8

Sales Communication

Norman B. Sigband

TEACHING A SEGMENT on sales writing can be most enjoyable and productive. Working in the area of sales requires imagination, creativity, and the desire to fulfill the needs of others. It is tremendously gratifying for an individual to develop the ability to use words that will persuade and motivate others to take a specific course of action.

In this chapter, we will use what industry calls a "systems approach." Our first step will be to briefly review the background of sales writing:

1. Requirements of successful sales writing
2. Initial steps of selling
3. Parts of the sales letter
4. Cover letter and enclosure
5. Direct mail

This review will be brief and is designed to ensure that all instructors reading this chapter possess the same general knowledge level of the topics.

Our second major step will then be to make specific recommendations of teaching methodologies for the areas noted above so that students will be competent in designing sales communications.

Let us now move immediately to our reviews.

Background of Sales Writing

Requirements of Successful Sales Writing

In order to do a good job in writing the letter which sells a product or service, there are three basic requirements: (1) a vivid imagination, (2) skill in the basic concepts of written communication, and (3) the sales ability to create desire through words.

Imagination is needed so that the writer is able to see things from the potential reader's position and perceive the reader's values, needs, and desires. The writer must use his or her imagination in recognizing and anticipating potential new needs, uses, and reasons why the reader should purchase the product or service.

Skill in composition is required in every communication, but especially the sales letter. The organizational development must be logical and smooth, the sentences must be crystal clear, and the word choice must be accurate and precise to evoke the exact response desired.

The sales correspondent must combine imaginative ability with communication skill to build desire. The words that are used must be able to provide a response that will result in the reader's favorable action.

Initial Steps of Selling

There are several steps the sales writer must carry through before writing the letter. These include:

1. Conducting a product analysis
2. Completing a market analysis
3. Reviewing the needs of the buyer
4. Selecting the attribute(s) of the products which fulfill the need—central appeal

Product Analysis

The sales-letter writer who hopes to sell a product successfully must know it intimately and thoroughly. He or she must know how it is produced, what components are used, where the raw materials came from, what the product or service will do, how it will do these things, and many other factors.

Knowing all these—thoroughly—not only permits the sales writer to talk knowledgeably about the product or service, but it also adds two vital selling factors to the sales presentations:

1. Sincerity and belief in the product
2. The ability to anticipate questions or objections which the prospect might raise

There are various ways in which a product analysis may be conducted. The sales writer may visit the manufacturing and office areas of the company producing the product. Through observation and discussion with those directly involved with the product or service, information about the product can be secured.

Data may be gathered and entered on chart forms concerning the quality level of the raw materials used and their sources, the production techniques employed, the quality control imposed, the method of operation of the product, the performance levels of the product, its design and appearance, the particular product's differentiating features, repair and service facilities offered, and prices and terms. The areas examined can be used as headings on a chart, and the data filled in under each head. When the work is completed, the sales writer possesses an excellent resource chart from which to draw information for sales letters and sales promotion pieces of various types.

Market Analysis

Most companies will bring a new product out only after very sophisticated market analysis. Since a great deal of money is involved in producing a product, it would be foolish to spend these huge sums without first determining whether or not a profitable market exists for the product. Such a market analysis will determine:

- The potential number of buyers
- Present sales and acceptance of competitive products
- Present buying habits and geographical concentrations of potential buyers
- The likes, desires, and status symbols of the potential buyers
- The buyers' purchasing power
- Under what conditions and terms the buyer will act
- The short- and long-range selling potential of the product
- Possible tie-ins with other products

Answers to these questions and many others may be secured from secondary as well as primary sourcs.

Company records, earlier market studies for similar products, government statistics on buying habits, and journal articles which discuss the future sales potential in various fields are only some of the secondary sources which are easily available. Primary sources of information are also extremely valuable. Interviews and questionnaire surveys of a sample of the potential buyers are frequently used. Personal and unobtrusive observation of how or why a buyer decides to purchase one product instead of another is also valuable.

Needs of the Buyer

A market analysis should indicate whether or not our product or service will sell and which groups in the population will become our market segment. At this point we must place these specific groups under the magnifying glass in order to determine what their needs and desires are and what specific appeals we should use to motivate them to select our product.

Most of people's daily activities revolve around efforts to fulfill their needs. These needs are usually divided into physical, social, and egoistic needs. In an affluent society, physical needs—food, shelter, clothing, etc.—are usually met easily; thus, people concentrate on their social and egoistic needs. Social needs include the desire to give and receive affection, to affiliate and be affiliated with others, and to care for others and be taken care of (nurturance).

Unlike the social needs, which concern a person's relationship with others, egoistic needs involve one's relationship with oneself. These needs may be filled by recognition received, status symbols, positions of authority a person occupies, the achievements the person secures, and similar situations of concern to oneself.

Specialists in consumer motivation have produced lists of human drives or motives which include from fifty to several hundred items. Most people desire to secure love, security, social distinction, comfort, pleasure, efficiency, position of authority, saving of time, good health, warmth, approval from others, respect, prestige, and delicious food. All of these drives and motives must be taken into account, for consumers will frequently buy on the basis of the need which the product will fulfill rather than the product itself. The purchaser of an expensive automobile is sometimes purchasing prestige and respect rather than basic transportation; a woman may want from her mink coat status and position instead of warmth. And so it goes, very well exemplified in the timeworn phrase: "Sell the sizzle—not the steak."

Central Appeal

In selling, it is necessary to select one or two outstanding attributes of the particular product or service offered and emphasize these attributes in the sales message. The characteristics chosen will help fulfill the needs—real or imagined—of the prospect.

This central appeal concept is necessary for two primary reasons. First, in today's fast-paced society, the purchaser doesn't have the time or the inclination to examine and weigh the various attributes of the products against other products on the market. Second, the seller is interested in showing the prospect how his or her product surpasses competing items. By selecting and emphasizing one or two attributes which this product has, and competing products do not have, the seller draws attention to so-called superior features. But this central appeal is based on the needs—real or imagined—of the prospect.

Different groups of people will be motivated to purchase by selecting different central appeals and matching these with what we hope are our prospects' needs. This means that a different central appeal may be used in four, five, or six different sales letters—all selling the same product at the same price.

It is interesting to see how the advertisements for the same cars, soaps, cigarettes, and a thousand other items change from magazine to magazine. This is obviously because the readers of *different magazines* have different needs. However, the readers of *a particular magazine* frequently have similar needs based on similar educational, economic, and social background.

The messages and appeals present various selling points of the product in an effort to match the different needs of the various market segments. Changes in the central appeal are made in the sales letters according to the prospect group or market segment which is being addressed.

Parts of the Sales Letter

Opening Section: To Arouse Attention and Interest

Because everyone receives so much mail these days, it is necessary for the sales writer to come up with an unusual sales message if he or she wishes to attract the reader's interest. The sales correspondent should be careful that this attention-catching idea isn't so arresting as to be classified as a tasteless gimmick. It also shouldn't be so unusual that the reader's interest focuses on the attention device and not on the items to be sold.

The sales correspondent may consider using the following ideas to gain attention and interest:

1. Samples of the product
2. Photographs or sketches of the product
3. Gadgets or gimmicks
4. Different openings to attract attention

Openings of sales letters should be positive and designed to awaken in the prospect favorable associations with the product or service. They should also be pertinent and concerned with the sales item, since readers become irritated if they find their interest has been aroused by a device that has nothing to do with the product.

Description and Explanation

Once interest has been aroused and we have the prospect reading, our next task is to describe the product carefully and show how its purchase will be beneficial. We must not only describe the product so that the prospect can almost see and feel it, but we must do this in such a way that leads to a *desire* to purchase it. In our description we answer the questions "What does it look like?" "How is it made?" and "'What is it made of?"

The words that are used to describe the product or service must evoke a real picture in the prospect's mind. There should be enough details so he or she can visualize the item, but they should be presented in such a way as to add strength to the central appeal. If the letter is accompanied by an enclosure, the details and sketches can go in there. If there is no enclosure, the details must be carefully selected and presented in the letter.

The questions "What will it do for me?" and "How will I benefit?", asked by the prospect while reading, must be answered early in the letter if we are to hold interest. He or she must be told how some personal need will be fulfilled. In handling the description of the product and the explanation of the prospect's benefits, it is again wise to be specific, positive, and detailed in reference to the central selling appeal.

Proof

Since Americans are a skeptical lot, they often say, "Sounds great, but I don't believe it will do all that. Prove it!" A dozen different methods can be used to secure belief in what has been said. The type of proof selected will depend in part on who the prospect is and the nature of the product.

Some common types of proof are:

1. Samples
2. Guarantees
3. Free trial
4. Names of previous purchasers
5. Testimonials
6. "Outside" agency records
7. Money-back guarantees

The proof in a sales letter should be restrained, specific, and well documented. It should overcome any doubts the prospect has, and it should convince him or her that the product or service will prove of value.

Although proof is normally placed after the description, it need not be. Sometimes the proof can be so startling and dramatic as to serve the twofold purpose of arousing interest and convincing the prospect to make the purchase.

Like everything else in the sales letter (interest, description, action, central appeal, etc.), the proof is selected according to who the prospect group is. With one group, a movie star's testimonial is excellent; with another, records of tests at a leading university are much more effective.

Action

Let us assume that we have aroused the interest of our prospect through a well-written opening; we have created a desire to possess the product or service through our description of it; and we have proved that it will give full value. Now the prospect must take the most important step of all—he or she must buy it. Most people hesitate before they buy. This, of course, is to the good. Our only concern is that they may delay purchase to the point where the desire or the impulse to buy may disappear. For this reason, the "buy" section of the sales letter should reflect an appeal sufficiently strong to move the prospect to action. We hope for immediate action, since the longer the delay, the less likely the prospect is to act favorably.

The action does not necessarily have to be the purchase of a product. It may simply involve "purchasing" the next step. It may be sending for a brochure, agreeing to see a sales representative, or accepting a demonstration.

The type and tone of the approach to use in the action section depends on the prospect. Sometimes incentives are offered so the potential buyer will act quickly. It is also important to tell the prospect *what* to do and *how* to do it.

Cover Letter and Enclosure

Most sales letters cover one page, although in some cases a sales letter of several pages has proved successful. Most experts, however, prefer to use a variation of the basic sales letter when length is required. This usually consists of a letter accompanied by a brochure, a pamphlet, or a flyer and is referred to as a sales promotion piece. Prospects do not object to reading through an attractively laid-out and well-written enclosure if it is concerned with a product they are seriously considering buying. However, they do object to reading through six pages of a sales letter.

Authorities in the field of direct mail seem to feel that the cover letter can be designed in either of the following two methods:

1. Very general and designed to arouse sufficient interest in the reader so that he or she will be motivated to turn to the enclosure.
2. Containing the four parts of the sales letter—interest, description, proof, and action. However, each section is treated so briefly that the total letter would be inadequate were it not for the enclosure which expands on each of the parts.

The design, layout, color, and copy of the enclosure can be as imaginative as the writer wishes it to be. The writer will be governed by knowledge of the prospect group and by budget limitations.

Direct Mail

Direct mail is not limited just to the selling of products and services. It can pave the way for salespeople, keep contact with customers between a salesperson's calls, get new accounts signed up, stimulate the inactive customer to return, develop interest among prospects not yet visited by salespeople, answer inquiries, build goodwill, distribute samples, and scores of other profit-building activities.

Advantages

On the whole, direct mail selling has proved to be an effective, inexpensive, and profitable method of doing business. Direct mail, when compared with other sales media (such as newspaper or magazine ads), has several distinct advantages:

1. You can be exact in the selection of the market you wish your advertising to reach.
2. You can be personal and confidential.
3. You have less competition for the reader's attention because there are fewer "distractions."
4. You have few limits in formats to restrict the creative expression of your advertising ideas.
5. You have great flexibility in the selection and use of creative materials and reproduction processes.
6. You can interpret your advertising story with a "reader-only" individualism.
7. You can produce direct mail as you need or want it.
8. You can use the "control" inherent in direct mail for research and testing of highly selective audiences.
9. Your timing of mailings can be accurate, exact.
10. You can offer a complete "reply" package so that the reader has ease of answering.

Other advantages include the following: a sales letter will frequently penetrate where other advertising media might not, it can be directed to widely separated geographic areas for less money than sales personnel; it can introduce a product prior to the personal call; and it can update information about the product or service for those already utilizing the product.

Mailing Lists

The best sales letter will be of no use unless it gets in the hands of your potential buyer. For this reason, the mailing list is extremely important.

The competent sales writer examines the names on the list periodically to be sure that it reflects the characteristics of a good mailing list.

1. Is each name correctly spelled?
2. Is every person a good prospect for the product or service?
3. Do all persons listed have common basic attributes?

4. If the list is large, has it been divided into logical divisions such as geographical location, economic level, etc.? When this is done, different central appeals can be used in different sales letters.
5. Has the list been revised so that it does not include the names of those who have moved, died, or expressed no interest in the product?
6. Have new accounts', customers', and prospects' names been added?
7. Have those names of persons requesting *no* direct mail *of any type* been removed from the list?

There are many methods of developing a mailing list, including developing your own prospect group, utilizing company records pertaining to their customers, utilizing public rosters, using various directories, and purchasing a list. Building a mailing list is therefore dependent on one's ingenuity and efforts, if not an ability to purchase a list from a commercial firm.

Now that we have reviewed the basic factors in sales writing, we are ready to move into our next step. That step is the discussion of teaching methodologies to help make the student a competent sales writer.

Teaching Students to Write Effective Sales Letters

Research

Because effective sales management is often based on research, it is imperative for the student to work on the areas of:

1. Consumer research
2. Product knowledge
3. Prospect (customer) knowledge

Exercises

The following are geared to make the student more aware of the three areas of sales research work mentioned above.

CONSUMER RESEARCH

Write a brief paper (three to five pages) on the topic of consumer behavior. Deal with such terms as *market-segmentation, product differentiation, demographics,* and *product life cycle.*

PRODUCT KNOWLEDGE

Select a consumer product or service. This may be one that is already on the market or a product or service that you feel can be sold to consumers. It may be a briefcase, a home appliance, an accounting service, a garden item, a piece of apparel, or any one of a thousand-and-one other items. Research that product or service thoroughly so that you can write about it (sell it) with authority and sincerity. Some of the factors you will want to look into are:

The various materials that go into the product
The source of supply of the materials
The method of manufacture
The competition which the product or service faces
The advantages the product or service has over its competition
The present and potential market which exists for the product or service
The various prices the product or service commands in today's market
The present and potential international market that exists for the product or service
The various types of proof (and which is the most effective) which are used for similar products and services
The sales history for similar products or services
The attractiveness the product or service has for any specific educational, economic, social, or ethnic group

In the process of gaining product knowledge, it is also wise to secure a sample product for careful examination and disassembly. In the case of a service, it may be possible to secure a demonstration or explanation of the service from a using agency.

PROSPECT KNOWLEDGE

Determine one or more groups of individuals who would be likely candidates to purchase the product or service. Examples might be students (high-economic-level black undergraduates, extension students over age thirty-five of various ethnic groups), professional personnel (urban-centered lawyers), individuals in the health care field (nurses, X-ray technicians), executives, housewives, aviators, engineers.

Now carry through research concerning the prospect group(s) you have selected. Some of the factors you will want to look into are:

Income level and source of income
Educational, economic, and social levels
Recent motivating incidents for this type of prospect
Trends in society which may impact on this level
What type of proof (testimonial, records of performances and tests, guarantee) seems to motivate this prospect best

Selecting the Central Appeal

Now that the student is knowledgeable of the product or service and the prospect, he or she can select the appropriate central appeal. Filling in the table below (or one the instructor designs) helps the student to appreciate the connection between product or service, prospect, and central appeal. The refrigerator segments have been completed as an example.

Product or Service	*Prospect Description*	*Central Appeal*
Refrigerator	Upper-income couple	New features, design, decor
Refrigerator	Upper-income family of 4 to 6 members	Capacity, new features, convenience
Refrigerator	Lower-income family of 4 to 6 members	Economy of operation, price, time payment plan
Attache case	Executive	____________
Attache case	Student	____________
Attache case	Urban home owner	____________
Automatic garage door opener	Urban home owner	____________
Automatic garage door opener	Rural home owner or farmer	____________
Automatic garage door opener	Unmarried woman	____________
Automatic garage door opener	Owner of a small factory	____________
Telephone answering service	Homemaker	____________
Telephone answering service	Lawyer	____________
Telephone answering service	Owner of small business	____________

After completing the table, students, in groups of four, should then discuss and evaluate their selections.

Evaluation of Actual Sales Letters

Another exercise which can prove very instructive is to have each student evaluate one or more actual sales letters. These can be "form" or individually typed letters. However, they should *not* be cover letters for sales flyers or sales literature. Every family receives one or more of these in the daily mail. If the student wishes, he or she can secure sales letters from almost any company, firm, or organization.

CRITERIA FOR EVALUATION

1. Total appearance and attractiveness
2. Tone of letter
3. Effectiveness and identification of interest/attention
4. Effectiveness and identification of description/explanation
5. Effectiveness and identification of proof
6. Effectiveness and identification of action
7. Effectiveness and identification of central appeal
8. Effectiveness of product-prospect match (explain)
9. Overall sales letter evaluation

Now that students (1) feel knowledgeable and (2) have evaluated others' sales letters, they will feel confident in creating their own sales letters.

Writing the Sales Letter

The student should be familiar, at this point, with the various attributes of the sales letter. This knowledge should now be applied to designing and writing the sales letter.

An initial determination should be made as to whether the sales letter will be distributed through a mass mailing, with no attempt at individuality, or whether a select list will be used. In this case of the latter, prospect names can be automatically typed in from computer records or individually typed in from a master list.

The writer should then compose the sales letter, keeping all the attributes of the prospect in mind as the following are selected:

Attention and interest
Description and explanation
Proof
Action

Auxiliary Items to the Sales Letter

The writer may wish to consider including samples, coupons, photos, or "gimmicks" which may arouse interest. For example, a swatch of leather may be effective in selling an attache case; a small square of plywood paneling may be valuable in discussing room additions or home remodeling. An excellent photo or a tiny plastic telephone "tipped" (pasted) on the stationery may also prove effective for the proper product or service.

Writing Style

In selling a consumer product in a sales letter, the writer should be especially aware of (1) using words that will arouse the proper picture in that prospect's mind and (2) noting how the prospect will benefit by purchasing the product or service.

Critique

Students should then carefully evaluate each other's sales letter using the same criteria employed when evaluating the actual sales letter written by someone else.

Sales Letters to Commercial and Industrial Prospects

Up to this point, the student has probably written and evaluated sales letters directed to consumers. A challenging and valuable experience is to now aim a sales letter at a commercial or industrial account.

All the exercises listed above can be repeated when trying to sell—for example—a machine tool to a corporation, or a copy machine to an organization. Of course, the student should keep in mind that, when selling to these types of prospects, the usual goal is to open a door for a salesperson (or some follow-up action) rather than to sell a product. It is obvious that it is possible to sell a $25 attache case by mail but not a $17,000 copy machine.

Teaching Students to Write Effective Sales Promotion Pieces

In many respects, the exercises used above can be adapted in this area. However, a sales promotion piece is usually designed in one of the following ways:

1. One design employs a cover letter and enclosure. In this instance, the usual function of the cover letter is to arouse interest. The other areas—description, proof, and action—are usually contained in the enclosure. The letter further gives dignity to the entire communication and lessens the "flyer, handbill, and circular" impression.
2. Here the cover letter is an integral part of the enclosure. It may be the first of a four-page communication with pages 2, 3, and 4 serving as the

enclosure. Or it may be reproduced and reduced on the top or cover of the enclosure.

3. The cover letter is dispensed with and only the enclosure is mailed. In some instances these sales pieces are one page; in others, two or more. They may be a series of sheets or a broadside (very large sheet) that has been folded two or more times.

Exercise

STEP 1

Ask all students to form into teams of three.

STEP 2

Have each team secure an example of each of the above sales promotion pieces.

STEP 3

Have each team submit its three examples with an evaluation for each of the three sales pieces based on:

1. How well has the product or service been matched with the prospect?
2. How effectively has the central appeal been selected in consideration of the prospect? (Also identify the central appeal.)
3. Identify and evaluate the effectiveness of (a) interest/attention, (b) description/explanation, (c) proof, and (d) action in relationship to the prospect.
4. Evaluate the visual attractiveness, format, and general appeal of the total sales promotion piece.

Exercise

Several of the above teams should be requested to mount their three examples on poster board and make presentations to the class. The presentations should follow the four-point evaluation suggested above.

Exercise

Each student should create, design, and write a sales promotion piece according to the following directions:

1. On one sheet of paper, list (a) the product, (b) the prospect (or prospect group), (c) the central appeal selected, and (d) the proof selected.

2. Write a cover letter.
3. Create, design, and write the sales promotion piece. Obviously, most students cannot draw the artwork required. However, they should designate space and "tell" the printer or art director what they wish to have in a sketch or a photograph. The colors should be indicated and the type size desired (large, small, bold face, etc.) should be noted.

Because this is an exacting, creative, and time-consuming assignment, the instructor may wish to ask students to work in pairs. However, since, in this case, individual effort is so personally rewarding, it may be wise to allow students a week or ten days for the assignment and let each one create his or her own.

Exercise

As an alternative to the above exercise, the instructor may wish to secure the cooperation of a firm in the city. In this instance, every student or team in the class prepares a sales promotion piece selling the firm's product or service.

The students (or a jury of three faculty) should select the three outstanding sales promotion pieces for small gifts or awards which the firm should agree to supply.

Teaching Students about Effective Direct Mail Communication

This segment of sales communication instruction can be the most exciting and interesting for students. The reason is obvious: direct mail is a vital industry involved in hundreds of millions of dollars in sales each year and thousands of people, products, services, and companies.

Exercise

Ask each class member to carry through research and write a brief paper on any one of the following topics:

1. How direct mail companies secure mailing lists
2. The cost and variety of mailing lists available
3. Equipment used for mass mailings
4. Methods of letter reproduction used in direct mail
5. Direct mail and the law
6. The role of the U.S. Postal Service in direct mail

7. Publications in the field of direct mail and their use
8. Outstanding success stories in the field of direct mail
9. Direct mail and international use
10. An analysis of a successful direct mail company (its product or service, method of operation, growth, etc.)
11. How and why major firms (TWA, Shell, Mobil, etc.) use direct mail
12. Present legislation concerning direct mail or the argument for or against so-called junk mail

EXERCISE

Request several students to make oral reports on their topics chosen from among the twelve above.

EXERCISE

Arrange a class tour through a firm that (1) is in the direct mail business, or (2) is a mailing company for firms in the field of direct mail.

EXERCISE

Request a businessperson or member of an advertising company in the field of direct mail to make a presentation to the class.

EXERCISE

Ask each student to select a product presently sold in stores and write a brief paper entitled "How (Product Name) Can Be Adapted for Direct Mail Sales." Note in this paper:

1. The type of direct mail piece used
2. The prospect group
3. Why a direct mail approach would prove successful for that product

Concluding Comments

All the exercises in this chapter will prove extremely valuable to the student not only for the field of sales, but for business in general. In addition, the instructor will find it relatively simple to adapt all the written exercises into oral presentations. Thus, the student will have adequate opportunity to enhance speaking as well as writing abilities.

The entire field of sales and sales promotion writing can be exciting and challenging. Furthermore, it can lead to a career path for someone who wishes to devote full time to it.

Acknowledgment

The contributions of Thomas O'Connell, a University of Southern California teaching assistant, proved extremely valuable in the writing of this chapter. I am indebted to him for his work.

Bibliography

BROCK, LUTHER. "Emphasize Key Points in a Sales Letter." *Direct Marketing,* vol. 43, no. 1 (May 1980).

———. "Free Samples Are One of the Best Attention-Getters." *Direct Marketing,* vol. 41, no. 8 (December 1978).

———. "How to Guide Your Reader Through Your Sales Letter." *Direct Marketing,* vol. 54, no. 1 (May 1982).

———. "Turn 'Covering Letters' into Sales Letters." *Direct Marketing,* vol. 44, no. 2 (June 1981).

———. "What Makes People Buy." *Direct Marketing,* vol. 42, no. 10, (February 1980).

FARRANT, ALAN W. "Use the Mail to Get Sales." *American Salesman,* vol. 25, no. 1 (January 1980).

INHOFE, ROBERT. "Selectivity Will Be Key to Mail Order Success." *Direct Marketing.* vol. 45, no. 3 (July 1982).

SIGBAND, NORMAN B. *Communication for Management and Business.* 3d ed. Glenview, Ill.: Scott, Foresman and Co., 1982.

———, and DAVID BATEMAN. *Communicating in Business.* Glenview, Ill.: Scott, Foresman and Co., 1981.

STONE, ROBERT. "Direct Marketing Sales Top 120 Billion." *Marketing Communications.* vol. 7, no. 6 (June 1982).

Section III

Interactional Communication

Chapter 9

Techniques of Effective Speaking

David E. Gootnick

Margaret Mary Gootnick

SPEECH COMMUNICATION IS essential for full and effective participation in group activities and organizational life. On the job, at social and community events, or at professional meetings, the ability to talk to groups is a social skill in great demand.

Business communication instructors recognize the impact of effective speaking on the business careers of students and the relevance of speech training to the business communication area. Without a doubt, a well-presented unit on effective speaking enhances student interest and satisfies an important business need.

The instructional concepts, strategies, and exercises presented in this chapter can be used to help you prepare and deliver an exciting business communication unit on effective speaking. The extent of unit coverage depends, of course, on your teaching goals and the time available for speech training.

The basic approach to the speaking unit is an active involvement of all students in the preparation, presentation, and analysis of talks. No "sleepers" are allowed. When a student is not presenting before the group or on television, that individual should be serving as an active member of the listening audience and evaluating other student presentations.

One very important point must be understood. Speaking before groups is one of the most dreaded acts known. Because the fear of speaking is so intense and so real, it may, for some, be a significant factor in high-stress reactions. It is not unheard of for a bright student or an up-and-coming executive to walk up before a group and then, without a blink, hyperventilate and faint.

Deal with this issue of student nervousness early in your unit. Help relieve anxiety by explaining that many skills used daily in our conversational communications and many techniques learned in other units of the business communication course can be applied to effective speaking as well. Inform your students that thorough speech preparation and subject familiarity will relieve nervousness and help build confidence.

Introducing the Speaking Unit

Kick off this unit by discussing the need for and importance of speech communication in the corporate business world and job market. Ask students to share incidents from their experience in which group speaking ability personally helped them. Next, ask the class to name instances in which public figures succeeded or failed to meet goals because of the level of their group speaking skills.

Give examples of various types of speaking situations. You may include examples from the following list:

1. Introduction of an individual at a business, professional, or civic meeting
2. Speech of recognition about an individual receiving a special honor or award
3. Progress report conveying the status of a particular effort to a management group
4. Authoritative presentation about one's area of expertise to a civic group
5. Persuasive request for budget approval to one's company
6. Product sales presentation to a new customer's purchasing team
7. Fund-raising appeal to a group of prospective contributors
8. After-dinner speech at a business conference
9. Educational talk at a professional seminar or trade show
10. Management briefing to company employees to explain an upcoming change in procedure or policy

At this point, inform your students of the goals for this unit:

1. To learn how to prepare and deliver effective speeches
2. To gain valuable experience by speaking from manuscript, giving impromptu talks, and delivering presentations extemporaneously
3. To give speeches before the class and on videotape
4. To give and receive constructive feedback for speech improvement

Explain that impromptu speaking—spur-of-the-moment speaking—involves little or no preparation, while extemporaneous and manuscript speaking require a good deal of preparation. Yet all three types of speeches are best delivered when one uses a natural, conversational speaking style. Because of this, request that during the delivery of all speeches, students do not attempt to immitate others or assume unnatural or highly formal speech patterns.

Speaking from Manuscript

Tell the class that they will now do a loosening-up exercise in group speaking. Some of them will come to the front of the room and practice an old and familiar skill—reading—but in a new and unfamiliar position—in front of the class.

Basic Reading Exercise

Call on four or five people for this exercise. Have each person read a few paragraphs from any book while in a standing position in front of the class. After each reading, find out what the student felt and thought. Also ask the members of the class for their feelings and thoughts about each reader's effectiveness.

The feedback will be mixed, ranging from "I was great" and "Jan's a good reader" to "he didn't project his voice" and "she seemed bored with the reading."

With this exercise, you have created the opportunity to explain the important difference between a private act intended for the doer alone and a public act intended for an audience. Emphasize that in effective group speaking, whether the speaker is reading from manuscript, talking from cue cards, or just weaving thoughts spontaneously, the message is intended for the listening audience—not for the speaker. Consequently, the message must be effectively directed to the listening audience with all the technique the speaker can muster.

With this explanation, students can better understand the importance of good eye contact and voice projection, as well as voice inflection. They can also become aware of the tendency to speak in monotone when reading and of the negative effect such a speech pattern has.

Review for your students the following list of typical problems associated with presentations delivered by untrained manuscript speakers:

1. The manuscript is read in a monotone, without apparent feeling for or understanding of the content.
2. The speaker lacks eye contact with the listening audience.
3. The speech sounds boring and stilted to the audience.
4. The speaker's voice is too low.

5. The speaker talks to the manuscript and not to the audience.
6. The speech is usually delivered with no rehearsal time invested.
7. The manuscript sounds as though another person wrote it without any input from the speaker—and often that is exactly what has occurred.

Effective Manuscript Speaking Exercise

Review the following list of manuscript speaking principles with your students:

1. When writing the manuscript, the speaker should use the lively words, phrases, and expressions of his or her own conversational style. The spoken manuscript should be an engaging and vital presentation, not a boring recitation of unnatural expression or unfamiliar language.
2. It is important to be a master of the manuscript message, not a prisoner of the manuscript words. Therefore, the speech should be read through several times until the message and feelings are clearly implanted in the speaker's mind. A mastered manuscript allows the speaker more freedom to speak to the audience rather than to the manuscript. In fact, the speaker who masters a manuscript should be able to look at an audience at least 75 percent of the time.
3. The speaker delivers the manuscript presentation using the natural pauses and inflections of his or her own speaking style.
4. The manuscript should be set up in large orator type and triple-spaced for easy reading from a lectern.
5. The speech should be delivered from behind a full or tabletop lectern.
6. Each page of the manuscript should be numbered in the upper-right-hand corner.
7. Because a speech is a group communication, volume has to be loud enough to be heard by all individuals present.

Now, have each student write a 150-word manuscript. It can be written on any subject at all and will be delivered to the class when completed. Give about fifteen minutes for writing the speech, and then start bringing your students to the front for their presentations. Be sure to provide a lectern and to properly position each student speaker behind it.

After each delivery, solicit class reactions. Comment on the need for manuscript mastery, good eye contact, good volume and projection, and a natural, lively speaking style.

Impromptu Speaking

On the spur of the moment, off the cuff, and *off the top of your head* describe the rapid speed and spontaneity required for creating and presenting the impromptu speech. There are no prepared manuscripts or cue cards to guide the speaker. Instead, the speaker relies on his or her subject mastery to help formulate an immediate and effective response to a question or situation.

One simple fact is clear: Many positive points can be scored in a business meeting by individuals capable of effective impromptu speaking.

Impromptu Exercise

Have each student in the class come to the front and talk for one minute on a subject of his or her choice. Following each talk, get audience feedback on the effectiveness of the student's delivery. Point out that impromptu speaking is natural, conversational, fluent, engaging, and interesting. Conclude that when a person has good subject knowledge and a point to make, the speech is usually successful.

In impromptu speaking, the problem arises when a person does not know the subject, does not have a point to make, and is suddenly placed into a position to say something intelligent. If such a situation occurs, it is better to defer a response until a later time so that some research can be done on the subject. Another approach is to refer the question to another person more knowledgeable on the subject. In any event, it is better to say nothing at all when one has little knowledge on a subject.

At this point, the students are ready to learn the principles for giving a successful impromptu talk. Tell them that the speaker:

1. Makes a quick decision and determines what to say about a subject
2. Is confident about the knowledge that is being shared, proud of personal opinions regarding it, and able to say what he or she wants to say
3. Uses everyday language and behaves in a natural manner
4. Maintains poise, good physical posture, and audible volume
5. Uses good eye-to-eye contact
6. Does not offer apologies for statements or discount personal opinions with such remarks as "I may be wrong, but . . . ," "There are more knowledgeable people on the subject, but . . . ," or "This may sound like a silly idea, but. . . ."

Videotaped Exercise

If your institution has video equipment or a television studio, you have the option, at this point, of recording student impromptu talks and allowing students to see and hear themselves in the playbacks.

Instruct each student to give a one-minute impromptu talk on "My most interesting experience." Tell the students to look at the people in the class during the taping and not into the camera. Playback and review of these impromptu talks provide a dramatic and effective method for student self-evaluation.

Extemporaneous Speaking

Extemporaneous speaking is the most important and useful speech style for delivering business presentations. Unlike the impromptu talk, the extemporaneous presentation involves much forethought, preparation, and rehearsal. In addition, the speaker writes up the key ideas, facts, and figures on cue cards which then serve as the cueing device for the presentation.

Explain to your students that the primary cueing medium for the extemporaneous speech is the cue-card deck. When properly prepared and used, cue cards allow the speaker to deliver a freestanding speech, without need for manuscript, lectern, or other notes.

Word-for-word speaking, as in manuscript speaking, is not permitted here. Instead, the extemporaneous speaker's mind is triggered by the carefully prepared cue cards. As a result, the speaker finds greater freedom of expression and spontaneity of word choice.

Cue-Card Preparation

Using the overhead projector, display the basic format for the cue-card deck. Note that the cue cards should be printed or typed in large readable letters or numbers. Only key words should be used to trigger the speaker's thoughts and words. Full sentences would only hamper freedom of expression. A direct quote, however, can be written out.

The position of the main idea and supporting facts and figures is important. Have students use the upper-left side of a card for the main idea and the space below for supporting thoughts.

Numbering each card in the deck is vital. The upper-right corner is the proper place for the card number. Should a deck be dropped by mistake or become disorganized, it can be quickly placed back into proper order by referring to the card numbers.

Using the overhead projector, show students the cue-card models, as well as examples of actual cue-card decks. You may also want to have your students examine the cue-card deck to be used for your model talk demonstration explained on pages 217–18.

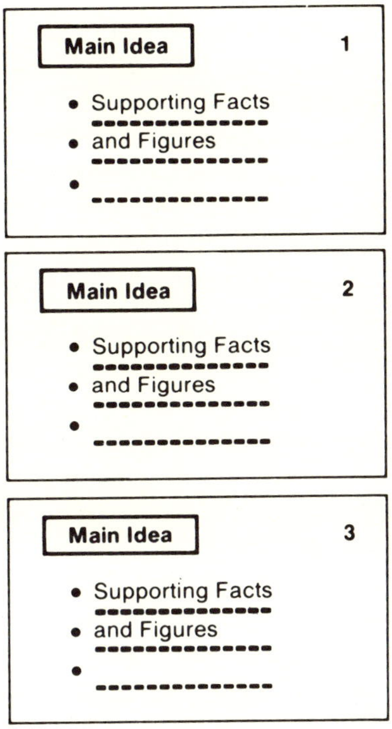

Cue-Card Use

If a student is right-handed, the cue-card deck should be held in the left hand. If a student is left-handed, the cue-card deck should be held in the right hand.

The cue-card deck should be held in front of the speaker in the same position one would hold a book to be read while standing. This book-reading position is natural and allows a speaker to be effectively cued by the cards.

The free hand is used for at least two purposes: (1) for hand gestures during the talk and (2) for moving completed cards from the top to the bottom of the deck. The free hand can also be used for pointing to audiovisuals or holding up props. In addition, when not in use, the free hand can help hold the cue-card deck or be dropped to one's side naturally.

Cue-Card Benefits

Explain the following three benefits of cue cards to your students:

1. The speaker is not a "prisoner of the word," as may be felt during word-for-word manuscript speaking. Properly prepared cue cards—with key words and ideas only—allow the speaker freedom of expression and naturalness of style.

2. With cue cards held in one's hand, the speaker does not require a lectern and may present the talk in "freestanding" position. Unobstructed by the lectern, the audience can see the speaker in full view, with that much greater visual impact. In addition, the speaker is free to move about without fear of losing his or her place.
3. When the extemporaneous presentation is fully rehearsed, the speaker should be able to easily look up at the audience at least 90 percent of the time. Eye-to-eye contact between speaker and audience is enhanced because of the nature of cue cards.

The Speech-of-Introduction Exercise

The speech of introduction is an excellent vehicle for exposing students to the extemporaneous speaking style. Because students will have many opportunities for using this type of speech in various business, educational, civic, and social situations, it is a relevant and interesting initial experience.

Inform the class that each person will be giving a one-minute introduction of another person to the class. The goal of this introduction will be to present the other individual as a unique, interesting, and capable person.

Pair off students for this exercise. Student A will be introducing Student B; then, Student B will be introducing Student A.

To prepare your students for their introductions, have Student A hold a five-minute information-gathering interview with Student B; then have Student B hold a five-minute information-gathering interview with Student A.

Advise students that upon completion of their information-gathering interviews, each speaker should write up the key ideas, facts, and figures on 3-by-5-inch cue cards which will serve as their cueing device for the talks. Make sure they do not write word-for-word copy on their cards, however.

After each introduction, solicit feedback about the talk from both the speaker and the class. In addition, give your impressions, making sure to comment on these points:

1. The quality of information-gathering interview significantly affects the quality of presentation. When conducting an interview, one must ask questions that probe the unique and interesting facets of the person to be introduced and identify accomplishments that support the person's capability.
2. The information acquired in the interview should be presented in interesting order. The boring and dull chronological organization pattern of presenting information should be avoided at all costs (She was born in. . . . She went to elementary school. . . . She graduated and went to high school. . . .).

3. When giving the introduction, the speaker should look up at the audience as much as possible and maximize eye-to-eye contact.
4. Only key words and figures should be placed on the cue cards, and these should be large enough to easily cue the speaker at about one-half arm's length.
5. Since there is no word-for-word copy to follow, a speaker should feel free to use natural language in expressing the planned ideas.
6. Extemporaneous speakers sometimes exhibit the problem of filler words, such as *ya know, like,* and *uh,* in their presentations. Such a problem often results from lack of familiarity with the material and lack of rehearsal with the cue cards. With the extemporaneous speaking style, practice definitely helps build speaker fluency and overcome the pauses and filler words of uncertainty.
7. Extemporaneous speaking is best done in a freestanding position with cue cards in hand. Since the speaker is not hidden behind a lectern, the audience has a full-body view. The extemporaneous speaker should, therefore, create the best physical impression through his or her posture, movement, and dress and nonverbally communicate a positive, confident, and professional attitude.

The Evaluative Checklist

This time-tested evaluative checklist, on page 218, contains sixteen criteria of effective oral presentations.

Hand out copies of this checklist to your students and make certain that each of the sixteen points is clearly understood. Also, review the directions for using the checklist in the evaluation of oral presentations.

Point out that this checklist will be used by the instructor as the formal evaluation device for rating student presentations during the unit. In addition, explain that all students in the class will gain experience using the evaluative checklist to give helpful feedback to student speakers.

The Model Talk Demonstration

Now that your students have discussed the sixteen criteria of effective speaking, it is recommended that they be given an opportunity to use the evaluative checklist in rating a model extemporaneous talk.

This demonstration talk can be presented by you or another person, live or on videotape. It should be a five-minute presentation and incorporate the proper use of cue cards, audiovisual aids, anecdotes, and statistics.

Inform students that immediately following your presentation, they will

The Evaluative Checklist of Oral Presentations

Directions: After participating in an oral presentation, you should have some feelings about most of the following important behaviors. Read a statement; then, check only one box reflecting your feelings about the behavior described. When a particular behavior does not apply to the presentation being evaluated, make no mark. If you observe a behavior that is either very good or very bad but is not listed below, write it down. Here are the definitions corresponding to the check points:

+2 = Strongly Agree 0 = Uncertain or Undecided −1 = Disagree
+1 = Agree −2 = Strongly Disagree

Observed Behavior	−2	−1	0	+1	+2
1. Clearly communicated purpose or objectives.					
2. Held attention and interest.					
3. Demonstrated knowledge of topic.					
4. Persuaded through evidence and support.					
5. Adhered to purpose and objectives.					
6. Organized presentation to achieve objectives.					
7. Clarified message through audio and visual aids.					
8. Maintained self-confidence, self-control, composure, and poise.					
9. Managed time limit and distribution.					
10. Spoke clearly, distinctly, and correctly.					
11. Avoided objectionable mannerisms and habits.					
12. Made favorable personal impression.					
13. Involved audience in presentation.					
14. Used helpful nonverbal cues.					
15. Clearly concluded talk.					
16. Achieved objectives of talk.					

David Gootnick, Even You Can Give a Talk (New York: David Gootnick Associates, 1975). Reproduced by permission.

be given time to rate your talk using the evaluative checklist. Ask them to give you their attention, as much as possible, during the talk. If, however, they do observe something of particular interest during the talk, they can, of course, make a note of it when it occurs.

After the students have completed their rating, hold an open discussion and solicit student ratings and feedback. The key to this exercise is to get your students actively involved in rating an actual presentation, thinking about the major presentational elements, and seeing—firsthand—a model talk.

Anecdotes

The anecdote is an important speaking technique that helps the speaker enliven the talk, involve the audience, personalize the material, and add realism to the subject. It is a short story about some human experience that points out a morale or teaches a lesson. Simply, it is a "slice of life" that makes a point.

Explain the two parts of the anecdote to your students: (1) the story and (2) the concluding point. A story without a concluding point is not an anecdote—it is merely a story. Also explain that in a presentation, anecdotes serve—as do examples, illustrations, facts, and figures—as verbal supports to main ideas. The anecdote is used to deepen an audience's understanding of a main idea and perhaps to help support its validity.

Structure of the Anecdote

To help students understand the anecdote's structure, give the following examples of typical lead-ins to the story and the concluding point:

STORY LEAD-INS

That reminds me of the time I. . . .
Something happened to me just the other day that would help illustrate this point. . . .
In this regard, I recall a story about. . . .

CONCLUDING-POINT LEAD-INS

As you can see from this story. . . .
In conclusion, this story points out that. . . .
This experience taught me one very important lesson. . . .
The moral of this story is. . . .

The Anecdote Exercise

Have each student present a one-minute anecdote in class. Following each anecdote, solicit class feedback. Be sure to comment on the need for clear anecdotal structure (story plus concluding point), sincere and natural delivery, and brevity.

The Anecdote Report

Have each student prepare an anecdote report containing twenty original anecdotes. Students should write down interesting experiences happening to them or others they know. They should also write down the lessons taught or morals pointed out next to each story.

This assignment is excellent for showing how easy it is to capture a human experience on paper and convert it into a useful presentational device.

Audiovisual Aids

Introduce audiovisuals (A/Vs) as aids to the speaker and not substitutions for good speaking. Stress that the speaker should be the focus of an audience's attention and that the primary audiovisual in any talk is the speaker.

Properly prepared and used, audiovisual aids help a speaker achieve the following goals:

1. Clarify main ideas
2. Dramatize main ideas
3. Add variety and sparkle to presentations
4. Persuade about the validity of a position

The guiding principle in preparing any audiovisual aid is the word KISS—"Keep it simple, stupid!" In other words, any audiovisual a student uses should clearly keep the audience's attention focused on one overriding message, concept, or relationship. When the KISS principle is not adhered to, audiovisuals tend to confuse rather than clarify.

Audiovisuals for Review

Review the following seven graphic devices and display examples of each on your projector:

1. Pie chart
2. Bar chart
3. Line chart
4. Organization chart
5. Flowchart
6. Pictogram
7. Table

As you display the various graphic devices, point out the key concepts or relationships that can be highlighted. For example, the pie chart highlights the parts of a whole, while the line chart features trends or directions of change. And, of course, the organization chart points out lines of authority and spans of control, while the flowchart describes sequence in an operation.

Review the various types of electronic audiovisual equipment, including overhead projector, 35-mm projector, movie projector, audiotape recorder, and videotape recorder. Also review the following audiovisual aids: chalkboards, flipcharts, posters, handouts, and props. Discuss the advantages and disadvantages of each audiovisual medium and how it can be used individually or synchronized with others into a multimedia presentation.

The Audiovisual Exercise

Have each student prepare one of the seven graphic devices discussed and present it to the class using his or her choice of delivery medium, such as overhead, chalkboard, or flip chart. Each speaker's visual should be focused on one clear concept or relationship. The speaker should open the talk with a few introductory words and close the talk with a brief concluding remark.

Following each brief audiovisual presentation, solicit feedback from the class and provide comment in two areas: (1) content and (2) delivery. From a content point of view, comment on how well a single concept or relationship is communicated. From a delivery point of view, comment on such matters as:

1. Eye-to-eye contact with audience
2. Position of body while referring to the audiovisual
3. Direction and projection of voice
4. Visibility of graphics to audience
5. Incorporation of audiovisual into talk

Extemporaneous-Talk Preparation

ADSOC Planning Procedure

Introduce the ADSOC formula as a five-step planning procedure for preparing talks quickly and effectively. Discuss the formula as follows:

A: Analyze speech assignment in terms of your background, subject, audience, occasion, time limits, and room setting.
D: Decide on purpose of talk.
S: Select main ideas for talk.
O: Organize main ideas in logical arrangement.
C: Choose verbal and audiovisual supporting materials to develop main ideas. Verbal supporting materials include facts, statistics, examples, illustrations, comparisons, testimony, and anecdotes. Audiovisual supporting materials include movies, graphs, charts, slides, diagrams, and maps.

The result of using the ADSOC formula in speech preparation is a clearly organized speech outline which can be transferred to cue cards for extemporaneous delivery before an audience or expanded directly to manuscript form and placed on a lectern for presentation.

Demonstration of the ADSOC Formula

Lead your class in the development of an ADSOC outline. Explain to the group that you will play the role of a hotel-chain marketing manager and that you have been asked to speak at a luncheon meeting for one hundred business executives. Your host has asked you to inform the group on how to select appropriate business meeting sites and conference facilities.

You have been given forty minutes for your entire group presentation. With this time frame in mind, you have decided to develop a twenty-five-minute prepared talk and to use the remaining fifteen minutes for a question-answer session.

Following your description of the case situation, explain that you have now discussed the A and D steps of ADSOC. On the board write the purpose of your talk: "to help business executives better understand how to select appropriate business meeting sites and conference facilities."

Now you are ready for the S step of ADSOC. Using brainstorming technique, ask the class to volunteer any ideas they believe should be conveyed in the talk. As ideas are brought forth, write them on the board. Once several thoughts are on the board, you can develop them as main or supporting ideas, combine them into larger ideas, or eliminate them from consideration. Be sure to consider ideas for both the opening and the closing remarks.

Below is one list of raw ideas which was generated for this talk by a group of students:

Location	Closing of talk
Accessibility	Food facilities
Costs	Sleep-over facilities
Purpose of meeting	Parking facilities
Entertainment facilities	Availability of site
Meeting-room sizes	Number of people attending
Opening of talk	Special meeting needs

As soon as ideas have been selected and refined into a number of clear main ideas, perform the O step of ADSOC and organize the ideas in logical sequence. Along with the help of your students, decide on the position for each idea within the presentation and place the appropriate number next to each idea. If you would like, at this point you can rewrite the main ideas on the board in the proper order.

The final step of ADSOC is choosing verbal material to develop the main ideas and audiovisuals, if used, to enhance the message. Briefly discuss each main idea to generate some thought on appropriate verbal and audiovisual supporting materials.

The Live Three-Minute Talk

Have each student prepare a three-minute extemporaneous talk using cue cards for presentation in class. Students can choose their own topics but must include in each presentation one audiovisual, one anecdote, and one use of statistics.

Before each talk, hand out evaluative checklists to the entire group. Following a talk, have the class rate and give immediate feedback to the speaker about the presentation.

After each brief feedback discussion, have the speaker collect all student checklists and prepare a brief written report containing tabulated ratings and recommendations for improvement.

The Question-Answer Session

The question-answer session that usually follows a prepared presentation is a good opportunity for the speaker to further demonstrate expertise in the subject matter. In addition, by adeptly fielding questions from the audience, the speaker can further bolster the favorable impression achieved by the prepared presentation.

Inform your students that they will be conducting question-answer sessions at the conclusion of their next talk. Then review the following rules for handling special problems and situations that arise within question-answer sessions:

1. The conscientious group speaker prepares for the question-answer session by trying to anticipate the questions that may be asked and by formulating responses to these questions.
2. The speaker should not allow any member of the audience to take more than thirty seconds to state a question.
3. No individual from the audience should be permitted to monopolize the question-answer session by dominating the floor.
4. A hostile question should be answered as positively and confidently as conditions allow.
5. If at all possible, the speaker should not answer more than one question from a hostile person.
6. The best time to end a question-answer session is at the peak of audience interest or immediately following a brilliant response.

The Live Five-Minute Talk

Following the live three-minute talks, step up your speech requirements to a live five-minute presentation. In this activity, have each student prepare a five-minute extemporaneous talk using cue cards for presentation in class.

Students must choose topics from within their business majors, such as accounting, business education, economics, management, or marketing. The topics must be current and of some interest and relevance to the entire group. Each talk must include two audiovisuals, two anecdotes, and two uses of statistics.

Immediately following the prepared part of each talk, have each speaker hold a two-minute question-answer session. Members of the audience should be encouraged to participate actively in this session.

Finally, solicit feedback from the students about each speaker's presentation and question-answer session. Be certain to comment on the sixteen major criteria of effective oral presentations listed on the evaluative checklist.

The Graded, Videotaped Five-Minute Talk

Have each student prepare a five-minute extemporaneous talk using cue cards for videotaped presentation. Students must choose business communication subjects and must include in each presentation two audiovisuals, two anecdotes, and two uses of statistics.

Whether the tapings are done during or after class, be sure to have several students present to serve as members of the audience for each speaker. In addition, your pretaping instructions should advise each speaker to direct his or her attention to the audience and not to the camera lens.

Tape the presentations in one continuous flow. Following this, play back and review each presentation with the speaker. You may have other students present if you wish. Following each playback, fill out an evaluative checklist and briefly discuss it with the speaker.

You may assign a grade to each presentation by examining the dispersion of ratings on the evaluative checklist. If most of the ratings fall on the right side (+1 and +2), you can assign grades of B and A. If most of the ratings fall on the left side (–2 and –1), you can assign grades of F and D. If you notice great dispersion (–2 to +2), assign a grade of C.

Everyone Wins with Effective Speaking

In organizational life, a key to business success is the ability to express oneself and extend one's sphere of influence into the public arena. There is no doubt that, within a business environment of growing complexity and misunderstanding, individuals who are comfortable and skilled when speaking in group situations are literally swept along from one success to another.

Because of this, and because of your commitment to relevancy and quality in business communication, some of your best teaching moments will be spent observing, guiding, and directing your students as they stand before your class gaining self-confidence and speaking skill.

Acknowledgment

Discussion of the ADSOC formula (pp. 221–23) reproduced from David Gootnick, *Even You Can Give a Talk* (New York: David Gootnick Associates, 1975). Used by permission.

Bibliography

CARNEGIE, DALE. *Effective Speaking*. New York: Pocket Books, 1962.

FLESCH, RUDOLF. *The Art of Plain Talk*. New York: Macmillan Publishing Co., 1951.

FLUHARTY, GEORGE W., and HAROLD R. ROSS. *Public Speaking*. New York: Harper & Row, 1981.

GOOTNICK, DAVID. *Even You Can Give a Talk*. New York: David Gootnick Associates, 1975.

PROCHNOV, HERBERT V. *The Complete Toastmaster*. Englewood Cliffs, N.J.: Prentice-Hall, 1960.

QUICK, JOHN. *A Short Book on the Subject of Speaking*. New York: McGraw-Hill Book Co., 1978.

ROGERS, NATALIE H. *Talk Power*. New York: Dodd, Mead & Co., 1982.

SARNOFF, DOROTHY. *Speech Can Change Your Life*. New York: Dell Publishing Co., 1970.

STONE, JANET, AND JANE BACHNER. *Speaking Up*. New York: McGraw-Hill Book Co., 1977.

VALENTI, JACK. *Speaking Up with Confidence*. New York: William Morrow & Co., 1982.

Chapter 10

Parliamentary Procedure That Pays Off

Dorothy L. Travis

Lorraine Missling

The "Why" of Parliamentary Procedure

"The meeting will now come to order." What a familiar statement and yet how few individuals recognize the need for parliamentary law. Many situations could be cited in which one side cleverly gained tremendous advantage because of its ability to properly execute parliamentary procedure. This should not happen if all were equally knowledgeable of parliamentary law.

Although the business of a chapter or club may proceed smoothly for long periods of time with only a minimum need for knowledge of parliamentary law on the part of its members, a problem may suddenly develop which can be satisfactorily resolved only by the proper application of parliamentary rules. Misunderstandings and friction between groups and individuals can be avoided when the rules of the game are followed. Parliamentary law does just that—it provides the rules for the game. These rules are as needed by the small club as they are during the proceedings of a state or national convention.

As in any game, the proper use of the rules of parliamentary procedure pays off in many ways. Respecting the rights of all individuals is the responsibility of every citizen. The rights of the minority as well as those of the majority must be recognized.

It appears that every individual today is involved in "too many meetings." However, through the implementation of parliamentary procedure it is possible to expedite business, which, in turn, saves considerable time.

The "Musts" of Parliamentary Procedure

Every organization must have a set of bylaws appropriate to its needs. The bylaws are concerned with the rights of the members and place limitations on the powers of the assembly. They usually include one provision designating a current edition of an accepted manual of parliamentary law as the organization's parliamentary authority.

The society may then adopt special rules of order to supplement or modify the rules in the adopted manual. As the need arises, the assembly may establish *standing rules.* These are concerned with the details of the administration of the association and can be changed rather easily as conditions dictate.

These documents state the rules of the game adapted to the particular needs of the organization. These should be reviewed frequently, even to the point of devoting meetings periodically to their study so that all members are fully aware of their significance.

Order of Business

Members of an organization should understand that there are certain basic procedures to be followed in any meeting in order to expedite the business. For example, every meeting should follow a prescribed order of business. After the presiding officer has called the meeting to order, there may be some sort of opening ceremonies and a roll call may be customary. However, the most common order of business after the meeting has been called to order follows:

1. Reading and approval of minutes
2. Reports of officers, boards, and standing committees.
3. Reports of special committees
4. Special orders
5. Unfinished business and general orders
6. New business

The chair or other officers or members may make any necessary announcements following the completion of new business. If a program has been planned, it generally should be presented before adjournment. The meeting may be closed by a motion to adjourn, or, if there is no further business, the chair may simply declare the meeting adjourned.

The president and secretary, or someone designated as such, must be present before the meeting can be called to order. The bylaws should specify the minimum number of members who must be present at meetings for business to be legally transacted. This number is known as the *quorum.* If a quorum is not present, no official business can be conducted. Any action that is taken at such a meeting must be ratified at the next meeting, provided a quorum is then present.

Proper terminology is an important "must" in conducting a meeting. For example, the presiding officer should be referred to as "the chair." However, when a member wishes to speak, the chair is addressed as "Mr. President" or "Madam President." All questions should be asked through the chair, and individual's names should not be used. Rather, the individual might be referred to as "the member who just spoke."

The members of an organization must be aware that there are different types of meetings. Probably the most common is the *regular meeting,* which is held periodically as specified in the bylaws, such as the second and fourth Tuesday of each month. Sometimes it is necessary to hold a *special meeting* for the consideration of issues which must be taken up before the next regular meeting.

A *convention,* on the other hand, is a meeting of individuals having a common interest and usually includes an assembly of delegates. As a rule, a convention is held only annually or biennially.

Classification of Motions

Too often one underestimates the importance of recognizing that there are five special classifications of motions, and within some of those classifications the motions have rank, thereby taking precedence over other motions. A meeting cannot be properly conducted unless the membership is familiar with the classifications and the order of precedence within them. The five classifications are:

1. Main motions
2. Privileged motions ⎫
3. Subsidiary motions ⎬ Secondary motions
4. Incidental motions ⎭
5. Motions that bring a question again before the assembly

The *main motion* is the lowest in rank of all motions although it is the one that introduces business to the assembly. Before a proposal can be considered, it must be presented in the form of a motion.

Privileged, subsidiary, and *incidental motions* are known as *secondary motions.* A main motion can be made only when no other motion is before the assembly, but secondary motions can be made and considered while a main motion is on the floor.

Privileged motions are highest in rank. They do not relate to the pending business but they must be considered immediately because they concern the welfare of an individual or the entire membership. The order of precedence for privileged motions is:

1. Fix the time at which to adjourn
2. Adjourn
3. Recess
4. Raise a question of privilege
5. Call for the orders of the day

Subsidiary motions also have rank. They are motions which are always applied to other motions and which assist in the action on or disposal of the main motion. The order of precedence for subsidiary motions is:

1. Lay on the table
2. Previous question
3. Limit or extend limits of debate
4. Postpone to a certain time (or postpone definitely)
5. Commit (or refer)
6. Amend
7. Postpone indefinitely

Incidental motions relate to the pending business and have no rank in themselves. Generally incidental motions are related to the main question in such a way that action on them is required before business can proceed. Some of the incidental motions are:

Point of order
Appeal
Suspend the rules
Objection to the consideration of the question
Division of the question
Division of the assembly
Requests and inquiries
Motions related to nominations and methods of voting

Motions that bring a question again before the assembly are those that have been acted upon previously but to which the membership wishes to give further consideration. They have the same low rank as main motions; and, like main motions, they are generally made while no business is pending. This classification includes the following motions:

Take from the table
Reconsider
Rescind (to repeal or annul or to amend something previously adopted)
Discharge a committee

There are certain basic rules or procedures all of which may or may not apply to each motion. In addition to knowing the precedence or rank of motions, a member should know to which motions or situations other motions are applicable, whether the motion is in order when another member has the floor, whether the motion requires a second, whether it is debatable or amendable or can be reconsidered, and what vote is required for its adoption.

Consideration of Business

When a member wishes to bring business before the assembly, a main motion is in order. The member rises and addresses the chair. Upon recognition by the presiding officer, the member states the motion, always beginning with the three words "I move that. . . ." Before the motion can be discussed, it must be seconded. Any member, whether in agreement with the motion or not, can second it.

Discussion cannot proceed until the chair has stated the question as presented by the member. Debate follows. The maker of the motion has the right to speak first.

Every member has the opportunity to speak twice on the same motion on the same day but may not speak a second time on any motion until every member desiring the floor has spoken once. Usually members participating in the debate speak briefly. No one may speak more than ten minutes unless he or she obtains the permission of the assembly or the standing rules specify some other time limit. Permission to speak longer may be given through general consent or by means of a motion to extend the limits of debate.

In the event that any member wishes to modify the motion, an amendment can be proposed. Discussion is then in order on the amendment, after which a vote is taken on the amendment only. If there is a favorable vote on the amendment, discussion follows on the amended main motion. When discussion has terminated, a vote is taken on the amended motion. Should the amendment have failed, the discussion and final vote would be limited to the original main motion.

Other methods of disposing of motions may include referring to a committee, laying on the table, postponing to a definite time, or postponing to an indefinite time. If a member wishes to bring a motion to an immediate vote, the previous question would be moved.

Members should be cognizant of the fact that most motions require a majority vote. However, a motion affecting the rights of the membership requires a two-thirds vote. Motions requiring a two-thirds vote include those that (1) prevent the introduction of a question for consideration; (2) close, limit, or extend time for consideration of a question; (3) limit nominating or voting procedures; (4) close nominations or the polls; (5) take away a membership or office; or (6) suspend or modify a rule previously adopted.

Reports

The reports prepared by officers and committee chairs and presented at the regular meetings are important in keeping the membership informed as to what the organization is doing.

MINUTES

Generally one of the first items of business is the reading by the secretary of the minutes of the previous meeting. The presiding officer says, "The Secretary will read the minutes." After they have been read, the chair asks, "Are there any corrections to the minutes?" If there are corrections, they are usually accepted by general consent rather than by motion. The chair then says, "If there are no corrections [or "no further corrections"], the minutes are approved as read" or "approved as corrected." This does not require a motion.

If there are minutes of other meetings which have not been read previously, they should then be read in order of date.

The minutes should record what was *done* at the meeting rather than what was *said*. The introductory paragraph should give the kind of meeting (regular, special, adjourned regular, or adjourned special); the name of the assembly; the date and time of the meeting, and the place (unless the meetings are always held at the same place); the fact that the chairperson and secretary were present or the names of those substituting for them; whether the minutes of the previous meeting were read and approved—or corrected if this was necessary.

In the body of the minutes, there should be a separate paragraph for each item of new subject matter. The report should show all main motions or motions that bring a question again before the assembly, giving complete and accurate wording of each motion as adopted or otherwise disposed of; the disposition of the motion with any amendments and adhering secondary motions; generally the name of the mover (but not the seconder); and all points of order and appeals.

The closing paragraph should give the hour of adjournment.

The minutes should be signed by the secretary, and also by the president if the assembly so wishes. The words "respectfully submitted" before the secretary's signature are no longer used.

The accompanying excerpt illustrates the minutes of a meeting.

> The regular meeting of the __________________ Chapter was held on Tuesday, March 14, 19__, at 7:30 P.M. at the chapter headquarters. The president and the secretary were present. The minutes of the previous meeting were read and approved as corrected.

The treasurer reported a balance of $154.35 and presented a bill for $42.00 for stationery.

The reports of the Membership Committee and the Program Committee were received and placed on file.

The chair of the special committee which was appointed to investigate the cost of a filing cabinet for the storage of the chapter records reported that the committee wished to check the costs at a new office-furniture store that is to open within a week.

Mary Smith moved "that the chapter pay for travel and lodging for five delegates to attend the state convention to be held on May 5." John Adams moved to amend by adding "and registration fees" following the word "lodging." After debate and amendment, the motion was adopted as follows: "That the chapter pay for travel, lodging, and registration fees for five delegates to attend the state convention to be held on May 5."

Paul Miller moved "that the next chapter dance be postponed one week" because of the Community Theater Series program on the night the dance was scheduled. The motion was adopted.

The chair of the Program Committee introduced the speaker, Mr. A. M. Walsh, whose subject was ________________.

The meeting adjourned at 9:15 P.M.

M________ D________, Secretary

Treasurer's Report

The chair may ask for a treasurer's report. The treasurer may give an oral report of the balance on hand or may read a report which includes the major receipts and expenditures. This report requires no action by the assembly. In a small chapter, the report may take the form shown in the "Report of the Treasurer" on page 233.

In most organizations the treasurer is expected to prepare an annual report which is then audited for accuracy. In a large association the auditing is usually done by accountants, but in a small chapter or club an auditing committee consisting of two or three members may check the report and financial records for accuracy. The report of the auditors or the auditing committee should be accepted by the assembly. Or if the annual report has not been audited at the time it is presented to the assembly, the chair may announce that it will be referred to the auditing committee.

Reports of Other Officers and Committees

The bylaws may require annual reports from other officers and from committees. Brief reports presented to small assemblies may be given orally. The

Report of the Treasurer
For the Month Ending March 14, 19__

Balance on hand February 14, 19__		$182.50
Receipts		
Dues received from 8 members	$24.00	
Proceeds from Valentine Dance	35.50	
Total Receipts		59.50
(Total)		$242.00
Disbursements		
Postage and telephone calls	$10.15	
Stationery	22.00	
Total Disbursements		32.15
Balance on hand March 14, 19__		$209.85
(Total)		$242.00

C________ R________, Treasurer

substance of such reports is to be recorded in the secretary's minutes. However, committee reports should usually be submitted in writing. These may be for information only, or they may contain recommendations requiring action by the assembly. If a recommendation is made by an officer, some other member should move the adoption or implementation of the recommendations.

If a committee report contains recommendations, the reporting member usually makes the necessary motion to implement the recommendations at the conclusion of the report. This motion does not require a second. However, if some other member makes the required motion, it should then be seconded. Or if no motion is made, the chair may expedite matters by assuming the motion and stating the question.

In the usual order of business, the chair calls for reports from standing committees first, in the order in which they are listed in the bylaws, and next the reports from the special committees in the order of their appointment. The chair does not call for a report from a committee that has no report to make.

Techniques in the Teaching of Parliamentary Procedure

Although ability in conducting a meeting according to correct parliamentary rules may usually be an individual responsibility, successful teaching procedures often involve team instruction and practice. The instruction may be given to an entire class or chapter, but competition provides motivation.

Providing actual practice in using parliamentary law is basic to successful teaching. Merely studying a parliamentary manual can be dull, but by using situations or problems requiring the application of the rules, their importance and need is emphasized. These problems may be fictitious or real situations which are likely to occur or have occurred within the organization or class receiving the instruction. These situations are similar to case studies and typical of the type of problems used in the parliamentary procedure competitive events of several of the student organizations.

The problem should progress from the simple to the more complex. In the early stages of instruction, the problem might be discussed first and then practiced, using the members of the class as the assembly and one student as the presiding officer. Or the problem might be demonstrated by small teams of students.

Self-evaluation by the students of their own work is especially profitable. They should be given opportunities to cite what they consider to be the strong points of their demonstrations and those which could be improved. Others in the class may add their observations of the performances and make suggestions as to ways the presentations might be refined. The criticism should be constructive and helpful.

When practical, the demonstrations should be recorded. The recordings will provide opportunities for further self-evaluation, review, and study.

In addition to authentic application of parliamentary rules, correct use of parliamentary terminology should always be emphasized. The practice meetings should be properly called to order by the presiding officer. A gavel should be used.

According to *Robert's Rules of Order Newly Revised,* the gavel is rapped once to call a meeting to order, and it may be rapped once to signal adjournment. If a member commits a slight breach of order during a meeting, the presiding officer may tap the gavel lightly and then point out the error to the member. Some organizations have established their own rules involving more use of the gavel.

In the demonstration sessions, the presiding officer should stand when calling the meeting to order and when adjourning the meeting. The chairperson should also stand when putting questions to a vote or, in general, when speaking to the assembly, but may be seated while members are speaking in debate.

Members should never speak to the assembly without first rising and addressing the chair in order to obtain the floor, thus being recognized by the chair as having the right to be heard. However, it is not necessary to obtain the floor when seconding a motion, nor is it necessary to be recognized by the chair when making a nomination.

Several sample problems of increasing difficulty, with built-in review to provide reinforcement, are presented here with comments as to points to be emphasized. The main motions may be changed to better fit the class or group receiving instruction.

PROBLEM 1

a. Move that the class have a dinner a week from Friday evening at the Hilltop Motel.
b. Move to amend by striking out "Friday" and inserting "Saturday."
c. Adopt both motions.

Points to Emphasize. Each motion must be seconded and stated by the chair before there can be discussion. The amendment must be voted on first, to be followed by a vote on the amended motion, which would then become a motion "that the class have a dinner a week from Saturday evening at the Hilltop Motel."

Amendments—and also debate—must be germane. In other words, they must be related to and involve the subject matter of the motion. An amendment to insert "and have a car wash on Saturday" would not be germane.

PROBLEM 2

a. Move to present a framed certificate of appreciation to Mr. John Alton, who is to be the speaker at the banquet.
b. Move to amend by substituting "metal plaque" for "framed certificate."
c. Move to refer the motion to a committee to be appointed by the chair.
d. Move to amend the motion to commit by inserting after the word "committee" the words "of three."
e. Dispose of the pending motions.

Points to Emphasize. The subsidiary motion to commit or refer takes precedence over the main motion and the subsidiary motion to amend.

The motion to commit should designate the committee, its size, and how it is to be appointed. For example, the motion or an amendment might specify a particular standing committee rather than a special committee, or some different method of selection, such as election after nomination.

The committee may present its report at the next meeting at the time designated for reports of special committees. The committee may recommend the adoption or rejection of the amendment and then present its recommendation as to the disposition of the main motion; or it may propose amendments or a substitute motion.

Following the report, the chairperson must start with the situation as it was when the referral occurred. The original amendment must be voted upon before the amendments or substitute motion proposed in the committee report can be acted upon.

PROBLEM 3

a–d. In a different situation, use the same steps *a–d* as in Problem 2. However, this time assume that it is necessary to halt temporarily consideration of the pending question.

e. Move that the pending motion be laid on the table because the speaker has just arrived and has another commitment in an hour.

f. Adopt the motion.

g. After the speaker has completed the presentation and departed, move to take the motion from the table.

h. Dispose of the motion.

Points to Emphasize. The main motion and the motions adhering to it all go to the table together. In this case, this would include the motions to amend, to refer, and to amend the motion to refer.

After the speaker leaves, the question with the motions adhering to it can be taken from the table by means of a motion with a majority vote, if no other question is pending; or it may remain on the table until the next regular meeting. If it is not taken from the table then, the question dies at the close of that meeting.

PROBLEM 4

a. Move that a team of members from the class present a parliamentary procedure demonstration before a community service club.
b. Move to amend the motion.
c. Move to amend the amendment.
d. Act on the amendments and the motion.
e. Immediately after the result of the vote on the main motion is announced, call for a division of the assembly.

Points to Emphasize. This problem includes a primary amendment—the amendment to the main motion, and a secondary amendment—the amendment to the amendment. A secondary amendment cannot be amended.

The secondary amendment must be voted on first. If it is adopted, then the next vote is on the amended primary amendment; if the vote is lost, then the next vote is on the primary amendment in its original form. The final vote is on the main motion in its amended form if the amendments have been adopted; or, if they were not, the main motion is voted on in its original form.

The division of assembly is called for when a member doubts the result of a voice vote or a vote by showing of hands, and it requires that the vote be taken again by rising.

PROBLEM 5

a. Move that the members of the chapter volunteer to assist with the annual United Way campaign for funds by typing envelopes.
b. Move to amend the motion.
c. Rise to a parliamentary inquiry.
d. Move to limit debate.

Points to Emphasize. A member may rise to a parliamentary inquiry when information is desired concerning parliamentary law or the rules of the organization. For example, the member might ask whether a certain motion would be in order at that time or whether that motion would require a two-thirds vote. The question would be addressed to the presiding officer.

The motion to limit debate may be used to limit the time spent in debate, to reduce or increase the number or length of speeches, to specify the hour for closing the debate and putting the question to a vote, or a combination of these. It requires a two-thirds vote because it deprives the members of their rights to full discussion.

PROBLEM 6

a. Move that a food sale be held in order to raise funds for sending a delegate to the national convention.
b. Move to amend the motion.
c. Rise to a point of information.
d. Move the previous question on the main motion and the amendment.

Points to Emphasize. A point of information is requested when a member wishes information concerning the business under consideration. The member might ask for additional information about the expected cost of a project which had been proposed or a date or deadline involved in the completion of the project. The question would be directed to the chair or through the chair to another member. This is similar to the parliamentary inquiry, but the question is not related to parliamentary procedure.

The previous question is a motion which immediately closes debate. Therefore, like the motion to limit debate, it requires a two-thirds vote. There may be no further amendments, and the motion itself is not amendable.

The motion, "I move the previous question" applies only to the immediately pending motion. However, the maker may specify that the motion is to apply to "all pending questions," or, may limit it, for example, to "the motion to commit and its amendment."

A member or members may call "Question!" to indicate a desire to end debate and proceed with a vote. Calling "question" is discourteous and out of order if someone has the floor or has already risen to ask for recognition, and it is not a motion for the previous question.

PROBLEM 7

In this problem the students are to set up the situation leading to the main motion and the amendment.

a. The main motion.
b. An amendment that is not germane.
c. Rise to a point of order concerning the amendment.
d. Move to postpone the question to a certain time.
e. Rise to a question of privilege. (For example, the band is practicing on the street outside making it difficult to hear the proceedings of the meeting, and a member wishes the window to be closed.)
f. Move to fix the time to which to adjourn.
g. Move to adjourn.

Points to Emphasize. A point or order must be raised promptly. After debate on the amendment has begun, the point of order is too late.

The chair rules as to whether the point of order is or is not "well taken." The chair may ask for advice from the parliamentarian before stating a decision; or, if the point is important, it can be submitted to the assembly for decision, whereupon the point becomes debatable. A decision made by the chair can be appealed by two members—one making the appeal and the other seconding it. However, no appeal can be made from the decision of the assembly.

Point of order and objection to consideration of a question are somewhat similar. The presiding officer can note a breach in the rules and correct the matter immediately; the chair can also submit an objection to a question. However, it is important to distinguish between the situations in which the two motions can be used. For example, objection to consideration of a question may not be used if the motion conflicts with national, state, or local law, or the bylaws or rules of the organization. This would call for a point of order.

A motion which has been postponed definitely or to a certain time will be taken up under unfinished business and general orders unless the question was made a special order for a certain hour. In that case, the motion might be stated, "I move that the question be postponed until 2 P.M. and made a special order."

Incidentally, the classification of "unfinished business" is often misunderstood. It includes questions which have come over from the previous meeting because that meeting adjourned before completing its order of business. The expression "old business" is not clear and is now considered obsolete.

The motion to fix the time to which to adjourn may also include the place in case there is no fixed place for the meetings. This motion has no effect on the present meeting. Its effect is to set up an adjourned meeting which will be a continuation of the present meeting.

PROBLEM 8

a. Move that funds be taken from the chapter treasury to send the newly elected president to the leadership conference next month and that a dinner be held to honor the outgoing officers.
b. Move to divide the question so as to consider the dinner separately.
c. If this motion is adopted, adopt or reject each part of the original motion.
d. Move that the chapter raise money by selling chances on a portable television set.
e. Move that the question be postponed indefinitely.

Points to Emphasize. The motion to divide the question is applicable only if each part of the motion can stand as a complete motion by itself. The motion to divide must specify how the question is to be divided.

The motion to postpone indefinitely applies only to the main motion. Its adoption kills the main motion for the duration of the session, and thus it can provide a method for avoiding a direct vote on the pending question.

Nominations and Voting

Some points not always familiar to members of an assembly include the following:

1. When nominations are made by a nominating committee, that committee should not be appointed by the president nor should the president be a member of the committee. The bylaws may specify that all committees except the nominating committee may be appointed by the president and that the president shall be an ex officio member of all committees except the nominating committee. The nominating committee should be elected by the members of the organization or by its executive board.

2. Following the presentation of the report of the nominating committee, the presiding officer must call for nominations from the floor. A member need not be recognized by the chair when making a nomination from the floor. As a general rule, no second to a nomination is necessary, although sometimes a member or members may use this method to indicate endorsement of the nominee.
3. A member may not nominate more than one person for a given office until every member who wishes to make a nomination has had the opportunity to do so.
4. It is permissible to nominate a person to more than one office, however, the bylaws may provide that a member can serve in only one office at a time. In that case, if a person is elected to more than one office, that member may indicate a preference for one of the offices; or if the individual is not present, the assembly may determine the issue by vote.
5. It is permissible for members of the nominating committee to be nominated for office.
6. As a matter of courtesy, the nominating committee, before making its report, should obtain the assurance from each of the nominees of acceptance of the nomination and willingness to serve in the office if elected.
7. A motion to close nominations is not necessary if it is evident that all who wish to make nominations have had the opportunity to do so. The chair may simply declare that nominations for that office are closed. However, if a motion to close nominations is made, it requires a two-thirds vote. A majority vote is necessary to reopen nominations.
8. When there are more than two nominees for an office, the balloting must be repeated until there is a majority vote for one candidate. Names receiving fewer votes may not be removed from the ballot unless it is so specified in the bylaws or the nominee voluntarily withdraws.
9. When the bylaws require that a vote be taken by ballot, this provision cannot be suspended. Under these circumstances, the motion that "the secretary (or other person) cast a unanimous ballot" is out of order.
10. In the case of a ballot vote, the tellers' report should be entered in full in the minutes to become a part of the official record. Similarly, the record of how each member voted in a roll call vote should be entered in the minutes.

The Bylaws

When a new organization is being formed, one of the first steps following the election of temporary officers is the designation of a committee to draft a set of bylaws. This committee should report at the next meeting of the organization. At that time each article or section is considered separately, after which an opportunity should be provided for making additions, corrections, or other changes. The bylaws are generally adopted at the second or third meeting of the society.

The bylaws usually include the following headings called *articles*.

I. Name
II. Object
III. Members
IV. Officers
V. Meetings
VI. Executive Board or Board of Directors
VII. Committees
VIII. Parliamentary Authority
IX. Amendment of Bylaws

Other articles may be added to fit the needs of the particular organization.

Whenever it is desired to change the bylaws, the motion to amend them is subject to certain special rules in addition to those applicable to any motion. The bylaws should specify that an advance notice and a two-thirds vote are required. The notice must specify each of the proposed changes. When the changes are extensive and would require many substitutions, the result is called a *revision* of the bylaws. There are certain restrictions to the extent of amendments to a proposed bylaw amendment in order to protect members who may be absent from the meeting. Reference should be made to the parliamentary authority adopted by the organization for regulations governing amendments and revisions of bylaws.

Parliamentary Procedure in Vocational Student Organizations

With the growth of student organizations has come a realization of the need for skill and ability in the application of parliamentary law. In some organizations the learning is rather haphazard in that the presiding officer and the members learn more or less by trial and error during meetings. However, in an increasing number of student associations, study and practice in parliamentary procedure are a part of the ongoing program for the organization.

In most of the vocational student organizations the need for the proper application of parliamentary law is emphasized. For example, the most-recent edition of the student manual for the Future Farmers of America includes an instructional unit on parliamentary procedure illustrated in color. In order to qualify for the Chapter Farmer (FFA) Degree, the students must be able to "demonstrate five parliamentary procedure abilities"; and to qualify for the State Farmer (FFA) Degree, a demonstration of ten parliamentary procedure abilities is required. These include making a motion, amending a motion, referring the motion to a committee, rising to a point of order, and other examples of parliamentary action.

In a similar way, the Vocational Industrial Clubs of America, Inc. (VICA) include parliamentary procedure development in their achievement program. Their manual provides parliamentary procedure references for study. For the first Leader Degree, Voice Classification, Citizen Rank, the student is expected to know the steps and rules for using the main motion. More advanced parliamentary procedure skills are required for the second Leader Degree, Inter-Community Classification, Committeeman Rank. The candidate for the third Leader Degree, Civic Classification, Leader Rank, must attend and complete a state workshop training session on parliamentary procedure and must be able to teach the basic principles of parliamentary law to younger members. For the fourth Leader Degree, Advance Classification, Patriot Rank, relative mastery of parliamentary procedure is expected.

Parliamentary procedure contests are a part of the national competitive program for the Future Business Leaders of America–Phi Beta Lambda (FBLA–PBL), the Office Education Association (OEA), and VICA. The state winners in these contests are qualified to enter the national contests. In some states, the Future Farmers of America (FFA) conducts competitive parliamentary procedure events, but the pattern for the contests varies from state to state. The manual for the Distributive Education Clubs of America (DECA) includes units of instruction on parliamentary procedure, but no parliamentary competitive events are held.

The parliamentary procedure events for FBLA–PBL, VICA, and OEA are similar in that teams of contestants are expected to conduct a typical chapter meeting during which they demonstrate parliamentary procedure abilities assigned to them in the form of problems. The details of the procedures followed in the contest, such as the length of the demonstration "meetings," the format of the problems, and the method of executing the meeting vary among the three organizations.

The number of members on the team varies from four to eight, depending upon the organization involved. Each team is given its problem and has a period of fifteen or twenty minutes in which to prepare for the demonstration meeting, which may be ten or fifteen minutes in length. The problems usually cover from four to six parts. Other items of business may or may not be included in the demonstration meeting as directed in the guidelines for that organization. Minutes of the "meeting," prepared by the secretary, are considered in the judges' rating of the team's work. *Robert's Rules of Order Newly Revised* is considered the parliamentary authority by all three organizations.

Examples of the competitive procedures and materials for FBLA–PBL, OEA, and VICA follow.

Future Business Leaders of America–Phi Beta Lambda (FBLA–PBL)

Participants in the FBLA–PBL competition are given an objective test on the principles of parliamentary procedure and the FBLA–PBL national bylaws. The ten teams achieving the highest scores on the written test are then scheduled for the performance of a demonstration test. The FBLA contestant and the PBL contestant scoring highest on the written test and having at least one year in school before graduation are appointed national parliamentarians for their respective organizations for the coming year. The judge's rating sheet for FBLA–PBL is shown on page 244.

A sample FBLA–PBL problem:

> Your chapter has decided to hold a recognition banquet for all area employers who had employed a chapter member this year. Your chapter has also decided to publish a monthly newsletter on business topics for all business students at your school. Incorporate at least four of the following motions into your performance:
>
> Amend
> Previous question
> Point of information
> Question of privilege
> Limit or extend limits of debate
> Division of the assembly

At least four of the five classes of motions—main, subsidiary, privileged, incidental, and motions that bring a question again before the assembly—must be introduced during the meeting, and at least one rule that might be applied to each must be demonstrated.

At one time the advisers for the ten FBLA and the ten PBL parliamentary procedure teams that qualified for the performance event through their scores on the written test were asked how they prepared their teams for the competition. A few are able to work this into class instruction. On the high school level this may be a part of the cooperative education block program. In some colleges parliamentary procedure instruction is given in business leadership or in business communications classes. However, a majority of the advisers reported that the instruction was done outside of class. Time might be arranged before school opens in the morning, during the lunch hour, or immediately after school, and sometimes there is evening practice at school or in homes. Among the more successful teams are those that begin their practice

STATE ______________________________

TEAM RANK ______________________________

PROPER ORDER OF BUSINESS

	Value	Score
Gavel—opening and closing meeting	1	
Reading and disposal of minutes	1	
Reports of officers	1	
Reports—boards and standing committes	1	
Reports—special committees	1	
Unfinished business	3	
New business	4	
Announcement	1	
Adjournament	1	
Totals:	14	______

MINUTES OF THE MEETING

	Value	
Completed within 30 minutes	1	
Spelling, grammar and sentence structure	2	
Type of meeting and name or organization	1	
Date, time, and place	1	
President and secretary or alternates present	1	
Minutes of previous meeting	1	
Main motions and action taken	4	
Other motions and action taken	4	
Adjournment time & Signature	1	
Totals:	16	______

MOTIONS

	Main	Subsidiary	Privileged	Incidental	Bring again	Value	Score	Comments
Made						5		
Seconded						5		
Stated						5		
Debate or no debate						5		
Put to vote						5		
Vote result announced						5		
Quality						20		
					Totals:	50	______	

GENERAL PARLIAMENTARY PROCEDURE

	Value	Score	Comments
Proper recognition, motions, and debate	15		
Proper use of parliamentary terms	8		
Clarity of expression, voice projection	5		
Presiding official impartial	2		
Members show initiative	5		
Each member speaks at least once	5		
Poise, dignity, and appearance	5		
Time: 9 to 11 minutes, no penalty; a 1-point penalty for each ½ minute or fraction thereof under 9 minutes or over 11 minutes (e.g. 11:05- -1 point; 11:35- -2 points)	5		
Totals:	50	______	

TOTAL SCORES

Proper Order of Business
Minutes of the Meeting
Motions
General Parliamentary Procedure
Performance Total
(____ points x 80%)
Test Total
(__ points x 20%)

Total Score ____________

early in the school year and meet regularly—some every day and some at a specific time every week.

Office Education Association (OEA)

Each team is given an assignment sheet containing three subjects. Each subject is to be used to demonstrate one or more abilities in parliamentary procedure. This becomes the order of business for each group.

A sample OEA assignment:

1. *Membership drive.* Abilities to be demonstrated must include:
   a. Make a main motion, offer an amendment
   b. Division of the question
   c. Postpone definitely
2. *Fund-raising project.* Abilities to be demonstrated must include:
   a. Make a main motion, offer an amendment
   b. Amend the amendment
   c. Parliamentary inquiry
3. *Employer-employee banquet.* Abilities to be demonstrated must include:
   a. Make a main motion
   b. Raise a question of personal privilege
   c. Previous question

Following the demonstration, five minutes is allowed each team for questions by the judges. Each team is asked the same questions. These questions will be about parliamentary procedures and may not necessarily be related to the abilities which were demonstrated.

The rating sheet for the OEA post-secondary competition is shown on page 246.

Vocational Industrial Clubs of America (VICA)

An identical agenda of the business meeting, secretary's minutes of the previous meeting, treasurer's report, and paper for preparing a report of the meeting is given to each team fifteen minutes prior to that team's demonstration. Each team demonstrates a complete business meeting from the call to order to adjournment. The procedures demonstrated during the simulated meeting are dictated by the items on the agenda and the minutes of the previous meeting which were given to the team prior to preparation time. The demonstration is to exhibit no fewer than six parliamentary procedures, including at least one motion from each of the five classes of motions.

JUDGE'S RATING SHEET
PARLIAMENTARY PROCEDURE CONTEST

TEAM NUMBER ______________________________

SCHOOL NAME ____________________ **STATE** ____________________

Directions: Judge #1 Score only columns 1, 2, 3
Judge #2 Score only column 4
Judge #3 Score only columns 5, 6

Ten bonus points will be given to each team completing its presentation within 15 minutes.

	Chairman's presiding ability (30)	Secretary's participating ability (30)	Clarity of business transactions (45)	Correctness of all transactions (105)	General participation by members (45)	Power of expression—voice, stage presence, and appearance (60)	Total Points	Maximum Points (315)	Comments
Subject 1	10	10	15	35	15	20		105	
Subject 2	10	10	15	35	15	20		105	
Subject 3	10	10	15	35	15	20		105	
Total Points									

Opening and closing ceremonies (maximum 10)
Points for response to judge's questions
(30 points maximum) __________
(each judge is requested to score own questions only, 10 points per judge)
Secretary's minutes of contest meeting
(30 points maximum) __________

Time ______

Bonus Points (max 10) ______

Total Points ______

Rank ______

Reprinted with permission from Office Education Association, Competitive Events Guidelines, OEA, Columbus, Ohio, 1981. The guidelines are revised annually.

The Excitement of Parliamentary Procedure

Most students who are deeply involved in parliamentary procedure agree that it is both very exciting and fun. Since various organizations are emphasizing that their meetings be conducted according to proper parliamentary procedure and since competitive events are a part of many student conferences, the excitement continues to grow at a fast pace. Students and teachers are beginning to recognize more fully how vital parliamentary procedure can be in the life of an individual.

The benefits from parliamentary procedure practice are very evident. Students who have participated in competition in previous years sell the idea to others and form a nucleus for building future teams. They are often given the responsibility for preparing new members and readily admit how exciting it is to disseminate parliamentary procedure knowledge to others and watch them progress. Parliamentary procedure competition appeals to students who prefer to participate in group rather than individual competitive events.

Groups of students training in parliamentary procedure often enjoy preparing their own problems. They use realistic situations that are typical of their own class or chapter activities. On occasion they use humorous or even ridiculous situations that make the practice more fun. Open-book tests and tests written by the students themselves help build confidence.

According to some of the advisers of successful teams, the key to developing winners is to encourage the participation of many more students than the number required for a team entering the competitive events. This leads to stiff competition among the members of the chapter for places on the team.

As the time approaches for the district or state competition, local elimination contests are held in order to select the members of the team. The elimination may be based on scores on written tests or there may be performance demonstrations before local judges. Those members who do not qualify for the contest team are frequently used as alternates if necessary, or they are good critics during practice sessions.

The teams get valuable extra practice and find it exciting to demonstrate before groups in the community such as the Chamber of Commerce, Kiwanis, Rotary, Lions, Masons, womens' clubs, and before school organizations and school administrators. Some chapters conduct parliamentary procedure workshops for other chapters and for civic or school organizations.

Correct parliamentary procedures should be practiced at all times in the regular chapter meetings. If the chapter is divided into interest groups, there are opportunities for more students to become involved in this practice. It is important that chapter officers on all levels have instruction and practice in parliamentary procedure.

Usually a great deal of closeness develops within a group striving to improve its parliamentary ability. There is a constant need to work as a team.

Cooperation and fair play are two other important qualities to be emphasized during the practice. Broad participation among the students in the chapter and in the school should be emphasized rather than merely the preparation of a winning team. Actually everyone who participates is a winner. The ability to conduct meetings with ease and to intelligently participate as a member are qualities important to leadership and good citizenship.

Other values resulting from participation include improved speaking ability, stage presence, and poise. A sense of organization and the power to think logically are obvious rewards. Working under pressure and improving finesse are still other benefits that will prove useful in later life.

The National Association of Parliamentarians and the American Institute of Parliamentarians are both strong supporters of parliamentary procedure activities in the student organizations. Experienced officers in organizations of all types are usually willing to assist with the instruction or to speak to the groups studying parliamentary procedure concerning values of the ability to apply parliamentary law correctly.

The National Association of Parliamentarians is encouraging students who are studying parliamentary procedure to take the NAP membership examination. Parliamentary procedure units are being formed throughout the country by students who have passed that test. Persons who have passed the membership examination may apply to take the examination to become registered parliamentarians.

There are many books and pamphlets on parliamentary procedure available. However, *Robert's Rules of Order Newly Revised—1981 Edition* is recommended since this is the latest edition of these rules and is the authority now used by many organizations.

Following is a list of other instructional materials that may be purchased from the National Association of Parliamentarians, 3706 Broadway, Suite 300, Kansas City, MO 64111:

General Henry M. Robert, *Parliamentary Law*

Congratulations Series (Revised):

- "You Are the *President*"
- "You Are the *Secretary*"
- "You Are the *Treasurer*"
- "You Are on a *Committee*"
- "You Are a *Member*"
- "You Want to Learn How to Make Motions and Amend Them"
- "You Want to Learn *Definitions*"

Pointers on Parliamentary Procedure

NAP Curriculum for Teaching and Study

Parliamentary procedure is a game. It is like chess: there always is a countermove. The challenges are endless. Knowing the rules really pays off—and it is most exciting.

Chapter 11

Dynamics of Nonverbal Communication

Malra Treece

THE DISCUSSION OF METHODOLOGY and subject content, as presented in this chapter, applies primarily to the inclusion of the study of nonverbal communication in a basic, comprehensive course taught at the undergraduate level. The suggestions presented here also apply to classes, workshops, and seminars emphasizing interpersonal communication.

Although entire courses, as well as many books, are based on nonverbal communication as the major area of content, such classes are not usually included in business curricula. We cannot teach any course in communication, however, without considering wordless messages.

Why Include Nonverbal Communication?

Nonverbal communication is inseparable from the total communication process. Ray Birdwhistell, a pioneer in the field of kinesics (body language), is said to have remarked that studying communication apart from its nonverbal aspects is like studying noncardiac physiology.

Nonverbal communication, which consists of many forms, permeates all speech and much, if not all, written communication. Various estimates from recognized authorities in the field indicate that nonverbal communication makes up about 70 to 75 percent of the transfer of meaning and emotions in face-to-face interaction. Some estimates are as high as 90 percent.

Much of nonverbal communication is unconscious. This factor is what makes it so sincere. We can improve interpersonal relationships by learning to receive the unspoken and unplanned messages of others, as well as by becoming aware of our own unspoken language. Developing students' understanding of messages sent and received is the most important result of including the subject as course content.

Most of us are far better at receiving the messages of others than we are in sending conscious nonverbal messages of our own. Usually we shouldn't attempt to send planned messages except by our confident and considerate attitude, by our smiles, or sometimes by a pat on the back or an arm around the shoulder. But we cannot fake these signals. As in all other methods of communication, sincerity is the most important element.

By becoming aware of the messages others are sending us, we can become more responsive to their needs. We will become more effective teachers, more-human human beings. We will become more receptive to our families and colleagues—and so will our students.

Many of the habits and attitudes we wish to instill in our students—promptness, courtesy, cooperation, responsibility, and others—are aspects of nonverbal communication. Preaching about these desirable qualities is less effective than building an understanding of their influence on the reception and effectiveness of all communication. We can best convey our conviction of the importance of these attitudes and actions by our own positive attitudes and actions—that is, by our own nonverbal communication of these attributes.

Students seem to be extremely interested in nonverbal communication. They are eager to choose aspects of this topic for reports on library reading or for longer research reports. Building and sustaining interest is in itself a worthwhile educational goal. Even more important, an understanding of the far-reaching effects of the many methods of nonverbal communication increases understandings and abilities in all other forms of communication.

Much of the research into aspects of nonverbal communication has been done by psychologists, psychiatrists, sociologists, and anthropologists. But, as you know, the study of communication of all kinds is interdisciplinary. This statement is true even when we limit the term strictly to business communication. In a basic course, we teach such diverse fields as English grammar, journalism, speech, semantics, psychology, ethics (which is in itself interdisciplinary, general business management, personnel management, office management, marketing (including retailing, advertising, sales promotion, and direct mail sales letters), research principles, logic, statistics, and half a dozen other subjects. Some kind of nonverbal communication enters into all these areas, with the possible exception of English grammar.

What Is Nonverbal Communication?

Although this chapter is planned primarily to discuss methods of presenting an understanding of nonverbal communication to students in your classes, the following summary of key concepts is included because the subject matter is relatively new to some business communication teachers, at least in comparison to more traditional content areas. In addition, the topic is omitted in some textbooks currently in use. In all textbooks planned for a comprehensive, one-semester course, space devoted to the discussion of nonverbal communication must be limited, although no topic is of more importance.

This summary is not intended to suffice as background reading for teachers who are preparing to present information about nonverbal communication to their classes. As with any other subject, the teacher should know far more than the content officially included in the course outline or in lesson plans.

Sources of Information

The bibliography at the end of this chapter will guide you in your reading. Because new publications appear frequently, however, this bibliography is of necessity incomplete.

A quick way to obtain an overview of the subject, in addition to reading the following pages, is to read fairly short, clear, interesting books on the entire field, books that summarize research studies without going into great detail on any one method or particular study. Some books planned for courses devoted to interpersonal communication contain one or several summarizing chapters on nonverbal communication. After reading these books or chapters, you are prepared to read further, and in greater detail, about the specific aspects of nonverbal communication of greatest interest to you. The card catalog of your library is likely to include a long list of books on the subject. You may not find these books immediately, however, for they are so popular that they are widely circulated.

These books are popular because we are all interested in getting to know one another better—in expressing our thoughts and emotions to other persons and in receiving the messages of others. Unfortunately, as we all know, perfect communication cannot be achieved by reading books, even the best ones.

As in any other field, books on nonverbal communication vary greatly in quality. Certain books on aspects of interpersonal relationships, especially communication through kinesics, or body language, seem to have been written only for the purpose of selling a large number of copies. Even these books, however, are not completely unscientific because they are based on the works of other writers in the field, including well-known and reputable researchers.

The popular books, often in paperback, tend to be overly simplistic and somewhat sensational. Even worse, some of them seem to imply that by learning the principles of nonverbal communication we can manipulate other people into doing what we want them to do, or that we can pry into their private lives and "read them like a book." Kinesics, like all other facets of communication of any kind, is far from being an exact science. Even if it were far more exact, to be effective—even to be real—communication must reflect an attitude of sincere cooperation.

Kinds of Nonverbal Communication

Nonverbal communication, in its broadest sense, includes all transmission of meaning except that which is expressed in oral or written words. The term *nonverbal* is sometimes misunderstood because the word *verbal* is thought to mean only oral communication, as the word is commonly used. Verbal comes from the Latin word *verbum,* meaning "word"; thus verbal means "with words" and nonverbal means "without words." (Another meaning of *verbal communication,* as listed in unabridged dictionaries, is "oral communication"; no doubt this definition developed because of popular usage.)

Perhaps you may feel that the preceding discussion of terms is obvious and unnecessary, but you are likely to find that your students are confused about the meaning of the words. Some students have assumed that nonverbal communication consists of written material, since it isn't oral communication.

Nonverbal communication is described in this way in the *Handbook of Communication:*

> The term nonverbal communication has been applied to a wide range of phenomena, everything from facial expression and gesture to fashion and status symbols, from dance and drama to music and mime; from flow of affect to flow of traffic, from the territoriality of animals to the protocol of diplomats; from extrasensory perception to analog computers, from the rhetoric of violence to the rhetoric of topless dancers.[1]

All of these methods of the transfer of meaning, as well as many more that you can think of, are forms of nonverbal communication. We are most concerned, however, with communication between humans—not communication between humans and machines, humans and animals, animals and animals, animals and machines, and machines and machines.

Human nonverbal communication will take one of three general forms, according to Ruesch and Kees in the book *Nonverbal Communication.*[2] These forms are sign language, object language, and action language.

Sign Language

Sign language is mostly conscious and consists of such things as a wave goodbye, the hitchhiker's familiar signal, the hand upraised to indicate "stop," the A-OK sign, the V for "victory" sign, and the complete and complicated sign language of the deaf. Sign languages, like verbal ones, differ from culture to culture. For example, in some societies a nod that we use to express "yes" means "no," and a shaking of the head means "yes." (Many, if not most, of the methods of nonverbal communication differ according to the particular culture.)

Object Language

Object language is made of such methods of communication as the arrangement and order of our homes and offices; our clothing, furniture, and automobiles; and other choices and displays of possessions. Object language includes status symbols and security blankets of all kinds, those which we consciously display to other persons and the ones which we do not consciously use to express our values and attitudes.

Action Language

Action language consists of actions of all kinds; kinesics, or body language, is only a part. It includes all movements that are not used exclusively as signals. Ruesch and Kees state: "Such acts as walking and drinking, for example, have a dual function: on one hand they serve personal needs, and on the other they constitute statements to those who may perceive them."[3] Action language also consists of such messages as arriving late for an interview.

Communication through the Use of Time and Space

The preceding listing of sign, object, and action language seems to omit the special interest of Edward T. Hall, communication through the use of time and space. But communication through the use of time and space consists of object language, action language, or both.

Edward T. Hall says of time:

> Time talks. It speaks more plainly than words. The message it conveys comes through loud and clear. Because it is manipulated less consciously, it is subject to less distortion than the spoken language. It can shout the truth where words lie.[4]

Edward T. Hall is well known for his theories concerning the use of time and space to effect nonverbal communication. Dr. Hall, a professor of anthropology, is especially concerned with the ways in which persons of different cultures respond to nonverbal communication. For example, he found that people from Arab and Latin American countries stand closer to other persons, when conversing, than we do here in the United States, and that people of some other cultures are much more casual than we Americans about the use of time.

Hall uses the term *proxemics* to describe his theories and observations about zones of territory and how they are used and defended by people of differing cultures. According to Hall, there are four kinds of interpersonal distance: (1) intimate distance, (2) personal distance, (3) social distance, and (4) public distance—with close and far phases in each zone.

For example, the far phase of social distance, seven to twelve feet, is the distance most appropriate for formal business relationships. Some executives use a desk large enough to keep visitors at this distance, or nearly so. At this distance a person can remain seated and look up at a guest without a loss of status. This distance is an adequate separation of a receptionist's desk from visitors' chairs. One can keep working without seeming rude or can talk without getting up.

Hall believes that, in addition to zones of distance, we establish our own personal territories, much as animals do. And we carry around with us an "invisible bubble" to protect our privacy.

Kinesics

Kinesics, or body language, is what most people think of when nonverbal communication is mentioned, without considering the many other forms.

As it was mentioned earlier, kinesics is far from being an exact science. (This is also true for the whole field of nonverbal communication and practically every other facet of individual or organization behavior, as well as many other areas of knowledge.) A great deal of research has been done in kinesics, especially by psychologists, psychiatrists, and anthropologists. Most formal research in human nonverbal communication has been done since 1940, although the study of nonverbal communication in animals goes back to the time of Charles Darwin.

Even without books or research studies, we would all realize the importance of kinesics to the transmission of ideas and emotions. You can tell a great deal about the feelings of others before they say a word. You learned to do so when you were very young.

Remember, though, that our judgments of the psychological meaning of such actions as the way a person sits in a chair or how one's hands touch the face, hair, or other parts of the body cannot be viewed as an exact interpretation or, in some cases, even an approximate estimate.

Birdwhistell says:

> Almost as soon as the linguist or the kinesicist meets someone he is asked, "What can you tell me from my speech or my body motion?" More fearful or more coquettish respondents manifest considerable anxiety that their behavior is going to reveal their deepest secrets to the expert. . . . However, the specialist cannot determine how distinctively individual any particular performance is before he knows his structure and individual range of behavior for a particular behavioral area . . . the scientific study of expressional behavior must await extensive experimentation before we can test productive value and reliability of clinical judgments.[5]

All nonverbal communication, as with all verbal communication, should always be considered in context. The title of one of Birdwhistell's books, *Kinesics and Context,* illustrates this important principle. Nonverbal communication is influenced by the environment, tone of voice, and previously established relationships. All these factors enter into nonverbal communication; they are, in fact, elements of nonverbal communication.

Paralanguage

We communicate through tone of voice and the hesitations, ohs, ahs, repetitions, clearings of throat, and other interrupting elements that we insert into our speech. These additions to oral communication are described as *paralanguage* and, logically enough, as "interrupters." These interrupters can also be considered as a form of action language, and they can function as a method of *metacommunication,* as discussed in the next subsection.

The term *paralanguage* is also used to describe nuances that surround the printed word, such as type and arrangement on the page.

Metacommunication

The term *metacommunication* is usually used to mean that spoken words carry different meanings, or supplemental meanings, from the obvious ones.

Silence

Silence can be used to send messages, sometimes most emphatic ones.

When, Where, and How Should Nonverbal Communication Be Presented?

No course in communication, business or otherwise, is exact or truly comprehensive if consideration of nonverbal communication is omitted. In fact, it is quite impossible to omit the influences of nonverbal communication in any course, even if it is described as business writing or business report writing. In courses in oral communication or interpersonal communication, nonverbal messages make up one of the most important areas of subject content. In courses described as basic, undergraduate courses in business communication, the study of theory also includes principles of nonverbal communication.

The following discussion of the presentation and evaluation of principles of nonverbal communication in a basic course in business communication also applies, for the most part, to the inclusion of the subject in any other communication course.

Teaching Nonverbal Communication in a Basic Business Communication Course

A basic, comprehensive course in business communication should include all the following areas of content: the theory of general communication, the theory of communication as it pertains to business situations and problems, and the application of general and business communication theory to the solving of business problems through messages presented in both oral and written forms. Written messages should include letters, memorandums, reports, and other frequently used media.

Where, then, does nonverbal communication fit into the suggested course content?

In its broadest sense, nonverbal communication is an essential part of most, if not all, of these suggested topics. An understanding of the concepts of nonverbal communication should be considered as a part of general communication theory. These concepts are also a part of business communication theory.

All aspects of communication are interrelated. Even if we tried, we could not teach the effective presentation of ideas in written form without also considering principles that apply to oral messages, and vice versa. We can teach neither oral nor written communication without also considering the influence of nonverbal messages.

We cannot approach the study or teaching of communication of any kind through the presentation of isolated segments of information. As we teach any aspect of the subject, which is broad and comprehensive, we must keep in mind all other aspects. We cannot discuss such topics as perception, barriers to communication, and feedback without including the effects of nonverbal messages. For example, much of an individual's perception is based upon information and attitudes received and sent other than through the use of words.

As a more pragmatic example, we talk about effective nonverbal communication as we discuss the process of obtaining employment through an interview. The applicant tells a great deal about himself or herself by the time of arrival, by the choice of clothing, and by posture, mannerisms, and facial expressions.

We are teaching nonverbal communication when we give the time-honored advice that written messages should be neatly typewritten, without strikeovers or obvious erasures, on good-quality paper and attractively arranged on the page. We teach that by making typewritten messages as attractive as possible we are sending messages in addition to the verbal ones expressed by our choice and arrangement of words. The appearance and timing of a memorandum, letter, or other communication can transmit silent messages to the effect that the writer cares enough about the reader to answer promptly and to present the words in an attractive form; that the writer is one who "does things right" or has them done right; that the writer and the employing organization are reliable and efficient. (That all of these descriptions are not necessarily exact is beside the point; all communication is imperfect.)

In addition to these methods of teaching nonverbal communication as components of written and oral messages that are ordinarily included in a basic course in business communication, we should add some formal study of the subject itself. We should work for an understanding of the importance and continuous effect of nonverbal communication. We should include a summary or research findings in the field, and, as discussed previously, develop the realization of the difference in quality, approach, and reliability of various books on the subject.

We should work for understanding, not for a memorization of details. But, as in all areas of knowledge, a specific vocabulary is an aid to understanding and to the effective transmission of ideas.

Concepts of nonverbal communication should be presented early in a basic course in business communication as part of the introductory theory upon which effective applications must be based. Then, as with all principles of communication, the follow-up lessons, lectures, and assignments should reemphasize and strengthen previously presented principles.

We should not, however, divide the course into discrete sections of theory and applications, although to obtain some measure of coherence and organization, we must at times during the semester emphasize differing methods, forms, and media of communication. At no time should one aspect of communication be "forgotten" as another form is presented. Both written and oral assignments can accompany the study of theory. Certain assignments pertaining to nonverbal communication can be used throughout the term or semester.

Often one short assignment can serve as instructional material planned to improve both written and oral communication and to develop an understanding of nonverbal messages. For example, the simple assignment of writing a one-page memorandum, with documentation, about some facet of nonverbal communication and presenting a one-minute summary of this information to the class provides experiences in all the following areas: library research, preparing footnotes and bibliographies, memorandum format, summarizing, writing, speaking to groups, principles of nonverbal communication, communicating nonverbally along with the oral presentation (students cannot do otherwise), and communicating nonverbally, along with written words, through the physical appearance of the memorandum.

As another example of how various aspects of communication can be presented and evaluated together, small-group communication, such as simulated committee meetings, can be videotaped and analyzed for effectiveness from several standpoints, including the effects of nonverbal communication. For practice in written communication, summaries and evaluations can be presented in various letter, report, or memorandum forms. Further practice in oral communication can be provided by asking group leaders to present reports to the class as a whole.

If no videotape equipment is available, some students can be "observers" during the simulated committee meeting and give their full attention to the words and actions of the small group, including instances of effective or ineffective nonverbal communication. They report their observations either to the class or to the small group, or they prepare written reports.

See *Communication for Business and the Professions,* revised edition, Chapters 1 through 18, for additional problems and assignments, to be used throughout the term or semester, that combine material ordinarily described as "theory" (including nonverbal communication), "written communication," and "oral communication."[6]

Concepts of nonverbal communication can be presented and discussed through reports of students' reading, as in the short memorandum previously mentioned, or through lectures, class discussions, films, filmstrips, transparencies, slide presentations, and videotapes made and analyzed during class sessions or as outside assignments.

Other methods include class feedback to students making oral presentations as to the effect of nonverbal communication—appearance, tone of voice, mannerisms, gestures, facial expressions—upon the favorable reception of spoken words.

In past years some instructors of speech classes, which were sometimes referred to as oratory training, taught students to use planned gestures to accompany their spoken words. The speaker was expected to memorize these movements along with verbal arguments. This approach is no longer widely used; speakers are advised to use their hands only as comes naturally, or, in some instances, to refrain from talking with their hands. Excessive hand movements can be meaningless and most distracting.

We cannot assign a nonverbal "message" in the same way that we assign a letter or a speech. Such an assignment, even if used, would be essentially an "act," not effective or sincere communication.

Emphasis throughout the course, in relation to principles of nonverbal communication, should be upon developing knowledge and understanding of the many and differing ways by which we send and receive wordless messages. Students should also be given an opportunity to evaluate the nonverbal communication of other persons and to evaluate and improve their own.

Using planned gestures or body movements to impress or to manipulate other people is far from what the study of nonverbal communication is all about. When we mention the topic as part of our course content, unfortunately, this approach is what some persons will understand the term to mean.

Teaching with Videotapes

The use of videotapes is especially helpful in teaching and evaluating nonverbal communication, as well as all facets of oral communication.

William C. Donaghy[7] states that he asks one of the campus recruiters (at the University of Wyoming) to schedule employment interviews in the videotape laboratory. Video cameras are mounted to show the interviewer on one half of the screen and the interviewee on the other half—as well as to show both participants from different angles in order to include facial expressions, appearances, distance between participants, mannerisms, and all other elements of nonverbal communication.

If actual employment interviews cannot be used, role-playing participants can be videotaped and the interview discussed from all standpoints of effective communication.

In relation to student response to videotaped presentations, Donaghy says that "They anxiously participate in their own education. Probably the hardest thing the instructor has to do with this particular approach is to get a word in edgewise."[8]

In addition to using videotape to record employment interviews, the method can be effectively used for group discussions or all oral presentations, including oral reporting, as discussed previously.

Richard A. Hatch[9] describes the use of videotape to teach report presentation. He asks groups of students to meet in the videotape lab for three 2-hour sessions outside class. These sessions are designed to polish the students' posture, gestures, and facial expressions; to improve the students' ability to respond to unexpected questions; and to provide practice in delivering a short business presentation.

Hatch suggests that videotape should not be used unless the student has had the opportunity to spend several sessions outside the classroom in self-observation. He believes that a single videotaping can do more harm than good because the first look at oneself on videotape is almost always depressing.

This opinion agrees with that of Doris Engerrand, who states that before the first taping, she spends ten to fifteen minutes scanning the class and allowing each member to observe himself or herself on television. "The purpose of this procedure is to help the student get over the initial shock.[10] She used role playing to act out one of the following situations: disciplining an employee, handling a customer complaint, firing an employee, and interviewing a prospective employee or interviewing an employee who had left the company. Immediately after the eight-minute taping, students evaluated the performance, including language, appearance, and body movements.

A consequence of nonverbal communication noted by Engerrand in her discussion of the tapes made by her students was that the placement of furniture at times became a barrier to effective communication.[11] This kind of barrier is mentioned by Hall as one of the elements of proxemics.

In addition to videotapes made in the classroom or in the video lab, videotape prints can be used to present principles of nonverbal communication, as well as other information and illustrations useful to business communication students.

Even television programs can be recorded and played in the classroom for student evaluation of the effects of nonverbal communication. Talk shows are sometimes particularly relevant, as are daytime serials and commercial advertising. (In addition to an analysis of nonverbal communication, students may comment on several other aspects of communication—perhaps on the desirability of logic and common sense.)

Although videotape equipment is desirable for use in business communication classrooms and in out-of-class labs, you need not feel that it is absolutely essential. If your school cannot afford the equipment, you can teach oral and nonverbal communication without it. Its greatest benefit—and this is an important advantage—is that students are far better able to evaluate their own appearance and actions.

How Can Instruction in Nonverbal Communication Be Evaluated?

Self-evaluation is a valuable method of measuring communication effectiveness, especially self-evaluation of performances as recorded on videotape. Self-evaluation can be used even when videotape equipment is unavailable; for example, students can analyze the results of their contribution to group discussions or the way in which their use of nonverbal communication affected their oral reporting.

Knowledge of the general principles of nonverbal communication, terminology, and significant research can be measured in all the ways that knowledge of any other subject area is evaluated.

Students can be evaluated by other students, especially after oral presentations. Comments from classmates are much more convincing than "criticism" from teachers.

As students watch films or videotapes, or perhaps slides, they can write down the nonverbal cues they identify and interpret these cues. Then the interpretations can be compared with those of other students.

Tests to measure sensitivity to nonverbal cues have been designed and used. Perhaps they will someday be on the market and available for classroom use.[12]

Shall We Do Further Research or Make Needed Changes?

Very little research has been done on nonverbal communication in business administration or business education. The many aspects of nonverbal communication that pertain to business or to business education offer numerous topics and questions from which your graduate students can develop research projects for theses or dissertations.

Shorter research projects can be undertaken by graduate or undergraduate students. For example, students at Memphis State University have used questionnaires and interviews to compare the opinions and actions of persons questioned with the principles of proxemics as presented by Hall. Although the people questioned had not read the works of Hall and did not know the meaning of the word *proxemics,* their opinions and illustrations of their actions regarding their use of personal space were consistent with Hall's theories. Other students have investigated the influence of appearance and dress on the outcome of employment interviews and the arrangement of the employment data sheet in relation to the preferences of personnel managers. (The arrangement of written information also constitutes a facet of paralanguage.)

Business education students and teachers should conduct research into methods of teaching nonverbal communication and into the effects of nonverbal communication on teaching success in various business subjects or in other fields. Students and teachers are needed to develop teaching aids for nonverbal communication, such as slide-sound presentations and other audiovisual aids. Research should be done to determine effective and efficient methods of preparing teachers of business communication to teach nonverbal communication. Textbooks written for general courses in business communication should include more material on nonverbal communication.

Throughout instruction in nonverbal communication, emphasis should be placed upon its importance to the reception of all other forms of communication.

Notes

1. Ithiel de Sola Pool et al., eds., *Handbook of Communication* (Chicago: Rand McNally Publishing Co., 1973). p. 93.
2. Jurgen Ruesch and Weldon Kees, *Nonverbal Communication* (Berkeley: University of California Press, 1970), p. 189.
3. Ibid., p. 189.

4. Edward T. Hall, *The Silent Language* (New York: Doubleday and Co., 1959), p. 23.
5. Ray Birdwhistell, *Kinesics and Context* (Philadelphia: University of Pennsylvania Press, 1970), p. 33.
6. Malra Treece, *Communication for Business and the Professions,* rev. ed. (Boston: Allyn and Bacon, 1983).
7. William C. Donaghy, "Using Videotape to Teach Nonverbal Communication," *ABCA Bulletin* (March 1975), p. 13.
8. Ibid., p. 15.
9. Richard A. Hatch, "Using Videotape to Teach Report Presentation," *ABCA Bulletin* (March 1975), p. 11.
10. Doris Engerrand, "Video Tape in the Business Communication Classroom," *ABCA Bulletin* (March 1975), p. 11.
11. Ibid.
12. Jean Voyles, "Evaluating Instructional Objectives in Business Communication" in *Evaluation and Accountability in Business Education,* NBEA Yearbook no. 16 (Reston, Va.: National Business Education Association, 1978), p. 276.

Bibliography

ARDREY, R. *The Territorial Imperative.* New York: Atheneum Publishers, 1966.

ARGYLE, MICHAEL. *Bodily Communication.* London: Methuen, 1975.

——. *Non-Verbal Communication.* Oxford: Blackwell, 1973.

BARNLAND, DEAN C. *Interpersonal Communication: Survey and Studies.* Boston: Houghton Mifflin Co., 1968.

BEIER, E. G. "Nonverbal Communication: How We Send Emotional Messages." *Psychology Today,* October 1974.

BIRDWHISTELL, RAY L. *Introduction to Kinesics.* Louisville, Ky.: University of Louisville Press, 1952.

——. *Kinesics and Context: Essays on Body Motion Communication.* Philadelphia: University of Pennsylvania Press, 1970.

DAVIS, FLORA. *Inside Intuition.* New York: McGraw-Hill Book Co., 1973.

DAVITZ, J. *The Communication of Emotional Meaning.* New York: McGraw-Hill Book Co., 1964.

DONAGHY, WILLIAM C. "Using Video Tape to Teach Nonverbal Communication," *ABCA Bulletin,* March 1975.

EISENBERGER, A. M., and R. SMITH. *Non-verbal Communication.* New York: Bobbs-Merrill Co., 1971.

EKMAN, PAUL, and WALLACE V. FRIESEN. *Unmasking the Face.* Englewood Cliffs, N.J.: Prentice-Hall, 1975.

ENGERRAND, DORIS. "Video Tape in the Business Communication Classroom," *ABCA Bulletin,* March 1975.

FAST, JULIUS. *Body Language.* New York: Pocket Books, 1971.

FROMM, ERICH. *The Forgotten Language.* New York: Rinehart & Co., 1951.

FUJIMOTO, EDWARD KUNIO. "The Comparative Communicative Power of Verbal and Nonverbal Symbols." Unpublished dissertation, The Ohio State University, 1971.

HALL, EDWARD T. *The Hidden Dimension.* New York: Doubleday & Co., 1966.

——. *The Silent Language.* Garden City, N.Y.: Doubleday & Co., 1959.

——. "The Silent Language in Overseas Business." *Harvard Business Review,* May-June 1960.

HATCH, RICHARD A. "Using Video Tape to Teach Report Presentation." *The ABCA Bulletin,* March 1975.

HAYAKAWA, S. I. "Postscript—Metamessages and Self Discovery." In *Poetry Therapy,* edited by J. J. Leedy. Philadelphia: J. B. Lippincott 1966.

HOPPER, ROBERT, *Human Message Systems.* New York: Harper & Row, 1976.

HUSEMAN, RICHARD C., JAMES M. LAHIFF, and JOHN D. HATFIELD, eds. *Interpersonal Communication in Organizations.* Boston: Holbrook, 1976.

KELTNER, JOHN W. *Elements of Interpersonal Communication.* Belmont, Calif.: Wadsworth Publishing Co., 1973.

KNAPP, MARK L. *Nonverbal Communication in Human Interaction.* New York: Holt, Rinehart and Winston, 1972.

LEATHERS, DALE G. *Nonverbal Communication Systems.* Boston: Allyn and Bacon, 1976.

MCCARDLE, ELLEN. *Nonverbal Communication.* New York: Marcel Dekker, 1974.

MEHRABIAN, ALBERT. *Silent Messages.* Belmont, Calif.: Wadsworth Publishing Co., 1971.

MORTENSEN, C. DAVID. *Communication: The Study of Human Interaction.* New York: McGraw-Hill Book Co., 1972.

ROSENTHAL, R. "Body Talk and Tone of Voice: The Language Without Words." *Psychology Today,* September 1974.

RUESCH, J., and W. KEES. *Nonverbal Communication.* Berkley: University of California Press, 1970.

SCHEFLEN, ALBERT E. *Body Language and the Social Order.* Englewood Cliffs, N.J.: Prentice-Hall, 1972.

——. *How Behavior Means.* New York: Gordon and Breach Science Publishers, 1973.

SOMMER, ROBERT. *Personal Space.* Englewood Cliffs, N.J.: Prentice-Hall, 1969.

TREECE, MALRA. *Communication for Business and the Professions.* Rev. ed. Boston: Allyn and Bacon, 1983.

——. "Teaching Nonverbal Communication in a Basic Business Communication Course." *ABCA Bulletin,* June 1977.

VOYLES, JEAN. "Evaluating Instructional Objectives in Business Communication." In *Evaluation and Accountability in Business Education* (NBEA Yearbook no. 16), Reston, Va.: National Business Education Association, 1978.

YOUNG, MARLEN CELESTE. "A Study of Four Problems Relating to Awareness of Metacommunication in Business Correspondence." Unpublished dissertation, Arizona State University, 1974.

ZIMPFER, FOREST A. "Attitudes of Selected Office Personnel Toward Nonverbal Communication Symbols and Actions." Unpublished dissertation, The University of Iowa, 1974.

Chapter 12

Effective Interpersonal Communication

William C. Himstreet

TODAY THERE IS INCREASING EMPHASIS on the nature of two-way, face-to-face communication in courses of study in both speech communication and business communication. Courses in organizational behavior were the first in business to incorporate large segments on interpersonal communication; as the organizational behavior field developed, however, more attention was given to organizational communication with lesser emphasis on purely interpersonal aspects. In many colleges and universities, courses in business communication have incorporated elements of interpersonal communication in the traditional written communication course. Additionally, separate courses in interpersonal communication have been developed.

Key Concepts and Learning Objectives

The single broad goal of instruction in interpersonal communication is to improve the individual's ability to function effectively in one-to-one and group communication situations. To achieve this goal, instruction is usually broken down into broad units covering the following areas:

1. Nature of the interpersonal transaction
2. Perception and its impact on communication
3. Sending skills and receiving skills
4. Leadership in group communication

A brief examination of these areas should be adequate to establish the key concepts and learning objectives of instruction in interpersonal communication. Any of the texts listed later in this chapter expands on elements of these areas.

Nature of the Interpersonal Transaction

Many authors describe an exchange between two people as an "encounter." Because *encounter* implies conflict, however, *transaction* is used in this discussion as a term interchangeable with *encounter.*

A.: Good morning.
B.: Good morning.
A.: How's everything?
B.: OK. How about you?
A.: Good.
B.: See you later.
A.: Adios.

This simple transaction is familiar to everyone. Reduced to its communication basics, it involves encoding and decoding of messages, provides open feedback, and permits observation of nonverbal aids. If the participants employ smiles, frowns, and other gestures, the transaction takes on added meaning. The transaction was perfunctory, and in fact, each comment was anticipated by the participants. Not all transactions, though, follow this simple pattern, as in the following example:

A.: Where did I leave my bracelet?
B.: On the dresser, stupid; can't you keep track of anything?

In this case, the transaction involves genuine information exchange, but it also contains implications about attitude, emotion, and perhaps lack of understanding in applied human relationships. The chapter bibliography lists books on transactional analysis by Eric Berne, Thomas A. Harris, and Muriel James and Dorothy Jongeward applicable in studying such transactions; however, most interpersonal communication texts devote little space to discussion of the ego-state approach used in transactional analysis. Rather, texts on interpersonal communication engage in a study of the needs of people and of establishing empathy. Social and egoistic needs, such as the need to be heard, the need to be wanted, and the need to be appreciated, receive emphasis. And empathy is usually defined as understanding another's state of mind or condition without actually experiencing the feelings of the other. The interpersonal communication course attempts to bridge the empathy gap by stressing experiential activities which lead to understanding of others.

The goals of improved interpersonal transactions are these:

1. To provide mutual pleasure
2. To develop mutual trust
3. To assist in improving psychological well-being

To understand the elements leading to improved interpersonal transactions, students are encouraged to engage in both classroom and out-of-class activities which lead to the development of trust and the habit of sharing through self-disclosure and to the identification of the needs of others through self-analysis.

Perception and Its Impact on Communication

Communication has a great influence on how people perceive others; and so, too, perception has a great influence on how people communicate with others. Although perception may be discussed in terms of *things* and *events*, the interpersonal communication course concerns itself with perceptions about people. How people perceive others during a first meeting determines how they will communicate with those others on a second transaction. Until something occurs in terms of behavior to change the perception, communication will continue to occur in terms of the original perception. Thus, the focus of a study of perception in interpersonal communication is on two areas: (1) perception of self and (2) perception of others. Class and out-of-class activities should be designed to assist the student in making accurate and positive perceptions about herself or himself and about others. The goal, of course, is to improve interpersonal communication through accurate perception.

Perception, by its nature, is influenced by (1) chronology (first impressions are important); (2) entirety (one could not perceive all that could be perceived about another); (3) reality (a person could seldom be perceived as the person really is); and (4) selectivity (some perceptual clues are accepted and others are ignored).

People gain perception about themselves from several sources. Self-perception may be influenced by one's recall of past performances. Successful *records* lead to favorable self-images and vice versa. At the same time, people constantly draw *comparisons with others*. Certainly, people gain perceptions about themselves based on the *feedback* they receive about themselves from others. These sources contribute to people's *attitudes toward themselves* and affect their feelings about self-confidence and objectivity.

Some of these factors in self-perception are obviously involved in how people perceive others. Attractive, well-behaved people are perceived favorably. This factor leads to one of "wholeness." People who have several desirable qualities for a certain task or position are perceived to have all the necessary qualities. Also, such factors as honesty, desire (people see what they want to see), and role and status contribute to perception about others.

The treatment of perception in the classroom may receive a wide range of emphasis—from a cursory first introduction to several class sessions. The important thing is that the student recognize the impact of perception on all communication activities throughout the course.

Sending and Receiving Skills

The "traditional" business communication course may contain relatively brief coverage of listening and speaking skills in addition to the study of written communication. While it includes information on how to listen to and deliver oral presentations, the interpersonal communication course spends considerable blocks of time on one-on-one listening and speaking, that is, interpersonal sending and receiving. Objectives for this portion of the course may be stated as follows:

1. To develop skill in techniques used in enhancing sending and receiving in interpersonal communication
2. To learn the methods used to clarify messages
3. To develop an understanding of the concept that one's encoding and sending occur simultaneously with another's decoding and receiving

Sending skills involve accurate symbol—usually word—selection and encoding, establishing credibility through crediting others and crediting self, and achieving accuracy through proper classifying, dating, and indexing. Words have meaning only when placed in the context of the experiences of both sender and receiver. As symbols, words are selected to describe some event or object external to the sender. Even when *what* symbols will be sent is decided, the problem of *how* to express them is pretty much a function of the interpersonal relationship existing between sender and receiver.

Credibility is achieved by crediting self (as in introducing a remark by "I believe") and by crediting others (as in introducing a remark by "Webster says"). Such references help separate fact from fiction and assist in avoiding being accused of dogmatism. In much the same way, classifying, dating, and indexing help clarify messages. Specific terms are better than general ones as are concrete terms superior to abstract ones. A "typewriter" is more accurately described as a "Royal electric typewriter," for example. "As sick as a dog" is not as accurate as "a temperature of 103 with chills and fever." Dating occurs when one says, "I learned to hate asparagus as a child and haven't eaten it since" rather than "Asparagus is terrible." Because all people have filing systems in their minds where they store all their past experiences, senders have a responsibility to qualify their remarks so the receiver knows from whose filing system the remark originated. No two human filing systems are identical.

Receiving skills include effective listening and conscious observing of the sender, of course. Additionally, however, the interpersonal communication course usually includes practice in paraphrasing another's remarks for clarification, questioning for further information, and making evaluative responses to clarify intended meaning. Although people engage in these activities often, they frequently are unaware that they are using a valuable technique. A major part of the treatment of receiving skills is devoted to *when* and *how* to use these techniques since each of them really is feedback to the message and should be adapted to the other person's needs.

By participating in two-person and small-group activities, students are able to practice these methods throughout the course.

Leadership in Group Communication

In addition to the development of improved one-to-one communication, the interpersonal communication area is concerned with the study of communication within groups. Group communication includes the behavior of individuals within such groups as committees, conferences, and social groups. Not included are formal organizations within industry, government, and education. A useful distinction might be that groups do not have a hierarchy of several status levels, but that organizations do have such a hierarchy.

The goals of group communication study and practice might be listed as follows:

1. To develop an understanding of the communication process within groups
2. To develop an ability to cope with barriers to effective group communication
3. To acquire an understanding of and practice in group leadership methods

Some key concepts in group communication can be described by the terminology used:

Task Goals. Most groups are formed to achieve certain tasks—to raise money for a church, to select a slate of officers for an organization, to develop a curriculum, to plan a party, etc. A primary purpose of a group is to accomplish a task.

Group-Maintenance Goals. A strong secondary goal, although not explicit, is to maintain the group and to provide self-maintenance for its members. Thus, most groups spend some time in activities not directly related to task goals.

Factors in group communication that influence the degree to which members communicate and the relative time devoted to either task or maintenance goals include the following:

Longevity. The length of time a group will function influences group communication. For example, a group formed to provide sandbags along a riverbank to thwart an impending flood would have a relatively short time span. More attention would be directed to task goals than to group-maintenance goals. The group would more likely have an autocratic, rather than a democratic, leader.

Size. The larger the group, the less the opportunity for individuals to communicate with all other members; smaller groups provide greater opportunity for interaction. As a general concept, problem-solving conferences benefit from small groups, and information-giving conferences could include much larger groups. Small groups tend to be informal; large groups tend to be more formal with strict rules of order.

Personal Expectations and Perception. Each group member comes with certain personal expectations and perceptions about how the group will operate, about the role of members, and about the leadership style to be used. The degree to which the assigned function of the group agrees with expectations and perceptions of the individual strongly influences communication. Agreement leads to harmony; disagreement leads to conflict and disunity.

Status of Members. Particularly when groups are formed from members of a larger organization, participants come with varying degrees of status. The member with the highest status is usually the one who is listened to most, is directly addressed most, and is most often called on for opinions and judgments.

Group Norms. As a group functions over time, certain standards of behavior and group conduct evolve. Starting on time or starting ten minutes late, joking about absent members, playing on words, and seating by status level are examples of norms that develop both from group behavior and from leadership style. As these norms become solidified, communication becomes greatly influenced by them and behavior patterns also become firm.

Communication Networks. The communication network evolves from the several factors just described, even though one particular network may have been designated in advance. Networks are usually described in terms of schematic models such as those shown in Figure 12–1. Communication networks are important to understand because (1) the number of other members with whom each member may communicate influences individual satisfaction; (2) short-term tasks, such as placing sandbags to prevent floods, are best accomplished with limited communication contacts; (3) the greater the number of communication contacts available for each member, the more effective will the group be in achieving group-maintenance goals. From a leadership point of view, the group leader can be more effective when the network and ways to control it are understood.

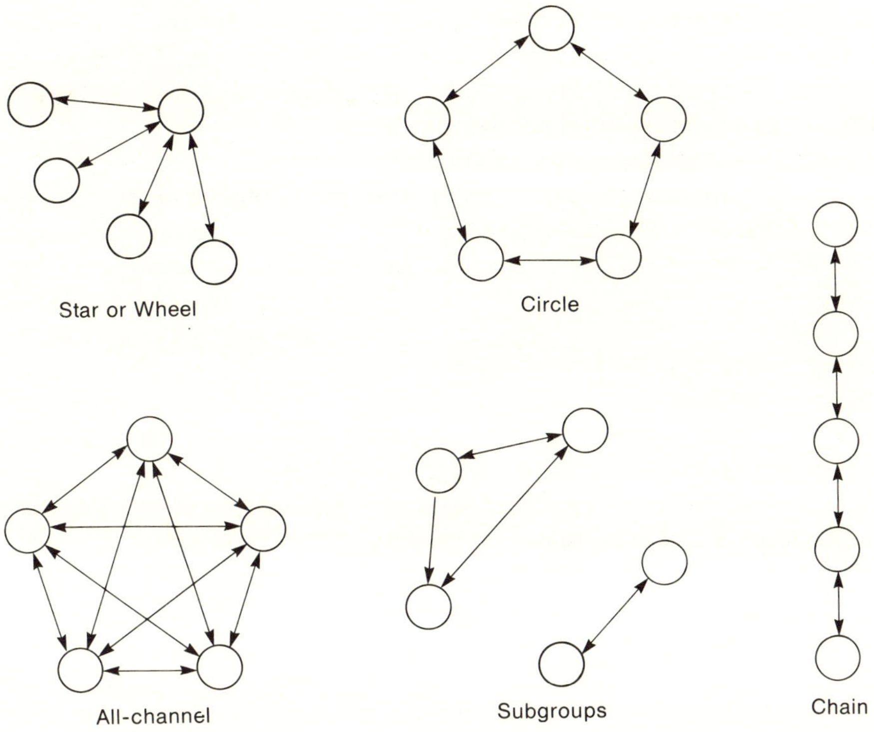

FIGURE 12–1 Group Communication Networks

Place in the Curriculum

Interpersonal communication study may be found throughout the curricula of colleges and universities in such a subject areas as speech, psychology, sociology, social work, and business. It is offered either as a separate course or as a portion of broader courses in communication.

Although it is generally a college-level subject, interpersonal communication can provide a valuable background for secondary school students studying business English. Perception, empathy, and an understanding of sending and receiving skills are critical factors in written communication planning and word selection.

Nature of Instruction

Although considerable lecture and discussion time should be devoted to the study of interpersonal communication, genuine understanding and skill in face-to-face communication are probably best developed through laboratory-type experiential activities.

The term *dyad* is used in most texts as a synonym for two-person groups which form the basis for much classroom activity. Additionally, three-, four-, five-, and six-person groups are used for discussion topics, interpersonal "games," and interpersonal behavior in groups.

In some schools where interpersonal communication receives considerable emphasis, "management" laboratories containing one-way glassed-in observation booths, sound systems, and videotape playback equipment have been developed. In any case, movable chairs in the classroom are desired for this purpose.

Sample Activities

Because the nature of instruction is activity-centered, this section will detail some typical activities. For further examples, instructors should consult any of the textbooks and accompanying manuals listed later in the chapter.

A First-Day Activity

Students generally are not familiar with their classmates on the first day of class and are, perhaps, hesitant to strike up relationships. At the same time, they probably are hesitant about accepting the role of feedback and the place of nonverbal communication in the communication process. A good first-day activity can be called the "mixer."

The mixer activity requires that all chairs be moved to the sides of the room. Then, ask students to rise and move or mill about the room for about three or four minutes. They cannot look at any others; they cannot touch others; they cannot speak to others. After the three or four minutes, instruct the class to continue doing the same thing, except that, during the next three or four minutes, they make physical contact—touch others—as they near them. At the end of this period, instruct the class to make eye contact with others and shake hands; however, no words should be spoken. After a couple of minutes of this activity, call "Stop!" Then instruct each student to retreat to the seats with the last person met. The pairs should then spend about five minutes learning all they can about each other.

At the end of the mixer exercise, hold a debriefing session built around these concepts:

1. The reaction of people to others at various degrees of contact—from situations where no feedback is possible, progressing to situations where somewhat intimate disclosures are made
2. The role of feedback—both verbal and nonverbal—in communication
3. The effect of being able to meet someone new during the first class session

Some authorities suggest that, after two people have had a discussion, two groups—four people—sit together to learn about each other. In this way, four will make new acquaintances. The mixer is a desirable activity for almost any course in communication or behavior where students will continue to interact throughout the semester.

Feedback Activities

The importance of feedback to effective communication is paramount, and several activities may be used to demonstrate the function of feedback. Such activities involve one activity without feedback possibilities and another with appropriate feedback.

Activity 1

Have a volunteer attempt to describe a figure which each class member will attempt to duplicate with a paper-and-pencil drawing, such as the following:

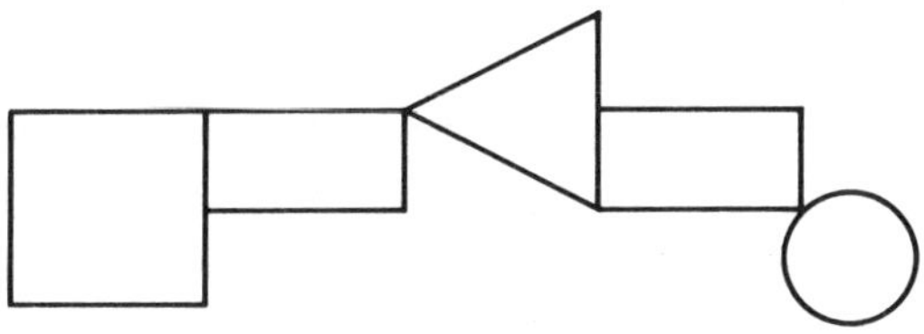

Give the volunteer the drawing with instructions that he or she should describe it as best as possible without the use of gestures and without entertaining any questions from the class. After the class has attempted this drawing, have the volunteer describe *another* drawing with a change in symbols and sequence. In this case, however, questions from the audience may be entertained and gestures may be used. The difference in accuracy will usually prove the value of feedback to communication effectiveness. This activity should be followed by class discussion.

Activity 2

Have the class form in groups of four or five to practice feedback. One member of the group should be given a statement in advance with which to open the discussion. Such statements may be on current events or about school situations. Examples are:

Accounting is the best major.
The Republicans have the best economic philosophy.

Equality of the sexes is an overdone theme.
College athletics should be eliminated.

Such statements are dogmatic and normally require some support if others are to accept them. The person making the statement should have given some thought to the topic and should be prepared to give it backing. During the group discussion, have one member act as an observer to note the kinds of actions that elicited a response. Were questions, rephrasing, or contradictory statements used to get the speaker to expand on the subject? The recorder should be informed that feedback is ongoing—once the discussion begins, everything said is a form of feedback to what was previously said. The recorder should also attempt to note any forms of nonverbal communication. Did some members simply nod their heads? Did some make facial gestures of agreement or disagreement? The key to the success of this exercise is to select controversial topics for discussion.

Perception Activities

Several perception exercises are available, and one of the all-time favorites is the serial communication activity. Select a picture from a magazine or newspaper showing people in action with background scenery. Many magazine advertisements could be used for this exercise. Select three or four volunteers who will leave the classroom. Then, show the picture to one volunteer. That person will then describe the picture to one of the others in front of the class. The class will not have seen the picture, of course. Then, the one who has just had the picture described will describe to the next volunteer, and the procedure will be repeated until the last volunteer describes it to the class. Finally, show the picture to the class. Hold a discussion about the various perceptions involved.

Another aspect of perception is the perceptual image people get when reading. One effective way to bring out such perceptions is to have students read a simple short story and then ask them to consider a series of response comments about it. In the following example, various perceptions are involved.

> A police officer arrested the owner of a company for breaking the law. His car was a late-model Mercedes. Officer Jones took caution to assure the accused of legal rights. Although the president of the company felt employees should support the image of the company during their off hours, no action was to be taken in this case.

A list of sentences related to the story follow. Students should be asked to indicate which ones are true (T), which ones are false (F), and which ones are questionable (Q).

1. Someone was arrested for a traffic violation.
2. A late-model car was involved.
3. The arresting officer used discretion in informing the violator.
4. The president's action protected himself.
5. The president wanted to protect the image of the corporation.
6. The man arrested was the owner of a company.
7. Officer Jones arrested the owner of a company.

All seven statements are questionable for these reasons:

1. The story made no mention of a traffic violation.
2. A car is described, but nothing in the story states that the car was involved in the incident. Who owns the car?
3. Officer Jones was not necessarily the arresting officer.
4. The owner was arrested, but the owner is not necessarily the president.
5. The company is not necessarily a corporation.
6. The owner may have been a woman.
7. Again, Officer Jones was not necessarily the arresting officer.

A follow-up discussion of this exercise will reveal several misperceptions. All owners are not necessarily men or presidents. Men are not the only ones to be arrested. All companies are not corporations. Generally, students will conclude that a good trial lawyer could tie knots in the typical witness by simply dealing with mistaken or generalized perceptions people have developed. A major advantage of using this type of exercise is that it lays the foundation for the development of effective sending and receiving skills.

Sending and Receiving Activities

Sending skills and receiving skills combine to form the crux of interpersonal communication. To say what one really means is the key to effective sending; to understand what has been sent is the key to effective receiving. Although this statement should go without saying, most communication inaccuracy results from lack of skill in sending and receiving. Expressing one's true feelings and emotions is most difficult at best. To understand another with empathy and consideration is also a most difficult task. Classroom activities directed toward the acquisition of these skills include self-disclosure through activities such as the consideration of circumstances under which a person is willing to disclose a series of personal biases, attitudes, and feelings. On the receiving end, students will benefit from an understanding of what is meant by effective listening, by appropriate responses to statements, and by assessing credibility. Some of the following exercises are typically used in this area:

Exercise 1

Because self-disclosure (the ability to reveal everything important to the message) is critical to effective communication, have the students indicate for each of the following topics whether they would practice self-disclosure to (*a*) a casual acquaintance, (*b*) a parent, or (*c*) a close friend:

Information about your income tax return
Your wildest fantasies
Your educational background
Things you like most about yourself
Things you dislike most about yourself
Your love affairs
Your views on politics
Your dietary habits
Your religious views and preferences

In this exercise, after individuals have made their analysis and responses, form groups of four or five to see if a consensus can be developed on each topic. The list of topics can, of course, be expanded to include a greater variety. Students will generally conclude that under certain conditions self-disclosure is extremely unlikely. Emotional states hinder the sending process; and, on the receiver's end, the development of empathy may be difficult.

Exercise 2

In groups of four, five, or six, have two members engage in a discussion with the remainder of the group serving as observers to record the kinds of feedback provided as the discussion progresses. Begin the discussion by having one of the pair make an opening statement such as:

The United States should have more nuclear-power plants.
Professional sports (athletics) do not serve the common good.
People who smoke should be permitted to do so when and where they please.
Police shows on television are a national disgrace.

Again, this list can be expanded. Controversial topics introduced by dogmatic statements are desirable, because they can generate serious discussion. Observers should attempt to isolate feedback statements that may be characterized by (*a*) empathy, (*b*) crediting self, (*c*) crediting others, and (*d*) time-dating, indexing, or classifying. Of course, statements may be characterized by lack of any of the above.

EXERCISE 3

This exercise is designed to introduce students to conflict and the difficulty of cooperating in the absence of feedback. It is called the "broken squares" exercise. (It was described by Kathleen S. Verderber and Rudolph E. Verderber in their *Instructor's Manual for Inter-Act: Using Interpersonal Communication Skills.*) The following is adapted from that source:

> Before class you will have to prepare as many sets of squares as you will need for the entire class [each set serving a team of five participants and one observer]. One set consists of five envelopes containing pieces of cardboard cut into shapes that can be used to form five squares that are 6″ by 6″. Although different combinations will produce some squares, only one combination of pieces will produce five squares.
>
> *Directions:* Cut each 6-by-6-inch square into the parts shown [here]. Like parts are lettered the same:

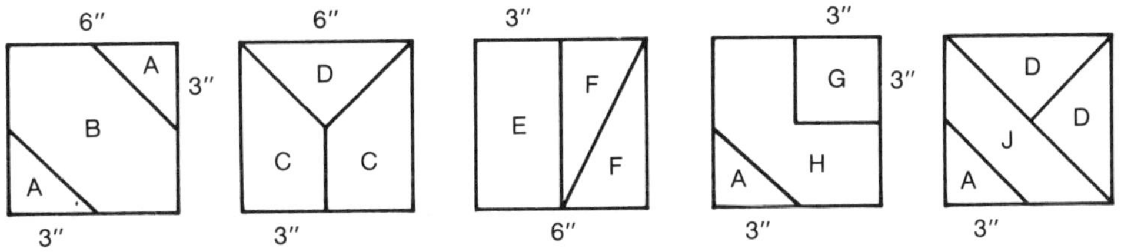

> Then mark five envelopes 1 through 5 and distribute the pieces as follows: Envelope 1: pieces D, H, and E; Envelope 2: pieces A, A, A, and C; Envelope 3: pieces A, D, and J; Envelope 4: pieces D, F, and B; Envelope 5: pieces G, F, and C. (When you have pieces distributed, write the numbers 1 through 5 on the back of the pieces going in those envelopes so pieces can easily be resorted for reuse.)
>
> Divide the class into groups of six—five participants and one observer. Distribute envelopes [one envelope per participant] but ask that envelopes not be opened until instructions have been given.
>
> *Instructions to be read and discussed with students:* "This is an exercise in cooperation. Each participant has an envelope containing pieces for forming squares. At the signal, the task for the participants is to form five squares of equal size. The group has not completed the task until every one of the participants has before him a perfect square of the same size as the other four. The observer is to watch what happens and see that the rules are observed. *Rules:* (1) Absolutely no talking; (2) you may not take a puzzle piece from someone else; (3) you may not indicate in any way that you would like a puzzle piece that anyone else has; (4) you may give away puzzle pieces to anyone, but you may not indicate where the piece might fit."

After most groups have completed the task (10–20 minutes), call for discussion. Have observers state behaviors they saw. Ask participants how they felt when they knew someone was holding a piece they needed; how they felt when someone had completed a square incorrectly, but thought they were right. Was there a climate that helped or hindered problem solution? How does this exercise demonstrate a cooperative versus a competitive orientation?

At the end of the exercise and the discussion, students should be aware of tendency toward competition even when cooperation is the goal; moreover, they should be aware of behaviors that can be identified as cooperative or competitive.

Exercise 4

A good exercise on establishing credibility of messages is to have students refer to statements such as those presented in Exercise 2 and to reword them in ways that are either self-crediting or crediting to others.

Group Communication Activities

Role playing is a characteristic of instruction in group communication. Here's a sample exercise that is designed to identify types of group leadership as well as to reveal group interaction.

Select three groups of about five or six students each. The remainder of the class will serve as observers. The purpose of each group will be to determine the amount of a dues increase for members of the student body. The student fee, which covers athletic tickets, the yearbook, and the student newspaper, is now $18 a year. An increase of at least $3 and possibly $5 is to be considered. The instructor will select one student to serve as group leader in each group. Give instructions to each leader as follows:

Group 1. This leader is to be authoritarian—even a demagogue. Rule the group with an iron hand. Be unprincipled. Cut off others when they are speaking. Attempt to get your own way. You want a $5 increase. Let the public be damned.

Group 2. This leader is to be weak and undecided. Let others do the talking; don't attempt to assist in reaching a consensus. Let the discussion wander off the topic. Even assist in the wandering.

Group 3. This leader is to be democratic and to practice desirable group-leadership traits. Permit others to make contributions. Call on those who indicate a desire to contribute and elicit a response from hesitant ones. Summarize the discussion frequently. Show respect for the contributions of others.

Within each group, assign roles as follows: (1) one participant should be steadfast in a desire to have no increase in the fee; (2) a second member should stand firm on a maximum of $3; and (3) a third member should argue for a $5 increase but be willing to accept $3 as a compromise. The other member or members should be undecided and willing to listen to arguments.

Some arguments for the increase are that the cost of athletic equipment and facilities has risen with inflation, and that advertising revenue is not adequate to cover the costs of the yearbook and the newspaper. On the other hand, arguments against an increase include the following: A reduction in the athletic program may be desirable; a more aggressive campaign to increase advertising revenue could offset added costs; the students who don't attend athletic events and don't care about the newspaper should not be forced to pay for the increase.

Following each presentation, have the observers as well as the participants rate the group process on a semantic-differential scale, such as:

cooperative	1	2	3	4	5	6	competitive
lively	1	2	3	4	5	6	drab
productive	1	2	3	4	5	6	nonproductive
warm	1	2	3	4	5	6	cold

Then, have the observers and participants rate the leader on a similar scale:

friendly	1	2	3	4	5	6	unfriendly
democratic	1	2	3	4	5	6	dogmatic
helpful	1	2	3	4	5	6	a hindrance
good	1	2	3	4	5	6	bad
persuasive	1	2	3	4	5	5	nonpersuasive

After a short statistical analysis of the three groups, the class could then engage in a discussion of leadership styles and of the decision-making process.

An alternative is to have the group undertake the problem without an assigned leader. The same evaluation could be made, but the class would then have an opportunity to analyze the factors that led to one person's assuming the leadership role.

Out-of-Class or Homework Activities

A common criticism of the teaching-learning process in interpersonal communication is that most learning takes place in the classroom and that students don't have to devote much time to work outside the class. However, every textbook in the field contains adequate out-of-class assignments in the form of case analysis. Most, too, have communication analysis guides for student use in evaluating communication transactions that occur outside the classroom.

Additionally, interpersonal communication does constitute a body of knowledge. The material in most texts is identical, but each author seems to have created a unique set of descriptive terms or labels. Thus, vocabulary becomes a major consideration in evaluating student knowledge. A good out-of-class assignment is to have each student accumulate on 3-by-5-inch cards a glossary of terms encountered during the course. Each card includes the term, a brief definition, and an example of the use of the term. In this way, students not only add to their own vocabularies, but also are better prepared for examinations.

Testing and Evaluation

Whether interpersonal communication is taught as a unit of a broader course or as a subject by itself, evaluation of student accomplishment may take several forms.

Objective Examinations

Objective examinations of the multiple-choice and true-false types are helpful in assessing mastery of subject matter. Here are examples of each as used in most courses:

Directions: Circle the correct response for each item.

1. When a person standing by the side of the road raises a hand with the fist clenched and the thumb pointing in the direction an approaching car is going, one of the following is not descriptive of the action:
   (*a*) Kinesic communication
   (*b*) Emblem usage
   (*c*) Nonverbal aid
   (*d*) A perception check

Answer: Responses *a, b,* and *c* are true; *d* is not descriptive of the action.

2. Which of the following is an empathic response to the statement: "I did such a terrible job on the exam; I'm afraid to see the teacher"?

(*a*) He won't even remember you.
(*b*) I felt the same way after my accounting exam.
(*c*) Maybe it's a good lesson; you might study harder next time.
(*d*) He's a lousy teacher anyway. I wouldn't be afraid.

Answer: Response *b* is the statement that gets in step with the speaker and is closest to a true supporting attitude.

Directions: Decide whether each item is true or false.

1. Empathizing is correctly identifying and responding to the affective state of another person. (*true*)
2. Body language is a form of nonverbal communication. (*true*)

Essay Examinations

Short-answer essay questions can help determine student understanding. Such essay items as the following are appropriate:

Discuss briefly what is meant by self-disclosure.
Distinguish among autocratic, democratic, and laissez-faire styles of group leadership.

Performance Evaluation

By establishing a point reward system for classroom participation, the instructor can stimulate activity and, hence, learning. Points can be earned for the quality of oral presentations and of role playing.

Self-Evaluation

Graded on composition quality as well as on the understanding exhibited, a written report on learnings acquired and skills developed can contribute to the evaluation of student performance.

Integration of Interpersonal Aspects in Other Courses

Several paperback texts and workbooks are available for the study of interpersonal communication and permit the topic to be included as part of courses in business communication. The content is readily adapted to a block of eight to twelve class sessions or to a portion of each class session throughout the course. Because the concepts are similar to many taught in planning and developing tone in letters, interpersonal communication can provide a sound background for those aspects of written communication. Much of the material can be developed by the teacher without the necessity of a required text.

Acknowledgment

Exercise 3, pp. 277–78, from *Instructor's Manual for Inter-Act: Using Interpersonal Communication Skills* by Kathleen S. Verderber and Rudolph F. Verderber. © 1977 by Wadsworth Publishing Company, Inc., Belmont, California 94002. Reprinted by permission of the publisher.

Bibliography

BARNLUND, DEAN, ed. *Interpersonal Communication: Survey and Studies.* Boston: Houghton Mifflin Co., 1968.

BERGER, CHARLES R., et al. "Interpersonal Relationship Levels and Interpersonal Attraction," *Communication Yearbook I.* New Brunswick, N.J.: Transaction Books, 1977, pp. 245–260.

BERNE, ERIC. *Games People Play.* New York: Grove Press, 1964.

BRAMMER, LAWRENCE. *The Helping Relationship: Process and Skills.* Englewood Cliffs, N.J.: Prentice-Hall, 1973.

COLLINS, B. E., and H. GUETZKOW. *A Social Psychology of Group Process for Decision Making.* New York: John Wiley and Sons, 1965.

FILLEY, A. C. "Committee Management: Guidelines from Social Science Research." *California Management Review,* vol. 13, no. 1 (Fall 1970), pp. 13–21.

HARRIS, THOMAS A. *I'm OK—You're OK.* New York: Harper and Row, 1969.

HOCHBERG, JULIAN E. *Perception.* Englewood Cliffs, N.J.: Prentice-Hall, 1971.

HUSEMAN, RICHARD C., et al. *Readings in Interpersonal and Organizational Communication.* 2d ed. Boston: Holbrook Press, 1973.

JAMES, MURIEL, and DOROTHY JONGEWARD. *Born to Win.* Reading, Mass.: Addison-Wesley Publishing Co., 1972.

JANDT, FRED E. *The Process of Interpersonal Communication.* San Francisco: Canefield Press, 1976.

KELTNER, JOHN W. *Interpersonal Speech Communication.* Belmont, Calif.: Wadsworth Publishing Co., 1970.

KLEIN, GEORGE S. *Perception, Motives and Personality.* New York: Alfred A. Knopf, 1970.

LARSON, CHARLES A. *Communication: Everyday Encounters.* Belmont, Calif.: Wadsworth Publishing Co., 1976.

LEAVITT, HAROLD J. *Managerial Psychology.* 4th Ed. Chicago: The University of Chicago Press, 1978.

LETH, PAMELA C., and J. F. VANDEMARK. *Small Group Communication.* Menlo Park, Calif.: Cummings Publishing Co., 1977.

LEWIS, PHILLIP V. *Organizational Communication: The Essence of Effective Management.* 2d ed. Columbus, Ohio: Grid Publishing, Inc., 1980.

MEHRABIAN, ALBERT. *Silent Messages.* Belmont, Calif.: Wadsworth Publishing Co., 1971.

NICHOLS, RALPH G., and LEONARD A. STEVENS. *Are You Listening?* New York: McGraw-Hill Book Co., 1957.

RICHARD, JUDY. *Communication* (Guide to Transparencies). San Jose, Calif.: Lansford Publishing Co., 1973.

RUBEN, BRENT D. *Human Communication Handbook: Simulations and Games.* Vol. 2. Rochelle Park, N.J.: Hayden Book Co., 1978.

———, and RICHARD W. BUDD. *Human Communication Handbook: Simulations and Games,* Vol. 1. Rochelle Park, N.J.: Hayden Book Co., 1975.

SCHNEIDER, ARNOLD E., et al. *Organizational Communication.* New York: McGraw-Hill Book Co., 1975.

SCHUTZ, W. C. *FIRO: A Three-Dimensional Theory of Interpersonal Behavior.* New York: Holt, Rinehart and Winston, 1958.

SILVERMAN, ROBERT E. *Psychology.* 2d ed. New York: Appleton-Century-Crofts, 1974.

STEWART, JOHN. *Bridges Not Walls.* 2d Ed. Reading, Mass.: Addison-Wesley Publishing Co., 1977.

——— and GARY D'ANGELO. *Together: Communicating Interpersonally.* Reading, Mass.: Addison-Wesley Publishing Co., 1975.

TIMM, PAUL R. *Managerial Communication: A Finger on the Pulse.* Englewood Cliffs, N.J.: Prentice-Hall, 1980.

VANDEMARK, JOANN F., and PAMELA C. LETH. *Interpersonal Communication.* Menlo Park, Calif.: Cummings Publishing Co., 1977.

VERDERBER, RUDOLPH F. *Communicate.* 2d ed. Belmont, Calif.: Wadsworth Publishing Co., 1978.

WEINTRAUB, DANIEL J., and EDWARD L. WALKER. *Perception.* Belmont, Calif.: Brooks/Cole Publishing Co., 1966.

WOFFORD, JERRY C., et al. *Organizational Communication.* New York: McGraw-Hill Book Co., 1977.

Section IV

Organizational Communication

Chapter 13

Organizational Communication

Raymond L. Falcione

For more than two decades interest in the area of organizational communication has been growing. Departments of communication, business, management, journalism, sociology, psychology, and secondary education, to name a few, are increasing their attention to this area. Surveys by Downs and Larimer and Pace and Feingold support statements of this quite phenomenal growth.[1,2]

Part of the reason for this growth is student demand for educational experiences which will have direct bearing on future employment. Since we are all members of organizations in one way or another, the development of effective communication skills within organizational contexts is extremely important. This emphasis on skill development can be helpful to the career-oriented student.

Philosophically, the emphasis on skill development and a career orientation can be troublesome for those who are concerned about sacrificing theory to teach skills. This is certainly a legitimate concern. However, it is my opinion that courses in organizational communication can be taught effectively by incorporating both theory and skill development. In fact, Spicer reports that instructors in organizational communication tend to perceive theory and skills as being equally important.[3] Using a modified Delphi technique to determine which communication competencies were most important for students to acquire, Spicer found of the forty-four competencies listed, eighteen could be viewed as primarily skills-oriented, nineteen could be viewed as primarily theory-oriented, and the final seven could be viewed as both theory-oriented and skills-oriented.

Eadie specifies three major end results for the student majoring in organizational communication:

1. The ability to display a broad-based conceptual understanding of communication as event and process
2. The ability to demonstrate proficiency in interpersonal skills
3. The ability to integrate this specialized knowledge about communication theory and skills with a general body of knowledge and [the ability] to apply this integrated knowledge in organizational settings[4]

While the above three end results suggested by Eadie are useful, they could apply to anyone majoring in communication generally. They don't sufficiently identify the specific areas of proficiency necessary for a student major in organizational communication.

The purpose of this chapter, then, is to develop a more comprehensive list of end results for a student majoring in organizational communication, recommend a classification system which purports to establish parameters for the field of organizational communication, and suggest some specific instructional strategies which are capable of integrating both theory and skill development.

End Results for Organizational Communication Majors

Below are the abilities which I feel a student majoring in organizational communication should possess:

1. Ability to display a conceptual understanding of intrapersonal, interpersonal, and group communication processes
2. Ability to display a conceptual understanding of organizational and environmental interface processes
3. Ability to display a conceptual understanding of behavior unique to the organizational context, with particular emphasis on end result or outcome variables such as job satisfaction, motivation, productivity, effectiveness, climate, change, and innovativeness
4. Ability to display a conceptual understanding of instructional paradigms and techniques designed to develop communication skills in organizational members
5. Ability to display a conceptual understanding of software/hardware media technologies in organizations such as written, audiovisual, and electronic media
6. Ability to display a conceptual understanding of systems theory as a means for viewing and diagnosing the nature of organizations
7. Ability to display a conceptual understanding of research methodology, including research design, instrumentation, data analysis, and field research strategies

8. Ability to integrate the above conceptual processes with specific behavioral skills as they relate to organizational settings and within organizational environments

The above list demonstrates for me those conceptual areas which should be required of an individual majoring in organizational communication. It requires an eclectic perspective which reaches far beyond the traditional speech communication emphases. If these end results are to be obtained, the student may take course work in fields such as journalism, organizational behavior, industrial and organizational psychology, social psychology, instructional technology, statistics, and computer science.

Organizational Communication Classification

In his study of communication as a scholarly discipline, Mortensen notes that "since the subject lacks either fixed boundaries or universally recognized dimensions of inquiry, the search for fundamentals required some arbitrary decisions about what to underscore and what to omit."[5] What is suggested of the general field of communication is equally applicable to the narrower area of organizational communication. The purpose of this section is to recommend an organizational communication classification system which can be viewed as major areas of concern in the teaching of organizational communication.[6-8] These classifications will hopefully provide parameters for what should be covered in an organizational communication program.

1. *Interpersonal Communication in Organizations.* This classification deals with the analysis of factors relative to the interpersonal situation in the organization, originating in the dyadic relationship, the work group, or in conferences.

   The concepts analyzed may include credibility, interpersonal trust, status, nonverbal variables, cognitive similarity, roles, redundancy, feedback, listening, and semantics.

   The topics in this classification may include superior-subordinate relationships, transactional analysis, counseling, conflict, perception, human relations, managerial style, and personal characteristics of managers and subordinates.
2. *Intragroup Communication in Organizations.* The literature in this classification may include the dimensions of interpersonal communication already discussed with regard to organizations, but are distinguished by the fact that the interacting parties are members of the same group.

   The groups analyzed may include specific functional departments, line, staff, labor, management, consumers, government bodies, project groups, and small work groups.

The topics in this classification may include participation, conflict, cohesion, task or maintenance roles, group size, individual behavior in groups, and group productivity.

3. *Intergroup Communication in Organizations.* The literature in this classification may include the same dimensions of interpersonal and intragroup communication, but the distinguishing element is that the interacting parties are representative of different groups.

   The groups considered may be different departments in the same organization, line-staff relationships, labor-management relationships, organizational interface with customers, and governmental interface with taxpayers, other agencies, or both.

   The topics in this classification may include coordination, collaboration, intergroup conflict, interorganizational conflict, negotiation, effects of hierarchical organization, influence of interest groups, and external communication such as public relations and advertising.

4. *Communication Factors and Organizational Goals.* This classification may include analyzing the influence of causal communication factors on the intervening and end-result variables in the organization.

   Some of the causal communication factors may include communication attitudes, communication satisfaction and expectations, and communication planning.

   Some of the intervening and end-result variables may include organizational performance, morale, conformity to plans, adaptability, organizational change, productivity, and organizational effectiveness.

   The topics in the classification may include organizational climate, job satisfaction, decision making, problem solving, organizational change, participation, leadership, motivation, innovation, adaptability, productivity, and effectiveness.

5. *Skill Improvement and Training in Organizational Communication.* This classification is concerned with communication skill improvement (verbal, written, and nonverbal), including public communication, meetings, group process, writing skills, listening, and interpersonal skills applicable to persuasive contexts, interviewing, and counseling.

   Areas dealt with may be oriented toward individual communication-skill development as well as an emphasis on the techniques of training within organizational contexts.

   Topics in this classification may include the design of training needs, materials, techniques, learning principles, training laboratories, games, role playing, programmed instruction, discussion techniques, and the use of the film and videotape.

6. *Communication Media in Organizations: Software and Hardware.* This classification may relate to both software and hardware including oral media, written media, telephonic media, audiovisual media, and electronic media.

   Some of the topics in this classification may include document retrieval systems, information systems, and computer capabilities.
7. *Communication System Analysis in Organizations.* This classification is concerned with the overall organization or subunits thereof: communication evaluation, communication audits, communication networks, communication diffusion, and organization development.

   Some of the topics in the classification may include communication network structures, information requirement analysis, data base models, change-agent topics, general systems theory, cybernetics, and organizational climate.
8. *Research Methodology in Organizational Communication.* This classification emphasizes research instruments and scales employed in the diagnosis of organizational communication. Emphasis is placed on specific field research strategies, including problems, techniques, and data analysis.

Obviously, the eight classifications are not being suggested as areas to be covered in a single course. They do, however, represent for me, at least, the rough parameters of organizational communication. A graduate of an organizational communication program should possess a theoretical and behavioral understanding of the above classifications.

Instructional Strategies Which Integrate Theory and Skill Development

There are many possible strategies for the integration of theory and skills, but, for the purpose of this chapter, I would like to discuss three designs which, in my opinion, are essential to a viable organizational communication program. They are (1) field research, (2) course work which integrates theory and skill development, and (3) internships in organizational communication.

Field Research in Organizational Communication Classes

One of the best ways to augment and integrate the theories presented in organizational communication is to test some of those theoretical assertions in an ongoing organizational environment, by conducting correlational analyses which measure various end-result or outcome variables as a function of communication variables.

Another way is to conduct field research which is primarily descriptive of perceptions, attitudes, and behavior. A communication audit is an excellent procedure to be used in this type of analysis.

A course incorporating field research activities allows for an integration of theory and skills in a very meaningful way. If it is assumed that the research eminates from the theory, this type of course provides both students and instructor with opportunities to develop relevant skills in analyzing theoretical premises. Depending on the specific nature of the research activity, a course of this type allows for development in most, if not all of, the above classifications. This kind of activity could prove invaluable to students by exposing them to literature review, research design and implementation, data analysis, and data presentation, which go beyond the classroom environment.

Guidelines in Selection of the Client Organization and Instructional Strategy

There are several critical factors which an instructor must deal with prior to and during a course designed as a practicum in field research. They are reflected in the following steps:

1. Establish contact with a client organization long before the course begins. If contact is made during the semester prior to the course offerings, you will have enough time to negotiate mutual expectations with the organization's representative and structure the time schedule prior to the beginning of the course. This schedule should be part of the syllabus so that the students will know from the first day of class how extensive the time and energy requirements will be.
2. Make every effort to contact the individual who is in a position to make a decision concerning entry in the organization. It is a waste of time and energy to negotiate with an organizational representative who does not have the power to grant permission to do the research.
3. During the period of negotiation, be sure you can meet some need of the organization. Some time ago, I was negotiating a research project with a personnel director who asked what my research could do for the company, a large manufacturing firm. I said that I could provide information concerning employee satisfaction and how it may relate to certain communication variables. The personnel directed then expressed some misgivings about finding out how satisfied the employees were: "If you ask them how satisfied they are, they may begin to realize just how dissatisfied they really are. I'd rather not open a can of worms." With that remark, I realized that mutual expectations would not develop very quickly, and that I probably couldn't meet the company's needs. As it turned out, the personnel director was concerned about

how productivity might be a function of communication. We therefore negotiated an agreement so that those concerns could be met.

4. Realize the limitations you are working under and don't try to promise too much. For whatever reason, there may be the tendency to promise results which are beyond the capabilities or scope of the project. This should be viewed as a learning experience which is to be carried out in an organizational environment. For most of the students it will be their first exposure to this type of activity. I am suggesting that their inexperience should be seriously considered when mutual expectations are determined.
5. A liaison team comprised of organizational representatives should be formed. Once mutual concerns have been dealt with and the project has been conceived, it is important to work directly with a liaison group. Their internal contacts with other organizational personnel can be a tremendous help in setting up schedules, meetings, feedback sessions, establishing time parameters, and disseminating information.
6. Once the project parameters have been established and the liaison team formed, the nature of the research project must be clear to all parties involved. The client organization needs to know exactly what the research team is going to be doing, the method of data collection, time parameters, and who is going to be involved. A letter from the person in charge should always be disseminated throughout the organization to inform the parties of the research project and to stress its importance for the entire organization or unit involved.
7. A guarantee should always be made concerning anonymity, and should be adhered to at all times by everyone involved.
8. Clarify responsibility for costs. It has been my experience that the client organization is normally willing to assume certain costs such as postage, stationery, reproduction, computer time, and travel expenses. This is not always the case, however. Be sure financial requirements are mutually understood from the beginning.
9. Students should have as much opportunity as possible for participating in the decision-making processes throughout the semester. The instructor must do much of the initial work and establish some guidelines, but the instructional design should allow the students to carry most of the responsibility while the instructor acts more as a resource.

Advantages of Field Research Activities in Organizational Communication Classes

The advantages of doing field research in organizational communication classes can be significant. Such activities allow the student to

1. Integrate theory with practical application.
2. Participate in and experience their own "mini-organization" consisting of the class, which has goals, norms, status variables, conflict, leadership, coordination of activities, and delegation of authority and responsibility.
3. Observe the internal organizational communication system firsthand.
4. Diagnose the viability of the internal organizational communication system and apply theoretical criteria to real recommendations designed for the system's modification.
5. Actively participate in various types of data collection methodologies. The two methods which have worked well in the past is the combination of interview and questionnaire. The interview in particular provides the student with an excellent opportunity to gain insight into the dimensions of organizational behavior.
6. Interpret qualitative and quantitative data to be used as a basis for specific organizational change recommendations.

The above advantages exemplify my biases for conducting field research in organizational communication classes. It can be an exciting learning experience for all involved.

Course Work Which Integrates Theory and Skill Development

The purpose of this section is to describe a seminar in organizational communication taught at the University of Maryland and at the State University of New York at Buffalo during the spring semester of 1977. Prior to the beginning of the spring semester, Dr. Gerald Goldhaber, associate professor and chairman of the Department of Communication at SUNY-Buffalo, and I collaborated on a course design which, in my estimation, was both exciting and mutually rewarding. The course was a pilot endeavor, and has since been incorporated at the University of Maryland.

Course Objectives

The course explored the role of the internal and external communication consultant as an organizational change agent who relies on data gathered with social science tools and techniques to facilitate the communication development of an organization.

The specific course objectives were to:

1. Describe organization development (OD) as a framework with which communication consulting may occur

2. Define, diagram, and exemplify five different types of intervention used by consultants
3. Define, describe, and illustrate survey-guided development of organizations within the "catalytic" intervention model
4. Describe and illustrate the factors affecting the establishment of the consultant-client relationship
5. Define and illustrate the diagnostic and prescriptive functions of communication consulting
6. List, describe, define, and illustrate the types of communication-consulting intervention activities
7. Describe and illustrate intervention activities useful in managing organizational and interpersonal conflict
8. List and illustrate problems encountered by the communication consultant during intervention activities
9. List and illustrate ethical considerations of the communication consultant during intervention activities
10. Describe and illustrate the factors affecting the termination of the consultant-client relationship

Course Sequence and Activities

The purpose of this section is to provide a description of specific activities conducted throughout the course.

During the first ten weeks of the seminar, the six students enrolled in my class at Maryland and the six students enrolled in Professor Goldhaber's class at Buffalo became well grounded in theories, models, and methodologies of organization development.

The class format consisted of lecture/discussion of consultation theory as well as the use of relevant case studies for analysis. Only the students in the University of Maryland class participated in a three-hour-per-week internship with various government and private organizations. These internships were part of the course requirement and were conducted in the organizational development, personnel, or staff development departments of various organizations. Each week the students would keep a brief log of their activities, and a portion of each class was devoted to exchanging feedback on their experiences.

While the students were becoming familiar with consultation theory, Professor Goldhaber contacted four large, New York–based corporations with OD departments and a private New York–based communication consultant. We arranged for both classes to meet with the corporations' key OD department personnel and the communication consultant. The corporations consisted of two large chemical companies, a large insurance company, and a large consulting firm with a wide range of consulting activities.

In preparation for our meeting with the four corporations and the private consultant, both groups of students were to develop a series of questions to be answered by the corporate representatives and the private consultant. The questions fell under the following main categories: (1) structure; (2) personnel; (3) selection process, contact, and solicitations; (4) contracts; (5) nature of interventions and data gathering; (6) evaluation; and (7) ethics.

Both student groups exchanged the questions they developed, synthesized them, and drew up a final list. During the seventh week of class, the questions were sent to the corporate representatives and to the private consultant, each of whom in turn sent both classes real or hypothetical cases pertinent to their organization or situation. The students from both classes were to analyze the cases and make specific recommendations to the corporate representatives and private consultant during the meetings in New York. In other words, the students were being asked to apply their knowledge of consultation theory in the form of specific feedback to the individuals involved. The feedback was first presented in written form approximately one week prior to the trip to New York. During the week of the trip, four-hour meetings were scheduled with each organization and the private consultant. The meetings allowed the students to provide feedback and recommendations on the cases. Essentially, the students participated as consultants to the organizations and to the private consultant.

Also, during the meetings, the organizational representatives and the private consultant exchanged ideas and perceptions concerning the list of questions. Each of the seven main topics was thoroughly discussed.

During the last four weeks of class, the students continued their reading assignments and case analyses. We also spent a considerable amount of time processing our experiences. After the trip to New York, the students were in a much better position to understand consultation theory from an experiential perspective.

They were also in a better position to understand and empathize with some real problems encountered by internal and external consultants. One particular benefit derived from this experience was that the students were able to see some of the disparities between theory and practice *without* negating the viability of theory as a basis for skill development. Once the students became grounded in theory, their firsthand experience exemplified the theory and helped them to identify with it in a more realistic way.

Internships in Organizational Communication

In a recent article by Zimmerman, four "guiding principles" for organizational communication instruction were outlined: (1) academic programs should emphasize skills training, (2) academic programs must be constructed on solid principles of adult education, (3) academic programs should become more interdisciplinary, and (4) academic programs should help develop a commitment to responsible communication, to ethical professional behavior.[9] In my estimation, one of the more viable means of adhering to the above principles is through the initiation of an internship program. An internship in organizational communication can be described as a period of service which calls for practical and intensified student involvement in the ongoing activities of a specified organization. This involvement may take the form of conducting research and/or participating in organizational activities which mutually benefit the student, in specific learning, and the organization, in meeting its objectives.

Characteristics of Internships

Wolvin and Jamieson have provided six objectives of internships generally:

1. To learn specific components of the communication process
2. To develop and test concepts involving the communication process
3. To develop interpersonal (and organizational) facility in a communication work environment
4. To gain professional feedback on communication work
5. To provide an opportunity to develop and to demonstrate competence in communication
6. To contribute to career decision making[10]

Internships have become more relevant for students as well as academicians.[11] They provide the student with practical, on-the-job experience in numerous communication-related settings, and opportunities for career decisions through increased awareness and preparation.

At the University of Maryland, internships are taken for academic credit during one or more semesters. The student spends an average of eight hours per week at a client organization, and receives up to three hours of academic credit.

Students majoring in organizational communication at the University of Maryland have participated in internships by working directly with the director of communication in a major retail organization, have developed in-house newsletters, conducted attitude research, taken readership surveys, worked in training and development programs, and developed and conducted various organization development activities within private and public sector organizations.

Guidelines and Specific Characteristics of the Internship

The three key people in each internship are the academic adviser/coordinator, the field coordinator, and, of course, the student. After making initial contact with a client organization to determine the organization's needs, the instructor (academic adviser/coordinator) then selects a student who can meet the academic, emotional, and motivational requirements of the internship. It is important to note that the needs of the client organization must be very clear and the capabilities of the student intern must be known well enough so that the attainment of the internship goals can be assured.

After a judgment has been made about the organization's needs and the selected student's capabilities, a contract is negotiated among the three parties involved. The contract (see sample) states the specific nature, objectives, responsibilities, and mutual expectations of the internship. Upon completion of the internship, the student is required to submit a detailed account of his or her activities at the client organization. The account is evaluated by the

University of ——
Speech Communication Division
Communication Internship Contract

This agreement is made by and between the Division of Speech Communication (hereinafter called the "Division") and ____________________ ________(hereinafter called the "Organization").

The Division and the Organization hereby agree as follows:

1. To participate in the communication internship program, the purpose of which is to provide students of communication with an opportunity to receive practical experience in analyzing, preparing, presenting, applying, engaging in, and studying communication in all types of agencies, businesses, industries, and other organizations.

2. That the Speech Communication Division at the University of —— is recognized as the credit-granting, coordinating, and supervising sponsor of the communication internship program.

3. That qualified students will be selected for participation in the communication internship program. Interns shall be screened for specific skills relevant to the needs of the Organization.

4. That the Organization will accept an Intern only after an official representative of the Organization has interviewed the prospective Intern and given formal approval of the applicant.

5. That Interns shall be assigned to the Organization for approximately twelve weeks commencing at the second week of a semester and terminating at the end of the thirteenth week. Changes in the length of an assignment may be made when acceptable to the Division, the Organization, and the Intern.

6. That the Organization agrees to accept [number] Intern(s) for the ______ semester of the ______ school year for ______ hours per week. Each Intern will receive ______ credits for satisfactory completion of the internship.

7. That both the Organization and the Division have the right to release or dismiss an Intern from his or her duties at any time. Violations of the rules, regulations, or requirements of the Organization, the University and/or Division will be considered sufficient cause for dismissal.

8. That the Organization will provide direct supervision of the Intern.

9. That the Division will provide an academic adviser who will be responsible for coordinating the academic activities of the Intern.

10. That the Organization may provide compensation to Interns for services provided. Nothing in this agreement shall be construed so as to imply that providing compensation is obligatory or even desirable. This provision is permissive only.

11. That the Organization, the Division, and the Intern shall be responsible for providing the following evaluations of Intern performance:
    a. The immediate supervisor of the Intern in the Organization will submit to the Division a report evaluating the performance, progess, and accomplishments of the Intern no later than one week following the Intern's exit from the Organization. A copy of the report will be given to the Intern.
    b. The academic adviser of the Intern will make periodic on-site observations of the Intern's work, and will meet with the Organization supervisor to review the work of the Intern.
    c. The Intern will submit a written report of his or her assignment, performance, organizational relationships, and progress to the Divisional academic adviser. The report should include sections describing tasks, experiences in residence, ideas for improvement, training received, and abilities utilized. The report must be submitted within one week following the Intern's exit from the Organization.

Date: ____________ By: ________________________________
Chairperson, Speech Communication Division

Date: ____________ By: ________________________________
Academic Adviser

Organization ________________________________
(Name)

Date: ____________ By: ________________________________
Organization's Immediate Supervisor

Title: ________________________________

Intern ________________________________

Date: ____________ ________________________________
(Signature of Intern)

The Communication Internship Contract is a modification of the one developed at the University of New Mexico.

academic adviser and discussed with the student. A letter from the field coordinator is also requested. It is sent directly to the academic adviser, who makes a copy for the student, to be placed in the student's personal portfolio.

Advantages of the Internship

The benefits of the internship are obvious. It provides the student with opportunities unavailable within a classroom environment. The student is able to move away from the theoretical and simulated activities in the classroom to the real-world problems of communication in organizations. Additionally, the student has the opportunity to become a participating observer and facilitator of the ongoing activities and relationships which impact on organizational goals.

Further, it provides the student with a better awareness of career objectives and interests. Pragmatically, it also provides an opportunity for contact with professionals who could give the student insights into specific career goals.

Summary

The nature of instruction in organizational communication can take many forms. This chapter has considered three that are useful in learning about communication in organizations, and has attempted to deal directly with the theory-versus-skill development dilemma encountered by many instructors. Hopefully, with the presentation of the end results, the classification system, and the integrative instructional strategies, the organizational communication instructor will be more prepared to deal with this dilemma.

The field of organizational communication offers numerous possibilities for innovative instructional techniques which go beyond the constraints of the classroom environment. With the increased emphasis on career-oriented education, the employment of theory-based skill development makes considerable sense both philosophically and pragmatically.

Notes

1. C. W. Downs and M. W. Larimer, "The Status of Organizational Communication in Speech Departments," *Speech Teacher*, vol. 23 (1974), pp. 325–329.
2. R. W. Pace and P. C. Feingold, "Curricula in Organizational Communication," *Communication Education*, vol. 25 (1976), pp. 323–327.
3. C. Spicer, "The Identification of Communication Competencies Required by Future Business-Persons: An Application of the Delphi Method" (paper pre-

sented at the annual convention of the International Communication Association, Chicago, 1975).

4. W. F. Eadie, "Training Undergraduates in Organizational Communication" (paper presented at the annual convention of the International Communication Association, Berlin, 1977).
5. C. D. Mortensen, *Communication: The Study of Human Interaction* (New York: McGraw-Hill Book Co., 1972), p. ix.
6. H. H. Greenbaum and R. L. Falcione, *Organizational Communication 1974* (Urbana, Ill.: American Business Communication Association, 1975).
7. R. L. Falcione and H. H. Greenbaum, *Organizational Communication Abstracts 1975* (Urbana, Ill.: American Business Communication Association, 1976).
8. ———, *Organizational Communication 1976: Abstracts, Analysis, and Overview* (Urbana, Ill.: American Business Communication Association, 1977).
9. G. I. Zimmerman, "Future Trends in Academic Training in Organizational Communication," *Association for Communication Administration Bulletin,* vol. 25 (1978), pp. 19–23.
10. A. D. Wolvin and K. M. Jamieson, "The Internship in Speech Communication: An Alternative Instructional Strategy," *Today's Speech,* vol. 22 (1974), pp. 3–10.
11. For statistics on teacher demand, see U.S. Department of Labor, *Occupational Outlook Handbook* (Washington, D.C.: U.S. Department of Labor, annually).

Bibliography

GREENBAUM, H. H., and R. L. FALCIONE. *Organizational Communication 1977: Abstracts, Analysis, and Overview.* Urbana, Ill.: American Business Communication Association, 1979.

Chapter 14

Conducting Research in Business Communication

James M. Lahiff

THE COMMUNICATION RESEARCHER, like any other researcher, is seeking answers to questions. Regardless of the setting of the research or of the procedures to be employed, the researcher first observes some communicative behavior and then makes some sort of statement about the observations. The communicative behaviors being observed are limitless in possibilities, the main constraints being such factors as the imagination of the researcher and the willingness and accessibility of the subjects.

Dewey's steps of reflective thinking accurately describe the path followed by the communication researcher or, for that matter, by any scientist.[1] Since these steps have been widely incorporated into the teaching of problem solving in particular and group discussion in general, this is a natural approach for the communication teacher to take in explaining the scientific method of investigation. It is the scientific method which the communication researcher follows.

Basic Research Concepts

Independent, Dependent, and Intervening Variables

One of the most frequently used terms in the researcher's lexicon is "variable." The term is used broadly and without unanimous agreement as to its meaning. In general, however, a variable may be thought of as any thing or event that is distinguishable from other things or events. Implicit in the term is the notion that it may vary or change.

Although Kibler noted other types of variables also, it is most important that the researcher be familiar with independent, dependent, and intervening variables.[2] Independent variables are those which the researcher manipulates with the expectation that a changed dependent variable will result. Where a researcher attempts to measure the effectiveness of two different styles for counseling problem employees, for example, the independent variable would be the styles of counseling.

A dependent variable is one that is expected to change as a result of manipulating the independent variable. It is the change of the dependent variable that will be measured by the researcher. When a researcher attempts to determine the effect of different persuasive messages on life insurance sales, sales would be the dependent variable.

Intervening variables are used to explain the different dependent variables which sometimes result from the manipulation of the same independent variables. Since various factors may intervene in the relationship between the independent and dependent variables, their presence is used to explain disparities in the results. A researcher may attempt to measure the effectiveness of various methods of communicating compensation information to employees and use the retention of such information as the dependent variable. A possible intervening variable would be the differing motivations of the employees to retain the information. Intervening variables cannot be measured directly, but their presence is frequently inferred in research studies.

The Hypothesis

It is through a hypothesis that a researcher predicts the relationship between the variables under investigation. A hypothesis is an unproven guess by the researcher, and it is used to confirm or refute a theory. There are several possible sources of a hypothesis. It may develop from personal hunches or follow naturally from the result of some earlier research. Regardless of its source, however, it is a prediction by a researcher.

Internal and External Validity

A prime concern of any researcher is that the research be valid both internally and externally. Internal validity refers to the effect that the researcher's manipulations have on the results of the research. The greater the number of variables that are beyond the researcher's control in an experiment, the more possible it is that the effect of such variables will be mistaken for the effect of the researcher's manipulation. By questioning the internal validity of a study, one is asking if the experimental treatments made a difference in a specific experimental instance.[3]

External validity is concerned with generalizability, which answers the question "To what populations, settings, treatment variables, and measurement variables can this effect be generalized?"[4] In investigating the external validity of a study, one seeks to determine if the findings of the study are representative of more than the situation or environment in which the research was conducted, and, if so, to what extent could the findings be generalized. Goldhaber recognizes the lack of external validity in much of the research done in organizational communication. He cites the unwillingness of communication researchers to replicate earlier research as a major part of the problem of external validity.[5] Campbell and Stanley present an excellent treatment of factors which jeopardize either the internal or external validity of research.[6]

In order to ensure a basic understanding of the research process, the teacher should acquaint the student with the meaning of certain terms. The student should be able to read research studies in communication and identify the independent and dependent variables, as well as any possible intervening variables and their influence. The function of the hypothesis should be clear to the student, who should also be able to explain the concepts of internal and external validity.

Steps to Effective Research

Regardless of the nature of a research study, there are certain steps that the researcher should follow. While the emphasis on the steps may vary according to the research methods used, the sequence of those steps is quite uniform. These are the steps that are comprised in the research process:

1. Develop the problem statement. A researcher is able to make a problem statement only after extensive research into the area. As a result of intensive investigation into the related studies that have been done, as well as personal hunches, a researcher is able to progressively narrow the focus of the problem statement until it is as specific as possible. The researcher should continue to rework the problem statement until it is phrased in a concise and unambiguous fashion. An appropriate problem statement for a communication researcher might be that line workers experience difficulties in understanding and retaining the provisions of their group insurance plan.
2. Develop the hypothesis. Once the problem statement has been developed and refined, the researcher next develops a hypothesis or a set of

hypotheses. The hypothesis tentatively explains the problem posed in the problem statement and frequently suggests a solution to it. Ideally a hypothesis will include variables which can be observed and measured. Simplicity is a desirable characteristic in any hypothesis. The fewer the number of variables included in a hypothesis, the simpler it is thought to be. After having developed the problem statement indicated in item 1, the researcher might hypothesize that when line workers are presented insurance information in small groups, there will be better understanding and retention of that information.

3. Plan the research strategy. After the researcher has developed a hypothesis, the next step is to plan a strategy for testing the hypothesis. It is only through a well-thought-out strategy that a researcher is able to answer research questions in an objective fashion.

   According to Stone there are a number of questions for which the researcher seeks answers at this stage. These include:

   (*a*) Who or what shall be the focus of the study?
   (*b*) What attributes shall be observed?
   (*c*) In what setting shall the observations be made?
   (*d*) What method shall be used to analyze the data produced by the research?[7]

   In responding to these questions, the researcher is faced with various alternatives. The research process would be greatly simplified were there only one possible answer for each of the above questions; however, there are many from which the researcher must choose. It is not as though there is only one "correct" strategy, or design, to employ to test a given hypothesis. The researcher's major consideration at this point must be whether or not the strategy developed will elicit data appropriate for testing the hypothesis.

4. Conduct the research study. When the research strategy has been completely developed, the researcher is ready to study the relationship between the relevant variables. As a result of this study, the researcher will learn the extent to which the hypothesis is supported by the "facts" or data generated by the study. The researcher interested in the line workers' understanding and retention of insurance program information might first test all the participants about their knowledge of the insurance program and then divide the workers into two groups. The members of the first group might receive such information as they customarily do, through the usual formal channels. The members of the second group might be placed in small groups of workers where they would participate in question-answer sessions about their insurance with representatives of management. The researcher would then test the participants again in order to determine how much each individual had improved and how the two groups now differed in their knowledge

of the insurance program. The researcher would then determine if the data supported the original hypothesis—if those who received the insurance information in small groups did show greater understanding and retention than those who received it in the conventional way. There are numerous ways of testing such a hypothesis. A simple one would be to compare the mean scores of the first group to those of the second group.

5. Prepare the research conclusions. Having analyzed the data and the apparent relationship between variables the researcher now determines what conclusions appear to be justified. The researcher ascertains exactly what can be said concerning the results of the study. While it rarely happens that the truth or falsity of a hypothesis can be conclusively determined in a single research study, the results of a single study may indicate the profitability of pursuing the present line of research.

   The presentation of research conclusions should not be viewed as an end in itself but as the introduction of additional problem areas to be investigated. The step which actually follows the research conclusions step is the problem statement step, for the research process is both cyclical and unending.

Research Methods

Once the researcher has refined a problem statement into a hypothesis or into several hypotheses, the research strategy must be developed. The selection of an appropriate method for conducting research is a vital part of the research strategy. The researcher has the choice of a variety of research methods and, before making a selection, the researcher should be aware of the strengths and weaknesses of the different methods. Emmert has criticized much of the research in communication for the practice of relying on a single research method.[8] He believes that the research methodology used in a study will itself tend to distort the observations made. By using several methods instead of one, the researcher should get a more complete picture of the subject of the investigation. Emmert terms this "complementarity in measurement." Regardless of whether the researcher uses one or more than one method, however, the selection will probably be made from the following methods: surveys, interviews, observations, or methods of interaction analysis.

Surveys

Surveys represent the most commonly used method of collecting data. In many cases these are sample surveys. A sample survey is one in which the researcher surveys a representative part of the population of interest. There is usually an implicit assumption that the selected sample truly represents the population from which it was drawn and that the findings of the sample survey may be generalized to the population. In order to ensure the representativeness of the sample, care must be exercised in the sampling procedure. The sample used in a study may range from that which is completely random to that which is highly systematic. Warwick and Lininger provide thorough coverage on this topic.[9] An alternative to the sample survey is the survey in which an entire population is polled. While surveying all of the insurance executives in the United States may be too formidable a task, surveying those from a given company would be more easily accomplished. In the former situation a sample survey would probably be used, while in the latter case the entire population in question might be surveyed.

Surveys are conducted for a multitude of different reasons, but they are usually a search for facts, opinions, or attitudes. They may be conducted face to face through interviews or impersonally through the mail. The telephone is another frequent medium for conducting surveys. The interview and the questionnaire will be subjects of consideration in subsequent subsections of this chapter.

The Questionnaire

Since questionnaires are extremely popular for data collection purposes, it follows that thousands have been developed for use in organizations of all types. Job satisfaction and leadership styles have been popular subjects for questionnaires; however, communication has not been ignored. Many questionnaires have also been developed for the study of communication in general or for the study of specific aspects of communication. After determining the purpose of the study and the desirability of using a questionnaire, the researcher must determine the type of questionnaire to be used. The issue of structure must be resolved at this point. If the researcher is seeking very specific information, the questionnaire will probably be highly structured. If the researcher is using a questionnaire to get a global or general view of the respondents, the questionnaire will usually be less structured.

Guidelines for Developing Questions

An issue closely related to that of structure is that of the form of the questions to be used. Kahn and Cannell maintain that the appropriateness of open questions or closed questions depends on several factors.[10] By learning the answers to these questions the researcher will be able to decide on the most appropriate type of questions:

1. What is the purpose of the interview? If the researcher is primarily interested in classifying the respondents or placing their responses into predetermined categories, closed questions are superior. The open question is more appropriate when the researcher is attempting to get a broader picture of the respondent. It is through open questions that a researcher can learn how the respondents' attitudes are formed as well as the individual respondent's own unique frame of reference.
2. How knowledgeable is the respondent on the subject? By using open questions the researcher can accurately learn how much the respondent knows about the subject in question. When the researcher asks an employee of Company X, "Do you approve of the open-door policy at this company?", the employee's answer will reveal little. The researcher can't even be certain that the respondent understands the open-door policy. If, instead, the researcher asked, "What do you like or dislike about the open-door policy at this company?", much more will be learned. If one is constructing a questionnaire to be answered by personnel administrators regarding the effect of EEO regulations on hiring practices, more closed questions would be appropriate than if the questionnaire were to be administered to a random sample of business executives. Since the levels of knowledge about EEO would be more variable among the executives, the researcher should rely more on closed questions.

   This is not to say that it is not possible to determine the respondent's level of knowledge through closed questions. A series of well-planned closed questions can be used to ascertain the respondent's level of knowledge; however, it may take longer. It may also be more threatening to those respondents whose ignorance is slowly and painfully revealed.
3. How thoroughly has the respondent thought through the topic? The more clearly the respondent has thought through a topic, the more probable it is that closed questions will be successful. If, as with the subject of EEO regulations and business executives, the respondents have not thought much about the topic, the researcher can guide the respondents through the cognition process. When the researcher uses a closed question to learn the respondent's attitude toward a topic which has not been heretofore thought about, the respondent's comments may differ greatly from what they would have been if the respondent had been given the opportunity to ponder it beforehand.
4. How easy will it be for the respondent to talk about the topic? It is generally easy to respond to closed questions. Because of the ease in responding, it is less likely that the respondent will decline to answer. This same ease is responding, however, also allows unknowledgeable and unmotivated respondents to provide answers.

Open questions require more of a commitment by the respondent, for they are more difficult to answer. In using open questions the researcher must often motivate the respondent to answer, and success in using open questions frequently depends on the relationship established between researcher and respondent.

5. Does the researcher truly understand, prior to the interview, the environment in which the respondent functions? The more familiar the researcher is with the population being investigated, the more likely it is that the researcher can structure closed questions which will elicit the desired information. When researchers understand the background and present environment of the respondents, the researchers are better able to safely make assumptions about the respondents and to pattern the questions accordingly.

On the basis of the answers to these questions, the researcher should determine the extent to which open and closed questions will be used in the questionnaire. This is not always a clear-cut decision since an element of risk remains inescapable. It sometimes happens that a researcher, after considering those questions, concludes that closed questions are appropriate for the topic and population in question. A follow-up study may reveal, however, such a high degree of heterogeneity among the respondents that there had probably been great disparity in their interpretation of the closed questions asked of them. The information elicited through the closed questions would then be of questionable value. Conversely, it may happen that the decision to use open questions may be incorrect for the respondents, already very familiar with the topic and unwilling to devote the time required to providing complete answers.

It frequently happens that a researcher rightly chooses to use a combination of closed and open questions. When a questionnaire encompasses a variety of topics, the above questions should be answered by the researcher as they pertain to each individual topic. Thus, some topics may warrant closed questions and others require open questions.

Guidelines for Preparing Questionnaires

After recognizing the specific purpose of the questionnaire and identifying the probable respondents, the researcher will be able to ascertain the structure necessary to accomplish the goal of the study. There will remain, however, many other decisions to be made. These questions suggest some of the significant ones:

1. Is a questionnaire necessary? By this point the researcher is often so immersed in the project that a tunnel vision has replaced the detached objectivity which originally characterized his or her approach. Hell-bent

to begin the data collection, the researcher puts completion of the questionnaire above all else. It is not surprising that in this sort of a climate one is not inclined to debate at length whether a questionnaire is actually necessary. A little spadework at the library may reveal that others have already collected the same information. The findings from a variety of polling organizations, including the U.S. Census Bureau, are readily available and may eliminate the need for a questionnaire or at least may suggest modifications in the planned questionnaire.

2. Are any of the questions biased? A question is biased if it is easier for the respondent to give one answer than another. Two of the most common types of bias are content bias and timing bias. This question in a poll of managers, "Do you oppose the union as most managers do?" typifies content bias. If a questionnaire on labor-management relations were administered in an organization in the aftermath of a bitter strike, the results would be biased by the timing of the study.
3. Are the questions clear? The rules for good writing in general also pertain to the writing of questions. Is the vocabulary used appropriate for the educational level of the respondents? If the questionnaire is to be administered to a homogenous group of specialists, it is appropriate to use terminology unique to their specialization. If nonspecialists will also respond to it, the terminology must be equally understandable to either group.
4. Does each question clearly express the alternatives? In preparing a questionnaire the researcher must explicitly state whatever alternatives exist in the question. No matter how clear a given alternative seems to a researcher, unless it is stated as a part of the actual question, one can never be sure if the respondent perceives the alternatives as intended by the researcher. As an example, Payne presented these two questions:

   > Do you think most manufacturing companies that lay off workers during slack periods could arrange things to avoid layoffs and give steady work right through the year?
   >
   > Do you think most manufacturing companies that lay off workers during slack periods could arrange things to avoid layoffs and give steady work right through the year, or do you think layoffs are unavoidable?[11]

   In the first question the alternative of unavoidable layoffs was only implied. According to Payne 63 percent of the respondents said companies could avoid layoffs. In response to the second question 35 percent said layoffs could be avoided. By implying alternatives in a question the researcher relinquishes some control which should be maintained in order to ensure accurate responses.
5. What is the best form of response for a question? The "yes" or "no" format is probably the most frequently used format. While it is appro-

priate in many instances, there are occasions in which it is used when the situation is not appropriate. Instead of asking employees "Do you approve of this company's health plan?" and allowing for "yes" or "no" to be checked off, the questionnaire should also allow for a "don't know" or "no opinion" response. When a dichotomy is created where one does not actually exist, the responses generated will not reflect reality. A questionnaire should not force respondents into categories which do not accurately reflect them. Many times, of course, three response categories do not include all of the alternatives and it is necessary to provide more. A general guideline for structuring responses is that all alternatives should be included and that the choices should be mutually exclusive.

6. Is each question suitably precise? The employees of one organization were once given questionnaires which asked, "Do you approve of the fringe benefits provided by the company, or would you prefer a cafeteria approach in which employees have the choice of a variety of benefits?" When the results were being compiled it was discovered that the question was actually "double-barreled," having two questions under the guise of one. Since the question inquired into two areas, approval of fringe benefits and attitude toward the cafeteria approach, the researchers could not fully ascertain to which topic the respondents were responding.

The questionnaire is an effective instrument for data collection when used in a thoughtful manner. Its effectiveness depends in part on the researcher's willingness to heed suggestions such as those presented above. The mistaken notion that good questionnaires can be developed quickly and effortlessly has resulted in an overabundance of poor examples. Pretesting a questionnaire with a group similar to that which will eventually respond to it will also strengthen it as long as the researcher is willing to modify the questionnaire on the basis of feedback received from the pretest.

Interview

Because there are so many similarities between questionnaires and interviews the guidelines presented above pertain to both. A major difference between the two, however, is that in the interview the interviewer often reads the questions and records the respondent's answers, two functions performed by the respondent when answering a questionnaire. Another significant difference is the environment in which the interview is conducted. The face-to-face setting of the interview provides the researcher with additional opportunities to motivate the respondent as well as the chance to elicit additional information when it is felt necessary.

As with the questionnaire, the interview will vary according to the structure provided by the researcher. If the interviewer follows a schedule of closed questions, the interview is said to be highly structured. If, instead, the interviewer not only does not use a schedule but asks mainly open questions, the approach is unstructured. The more highly structured an interview is, the easier it is to quantify the findings. In order to develop a schedule of closed questions, it may be desirable to initially use open questions in a pilot test. On the basis of the respondents' answers to the open questions in the pilot test, it will be possible to construct questions which will include all the appropriate answer categories. In determining whether or not to use the interview for collecting data, the researcher should consider the strength and shortcomings of the interview as a research tool.

Strengths of the Interview

Researchers should use the interview for data collection if they are seeking:

1. A high rate of response
2. An opportunity for flexibility in approach
3. An opportunity to probe into responses
4. Interaction with a heterogeneous group

The response rate is usually better for interviews than for mailed questionnaires. It appears that people find it more difficult to turn down an interviewer than they do to discard a questionnaire. The interviewer is able to motivate the respondents and to clarify for them any questions which may be unclear. When the respondents' answers are incomplete or in some way inappropriate, the interviewer is able to get the respondent to elaborate. At times the researcher seeks information from respondents who may be illiterate or in some other way deficient in their use of the language. Although unable to respond to a written questionnaire, they may be able to contribute valuable information to an interviewer. It should be obvious that the interview does indeed have some unique advantages.

Shortcomings of the Interview

There are also shortcomings inherent in the use of the interview for collecting data. Some of the more commonly cited disadvantages of which the researcher should be aware are these:

1. Interviewer influence
2. Effect of the interview on interviewee
3. Expense of interviews
4. Variations in approach

There may be certain characteristics or traits in the interviewer which will affect the responses of the interviewee. Such variables as age, sex, and race of the interviewer may influence the respondents and their answers. For many respondents the interview itself constitutes an "event." Such individuals may respond to the uniqueness of the situation and provide those responses that they believe the interviewer wants. Interviews are time-consuming and are hence expensive. Also, interviewers must be trained, and that adds significantly to the total expense. With each successive interview interviewers may become more likely to alter their approach. Slight changes in factors such as emphasis, pace, or sequence of questions may result in altered responses. Before selecting the interview for data collection, the researcher should weigh its strengths against its shortcomings.

Direct Observation

In some research studies the researcher functions as a measuring instrument. After observing the behavior of individuals, the researcher records those behaviors which are relevant to the study being conducted. As with most research tools, one of the first issues which the researcher must address is that of structure. In highly structured observation the researcher has a well-developed plan for observing and recording those behaviors that are relevant for the study being conducted. In more unstructured studies there is less planning and a more open-ended approach. In determining the amount of structure that is appropriate, the researcher will consider such factors as the purpose of the study and the environment in which the research will be conducted.

As with any other research tool, there are certain limitations inherent in direct observation. Three of the most significant constraints are observer influence, observer inference, and sampling validity.[12]

It is indisputable that when people are aware that they are being observed, it will have an effect on their behavior. For that reason it is important that the researcher determine the extent of such influence and how best to minimize it.

One approach to recognizing such influence is to employ concealed observation. Through concealed observation the researcher is able to compare what was observed publicly with what was observed from concealment and thereby determine the differences between the two. There are, however, ethical questions surrounding the use of concealed observations, and the researcher should determine whether such an approach would be ethical.

Without concealed observation the researcher cannot accurately compare subject behavior in observer-free and observer-present situations. If the researcher determines that for ethical or other reasons that concealment is inappropriate, however, it appears that public observers have only a temporary effect on the behavior being observed. Research findings suggest that individuals quickly grow oblivious to the presence of observers.

It is possible for the researcher to minimize the effect of observer influence. Observing the behaviors of subjects in familiar surroundings is one way in which this can be aided. Another is by earning the acceptance of the subjects. If it is possible for an observer to become a routine fixture among the subjects before beginning to collect observations, that researcher will be more readily accepted by the subjects and hence will exert less influence on them.

The presence of a stranger in the midst of a work group may be perceived as threatening to some of the subjects. If subjects perceive an observer to be evaluating them, the feeling of threat may be exacerbated. If the observer refuses to interact at all with the subjects, that may be viewed as threatening. The observer must stress whatever procedures are unlikely to threaten people and likely to put them at ease and by so doing will be abe to minimize the effect of observer influence.

When employing direct observation the researcher observes behavior and records the observations. Between the observation and the act of recording, observer inference may be a mediating factor. As Kerlinger describes it, "The basic weakness of the observer is that he can make quite incorrect inferences from observations."[13] Observers sometimes allow their own preconceptions to "color" their observations. When the observer creates categories within which to record observations, the vaguer the categories, the more susceptible the observer is to the influence of observer inference. The more that the observer is expected to provide as the link between observing and recording, the greater the likelihood of observer inference.

The sampling procedure employed in direct observation is of critical significance. Invalid sampling may severely bias the data acquired or limit the generalizability of the conclusions drawn from the analysis of the data.

Two forms of sampling plans are especially recommended for field research involving the direct observation of behavior: event sampling and time sampling. Event sampling, as the name suggests, is the selection of events of a given class for observation. The communication researcher who observes all of the exit interviews conducted in an organization is doing event sampling. An obvious problem in event sampling is that of knowing when an appropriate event is to occur or of being able to recognize such an event when it does commence.

Time sampling is the selection of certain behavioral units for observation at different points in time. They can be selected in systematic or random ways in order to obtain samples of behaviors.

In summary, three basic considerations in the use of direct observation are observer influence, observer inference, and sampling validity. The researcher must also, of course, remain aware of such issues as reliability, validity, and proper categorization of observed behaviors.

Some other research methods closely related to direct observation are content analysis and the Q sort technique. In doing a content analysis the researcher creates categories and places units from a preselected stimulus into them. When a journalistic researcher analyzes newspapers for positive, neutral, and negative references to the stock market, content analysis would be an appropriate research method.[14] The Q sort technique is a way of rank-ordering items or stimuli and then subgrouping them for statistical purposes.[15]

Laboratory Research

In the minds of many, laboratory research and field research are exact opposites. As Miller points out, however, "all communication studies do not divide this neatly into scientific fish or fowl."[16] He has proposed that research be visualized on a continuum ranging from "pure" laboratory research to "pure" field research. There is no absolute difference between the two types. Whatever differences exist are matters of degree rather than of kind.

Characteristics of Laboratory Research

Laboratory research has three important characteristics:

1. *Structured Environment.* When the researcher creates communication networks and assigns subjects to them, that researcher is structuring the environment. The Leavitt study and those by Shaw illustrate some of the kinds of structuring that a researcher might do.[17]
2. *Use of Controls.* The second characteristic of laboratory research is that the researcher uses controls to identify source of variation. The physical manipulation of subjects within a given group is an example of control.

   Moreover, the selection procedures employed by the researcher can be used to exert control. These may govern the selection of subjects or of such things as selection of materials or selection of data. Control may also be exerted through the application of certain statistical tests deemed appropriate by the researcher. While the student should be able to think of other types of control, these are the ones found with the greatest frequency.
3. *Sample from Limited Population.* Another characteristic of laboratory research is the use of samples drawn from narrow parent populations. There are usually economic reasons for this; however, it presents a problem that the laboratory researcher must face. To how broad a population might the findings be generalized? Although the problem is

not restricted to laboratory research, it is especially severe in the laboratory.

Adapting the Laboratory to Business Communication Problems

A basic problem in laboratory research is that of simulating the business environment in the laboratory. The researcher should attempt to incorporate the most significant organizational variables into the laboratory setting. Two such variables of significance to the communication researcher are organizational size and the serial nature of communication.

While it is seldom possible to mirror actual organization size in the laboratory, the researcher should strive to preserve the effects of organization size. As an organization grows, subgroups are formed and hierarchies established. These features can be made a part of a laboratory study. It should not be difficult for any researcher to arrange an orderly division of subjects into subgroups or to provide the subjects with role descriptions and, thereby establish a hierarchy.

Much of the communication in any organization is of a serial nature, that is, it is transmitted through a number of links in the organization before reaching the intended receiver(s). For that reason it is an organizational characteristic that the communication researcher should be able to simulate. Researchers are able to do this through the creation of networks and the introduction of whatever types of obstacles which would be appropriate for the study being conducted. It is also possible to incorporate such variables as task interdependence or independence, career orientation, or feedback.

Since it is relatively easy to create an organizational environment there, the laboratory is an ideal site for conducting research in business communication. Through the provision of structure and controls the communication researcher is able to go beyond the description of that which has occurred and to explain communication behaviors.

Field Research

While it has already been pointed out that laboratory research and field research are not direct opposites, differences certainly do exist between them. When research is performed outside of the laboratory and in a more natural setting, there are certain characteristics that become significant. Foremost among them is the common network of which all of the subjects are a part. Unlike laboratory groups, which are structured for the purpose of research, field groups are natural in makeup and in environment. In addition to that, the group members share similar values and norms. It is not necessary for the researcher to attempt to create artificial varieties of such factors. The field researcher in organizational communication need not attempt to simulate differentiation between subjects because such differentiation is inherent in the organization in which the research will be conducted.

Advantages of Field Research

Such characteristics of field research suggest certain major advantages to it. Realism is one of the most significant of these advantages. Since the setting is a natural one, realism will be high. Another important advantage is that the research can be conducted inobtrusively with the research having minimal personal effect on the environment or on the subjects. Through field research it is also possible to collect data on a large number of variables.

One of the most significant disadvantages is that measurement is not as precise in field research as in laboratory research. It is often difficult to assess the influence of a given variable in field research. Also, it is often difficult to obtain the cooperation of organizations for field research since such cooperation often entails considerable effort on the part of the organization.

Field Experiments Versus Field Studies

To many, the idea of field research connotes situations in which the researcher has completely relinquished control, but such is not necessarily the case. Field research can be most accurately described by identifying the two distinct approaches which constitute it: field experiments and field studies.

Field experiments are characterized by carefully controlled conditions in a realistic situation; within that situation the experimenter manipulates one or more independent variables. Since field experiments involve the systematic investigation of phenomena in natural settings, external validity may be less of a problem than in laboratory research. Field experiments also lend themselves to the solution of practical problems.

A prime disadvantage of field experiments is that they are usually more expensive to conduct than are laboratory studies and they entail more of a commitment on the part of the cooperating organizations. Since field experiments often require extended contact between the researcher and the organization being investigated, there is also the possibility that the researcher's objectivity may diminish. Cook and Campbell provide thorough coverage on the subject of field experiments.[18]

Field studies are similar to field experiments in that variables are systematically measured in a natural setting. Field studies, however, are ex post facto in nature. Instead of manipulating independent variables the researcher observes and records some aspect or aspects of the present state of affairs in the organization. In most field studies the presence of confounding variables makes measurement less precise than for field experiments.

Much of what has been learned about organizations and about human behavior in organizations has been learned through field studies. Neither field studies nor field experiments, however, are themselves research methods. When discussing field research or laboratory research, the issue is mainly the locale in which the research will be conducted. On the basis of locale and whatever other factors are important, the researcher must select a research method such as those described earlier in this chapter.

Instructional Note

This chapter has presented those basic concepts in research with which the student should be familiar. The endnotes and the bibliography suggest sources which will provide the student with greater depth in the respective areas. The following describes some assignments which would be appropriate to reinforce the materials included in this chapter:

1. In groups of five the students should develop a strategy for a survey to be conducted on the campus. What will be the purpose of the survey? How will the respondents be selected? What barriers may be expected and how will they be overcome?
2. The groups of five used in the first question must now construct the questionnaire to be used in the survey. Group members should be able to provide a rationale for each question.
3. Each student should design a study in which direct observation is the resource method used. (Prior to this assign Webb et al., *Unobtrusive Measures: Nonreactive Research in the Social Sciences* as required reading [see bibliography at end of chapter].)
4. Each student should become familiar with one article describing a research study in communication which was conducted in a laboratory. Describe the study in detail to the class. Next, describe how this study might have been conducted in the field.
5. As in assignment 4, each student should learn about and describe a research study, but this time the focus is on a research study conducted in the field. The student must describe how the study might have been conducted in the laboratory.
6. Ask students to explain the following terms:

independent variable	dependent variable
intervening variable	hypothesis
internal validity	external validity
event sampling	time sampling

Notes

1. John Dewey, *How We Think* (Boston: D. C. Heath, 1933).
2. Robert J. Kibler, "Basic Communication Research Considerations," in *Methods of Research in Communication,* edited by Philip Emmert and William D. Brooks (Boston: Houghton Mifflin Co., 1970).
3. Donald T. Campbell and Julian C. Stanley, *Experimental and Quasi-Experimental Designs for Research* (Chicago: Rand McNally & Co., 1963), p. 5.
4. Ibid.
5. Gerald Goldhaber, *Organizational Communication* (Dubuque, Iowa: William C. Brown, 1974), p. 276.
6. Campbell and Stanley, p. 5.
7. Eugene Stone, *Research Methods in Organizational Behavior* (Santa Monica: Goodyear, 1978).
8. Philip Emmert, "Complementarity in Measurement," in *Methods of Research in Communication,* edited by Philip Emmert and William D. Brooks (New York: Houghton Mifflin Co., 1970).
9. D. P. Warwick and C. A. Lininger, *The Sample Survey: Theory and Practice* (New York: McGraw-Hill Book Co., 1975).
10. Robert L. Kahn and Charles F. Cannell, *The Dynamics of Interviewing* (New York: John Wiley & Sons, 1957).
11. Stanley L. Payne, *The Art of Asking Questions* (Princeton, N.J.: Princeton University Press, 1951).
12. John D. Hatfield, "The Development of a Category System for Analyzing Superior-Subordinate Communication Behavior" (unpublished dissertation, Purdue University, 1976). Most of the material on the direct-observation method was adapted from this dissertation.
13. Fred N. Kerlinger, *Foundations of Behavioral Research,* 2d ed. (New York: Holt, Rinehart & Winston, 1973), p. 538.
14. For thorough coverage of this topic see: O. Holsti, "Content Analysis," in *The Handbook of Social Psychology,* 2d ed., edited by G. Lindzey and E. Aronson (Reading, Mass.: Addison-Wesley, 1968).
15. Kerlinger.
16. Gerald R. Miller, "Research Setting: Laboratory Studies," in *Methods of Research in Communication,* edited by Philip Emmert and William D. Brooks (Boston: Houghton Mifflin Co., 1970).
17. H. J. Leavitt, "Some Effects of Certain Communication Patterns on Group Performance," *Journal of Abnormal and Social Psychology,* vol. 46 (1951), pp. 38–50. M. Shaw, "Some Effects of Unequal Distribution of Information upon Group Performance in Various Communication Nets," *Journal of Abnormal and Social Psychology,* vol. 49 (1954), pp. 547–553; and "A Comparison of Two Types of Leadership in Various Communication Nets," *Journal of Abnormal and Social Psychology,* vol. 50, (1955), pp. 127–134.
18. T. D. Cook and D. T. Campbell, "The Design and Conduct of Quasi-Experi-

ments and True Experiments in Field Settings," in *Handbook of Industrial and Organizational Psychology* edited by M. D. Dunnette (Chicago: Rand-McNally, 1976).

Bibliography

EMMERT, PHILIP, and WILLIAM D. BROOKS. *Methods of Research in Communication.* Boston: Houghton Mifflin Co., 1970.

FESTINGER, L. "Laboratory Experiments." In *Research Methods in the Behavioral Sciences,* edited by L. Festinger and D. Katz. New York: Holt, Rinehart and Winston, 1953.

GUETZKOW, HAROLD. "Communication in Organizations." In *Handbook of Organizations,* edited by James G. March. Chicago: Rand McNally, 1965.

JABLIN, FREDRIC M. "Superior-Subordinate Communication: The State of the Art." *Psychological Bulletin,* vol. 86, no. 6, (1979), pp. 1201–1222.

MUCHINSKY, P. M. "Organizational Communication: Relationships to Organizational Climate and Job Satisfaction." *Academy of Management Journal,* vol. 20 (1977), pp. 235–243.

NEUMAN, ELISABETH NOELLE. "Wanted: Rule for Wording Structured Questionnaires." *Public Opinion Quarterly* (summer 1970).

ROBERTS, K. H., and O'REILLY, C. A. "Measuring Organizational Communication." *Journal of Applied Psychology,* vol. 59 (1974), 321–326.

SCOTT, W. RICHARD. "Field Methods in the Study of Organizations." In *Handbook of Organization,* edited by James G. March. Chicago: Rand McNally, 1965.

WEBB, EUGENE J., DONALD T. CAMPBELL, RICHARD D. SCHWARTZ, and LEE SECHREST. *Unobtrusive Measures: Nonreactive Research in the Social Sciences.* Chicago: Rand McNally, 1966.

WEICK, KARL E. "Laboratory Experimentation with Organizations." In *Handbook of Organizations,* edited by James G. March. Chicago: Rand McNally, 1963.

Chapter 15

Data-Based Communication Consulting

Gerald M. Goldhaber

Donald P. Rogers

Most courses in business, professional, technical, or organizational communication that are taught in our colleges are of the service-and-skills type. They are offered not for communication majors, but for students from other departments. They are intended not to increase understanding of organizational communication, but to develop specific communication skills (e.g., report writing, interviewing, and layout). While we find nothing wrong with the how-to-do-it courses, we are uneasy about their tenuous theoretical base. We are made even more uneasy by the growing recognition in the literatures of accounting, economics, finance, industrial engineering, marketing, and organizational behavior that *communication has organizational consequences.*

Other functional areas are beginning to recognize that communication (and its twin dimensions of information and interaction) is important to the organization, not just as an interpersonal skill, but as a tool of management, a source of power, and a constraint on events. As other areas "discover" or "invent" the importance of communication (*we* knew it all along), they are turning to the specialists in communication (*us*) for explanations of these phenomena. While this is a great opportunity, it is not without risk. Specifically, most of our theories of communication are prescriptive. They are how-to-do-it theories. They are theories grounded in a pragmatic idealism. They focus on the individual and what the individual ought to do. Our theories are value-centered, which is a nice way of saying that they contain an implicit (humanistic) bias. Try this in your classroom.

Take some aggressively publicized product (like light whiskey), concept (like the Equal Rights Amendment), or technology (like video teleconferencing) which has floundered or failed. Ask your students, "Why?" Chances are that if your students have really internalized the idealistic model of communication, they will answer, "The idea failed because the public [or the special interests] resisted it." That answer is tautological. It says, "The idea wasn't accepted because people didn't accept it."

Most of our theories of communication are *personifications* of the obvious. Our theories replace the abstractions of the rationalists (like economists) and the objects of the empiricists (like the behavioralists) with the persona of the humanists (who are not otherwise represented in the administrative sciences).

The risk, as we see it, is that our theories of communication as a critical organizational process will not be accepted by our colleagues because there are neither rational explanations nor empirical descriptions of the phenomenon. In other words, we don't speak the same language as our colleagues. We are not going to recommend the development of rational or empirical theories of organizational communication. We expect those to emerge as our field matures. Instead, we are going to propose a strategy for teaching our students to produce humanistic effects by using rational techniques and empirical methods.

We suggest teaching students to use the communication audit to intervene in organizations. The communication audit uses rational techniques to plan the intervention and to develop strategies for improvement. The communication audit uses empirical methods to gather data and provide feedback. The important humanistic effects of a communication audit are (1) the pursuit of truth in the meanings which people ascribe to their organizations; (2) the defense of democracy through participation in planning, administering, and evaluating the audit; and (3) the enhancement of personal freedom in the development of a sense of responsibility for self-actualization. Stated less euphemistically, a communication audit can produce valid information, arouse interest and involvement, and strengthen the commitment and motivation to organizational change.

Auditing Organizational Communication

As Greenbaum and White have noted, "There is no generally accepted format for a communication audit."[1] However, there are some general approaches. The first is the conceptual approach. This approach starts by selecting a set of standards for organizational performance (measures of goal attainment) and then assesses organizational performance according to those standards. The most common standards for such an audit are efficiency and effectiveness.

Efficiency Criteria

As the name suggests, these are the criteria for determining how efficient (in a technical sense) the diffusion system is.

Cost. The cost criterion compares the expected or planned cost of disseminating certain information with the actual costs of the dissemination. Cost would be measured in dollars and cents.

Time. The time criterion compares the amount of time expected or planned for the distribution of certain information with the actual amount of time that the distribution takes. Elapsed time would be measured in days, hours, and minutes.

Accuracy. The accuracy criterion compares the minimal number of acceptable errors in content with the actual number of errors. This would be measured in terms of number of errors.

Intelligibility. The intelligibility criterion compares the intended level of difficulty of a message with the actual level of difficulty. Intelligibility would be measured in terms of audience level (education, experience, etc.), audience comprehension of the message, or both.

Effectiveness Criteria

These criteria are intended to determine how effective the information diffusion system is in providing the information that the users feel they need.

Receiver/User. This criterion compares the intended receiver(s) of certain information with the actual receivers. The concern is both that those who should get information get it, and that others might get it (whether or not these others ought to have the information would be a decision left to the organization).

Content. The content criterion compares the data intended to be transmitted with the data actually received (according to receivers).

Timing. The timing criterion compares the time at which information is needed with the time at which it is received.

Media. This criterion compares the media used to transmit some amount of information with the media through which the information is received (the plural word *media* is used because information is generally transmitted in an organization through a combination of media).

Format. The format criterion compares the format in which the information was sent with the format in which the information was received.

Source. The source criterion compares the intended or responsible source of certain information with the actual source. A conceptual audit form appears in Table 15–1.[2]

TABLE 15–1 Conceptual Audit Form

Efficiency Criteria (Planned vs. Actual)	Variance
Cost	Above/below planned cost
Time	Received before/after intended time of receipt
Accuracy	Number of errors more/less than acceptable
Intelligibility	Understanding level above/below that desired
Effectiveness Criteria	**Variance**
Receivers	1. Did all intended receivers get the data? 2. Did any unintended receiver get the data?
Content	1. Were all necessary data transmitted? 2. Were any unnecessary data transmitted?
Timing	1. Were data available when needed? 2. How long were data stored before use?
Media	1. Through what media were data received? 2. Were more efficient media available?
Format	1. In what format were data received? 2. Were more efficient formats available?
Source	1. Who was the immediate source of the data? 2. Were more credible sources available?

The second approach to auditing organizational communication is the single-instrument survey. This approach starts with a research instrument and then applies that instrument to assess the organization according to the instrument. Most field research in organizational communication falls (or could fall) into this category. The basic (and critical) difference between ordinary survey research and auditing is the meaning of the data. Survey research focuses on *generating* data (the data are an end in themselves), while communication auditing focuses on *using* data to improve the organization (the data are a means to an end).[3]

The third approach to auditing organizational communication is the procedural approach. This approach focuses on the process of conducting the communication audit rather than on the research instruments employed. This is the most complex approach to auditing, involving a team of auditors with multiple instruments in the organization over an extended period of time. Many consulting firms use the procedural approach, but the only standardized procedure with instruments in the public domain is the International Communication Audit, developed by the Organizational Communication Division of the ICA. Since both of the authors have been involved in developing the ICA Communication Audit, we will focus on it for the rest of this chapter.[4]

The ICA Communication Audit

The ICA Communication Audit is designed to provide reliable, factual, and reportable data about internal communication and to do so in a way that will permit comparability with similar organizations. It is unique as a measuring system in that it:

1. Measures information flow, message content and communicator attitudes and perceptions of both
2. Provides attitudinal, perceptual and behavioral data
3. Uses a variety of measurement techniques, allowing any combination of instruments to be used in data-gathering
4. Allows for measurement of communication over time
5. Uses standardized procedures for administration of instruments and collection and analysis of data
6. Allows for limited organizational input to customize the instruments and administration procedures without disrupting the standardization needed for organizational comparisons
7. Uses trained and credentialed ICA communication auditors with knowledge, experience and competencies in the audit to design and direct all audits
8. Uses original computer programs for data analysis and report feedback
9. Allows organizational comparisons on specified communication behaviors, perceptions and attitudes by norming audit data[5]

The overall objective is to evaluate the organization's communication system, providing information and recommendations which should help an organization improve both its communication practices and its overall effectiveness as an organization. Specific *objectives* during an audit are to:

1. Determine the amount of information underload or overload associated with the major *topics, sources and channels* of communication
2. Evaluate the *quality of information* communicated from and/or to these sources
3. Assess the *quality of communication* relationships, specifically measuring the extent of interpersonal trust, supportiveness, sociability and overall job satisfaction
4. Identify the *operational communication* networks (for rumors, social and job-related messages), comparing them with planned or formal networks (prescribed by organizational charts)

5. Determine potential *bottlenecks and gatekeepers of information* by comparing actual communication roles of key personnel (isolates, liaisons, group members, etc.) with expected roles (provided by job descriptions, etc.)
6. Identify categories and examples of commonly occurring positive and negative *communication experiences and incidents*
7. Describe individual, group and organizational patterns of *actual communication behaviors* related to sources, channels, topics, length and quality of interactions
8. Provide general recommendations, derived from the Audit, which call for changes or improvements in attitudes, behaviors, practices and skills[6]

When the above objectives are met, an organization will have the following *products:*

1. An organizational profile of perceptions of communication events, practices and relationships. This profile can be further analyzed according to such demographics as: age, sex, education, supervisory status, division or department (or any desired meaningful combinations). Specific products include lists of:
   (*a*) Topics, sources and channels of communication rank-ordered according to their need for improvement (based upon differences between current and ideal conditions)
   (*b*) Effective and ineffective major communication sources with respect to their message timeliness, accuracy, utility, excessiveness and follow-up
   (*c*) Effective and ineffective interpersonal and organizational factors affecting communication relationships
   (*d*) Job traits contributing the most and least to job satisfaction
2. A map of the operational communication network for rumors, social and job-related messages; for each of these three networks, the following are produced:
   (*a*) Lists of individuals in actual work or social groups, allowing comparisons with organizational chart assignments
   (*b*) Identification of all personnel as active members of work or social groups, as a liaison between groups, or as a communication isolate within the organization
   (*c*) Identification of potential communication bottlenecks and gatekeepers with recommendations for possible reorganization of personnel.
3. Verbal summaries of successful and unsuccessful communication experiences used to explain some of the reasons for problems or strengths identified on the survey and network analysis. Specifically, we provide:
   (*a*) A ratio of successful to unsuccessful communication incidents for the entire organization and important subgroups
   (*b*) An identification of the major communication categories which account for most of the incidents (also further analyzed, if desired, by important subgroups)

(*c*) A listing, by major sources (co-workers, subordinates, immediate supervisor, top management) or *all* successful and unsuccessful incidents

4. An organizational profile of *actual* communication behaviors (also further analyzed, if desired, by age, sex, education, etc.). Specific products, allowing comparisons between actual and perceived (from the survey) communication behaviors are:
   (*a*) An organizational summary of major message sources, receivers, topics, channels, lengths and qualities
   (*b*) Individual summaries (provided confidentially) of the above information
5. A set of general recommendations, derived from the results of the audit, indicating which attitudes, behaviors, practices, and skills should be continued, added, changed, or eliminated
6. Benchmarks on communication behaviors and perceptions to be used for possible pre–post measurement to diagnose organizational change or development (or to diagnose specific organizational changes needed) are developed.
7. Several personnel from the organization familiar with the ICA Audit instruments and procedures, helping the organization to take the major initiative in conducting future audits themselves.
8. Permanent future access (on a confidential basis) to the ICA Audit data bank, allowing the organization to compare the results of present and future audits with those of similar organizations[7]

Benefits of a Communication Audit

Organizations who conduct communication audits will collect valid information about their communication systems. With this information, they will be able to not only describe current behaviors and practices but also predict the likelihood of potential successes and failures. They will take the offensive in planning for their future rather than be on the defensive, reacting to communication crises. Valid information gives an organization the freedom to choose from a variety of alternatives what paths it should follow as it grows and develops. With the replacement of guesswork with accurate data, an organization can forecast problems rather than react with patchwork solutions. Specific organizational benefits include using audit data:

1. As a premeasurement or postmeasurement to determine the impact of new communication programs
2. To assess the impact of ongoing programs (such as those mandated by the 1974 Employee Retirement Income Security Act [ERISA])
3. As a premeasurement or postmeasurement to determine the impact of new organizational innovations (restructuring, addition of the computer, new organizational development program)

4. To identify the current organizational structure as an aid to successful reorganization
5. To identify key communication groupings prior to restructuring, especially for overseas assignments in large transnational corporations
6. To identify major communication costs (telephone calls, meetings, postage, air travel) involved in new expansions to other states or countries
7. To develop new communication training programs geared to solve real organizational problems identified in the audit[8]

Communication Audit Considerations

A communication audit is a very powerful research tool, but it isn't all-powerful. The ICA Communication Audit is one approach to measurement of organizational communication. There are other viable approaches which may be appropriate to a given organization at a given time.

Sincoff and Goyer have pointed out three cautions to consider before conducting a communication audit.[9] First, a communication audit should not be done for its own sake. The data from an audit may be of great interest to the academic researcher, but the information gathered, analyzed, and evaluated must be useful to the manager as well. Based on our experience, it would appear that the results and recommendations of an audit will be useful to a manager if at least two of these three conditions are met. One, the organization must be under pressure to improve performance. This pressure may come from within (management pressures for increased productivity, employee pressures for growth) or from outside (customer pressure for improved service, government pressure for social responsibility). There must be pressure to improve, to grow, to reduce costs, to increase profits, to increase output, to improve quality, etc. Two, the organization must be under pressure to coordinate and control complex operations. Operations may be complex because of uncertainty (manufacturing in an industry where technology is changing rapidly), size (large numbers of employees), or specialization (an urban hospital with many separate units, clinics, and services). The pressure must be for management of interdependence rather than management of autonomy. Three, the organization must have slack resources to support the audit. The audit is not a solution to any problem but the lack of information. The audit takes time, money, and people. It is not a quick-and-dirty approach to generating information. The organization must be able (and willing) to support a diagnostic procedure.

That third condition for conducting an audit relates directly to Sincoff and Goyer's second caution: A communication audit is a diagnostic technique—not a cure-all. The collection of data arouses interest. It gets people involved. It focuses attention on communication. It gets people stimulated and ready for change. But it does not produce change. The follow-through, the application of results, and the implementation of recommendations are the responsibility of management. No manager needs an audit if changes can't or won't be made. In fact, if change is not possible, it may be better not to begin the audit process at all because the audit may make things worse.

The third caution is that the communication audit is only one of many needs analyses available to an organization. This caution is probably more applicable to the auditor/researcher than to the manager. The organization may have needs in the areas of communication, information flow, or both, but it may also have needs in the areas like capital financing, personnel retainment, scrap losses, accountability, or government regulation where the audit is not likely to provide much useful information. Even if the greatest needs are in the area of communication, critical analyses of documents or of telephone charges may be more useful to the manager than a communication audit.

Our purpose in discussing cautions is not to disparage the ICA Communication Audit, but to give the manager or researcher contemplating an organizational communication audit a basis for informed choice. An audit can not be justified if its procedures, results, and recommendations cannot be useful. However, it is our opinion that most large organizations meet the conditions for justifying an audit. More importantly, most large organizations can benefit from the process of conducting a communication audit.

Teaching Auditing

In general, our philosophy of teaching organizational communication involves the progressive movement from the classroom, to the simulation, and then to the organization. In teaching auditing we follow the same philosophy. The first phase is the classroom introduction to the conceptual approaches, instruments, benefits, and limitations of communication auditing. The second phase is the classroom simulation of the planning, administering, reporting, and recommendation building processes. The third phase is the actual conduct of a communication audit (in a university department, for example). The first two phases can make up a one-semester course. The third phase is (and should be) outside the scope and structure of an ordinary course; it should be offered as independent or advanced study.

If the class has qualified people, it might very well do its own audit. Qualified people in this context means people who are:

1. Generally familiar with survey research methods.
2. Specifically trained in communication audit instruments and procedures. (Communication auditing courses are offered at several universities and two-day workshops are held throughout the year in various locations—several hundred people have already gone through this training.)

3. Experienced in conducting a communication audit. (Most of the courses actually conduct an audit.)

The advantage of do-it-youself auditing is the reduction of cash outlay because personnel, time, and facilities costs are already built into the organization's overhead. We would expect this advantage might be attractive to some kinds of organizations (mostly universities and consulting firms) which have experts in organizational communication systems (theory, research, and practice) on staff.

Planning

The best way to teach planning is to have a class go through the stages of actually planning an audit. The following sequence is based on Koontz and O'Donnell's strategic planning model.[10]

The first step in the planning model is to establish objectives for the audit. This requires the planner to ask, "What do I hope to achieve by conducting a communication audit?" In general, there appear to be three things a communication audit can do. First, it can generate valid information about an organization. It can generate information which can be used to define problems, identify opportunities, answer questions, make decisions, or suggest changes. If the planner's objective is to generate valid information, the communication audit is one way of doing so. Second, it can focus the attention of the organization. The communication audit is a very visible process. People become aware, interested, and involved in the process. We have often been told that the communication audit is perceived as a very effective mechanism for communicating an emphasis on participation. With all this activity focusing on communication, it is only natural that the organization begins to pay attention to its communication system. If the planner's objective is to focus the attention of the organization on communication, the communication audit is one way of doing so. Third, it can produce effects. The communication audit can have immediate effects in areas like morale, grievances, productivity, performance, or work errors. Through the implementation of recommendations and improvement of communication, it can have long-term effects on morale, turnover, absenteeism, productivity, errors, operating costs, and public relations. If the planner's objective is to produce change in the organization, the communication audit is one way of doing so.

There are probably other things that a communication audit can do, but not efficiently. More importantly, there are some things that a communication audit cannot do. It cannot substitute for sound thinking and executive judgment. It cannot be a cure-all. It cannot tell us everything that we may want or need to know. There are some things that a communication audit should not do. It should not gather information for the sake of gathering information. It should not be a strategy for impressing the boss. It should not promise more in the way of improvement than it can deliver.

The second step in the planning model is forecasting constraints. This requires the planner to ask, "What's going to happen that might affect the audit?" Since it may take up to six months to complete a large communication audit, the planner must be able to anticipate events. Obviously it would be foolish to conduct an audit on the eve of a strike or during contract negotiations. But there are other types of events which must also be considered. First, and foremost, there are the other plans or strategies of the organization. The communication audit focuses attention on communication. If the organization is introducing a new product or service, it may be better to focus its attention there. At the least, the planner must try to anticipate the other decisions, plans, programs, or projects which may affect or be affected by an audit. Some projects will conflict with the communication audit (e.g., layoffs, reorganizations, new products, other studies), but some programs will complement the audit (e.g., work force expansions; mergers or acquisitions; communication campaigns concerning ERISA, the Occupational Safety and Health Act [OSHA], equal employment opportunity, and affirmative action). Second, the planner must consider events which will require the organization to respond. Other people can do things which will command the attention of the organization. For example, new legislation may be passed, suppliers may close, competitors may cut prices, clients may make demands, etc. Uncontrollable events can occur. If the organization is expecting some event which will require a major response, it should not encumber itself with an audit. In general, a communication audit will not compete for attention with regular operations. It will, however, compete with some kinds of special events. By and large, this competition can be avoided by anticipating the other events in the planning of the communication audit. The audit should be scheduled when there is time to focus attention on communication. One of the best times to schedule an audit is *prior* to major changes, expansion, reorganizations, or growth—because the audit can prepare people for change and provide information useful to guiding growth.

The third step in the planning model is the determination of alternative courses of action. We have pointed out that the ICA Communication Audit is one way of gathering valid information, one way of focusing the organization's attention, one way of creating effects. It is not the only way. The planner must ask, "What alternatives to the communication audit are available?" We are again going to resist the temptation to provide a long, scholarly review of the data-gathering instruments, research procedures, and change strategies available to the planner. We assume that most of the readers of this book are managers, researchers, consultants, or teachers and therefore have some access to, or awareness of, alternative instruments, research methods, and development techniques. The planner must compare the alternatives available in light of the objectives. If the objective is to gather information to impress someone, the ICA Communication Audit is inappropriate. If the objective is to gather useful information, to focus attention on communication, or to improve organizational performance, the ICA Communication Audit may be appropriate. Criteria for evaluating alternatives in terms of objectives would include instrument coverage, instrument reliability and validity, information utility, instrument comparability, procedural reliability, participation and involvement, organizational expectations, positive gains, unsought consequences, and potential effects. Criteria for evaluating alternatives in terms of efficiency would include qualifications of personnel, contract provisions, time, space requirements, services and facilities, schedules, costs, and returns on investment.

The fourth step in the planning model is choice. It is up to the planner, manager, researcher, consultant, or teacher to decide whether or not to conduct a communication audit.

The fifth step in the planning model is the development of a plan for implementing the decision. This involves the class in making research and resource decisions.

The first decisions the class must make have to do with research. The class must decide what kinds of information will be most useful to that particular audit. This decision will influence the selection of specific instruments. The audit uses five separate but related data-gathering tools:

Questionnaire Survey. The questionnaire includes 118 items and 10 demographics plus up to 18 questions of any type determined by the organization. The reliability of the scales on the 118-item set ranges from a low of .70 to a high of .90. The validity of these scales is based upon their self-evident relationship to organizational communication and their ability to predict organizational outcomes. Respondents answer the survey anonymously in group sessions lasting about forty-five minutes. The survey allows respondents to indicate their perception of the *current status* of their communication system as well as their *desired or ideal status.* This helps the identification of communication needs in the organization. The comments on the following pages cover in more detail the content, reliability, and validity of the survey.[11]

Interviews. Randomly or purposively selected members of the organization are asked to participate in one-on-one interviews, the principal purpose of which is to corroborate and expand upon concerns reported in other audit tools. Two interview schedules are used: one that is structured to provide exploratory information, using open-ended questions; and a follow-up guide which is specifically tailored to each organization to explain findings revealed through the use of other audit tools. Most interviews last from 1 to 1½ hours, and all are conducted confidentially (sometimes using two interviewers, tape recorders, or both to facilitate data analysis).

Network Analysis. Respondents indicate the extent to which they typically communicate with each individual in their unit or department (or with key individuals outside their unit). A computer examination of all communication links identifies the operational communication network (for rumors, social messages, and job-related messages) and places individuals into communication roles of isolate, liaison, or group member. The instrument is completed in group sessions lasting about thirty minutes.

Communication Experiences. Respondents describe critical communication episodes which they feel are representative of typical successful or unsuccessful incidents. From these descriptions a set of examples are developed to help illustrate why a given unit or department is experiencing good or bad communication. These qualitative data add much richness to, and provide explanation for, information from other audit tools. Respondents complete this instrument in group or individual sessions lasting about one hour. All data are computer-analyzed confidentially.

Communication Diary. Each participant is asked to maintain a diary of specified communication activities (conversations, phone calls, meetings, written materials received and sent, etc.) over a one-week period. Forms are provided to simplify the recording of these communication events. Cumulative time required per person for the entire week is approximately 1½ hours, including a short training period. These data are confidentially analyzed by computer and provide indications of actual communication behavior among individuals, groups, and the entire organization.

The selection of specific instruments determines the information to be gained, the cost, and the length of a communication audit. Figure 15–1 shows factors to consider in selecting instruments.

When instruments have been selected, the class must decide who will participate in the audit. This process, called selecting the sample, is critical to survey research. The two components of a sample are its size (how many people) and its composition (what kinds of people). The decision about appropriate sample size is determined by organizational size, prior information, tolerable error, confidence level, and composition. In an organization of fewer than three hundred employees everyone should be surveyed, both to ensure reliability and to avoid bad feelings on the part of those not surveyed. As the number of employees increases the percentage sampled can decrease. For example, maximum sample sizes for organizations of 300–1000 people might be 50 percent; for 1000–2000 people, 25 percent; for 2000–5000 people, 10 percent; for over 5000 people, 5 percent. Prior information can also reduce sample size. The more information the organization already has (from prior studies) about the composition of its population (kinds of people), the fewer the number of factors it needs to consider. Tolerable error influences sample size as a function of the use to be made of the information. The more general the question asked, the greater the error which can be tolerated and the

	Orientation Interviews	Employee Interviews	Client/Customer Interviews	Survey Questionnaire	Experiences Questionnaire	Network Questionnaire	Personal Diary
Instrument characteristics							
Reliability	L	M	M	H	M	M	M
Validity	L	M	M	H	M	M	M
Richness	H	H	H	M	H	M	H
Flexibility	H	H	M	L	M	L	M
Codability	L	L	L	H	M	M	M
Ease of interpretation	L	M	M	H	M	M	L
Organizational costs							
Time	M	M	M	M	M	M	H
Effort	H	H	H	M	M	M	H
Money	H	H	H	M	M	H	H
Space	M	M	M	M	M	M	L
Disruption	M	H	L	M	M	M	H
Personal risk	L	M	L	L	M	M	H

H = high M = moderate L = low

FIGURE 15–1 Consideration Factors in Selecting Instruments

smaller the minimum sample needed. If we want to know how many people receive an adequate amount of information about advancement opportunities, we can tolerate a relatively high error. Suppose we find that 30 percent receive adequate information. Even with an error of 10 percent, we know that this is relatively low and more information needs to be made available. Most organizational researchers accept a maximum tolerable error of 10 percent, but prefer to limit tolerable error to 5 percent. Confidence level influences sample size as an estimate of the probability that the actual error is less than the tolerable error. The more we want to be certain that we are within the tolerable error, the larger the sample we need. Most organizational researchers accept a minimum confidence level of 95 percent, but prefer a confidence level of 99 percent.

Composition is both a component of the sample and a determinant of the necessary sample size for survey research. Composition refers to the kinds of people in the organization (or population). Composition influences sample size as a function of the number of categories necessary to describe the significant characteristics of the organization's people. The more categories necessary, the larger the sample size necessary. For example, most organizations have people who are new and people who have been there a long time. If the length of employment with the organization influences an employee's information, attitudes, or communication patterns, then the sample must be larger in order to categorize people by length of service and maintain tolerable error and minimum confidence levels.

The decision about sample size will influence the reliability of the information gathered (larger sample means higher reliability) and the cost of the audit (large sample means high cost). To a large extent the decision on sample size should be a function of the objectives of the audit. If the objective is to focus attention or produce results, we would strongly recommend that the sample be a complete census of the entire populations. Every member of the organization should participate. If, however, the objective is simply to ensure reliable information, we would recommend that the committee decide to aim for a minimum confidence level of 95 percent, a maximum error of 5 percent, and one or two sampling categories. This translates into a minimum sample size of about four hundred people (or everyone in the organization, if there are fewer) and a maximum sample size of about five hundred people.

From our experiences with other audits, we would expect that the research decisions would be made fairly quickly once the objectives of the communication audit have been specified. Ordinarily the class would make these decisions early in its discussions because they largely determine the resource commitments which will be required for the audit.

The second type of decisions that the class must make are resource commitment decisions. The basic question is "What resources are necessary to conduct the communication audit?" Obviously if the class members (including the auditors) are not willing to commit necessary resources, there is no point in trying to conduct the audit. Consideration of the resource requirements should be a part of the planner's decision to go ahead with a communication audit. Probably the most important resource commitment is time. The communication audit takes from five to six months (if all instruments are used). The instruments take people away from their work for up to 1½ hours for the surveys (total) and up to 2 hours for the interviews. A sample time line is shown on Figure 15-2.

A finer breakdown of the time line appears in Table 15-2. The total time for the audit could be shortened if not all instruments are used.

A sample resource fact sheet for all commitments appears in Table 15-3. This sheet reflects a number of decisions by the company to be audited including a desire for a great deal of involvement in the administration, collection, coding, and dissemination of the audit materials, data, and results.

From our experiences with other audits, we would expect that the discussion of resources would be fairly lengthy. As we mentioned earlier, analysis of the resources required for a communication audit should be a part of the plan-

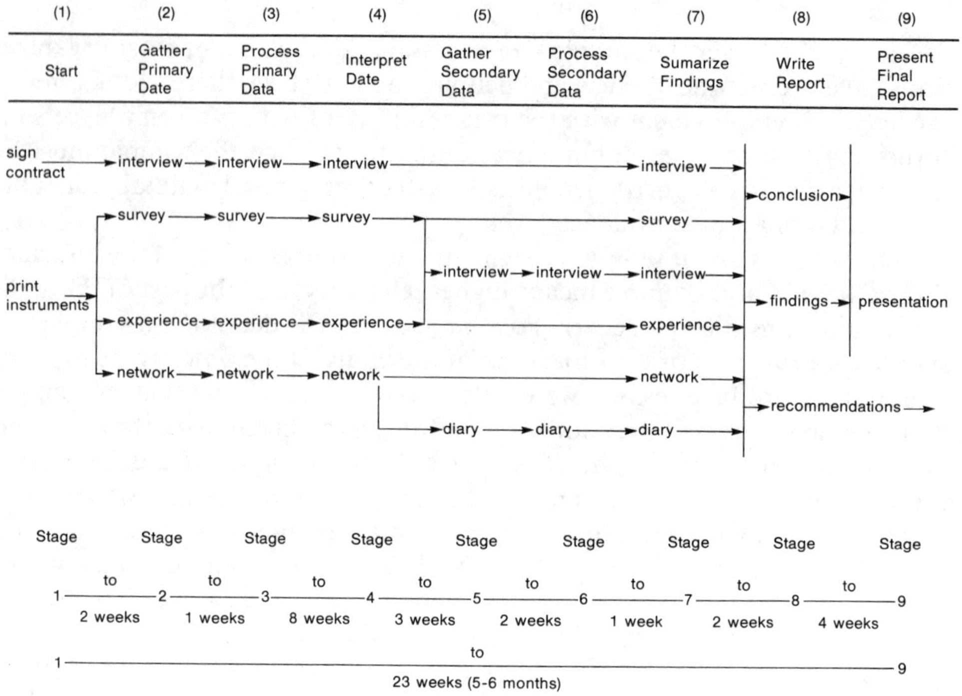

FIGURE 15–2 Sequence and Timetable of Events

TABLE 15–2 Breakdown of Sequence and Timetable of Events

Activity	Duration (weeks)
1. Finalize contract; prepare tools	2
2. Conduct exploratory interviews	1
3. Transcribe interviews and prepare for analysis	1
4. Analyze exploratory interviews	2
5. Administer survey, communication experiences, and network analysis questionnaires	1
6. Analyze survey, communication experiences, and network analysis data	6
7. Prepare preliminary interpretation of data, formulation of follow-up interview guide, communication diary log	3
8. Conduct follow-up interviews, administer communication diary	2
9. Transcribe interviews and prepare for analysis, prepare diary data	1
10. Analyze follow-up interviews, communication diary	2
11. Interpret data, draw conclusions, prepare recommendations, write final report	4
12. Present final report (orally and in writing), discuss future steps	0.3
Total elapsed time	25.3 weeks

TABLE 15–3 Sample Resource Fact Sheet for XYZ Corporation

Costs
- $15/person for a complete audit
- $12/person for an audit without network analysis

Terms
- 50% payable upon contracting
- 50% payable upon completion

Products/Service Provided to XYZ
1. Audit personnel to train XYZ personnel in administration preparation for analysis, and analysis of ICA Audit
2. Audit personnel to help interpret and provide recommendations to XYZ personnel
3. Use of ICA Audit instruments, computer programs, norms

Services Provided by XYZ
1. Preparation of Audit instruments
2. Dissemination of information to XYZ personnel about Audit (pre, during, and post)
3. Administration of audit
4. Preparation of Audit data for analysis by computer (i.e., coding, keypunching, placing of data on tapes)
5. Provision of feedback about Audit results to XYZ personnel (orally and/or in writing)

Timeline: XYZ will receive computerized results of Audit within 2 weeks of receipt of computer tapes from XYZ or within 4 weeks of receipt of uncoded data.

Follow-up
1. Future Audits. XYZ would have access to current versions of ICA Audit instruments and norms and computer programs for a charge of $11/person for a complete audit and $8/person for an audit without network analysis.
2. Implementation of Recommendations. XYZ could contract with any Audit personnel for additional help in the implementation of any Audit recommendations. Costs would be on a per diem basis according to the rate/day of the consultant. This service is beyond the scope of the ICA Communication Audit directly.

ning process. Our advice is simple: If the planner, manager, or researcher is not willing to commit the necessary resources (including his or her own time and effort), then an audit should not be done. The ICA Communication Audit is a very good research system, but not so good that it can be done badly.

Gathering Data

We are not going to suggest any classroom activities for gathering data. We firmly believe that there is no learning experience in the classroom which can substitute for actually gathering data in an organization. It is quite useful, however, for students in the classroom to analyze data previously collected in the organization. We have put together a number of artificial data sets for just this purpose.[12]

Providing Feedback

It is in this stage of an audit that we feel the greatest contribution to teaching business communication can be made. Analyzing the data generated by an audit is a powerful base for teaching students to report that data to the organization.

Weiner (1950) developed the notion of feedback as a measure of the actual performance of a system which, when analyzed by the system, would provide a basis for future action.[13] A feedback situation could occur when, for example, you go bowling. You get up to the lane and throw the ball. It curves to the left. That curve represents the actual performance of the system (throwing the ball). You have received feedback that the way you are throwing the ball is causing it to curve left. For your next throw, you will adjust something (your throw, your stance, etc.) to try and make the ball go more to the right. After you throw the next ball, you will get feedback on how successful your adjustment has been.

This same process is important to a communication audit. First, the people who participate in the audit probably choose to do so because they expect their own information about the organization to improve and because they expect the organizational communication system to improve. They expend effort because they expect results. If they do not see results in the form of findings or improvements, they are likely to conclude that their efforts were wasted. The next time they are asked to expend effort they might refuse, because they do not expect the results to be worth the effort. Second, the organization which conducts an audit needs feedback to energize itself to act. Feedback provides the organization with a sense of where it is "off-target." Feedback from the audit lets the organization learn what it is doing right. Feedback gives the organization a sense of where, what, and why problems exist. Feedback from the ICA Communication Audit gives the organization a ranking of its problems, so that it can focus its resources on its greatest needs.

Feedback from a communication audit should take at least three forms. First, a brief written report focusing on the conclusions and major findings of the audit should be prepared for distribution to all those who participated in the study. This report may or may not include recommendations. Second, a longer written report focusing on conclusions, recommendations, methods, and findings should be prepared for the administration and responsible committees of the organization. This report should include all supporting data, tables, charts, and instruments as appendixes. Third, an oral report, in the form of a feedback meeting, should take place to discuss the findings and implications of the audit. Participants in this meeting should include the research team, key managers, and the audit liaison committee which will study the reports and develop plans for implementing changes.

Brief Written Report

The brief written report is intended for circulation to all members of the organization (or, at least, all those who participated in the audit). It is probably most effective if it is written in a personal style and circulated as a letter or memo. It may, however, be written in an impersonal journalistic style as a straight (objective) report or as an interpretive (analytic) report and circulated as a story in the organization's internal publication or posted on bulletin boards.

The purpose of this report is to provide members of the organization with feedback of the results of the audit. This report helps to demonstrate that the effort of participating in the communication audit was not wasted. The report should be short and simple. It will probably be written after the longer final report and may be a summary of that report. This report should be very limited in its focus on the conclusions and major findings of the audit. It should avoid excessive reporting of findings in quantified form. One or two key numbers will be enough. A sample short report follows (page 340).

Final Written Report

The final written report is a long report intended for the top management of the organization and for the audit liaison group within the organization. This report should focus on the conclusions, recommendations, and findings of the audit. It should be a relatively complete report, but instruments, charts, tables, and figures should not appear in the text of the report. These should be included in a series of appendixes. This report is probably most effective if written in a personalized plain-English style—rather than an academic, research report style. The objective of this report is to be useful, not scholarly.

The final written report must provide readers with enough information to be useful, but not so much that they will be overloaded. This report can be very helpful. It can provide feedback to people who cannot be at the oral report meeting. It can give members of the organization something tangible to work with. It can allow people to digest the findings of the communication audit at their own pace. Most important, it can provide a starting place for a discussion of the communication problems and needs of the organization.

Sample: A Brief Written Report

TO: All MHA Employees

FROM: Communication Audit Team

RE: Conclusions of the Audit

We have now completed all phases of the Communication Audit. We have surveyed almost 300 employees, interviewed 20 employees, and interviewed over 230 tenants. We have analyzed these data and we have drawn the following conclusions:

1. *Internal Communication Strengths.* Interpersonal relations are excellent. People like one another and get along together. People like and trust their immediate supervisors. People like their jobs. They like the housing authority. People are receiving good information. It is useful and accurate.
2. *Internal Communication Weaknesses.* There is a serious lack of downward communication. People want information, but are not getting it. A number of channels of communication (like department meetings, letters, memos, and the telephone) are underused. Upward communication is sometimes discouraged. There seems to be a lack of timely response, of decisive action, and of clear authority. There is a definite lack of recognition and/or reward for quality performance.
3. *External Communication Strengths.* Tenants are getting good quality information and would like more. They are satisfied with their apartments and projects. They know where to go and who to see to make a suggestion or complaint.
4. *External Communication Weaknesses.* Tenants see the MHA as receptive to complaints, but not responsive. They feel that sometimes there is a "don't care" attitude in MHA.
5. *Recommendations.* While we have identified some serious communication problems, we do not think that these are beyond remedy. Quite the opposite, we feel that most of the communication problems can be solved by making more information available, by making it easier for people to communicate, by having more meetings, and by creating some internal publications.

   The MHA is basically a good organization, but it does have problems. These problems are serious, but correctable. We have recommended a number of measures for improving communication within MHA and between MHA and its tenants.

Oral Report Feedback Meeting

Almost from its inception one of the guiding models of the ICA Communication Audit has been the process consultation model.[14] This model is an alternative to the purchase model (the manager wants something done and hires an outside expert to do it) or the doctor-patient Model (the manager hires someone to diagnose and treat some organizational problem) of intervention. The process consultation model involves the organization and the auditors in a process of joint diagnosis so that the members of the organization can learn to see their own problems and can take responsibility for designing solutions suitable to their own special needs, conditions, and culture.

While the communication audit gets members of the organization directly involved in the collection and analysis of data, the implications of the process consultation model are most visable during the oral feedback meeting. Very clearly change begins to occur when people have an opportunity to discuss the conclusions, recommendations, and findings of the audit. We have known for many years that the best way to learn, comprehend, or understand something is to talk about it. The oral feedback session is a dyadic or small group meeting focusing on a discussion of the audit, rather than a presentation of it.

The oral feedback session can take many forms. Each of these sessions has actually been conducted in connection with at least two audits. The feedback session can be a private session for the organization's chief executive officer (CEO). The advantages of such a session are that it gives the CEO advance notice of reports, it allows the CEO to question the implications of the audit privately, and it prepares the CEO for questions about commitments to follow up. The major disadvantage is that it may give the CEO a false sense of control over the data. The feedback meeting may be a private session for other key members of the organization. This is most appropriate when findings of the audit are of specific relevance to the individual. The advantages, again, are focus, privacy, and the opportunity to plan a response. The disadvantage of most significance is that this session may produce defensiveness in the individual.

The feedback meeting may be a group session for key members of the organization. Such a session can focus on areas of common interest and deemphasize areas of lesser relevance. For example, it is common that some of the findings of a communication audit are true or important for only a part of the organization. The feedback session can be a press conference in which the findings of the audit are presented to the internal, local, or financial media. This type of session may help to disseminate the findings of the audit more quickly. To date, this type of feedback meeting has been conducted by only two public-sector organizations. The major disadvantage of this type of meeting is that the organization has little or no control over how the press will report the findings of the audit.

The instructor can have students do any or all of the following: write a short report, write a long report, conduct an oral feedback meeting. This provides a practical application of the things learned in business communication courses at the basic level.

Making Recommendations

The principal payoff of an audit comes not when the data have been gathered, but when the organization uses the data to improve organizational communication. Students can learn a great deal about communication strategies by developing recommendations for the organization based on the audit data.[15]

Examples of recommendations made and implemented include:

1. Addition of new formal channels of communication (newsletters, videotape playback of key memoranda, news bulletin boards, new meeting structures, new telephone systems, etc.)
2. Development of communication goals, objectives, and policies and the disclosure of these to employees
3. Open disclosure policies on certain topics of information
4. Improvements in informal communication (luncheons with key executives, social events, rap sessions, and open-door policies)
5. Hiring or shifting of personnel to improve the communication function in the company
6. Addition of liaison personnel to facilitate horizontal communication between computer users and computer personnel to improve understanding and reduce costly programming mistakes
7. Changes in the amount of information communicated about career paths and the personnel function (e.g., job postings, pay ranges for certain positions, training and development programs available for certain career paths)
8. Better upward input solicited by top management to improve the planning process, both short and long-range; development of specific mechanisms to generate such input in a nonthreatening way
9. Improvement in the quality of the quarterly officers' meetings, adding question-answer periods and open discussion
10. Retraining of certain management personnel in communication skills (writing, listening, public speaking, interviewing, group discussion, problem-solving, brainstorming, etc.)
11. Better and more periodic monitoring of the company's external image, as perceived by significant publics (consumers, stockholders, politicians, and community leaders)

Conclusion

We see the teaching of auditing with its commitment to organizational improvement as a logical capstone to a humanistically oriented program in business, professional, or organizational Communication. We have used the communication audit to teach graduate and undergraduate students. We have used the audit to teach interviewing, report writing, survey research, research methods, graduate field experience, strategic planning, group decision making, and consulting. We believe in the teaching of auditing because it integrates so much of the theory and method of communication with the consultant's philosophic orientation to improving the human condition within the organization.

Acknowledgment

This chapter presents an introduction to communication auditing. For a complete discussion of this topic the interested reader should see Goldhaber and Rogers, *Auditing Organizational Communication Systems: The ICA Communication Audit,* from which this chapter was developed. Lists in the preceding text are reprinted with permission from Goldhaber-Rogers: *Auditing Organizational Communication Systems: The ICA Communication Audit,* Kendall/Hunt Publishing Company, 1979.

Notes

1. Howard H. Greenbaum and Noel D. White, "Biofeedback at the Organizational Level: The Communication Audit," *Journal of Business,* vol. 13, no. 4 (1976), p. 10.
2. For more information on the conceptual approach to auditing organizational communication see: Howard H. Greenbaum, "The Audit of Organizational Communication," *Academy of Management Journal,* vol. 17, no. 4, (1974), pp. 739–754; Howard H. Greenbaum and Noel D. White, "Biofeedback at the Organizational Level," pp. 3–15; Donald P. Rogers, "An Audit Plan for the Internal Information Diffusion System of a Complex Organization," ERIC Document no. 904 425, abstracted in *Research in Education,* vol. 9, no. 12 (1974), p. 50.
3. For information on potential instruments see: Raymond L. Falcione and Howard H. Greenbaum, *Organizational Communication Abstracts,* published annually by Sage Publishers. For more information on the single-instrument approach to communication auditing see: George S. Odiorne, "An Application of the Communications Audit," *Personnel Psychology,* vol. 7 (1954), pp. 235–243; Karlene H. Roberts and Charles O'Reilly III, "Measuring Organizational Communication," *Journal of Applied Psychology,* vol. 59 (1974), pp. 321–326; Osmo A. Wiio, "Auditing Communication in Organizations: A Standard Survey—'LTT Communication Audit'," *Finnish Journal of Business Economics,* vol. 4 (1974), pp. 303–315.
4. For more information on the ICA Communication Audit, see Gerald M. Goldhaber and Donald P. Rogers, *Auditing Organizational Communication Systems: The ICA Communications Audit.* (Dubuque, Iowa: Kendall-Hunt, 1979).
5. Ibid.
6. Ibid.

7. Ibid.

8. Ibid.

9. M. Sincoff and R. Goyer, "Communication Audit Critique: The Researcher's Perspective," *Journal of Business Communication,* vol. 15, no. 1 (fall 1977), pp. 57–62.

10. H. Koontz and C. O'Donnell, *Principles of Management,* 3d ed. (New York: McGraw-Hill Book Co., 1964).

11. Complete information about the questionnaire survey referred to on page 332 appears in M. Yates et al., "The ICA Communication Audit System: Results of Six Studies" (paper presented at the International Communication Association convention, Portland, Ore., 1976); and G. Goldhaber, "The ICA Communication Audit: Rationale and Development" (paper presented at the Communication Association of the Pacific convention, Kobe, Japan, 1976; also presented at the Philippine-American Communication Conference, Manila, 1976, and the Academy of Management convention, Kansas City, Mo. 1976).

12. For more information see: Gerald M. Goldhaber and Donald P. Rogers, *Auditing Organizational Communication Systems* (Dubuque, Iowa: Kendall-Hunt, 1979).

13. N. Weiner, *Cybernetics* (Boston, Mass.: MIT Technology Press, 1950).

14. E. H. Schein, *Process Consultation: Its Role in Organization Development* (Reading, Mass.: Addison-Wesley, 1969).

15. For more information on teaching communication strategies, see: Donald P. Rogers, "The Content of Organizational Communication Texts," *Journal of Business Communication* (1979); "Teaching Organizational Communication: Philosophy and Commitment," *ABCA Bulletin,* vol. 40, no. 4 (1977), pp. 1–3; "Case Studies for Teaching Organizational Communication," ERIC/RCS Document #109 730, 22 pp., abstracted in *Resources in Education,* vol. 10, no. 12 (1975), p. 67; "New Directions in Teaching Organizational Communication," *ABCA Bulletin,* vol. 38, no. 2 (1975), pp. 22–25.

Bibliography

ARGYRIS, C. *Intervention Theory and Method: A Behavioral Science View.* Reading, Mass.: Addison-Wesley, 1970.

BARNARD, C. *The Functions of the Executive.* Cambridge: Harvard University Press, 1938.

BAVELAS, A., and D. BARRETT. "An Experimental Approach to Organizational Communication." *Personnel,* vol. 27 (1951), pp. 366–371.

BECKHARD, R. *Organization Development: Strategies and Models.* Reading, Mass.: Addison-Wesley, 1969.

BOULDING, K. E. *The Organizational Revolution: A Study in the Ethics of Economic Organization.* New York: Harper & Brothers, 1953.

———. *The Image: Knowledge in Life and Society.* Ann Arbor: University of Michigan Press, 1956.

BROOKS, K., J. CALLICOAT, and G. SIEGENDT. "The ICA Communication Audit and Perceived Communication Effectiveness Changes in 16 Audited Organizations." Unpublished monograph, Ohio State University, Columbus, Ohio, 1978.

CARTER, E. E. "The Behavioral Theory of Firm and Top Level Corporate Decision." *Administrative Science Quarterly,* vol. 16 (1971), pp. 413–428.

CONRATH, D. "Organizational Communication Behavior: A Systems Study and Its Relevance for Organizations." Paper presented at the International Communication Association convention, New Orleans, 1974.

CUMMINS, R. C. "Group Size, Task Structure and Productivity." Unpublished doctoral dissertation, Purdue University, Lafayette, Ind., 1970.

CYERT, R., and J. MARCH. *A Behavioral Theory of the Film.* Englewood Cliffs, N.J.: Prentice-Hall, 1973.

DAVID, I. "Channels of Personnel Communication within the Management Group." Unpublished doctoral dissertation, Ohio State University, Columbus, Ohio, 1952.

DAVIS, S., AND P. LAWRENCE. *Matrix.* Reading, Mass.: Addison-Wesley, 1977.

DENNIS, H. "Conceptualizing the Communication Audit." Paper presented at the International Communication Association convention, Montreal, 1973.

———. "The Construction of a Managerial 'Communication Climate' Inventory for Use in Complex Organizations." Paper presented at the International Communication Association convention, Chicago, 1975.

DENNIS, H., G. RICHETTO, and J. WEIMANN. "Articulating the Need for an Effective Communication System: New Empirical Evidence for the Communication Specialist." Paper presented at the International Communication Association convention, New Orleans, 1974.

DRUCKER, P. G. *The Practice of Management.* New York: Harper and Row, 1954.

FALCIONE, R. "A Communication Audit of an Academic Department." A report to the chairman of the department, June 1976.

———. "A Communication Audit of a U.S. Federal Agency." A report to the director of the agency, June 1976.

FALCIONE, R. L., and H. H. GREENBAUM. *Organizational Communication 1976: Abstracts, Analysis and Overview.* Urbana, Ill., and Austin, Tex., ABCA and ICA, 1977.

FARACE, R. V., P. M. MONGE, and H. M. RUSSELL. *Communicating and Organizing.* Reading, Mass.: Addison-Wesley, 1977.

FEINGOLD, P. "A Communication Audit of a Public Defender's Office." A report to the director of the agency, January 1976.

GOLDHABER, G. *Organizational Communication.* Dubuque, Iowa: W. C. Brown, 1974.

———. "A Communication Audit of a Canadian Hospital." A report to the director of the hospital, June 1975.

———. "A Communication Audit of a Florida School System." A report to the superintendent of schools, July 1975.

———. "A Communication Audit of a U.S. Senator's Office." A report to the Joint Congressional Operations Committee, October 1975.

———. "Organizational Communication: State of the Art—1975." Keynote speech delivered at the International Symposium in Communication, Monterrey, Mexico, October 1975. Reprinted in *Vital Speeches of the Day,* vol. 42 (1976), pp. 268–273.

———. "A Communication Audit of a Pennsylvania Manufacturing Company." A report to the vice president for industrial relations, December 1975.

———. "A Communication Audit of a Division of University Relations." A report to the vice president of university relations, June 1976.

———. "A Communication Audit of a University Personnel Department." A report to the director of the department, June 1976.

———. "The ICA Communication Audit: Rationale and Development." Paper presented at the Communication Association of the Pacific convention, Kobe, Japan, 1976; also presented at the Philippine-American Communication Conference, Manila, 1976, and the Academy of Management convention, Kansas City, 1976.

———. "Toward a Contingency-Based Theory of Organizational Communication," Paper presented at the Knoxville Conference Communication Theory, April 1977.

———, ed. *Improving Institutional Communication.* San Francisco: Jossey-Bass, 1979.

GOLDHABER, G., and P. KRIVONOS. "The ICA Communication Audit: Process, Status and Critique." *Journal of Business Communication,* vol. 15, no. 1 (1977), pp. 41–64.

GOLDHABER, G., T. PORTER, and M. YATES. "The ICA Communication Audit Survey Instrument: 1977 Organizational Norms." Paper presented to the 27th Annual Conference of the International Communication Association, Berlin, 1977.

GOLDHABER, G., O. WIIO, H. DENNIS, and G. RICHETTO. *Information Power and Management Function: Developing Organizational Intelligence.* Englewood Cliffs, N.J.: Prentice-Hall, 1978.

GOLDHABER, G. M., and D. P. ROGERS. *Auditing Organizational Communication Systems: The ICA Communication Audit.* Dubuque: Kendall-Hunt, 1979.

GOODNIGHT, G., D. CRARY, V. BALTHROP, and M. HAZEN. "The Relationship Between Communication Satisfaction and Productivity, Role Discrepancy and Need Level." Paper presented at the International Communication Association convention, New Orleans, 1974.

GREENBAUM, H. H. "The Audit of Organizational Communication." *Academy of Management Journal,* vol. 17, no. 4 (1974), pp. 739–754.

———. "Organizational Communication Practices—1975." Paper presented to the Eastern Communication Association, New York City, 1975.

GREENBAUM, H. H., and N. D. WHITE. "Biofeedback at the Organizational Level: The Communication Audit." *Journal of Business,* vol. 13, no. 4 (1976), pp. 3-15.

GUETZKOW, H. "Communication in Organizations." In *Handbook of Organizations,* edited by J. G. March. Chicago: Rand McNally, 1965, pp. 534-573.

HAIN, T. *Organizational Change Patterns.* Flint, Mich.: General Motors Institute, 1972.

HAIN, T., and S. TUBBS. "Organizational Development: The Role of Communication in Diagnosis, Change, and Evaluation." Paper presented at the International Communication Association convention, New Orleans, 1974.

HAIN, T., and R. WIDGERY. "Organizational Diagnosis: The Significant Role of Communication." Paper presented at the International Communication Association convention, Montreal, 1973.

KOONTZ, H., and C. O'DONNELL. *Principles of Management.* 3d ed. New York: McGraw-Hill Book Co., 1964.

LAWRENCE, P., and J. LORSCH. *Organization and Environment.* Homewood, Ill.: Richard D. Irwin, 1969.

LESNIAK, R., M. YATES, G. GOLDHABER, and E. RICHARD. "NETPLOT: An Original Computer Program for Interpreting NEGOPY." Paper presented at the International Communication Association convention, Berlin, 1977.

LIKERT, R. *New Patterns of Management.* New York: McGraw-Hill Book Co., 1961.

———. *The Human Organization: Its Management and Value.* New York: McGraw-Hill Book Co., 1967.

———. "Human Resource Accounting." *Personnel,* May-June 1973, pp. 8-19.

LIKERT, R., and D. BOWERS. "Organizational Theory and Human Resources Accounting." *American Psychologist,* vol. 24 (1969), pp. 585-592.

NADLER, D. A. *Feedback and Organization Development: Using Data-based Methods.* Reading, Mass.: Addison-Wesley, 1977.

ODIORNE, G. "An Application of the Communication Audit." *Personnel Psychology,* vol. 7 (1954), pp. 235-243.

PORTER, D. THOMAS. "CAAS—Communication Audit Analysis System." Unpublished computer program, Buffalo, N.Y., 1976.

PORTER, L., and K. ROBERTS. "Communication in Organizations." Technical Report no. 12, Contract #N00014-69-A-0200-9001 NR151-315, Washington, D.C.: Office of Naval Research, July 1972.

PRICE, J. *Handbook of Organizational Measurement.* Lexington, Mass.: D. C. Heath and Co., 1972.

REDDING, W. C. *Communication Within the Organization.* New York: Industrial Communication Council, and Lafayette, Ind.: Purdue Research Foundation, 1972.

REDDING, W. C., and G. SANBORN. *Business and Industrial Communication.* New York: Harper and Row, 1964.

RICHARDS, W. "A Conceptually Based Method for the Analysis of Communication

Networks in Large Complex Organizations." Paper presented at the International Communication Association convention, Phoenix, 1971.

——. *A Manual for Network Analysis: Using the NEGOPY Network Analysis Program.* Stanford, Calif.: Institute for Communication Research, Stanford University, 1975.

RICHARDS, W., R. FARACE, and J. DANOWSKI. "NEGOPY—Communication Network Analysis Program Description." Unpublished paper, Department of Communication, Michigan State University, November 1972.

RICHETTO, G. "Organizational Communication: An 'Unconventional' Perspective." In *Speech Communication: A Basic Anthology,* edited by R. Applbaum, O. Jenson and R. Carroll. New York: Macmillan Publishing Co., 1975.

ROBERTS, K., and C. O'REILLY. *Some Problems in Measuring Organizational Communication.* Technical Report No. 2, Contract #N000314-69-A-0200-1054. Washington, D.C.: Office of Naval Research, May 1973.

——. "Measuring Organizational Communication." *Journal of Applied Psychology,* vol. 59 (1974), pp. 321–326.

ROBERTS, K., C. O'REILLY, G. BRETTON, and L. PORTER. *Organizational Theory and Organizational Communication: A Communication Failure?* Technical Report No. 3, Contract #N000314-69-A-0200-1054. Washington, D.C.: Office of Naval Research, May 1973.

ROGERS, D. P. "An Audit Plan for the Internal Information Diffusion System of a Complex Organization," ERIC/RCS Document No. 094 425, 1974.

——. "Case Studies for Teaching Organizational Communication." ERIC/RCS Document No. 109 730, 22 pp., abstracted in *Resources in Education,* vol. 10, no. 12, (1975), p. 67.

——. "New Directions in Teaching Organizational Communication." *ABCA Bulletin,* vol. 38, no. 2 (1975), pp. 22–25.

——. An ICA Communication Audit of a Municipal Housing Authority." A report to the commissioners, 1977.

——. "Teaching Organizational Communication: Philosophy and Commitment." *ABCA Bulletin,* vol. 40, no. 4 (1977), pp. 1–3.

——. "The Content of Organizational Communication Texts." *Journal of Business Communication,* 1979.

——. "Effective Institutional Communication." In *Improving Institutional Communication,* edited by G. Goldhaber. San Francisco: Jossey-Bass, 1979.

ROGERS, E. M., and R. AGARWALA-ROGERS. *Communication in Organizations.* New York: The Free Press, 1976.

SCHEIN, E. H. *Process Consultation: Its Role in Organization Development.* Reading, Mass.: Addison-Wesley, 1969.

SEASHORE, S., and D. BOWERS. "Durability of Organizational Change." *American Psychologist,* vol. 25 (1970), pp. 219–226.

SIMON, H. *Administrative Behavior.* New York: Macmillan Publishing Co., 1945.

SINCOFF, M., and R. GOYER. "Communication Audit Critique: The Researcher's

Perspective." *Journal of Business Communication,* vol. 15, no. 1 (Fall 1977), pp. 57–62.

Steel, F. *The Open Organization.* Reading, Mass.: Addison-Wesley, 1976.

Taylor, J., and D. Bowers. *Survey of Organizations.* Ann Arbor, Mich.: Institute for Social Research, 1972.

Thayer, L. O. *Communication and Communication Systems.* Homewood, Ill.: Richard D. Irwin, 1968.

Weick, K. *The Social Psychology of Organizing.* Reading, Mass.: Addison-Wesley, 1969.

Weiner, N. *Cybernetics.* Boston, Mass.: MIT Technology Press, 1950.

Wiio, O. "Auditing Communication in Organizations: A Standard Survey—'LTT Communication Audit'." Paper presented at the International Communication Association convention, New Orleans, 1974.

———. "Organizational Communication: Interfacing Systems in Different Contingencies: Results of Three Years of Communication Auditing in Finnish Organizations." Paper presented at the International Communication Association convention, Portland, 1976.

Wilensky, H. L. *Organizational Intelligence.* New York: Basic Books, 1967.

Yates, M., D. Porter, G. Goldhaber, H. Dennis, and G. Richetto. "The ICA Communication Audit System: Results of Six Studies." Paper presented at the International Communication Association convention, Portland, 1976.

Chapter 16

Media: Getting the Message Across

Phillip V. Lewis

THE ROLE OF TODAY'S MANAGER involves more than determining what must be done and ordering it done. For each message sent, a decision must be made as to the best way to send that message. The media chosen may mean the difference between achieving success or failing to meet an objective. Hence, a very real need exists for managers acquiring a thorough understanding of the available communication media.

The word *media* (plural of *medium*) might be defined as the means of transmitting a message. Basically, we are concerned with who says what, in which channel, to whom, and with what effect—i.e., who is talking and what is being said, which channels are being used, who is listening, and what is the audience impact? In sequence, we are concerned with source analysis, content analysis, media analysis, audience analysis, and effects analysis.[1] Since you're already familiar with source, content, audience, and effects analysis, we are concentrating in this chapter on media analysis.

Before discussing the means available to organizational communicators (managers, public relations experts, company representatives, etc.), however, let's note three popular theories of message transmission practiced in some companies.

1. *Overpower 'Em Theory.* If you repeat something often enough and long enough and yell loud enough, the message is bound to get through.
2. *Glamour Theory.* If you take an idea and wrap it up in a very pretty

package with a very pretty bow, the receiver will be seduced into buying that idea.

3. *Don't Tell 'Em Theory.* If you "don't tell 'em" anything, they don't have anything to gripe about, and they don't have anything to ask questions about. If you don't tell 'em anything, they don't have anything to form negative opinions about.[2]

As you probably suspect, none of these theories works. Therefore, some company communicators may need to change their patterns of sending messages. For example, instead of overpowering, seducing, or ignoring employees, you should tell them what they want to hear, tell them what they already know, tell them what you're going to tell them, tell them with action words, and tell them what you told them.[3] This approach should enable all communicators to hit their target.

Regardless of what it is you tell them, though, the media choice is often critical. Thus, what are the media that may be chosen for any situation?

Communication Media

There are several dozen choices a communicator has regarding media selection. In general, we might say there are three basic alternatives—written, telephone, and person-to-person communication.[4] We will consider these three our major media choices in most businesses because of their familiarity. However, so that you might understand the broad spectrum of communication media, we will discuss a seven-class system first.

A Taxonomy of Communication Media

Usually, when someone speaks of "media," we think of some system of audiovisual presentation which does not require face-to-face interaction. Overall, communication media should meet the following criteria:

1. The system must be capable of conveying complete messages without face-to-face verbal narration at the point of reception.
2. The system must be capable of reproducing messages either simultaneously (by point-to-point, or point-to-many point, transmission) or sequentially (by recording or printing).
3. The system must involve a unique combination of sound, picture, line graphics, print, or motion.
4. The system must use a special equipment method, e.g., electrical, mechanical, photographic, and/or optical processes.

5. A single system includes only those elements that reach receivers via one transmission and/or recording and distribution system.[5]

From these criteria we might develop seven classes of communication media. Although there may be many ways of representing information, this proposed system seems to be the most encompassing. See Table 16–1 before reading further.

Now that you've become familiar with the general media available to communicators, let's look at those three systems used most frequently in organizations—written, telephone, and person-to-person.

Written Communication Media

Written communications include those written documents which convey organizational messages, e.g., letters, memos, reports, proposals, agree-

TABLE 16–1 Seven Classes of Communication Media

Class I: Audio-Motion-Visual Media
1. Television
2. Picturephone
3. Sound film
4. Film television recording
5. Electronic video recording
6. Holographic recording
7. Video tape

Class II: Audio-Still Visual Media
1. Still picture television
   a. Slow-scan TV
   b. Time-shared TV
   c. Recorded still TX
3. Sound slide-set
4. Sound-on-slide
5. Sound page
6. Talking book

Class III: Audio-Semimotion Media
1. Telewriting
2. Telewritervision
3. Recorded telewriting
4. Audio-pointer

Class IV: Motion-Visual Media
1. Silent film

Class V: Still-Visual Media
1. Facsimile
2. Printed page
3. Filmstrip
4. Picture set
5. Microfilm
6. Video file

Class VI: Audio Media
1. Telephone
2. Telelecture
3. Radio
4. Radiovision
5. Audio disc
6. Audio tape

Class VII: Print Media
1. Teletype

Source: Rudy Bretz, A Taxonomy of Communication Media. © 1971 Educational Technology Publications, 140 Sylvan Avenue, Englewood Cliffs, NJ 07632. Used with permission.

ments, directives, manuals, forms, and brochures. (Written communication is discussed in detail in Section II of this book.)

Letters find very high use in most organizations because letters can be personalized, are easy to use, and serve a documentary function. While letters usually serve as external media, memos serve internal needs. When detailed information is needed for decisions, reports are used to tie together the essential information. Employee publications can serve as a source of information. Policies, procedures, and future changes can be discussed in detail. Forms focus attention on the important elements of a message by eliminating unnecessary words.

Thus, written communication has several advantages and disadvantages that must be dealt with. For example, it is precise, leaves a record, is easily duplicated, can be prethought, is complete, and can be disseminated widely. On the other hand, it takes time to assemble, is one-way, is expensive, is sometimes uncontrollable, and does not require an instant response. These characteristics work for you when:

1. *You must choose your words carefully and precisely.* When you write something, you can do as many drafts as necessary to get it just right.
2. *It is an important occasion for the other person.* Putting something in writing gives some visible and lasting evidence of your appreciation or concern.
3. *It can save you time and energy.* Sometimes writing means you don't have to do it at all. Your secretary or assistant can draft a memo, and all you have to do is sign it.
4. *It can put you on firmer ground.* In situations where you are unsure of yourself in person, putting it in writing may make you more comfortable, thereby enhancing your chances of saying the right thing.
5. *It will help the recipient respond appropriately.* A written message gives the other person much more reaction time than even the most low-keyed oral approach.
6. *It will put it on the record.* Often, complex matters discussed in person ought to be followed up by a written summary. This helps ensure that you really agree.[6]

Overall, we might say that if documentation, distribution, and volume are important considerations, the written media should be used. If urgency and verification are more important, use the telephone.

Telephone Communication

A few uses of the telephone include transmitting or receiving instructions, securing information, and focusing attention. The telephone has several benefits—it is individual, flexible, private, convenient, and time-saving—and it may be the simplest method of sending messages because you don't have to go anywhere. Additionally, it is fast, permits questions and answers, and is two-way. However, there is no record of the conversation, and the message might be misunderstood. The beneficial characteristics will work for you when:

1. *You have a simple question or request and need a quick reply.* For example, telephone when you need a quick fact or figure for a report you are writing or to continue a discussion with someone in your office, and you know a person who has the information at his or her fingertips.
2. *You want to get to the point quickly.* You are very busy, or you know the other person is very busy. A personal visit might require extraneous chit-chat, while on the telephone a to-the-point message doesn't sound so abrupt.
3. *It is not critical that you talk with a particular person.* If you can get the information you need from any one of a number of managers or their secretaries, it is faster to switch around with your finger than run around on your feet.
4. *It is advantageous to be informal.* You don't want to seem to be pulling rank or standing on ceremony with official memo paper or letterhead. And the sound of your voice can communicate your relaxed intent best.
5. *You want to prod someone gently.* For a reminder of something you've agreed upon in person or have requested in writing, a telephone call can strike the right note. It reminds the person, but not in too heavy-handed a manner.
6. *You want to pave the way for a difficult encounter.* Instead of appearing on the scene with a complex or unpleasant message, you call ahead to give the other person time to get collected.[7]

There are times, of course, when both written and telephone media are unacceptable. You may need direct, face-to-face contact.

Person-to-Person Communication

Personal contact represents the most desirable medium because of the face-to-face interchange of ideas. It may occur individually between two people or in groups, such as in conferences, meetings, presentations, and speeches. Thus, a wider range of messages may be conveyed than was possible with written or telephone communication.

Facial expressions, gestures, and tone of voice contribute to messages. By combining the visual and oral aspects of a personal visit, you are able to show someone more easily what you are talking about. The advantages of face-to-face communication are that it is visual, provides personal contact, can show and explain, can set the mood, and is two-way. The disadvantages are that it has to take place at a convenient time, it requires spontaneous thinking, it may not be easy to terminate, one person may feel subject to pressure by power or status, and conversation may be heard by unintended receivers. Overall, the characteristics of person-to-person communication are in your favor when:

1. *You want to make contact.* The desire to get in touch with someone can often take precedence over the efficiency that a written or telephone message would provide.
2. *You want to sound people out.* There are times when you may not have anything concrete to say yourself, but you want or need to know what other people are thinking.
3. *You want to say something fairly complex.* You feel that personal give and take will get it across best.
4. *You want to discuss a confidential matter.* Private face-to-face communication can help ensure confidentiality.
5. *You simply want a break.* Dropping in on someone gives you a chance to unwind, to get other points of view, to gain perspective and to refresh yourself.[8]

Although these three areas—writing, telephoning, and face-to-face visiting—are the most common, they do vary in cost.

Cost Considerations

The actual costs of communication media have been a stimulus for some research. Obviously, the costs incurred in the purchase of television equipment or some of the other media listed in Table 16–1 would be expensive. We are concerned primarily with the costs of the above three media: written, telephone, and face-to-face. In Table 16–2, I have summarized various surveys of the costs of business correspondence. As you can see from the 1982 figure, business correspondence is more expensive than its weight in silver.

Certain conclusions are obtained by comparing the three media: First, if you have a thought to communicate to one other person, telephone is cheaper than other methods because you have nothing to prepare. However, if you want to communicate that thought to several people, the telephone may not

TABLE 16–2 Surveys of the Average Costs of Written Communication

Year	Cost
1953	$1.17
1964	2.32
1973	3.21
1982	7.11

be the cheapest method. Second, if you have already prepared typewritten information to communicate to one or more persons, mail it. If the mail is fast enough, don't use any other method. If mail isn't fast enough, then choose facsimile, teletype, mailgram, or telegram if you need a written record. Third, if you already have prepared handwritten information which must be typed and forwarded to one or more persons, it takes about the same effort to type the information for a memo, letter, or teletype message of the same length and degree of accuracy and format.

Thus, as you have seen, there are several types of and benefits to communication media. The choice of which to use is important, not only for getting the message through in the most efficient and effective method but also for saving money.

In addition, knowledge of media and the costs involved enable public relations personnel to make wiser choices regarding advertising. Overall, we might say that public relations is one of the newest and fastest-growing fields in communication. Because of that fact, it is important for us to see the role communicators play in public relations.

Public Relations Communication

Public relations might be defined as the planned effort of an organization to establish mutually beneficial relationships with its publics. Likewise, publics are the various groups of people affected by (or who can affect) the organization's operations. Obviously, with these definitions, public relations is based on two-way communication.

As our society becomes more complex, the public relations field is likely to continue its growth. This is precipitated by the need for effective communications between individuals and organizations. The importance of public relations can be further seen through the following objectives:

1. To interpret the firm's practices and nature of business operations to its publics.
2. To interpret to management the opinions and attitudes of the public about the company.
3. To discover and prevent internal, people-oriented problems that could cause business problems.
4. To obtain customer acceptance of products, increase sales, and gain other concessions by winning customer friendships.
5. To guide management in making decisions.
6. To personalize the company.
7. To focus on service.[9]

These objectives help to refine public relations practice by correlating the interests of management with those of the public. This growth and development process has been a long time coming, however.

Public Relations History and Development

Ivy L. Lee was perhaps the initiator of the modern public relations concept. Before his time, businesspeople seemed to care little for the public. Lee set up Business News Bureau to disseminate information to the press on behalf of business organizations. With the coming of World War I, another dimension was added with the establishment of the Committee on Public Information. Then, in the 1930s modern public opinion and marketing survey techniques added still a third dimension to modern public relations.

Today, public relations personnel are concerned with all the social, economic, and political trends (e.g., environment, inflation, equality). These trends affect the business organization, often in profound ways, and suggest a need for involving public relations personnel in long-range planning.

Public Relations and Long-Range Planning

There are a number of reasons for increasing the activity of the public relations department in corporate planning. First, long-range planning decisions affect the organization's long-run operations. Decisions change how the company interacts with the target audience. Keeping the public relations communicators in the dark until the last moment can stymie efforts and result in failure. Second, planning divisions need supporting services that public relations professionals can provide. Such services include:

1. Research to determine an industry's structure and a company's relative position within it
2. Surveys of users to discover needs for new products
3. Analysis of government regulations and attitudes toward a company considering doing business in a foreign country

Third, the rise in government regulation of business activity has increased the role of public relations people.[10] Because of these three realities, the communicative function of public relations has become an inextricable part of mass communications.

Public Relations and the Mass Media

The more commonly known mass media are printed media—newspapers, magazines, the Yellow Pages, business publications, outdoor advertising, transit advertising (bus, train, subway, taxi, etc.), point-of-purchase advertising, and speciality items (such as pens, pencils, and calendars)—and electronic media (television and radio). As we have already established, no single category of media is best for everything. Each has its place, depending on the circumstances. Generally, though, people will follow those media which provide them with the most complete and faithful treatment of the topics in which they are interested.[11] To see the advantages of the print media versus the electronic media, look to Table 16–3.

All mass media create opportunities for public relations communicators to employ effective techniques of merchandising their products. No doubt they will develop other techniques that will be equally effective in the future. To see what the future holds, however, we might review the changes that have taken place in the media. We will take a realistic view of what has actually been happening in public relations.

How the Media Have Changed

The biggest change in media is the development of cable TV and the prospects of cable TV in the next 10 years. Cable will grow by at least five times by the

TABLE 16–3 Advantages of the Print Media and of Television

Avantages of Print	Advantages of Television
1. Readers can control time, pace, and direction of their exposure. Readers can skim or read the material in depth at a time most convenient and appropriate to the occasion.	1. Advertisers can reach a large audience with a single advertising message.
2. Readers can develop a topic to whatever extent they wish.	2. Cost per exposure is relatively low.
3. Readers have the opportunity to closely examine the material in print at their own pace. Thus they can retain complex materials.	3. Sight, sound, motion, and color are utilized to get across a message.
4. Specialized appeals can be used to reach small, specialized audiences.	4. At the moment of exposure, a TV advertisement excludes competing messages.
5. Readers can reexperience the printed word days, weeks, or months after first exposure and can do so as often as they wish.	5. A select market target can be reached.
6. Prestige is quite high for some printed publications. A halo effect often results for the topics and writers found in some print media.	6. Dealer support is gained through TV advertising.
	7. Viewers are subject to inertia and will continue to watch TV through the commercial rather than change to another program.

Source: M. Wayne DeLozier, The Marketing Communications Process (New York, McGraw-Hill Book Co., 1976). Reprinted by permission.

end of the decade. However, the advent of cable TV will not become a significant factor in the practice of public relations. The twenty to one hundred channels that may become available will simply provide more places for a public relations practitioner to present material.

The use of videotape has brought about many changes in employee training and communications and other fields. But, so far, little interest has been expressed by public relations people.

Another dramatic change being talked about today in the media has to do with the technological developments in newspapers. But, so far, there is no evidence to suggest that these developments will result in any great changes in business.

Technological changes in book publishing—such as microfilm—also promise to alter that medium radically. Book publishing can be an important factor in public relations programming, but this field will not be any more significant to public relations than the technological developments in newspaper publishing.

Radio is another medium that has become more specialized in recent years. But, as with cable TV, radio broadcasting has not been a *major* factor in a public relations program. The fact is that radio and television departments at public relations agencies have grown very little during the last decade.

Film has become one of the most-creative media of our time, and there are always new directions to watch. Expensive productions for the commercial networks and even for educational television still tend to be advertising rather than public relations budget items. Less costly films which can be shown as part of museum exhibitions, retail store promotions, and educational programs continue to be a serious factor in public relations planning. But there are still few outlets for outstanding films that have a public relations purpose.

When we look at magazines as specialized publications, however, the story is quite different. The changes in the magazine publishing world during the past several years have already had a dramatic affect on the public relations business. In recent years there has been a tremendous upsurge in specialized magazines—something like seven hundred new magazines in the last ten years. Changing reading patterns now make it possible for a whole series of publications to emerge in a specialized field.

A few years ago, public relations experts would have been much less likely to develop a program with these media in mind. Now it is becoming commonplace, and this trend is going to increase greatly as time goes by. Specialized publications will, therefore, create many new opportunities in public relations. The reprint is one such technique that is already of great importance. Other techniques will be developed that will be equally effective as the multiplicity of specialized media increases.[12]

Reinforcement Activities for Students

1. Have the students discuss in small groups the reasons why the three popular theories of message transmission do not work.
2. Conduct a research project into the seven classes of communication media so that students can discover the advantages and disadvantages of each classification.
3. Take the class on a field trip to a large company that has a public relations department in order to see what kinds of media are actually used in business.
4. Have the students interview someone in a management position to determine the types of media used most often in his on her company. Discuss the advantages and disadvantages of those media. Determine the success of the various media used.
5. Ask each student to try to determine the actual costs of a specified media by researching, by interviewing, or by writing some research firm (e.g., Dartnell).
6. Invite a public relations expert to class to discuss public relations, mass media, or advertising and its application to communication.
7. Conduct a research project into the history and development of public relations. Ask the students to determine the changes in public relations work during the twentieth century.
8. Assign a research paper on the necessity for involving public relations departments with management's long-range plans.
9. Collect a series of advertisements from a category of print media and tell the other class members why you think they are effective or ineffective.
10. Create what you would consider an effective public relations communication program for a specified product.

Notes

1. Harold D. Lasswell, "The Structure and Function of Communication in Society," in *Mass Communications,* edited by Wilbur Schramm (Urbana, Ill.: The University of Illinois, 1960).
2. Owen A. Paul, "Communications in Changing Times," *S. A. M. Advanced Management Journal* (October 1971), pp. 59–65.
3. Ibid.
4. Robert D. Breth, *Dynamic Management Communications* (Menlo Park, Calif.: Addison-Wesley Publishing Co., 1969).
5. Rudy Bretz, *A Taxonomy of Communication Media* (Englewood Cliffs, N.J.: Educational Technology Publications, 1971).

6. Jane G. Bensahel, "Choosing the Right Medium for Your Message," *International Management* (May 1976), pp. 38–40. By permission.
7. Ibid.
8. Ibid.
9. S. Bernard Rosenblatt, T. Richard Cheatham, and James T. Watt. *Communication in Business* (Englewood Cliffs, N.J.: Prentice-Hall, 1977).
10. Jeffrey D. Bogart, "The Communicator's Role in Long-Range Planning," *Public Relations Journal* (September 1976), pp. 22–23, 33.
11. G. A. Steiner and B. Berelson, *Human Behavior: An Inventory of Scientific Findings* (New York: Harcourt, Brace & World, 1964).
12. David Finn, "How the Media have Changed," *Public Relations Journal* (October 1975), pp. 29–31.

Bibliography

LEWIS, PHILLIP V. *Organizational Communication: The Essence of Effective Management*. Columbus, Ohio: Grid Publishing, 1980.

Section V

Foundations and Frontiers

Chapter 17

Communication Theory

Leland Brown

Let's face the issue! Does a body of knowledge called communication theory exist? The answer is "yes, but. . . ." It is still in an integrative stage of development, for it is drawn from various disciplines that have contributed theories relevant to communication. The very nature of communication, if we define it simply as an interaction process or the ways one mind influences another, is in itself integrative. Just as everyone, however, will not agree to this definition, so not everyone will agree as to what is and what is not communication theory. Because communication theory is interdisciplinary, there is need for a pulling together of different viewpoints from the fields of psychology, sociology, English and speech, linguistics, semantics, organizational development and management, psychiatry, social sciences, and so the list goes on, into an integrated theory of communication.

The objectives of this chapter, thus, are to provide the reader/user with:

- A concept of theory
- A historical perspective of how communication theory has evolved
- An awareness of what elements make up communication theory
- An understanding of communication theory to be taught at undergraduate and graduate levels
- An understanding of what communication theory to include in a basic course in business communication or in additional courses
- Increased skill techniques and methodology for teaching communication theory to college and university students
- An insight into and appreciation for communication theory
- A challenge to become involved in communication theory, communication research, or both

Hopefully, this chapter will also provide a framework for understanding and applying the material presented in the additional chapters of this book, for communication theory, to be meaningful and useful, should be applied in various communicative situations and experiences. Good practice is built on sound theory, and an understanding of theoretical elements involved will prepare one to confront communication problems and to create alternative solutions.

A Concept of Theory

The *Encyclopedia Britannica* defines *theory* as the act of viewing. It derives from the Greek *theōria,* meaning "to look at, behold, contemplate, consider." The *Britannica* furthermore states it is the imaginative contemplation of reality, an intellectual insight, and lists several examples:

A *brief,* policy, or procedure proposed as a basis of action—a principle or or plan of action
An *ideal* or hypothetical set of facts, principles, or circumstances
A *body of generalizations* in association with practice of activity or field of study
A *conceptual, pragmatic principle* forming a framework of reference for a field of inquiry
A *judgment,* conception, or proposition or formula—a working hypothesis
An *unproved assumption,* conjecture, or supposition

From these ideas, we can conclude that many of the principles and concepts we have been teaching through the years to students in a business writing course, in oral communication, or in some other communication course can be presented in a theoretical framework common to all communicative acts.

According to Richard Hatch this does not mean adding another body of material to such courses but rather taking a theoretical approach.[1] Through a theoretical approach we can attach our material to ideas and concepts the students already have from having studied psychology, motivation, and other related areas. We can generalize material to fit all kinds of communication problems. When we deal with the psychological concepts in organizing unpleasant messages, for instance, we are also dealing with ways of organizing memos, speeches, reports, telephone conversations, interviews, TV commercials, and so forth. A good theory provides the student a workable and convenient analytical framework for solving communication problems. The fact is that a theoretical framework actually replaces many of the concepts we now teach with better, more generally useful ones.

Some Historical Perspectives

Following World War II, when a number of persons (including myself) began college and university teaching careers, we were teaching courses in business English, business letter writing, or business report writing, and a few people, considered the avant-garde for that time, may have specialized in direct mail advertising or business speaking. We were all engrossed in seeking principles and guidelines for helping students improve their writing and speaking skills, and in so doing were, without realizing it, formulating concepts common to all business letters, reports, etc., and we were researching businesses to determine what is good practice. Thus began the evolution of today's communication theory. Forerunners of textbooks in business English, letter writing, and report writing were authors such as "Andy" Anderson and Alta Gwinn Saunders at the University of Illinois, Robert Aurner at Wisconsin, Bill Boyd of Texas, Smart and McKelvey of Northwestern—several deceased, several retired, but their contributions are there. At the same time Carl Hovland, Irving Lee, Alfred Korzybski, Harold Lasswell, and others were exploring and writing from the points of view of psychology, linguistics, semantics, speech, psychiatry, and other disciplines. These two divergent groups of thinkers and writers illustrate the interdisciplinary nature of communication theory from the outset of its evolvement as this area has undergone substantial changes during the last twenty-five to thirty years.

With the advent of Shannon and Weaver's *The Mathematical Theory of Communication* in 1949, communication theory was considered strictly mathematical and was identified somewhat narrowly with technology and the technical aspects of communication. This emphasis had a direct impact on such concepts as measuring the unit of information transmitted over technical channels like the radio, telephone, etc., led to the development of information theory separately from communication theory during the 1950s, and influenced the development of computer science, data processing, cybernetics, and other studies—all as segments of information theory. Each discipline contributing to communication theory then went off in its own direction for research and theory development.

Also during the 1950s, Wilbur Schramm introduced mass communication theories, Wendel Johnson the use of communication for personality adjustment, and David Berlo the process theory and SMCR model. These authors presented process models which show a schematic diagram of the communication process as expressing an idea persuasively to another person (audience).

The models provided a theoretical framework for studying component stages and elements which were common to all communication. They compelled us to deal theoretically with how to get attention to the message, involving forensic, histrionic, and literary arts as developed and applied by different persons, cultures, and civilizations. They compelled us to deal theoretically with how to carry the message to a given recipient (audience), involving techniques of adapting messages to values, motives, background, knowledge, and experience of the receiver. Thus a whole body of theory developed dealing with the art of persuasion, motivation, and influence over another person through logical reasoning, facts, and psychology. This called for using linguistic and nonverbal symbols to encode messages to be decoded through the senses by the receiver who perceives according to personal experiences, background knowledge, and whatever else has gone into the makeup of his or her total personality.

Thus a whole body of theoretical knowledge developed dealing with transmission of communication through different media—oral, visual, written, mass, interpersonal, intrapersonal—from which the decoder interprets and understands what is being seen, felt, or heard, and dealing with the behavior of persons, how they react, why, to what, and with what effect. So at the end of the 1950s and throughout the 1960s, attempts were made to apply information theory from the early 1950s to the psychology of communicating and social sciences. This demonstrated a need for a behaviorally oriented synthetic theory of communication which permeated the late 1960s and 1970s.

Currently communication theory refers largely to the interdisciplinary, behaviorally oriented field of research dealing with the process of human communication and the nature of human interaction. A communication theory per se probably still does not exist. Current literature, however, indicates a core of theories related to particular phases of communicative behavior. Sereno and Mortensen identified these as four dimensions of communication theory and organized their book accordingly into four theoretical parts:

1. Communication as a system of behavior
2. Communication as decoding-encoding activity
3. Communication as interaction
4. Communication in social context[2]

In doing this they sought to provide resource material for study in courses in speech, social psychology, interpersonal communication, persuasion, and organizational communication by providing a core of fundamental concepts or theoretical framework for studying the nature and process of human communication. This approach focuses on the function of major determinates of communicative acts, the inner workings of communication, and the dynamics of interaction—forces affecting communication events and influencing communication outcomes.

Elements of Communication Theory

To determine what elements communication theory consists of, I analyzed the contents of the six books that are marked with an asterisk on the annotated bibliography at the end of this chapter. They provided a list of identified theories agreed upon fairly closely by all six authors:

Process	Mathematical
Stimulus-response	Models
Individual differences	Definition
Organizational	Information
Management	Mass
Behavior	Interaction
Two-step flow	

Further delving into those general theories, I sought what I considered elements in their makeup, such as "Process theory includes sender and receiver, message, channels." This search gave me a list of common elements contained within most of the labeled theories:

Sender/receiver characteristics	Channels
Language/symbols	Encoding/decoding
Media/method/form	Message
Perception	Feedback

Because concepts and principles are considered parts of theory, the following concepts were apparent also within either the so-called theories or elements thereof:

Motivation	Persuasion
Conflict	Understanding
Style	Listening
Tone	Nonverbal
Interpersonal behavior	Creativity
Small groups	Interviews
Leadership	Management styles
Problem solving and decision making	Environment
Oral	Written
Visual	

The theories listed here and elements in their makeup are common to all forms of communication media. The concepts, however, more or less deal with specific applications in particular communication situations calling for written or oral communication, interpersonal or small-group communication and, used in such situations, contain an entire separate list of principles or theories. For example, concepts of small-group communication involve a study of leadership and group member participation; techniques of discussion, creating ideas, and problem solving; the art of questioning; and management responsibilities of directing, stimulating, controlling, and other functions.

A survey of seventeen representative texts written for use in business communication classes revealed to what extent textbooks included these elements. (See "Representative Textbooks Surveyed" at the end of this chapter.) This survey also indicated the degree of agreement or disagreement among the authors and consequently inclusion in courses in communication, for those using the texts.

The labeled theories appeared in rank order as indicated below:

Theory	Number	Percent
Process	16	94
Behavior	13	77
Organizational	11	65
Management	11	65
Models	9	53
Stimulus-response	7	41
Interaction	7	41
Mathematical	5	30
Definition	2	12
Information	2	12
Mass, individual differences, two-step flow	1 (each)	5

The identified elements included in the above theories appeared in rank order as indicated below:

Elements	Number	Percent
Language/symbols	13	77
Perception	12	70
Media/method/form	11	65
Message	10	59
Sender/receiver characteristics	9	53
Channels	7	41
Feedback	6	35
Encoding/decoding	4	27

Likewise the concepts ranked as follows:

Concepts	Number	Percent
Small groups	12	70
Listening	11	65
Written	11	65
Persuasion	10	59
Motivation	10	59
Nonverbal	10	59
Interpersonal	10	59
Problem solving and decision making	10	59
Oral	10	59
Style	9	53
Tone	9	53
Understanding	7	41
Interviews	6	35
Environment	6	35
Visual	6	35
Leadership	5	30
Conflict	2	12
Creativity	2	12
Management styles	1	5

In all probability the concepts were treated according to the type of course the textbook was intended for. The books surveyed represented texts used in written communication, which are predominantly letter- and report-writing-oriented, texts on organizational and interpersonal communication, which have an oral orientation, and general texts. In ten of the texts surveyed, the authors integrated theory and practice throughout their works, and much of the theoretical considerations emphasized concepts and principles for improving communicative skills. In five of the texts, the authors separated theory from practice or application and dealt with it first. A few treated theory common to several forms or media of communication then later sought to discuss its applications, integrated with practice.

Since the survey was originally made in 1979 and 1980, I have examined four textbooks published in 1982, one in 1981, and one in 1980 to determine to what extent they agree or disagree with the original findings.[3] They represent the field of communication and provide excellent treatments of all the labeled theories, elements included in the identified theories, and concepts that are applicable—even to the extent that each of the six authors could have devised similar lists as used here in a survey of his or her own and come up with the conclusion to include all of them in one way or another. In my evaluation, these books represent the best that have been published in any one year.

Four of the authors treat theory in separate parts of their texts; Persing uses the process theory as a basis for organizing her divisions and chapter sequence. All six authors include the elements of theory and the concepts. Brown, Feinberg, Persing, and Sigband give more emphasis to the application of theory and skill building than do the other two authors. All six cover theory and applied theory in both oral and written communication, although by varying degrees of emphasis.

Communication Theory to Be Included in Various Courses

It was expected that an examination of the seventeen representative texts would reveal elements of theory which were to be a part of graduate or undergraduate courses in communication, used in a basic required course, or studied in specialized courses. Such was not true, however, because the texts were not selected for their functioning in any particular course or courses, but simply to provide a random sample, representative of more recently published texts available from which an instructor may select one according to the needs and purposes of the students. Therefore, any list of elements concluded from the survey shall of necessity be colored by subjective thinking on my part and will be substantiated by the thirty some years of my teaching in the field of business communication and by the growth and development of communication theory during the same period.

Any basic course in business communication, therefore, should deal with the process theory of communication. This was dealt with by practically all the authors surveyed. Consideration of models naturally follows to provide a schematic diagram of various process stages to provide a framework for analysis of elements with greater emphasis on language/symbols, messages, media/method/form, and sender/receiver characteristics than that given to channels and encoding/decoding. Communication should also be viewed as interaction, and one should emphasize behavioral theories and organizational and management theories. Information theory and mass communications should not be included. The basic theories thus presented can be discussed and applied in whichever direction the course needs to proceed, for example, courses in business letter and report writing, oral communication, persuasive communication, general business communication, or some combination of subject matter. These can be dealt with on either graduate or undergraduate levels. They can also be dealt with in depth in a foundation course in communication theory, preferably at the graduate level. For the latter, in my opinion, the Sereno or Anderson texts (listed in the bibliography on theory) would be appropriate.

Each of the concepts listed and surveyed in the representative textbooks could be the subject of a book or course of study by itself in which the theory pertaining to that area would be dealt with. For instance, a book on listening would include listening theory as well as practice and application; a book on nonverbal communication would include nonverbal theories; books on persuasion, or conflict, etc., would include theoretical concepts pertaining to those subjects. Also a book on interpersonal communication would include theory pertaining to each element dealt with—much the same as Richard Huseman does in *Interpersonal Communication in Organizations* or Malra Treece in *Communication for Business and the Professions.* One part might deal with theory, another with practice or applications, or the theory could be integrated with application in each chapter or division of the text. Theoretical concepts dealing with style, tone, visual aids, creativity, and the like would be treated in appropriate subject areas such as written or oral communication. Of the texts examined, six or seven dealt with theory separately from application or practice. Six or seven integrated theory with practice. Six fairly much ignored theory and dealt with skill development, and several of them dealt with theory more in depth, excluding practice and skill development. Needless to say, the texts available today give the professor a wide choice in selecting one to fit his or her purpose and the students' needs.

The four texts published in 1982, the one in 1981, and the one in 1980 which were examined substantiate the findings of the earlier survey, but they treat theory more comprehensively and emphasize application of concepts and principles in oral and written communication. The Association of Collegiate Schools of Business, American Business Communication Association, and American Management Associations advocate the inclusion of theory and oral and written communication in basic courses in business communication. They also advocate focusing on improving analytical and problem-solving abilities.

Teaching Methodology and Techniques

Behavioral learning theory provides the following principles for effective teaching-learning worthy for consideration:

1. Identify goals for the class.
2. Preassess students.
3. Set objectives to provide for learning to proceed in small steps.
4. Obtain active participation of students.
5. Provide for transfer of learning.
6. Plan for feedback to evaluate the instructional program.

Both instructor and student should know in advance goals that are to be achieved. Students need to understand clearly what the goals are. Three major goals in teaching communication theory might be stated as having knowledge of communication theory, developing the ability to bridge the gap between communication theory and practical application, and providing a conceptual framework for analysis and solving of communication problems.

Before teaching something, however, it is well to determine what prior knowledge somebody already has and how he or she will benefit from or use the new knowledge. Preassessment can be done by pretesting, filling out information data cards, oral questioning, holding conferences, and the like. It will give the instructor help in planning what to present and how to present it.

The goals stated above represent general, or overall, goals and need to be made specific. This can be done by formulating behavioral objectives that will relate the objectives to bits of learning in a progressive step-by-step process. The objectives should be specific statements that will identify the terminal behavior of the student as evidence of having achieved the objective. They will describe conditions under which the behavior is expected to occur and the criteria of acceptable performance. An objective will communicate your intent to the degree that you have described what the learner will be doing when demonstrating his or her achievement and how well you will know what is being done. Examples are:

1. The student should be able to understand communication theory. Evidence of understanding will be obtained from a written essay not to exceed five typewritten pages on communication theory.
2. The student should be able to explain correctly each of the elements presented in three different models of communication process. He or she will be held accountable for this on a test.
3. The student should be able to write a persuasive letter, within the business context, incorporating the five persuasive steps.
4. The student should be able to identify or list a dozen forms of nonverbal communication that are readily available to a manager in interactions with employees.

Active participation is dependent upon the instructor's presentation of material, involvement of students, and application of what is learned. Making use of self-study through study problems and exercises, through cases for analysis (discussed or written), through independent research, and through reading and making oral or written reports and annotated bibliographies will all involve the student actively and help in the acquisition of knowledge of communication theory. Principles and key points to be remembered can be brought about through demonstration and small group involvement. The discussion method can be used. Buzz groups, problem-solving groups, and idea-generating groups provide other means for student participation, as do games, panels, role playing, and so forth. Forums, seminars, and lectures can be supported by audio-visual aids such as:

Films	Charts
Slides	Tapes
Handouts	Videotapes

They may also be supported by presentation techniques such as:

Personal experiences	Relevant humor
Illustrations	Questioning to stimulate, coordinate, or direct
Examples	
Pace changers	

Structured notes can also be used. Such notes force participation, which in turn boosts learning and retention. "Programmed" notes, which the student completes as the professor proceeds with the lecture or discussion, enable the student to record all key points according to the instructor's presentation. The notes can be distributed as a handout, written on the board, or projected on the screen. Visual aids may accompany the notes to reinforce the learning process. Structured notes also force the instructor to weed out the unimportant and to organize the important into meaningful areas for presentation.

"Keep them laughing and learning" is a fallacy. Studies have shown that humor can increase attention to and interest in a topic. But they do not prove that comprehension and acceptance of factual knowledge improve when the message includes humor. Somehow humorous examples detract, for a person recalls the example and not the concept for which it was given. You may leave them laughing but not the wiser. Humor does have, however, a positive effect as an icebreaker.

Further tips for teaching follow:

1. Stimulate students to ask questions. Examinations produce material for discussion. Discussion clarifies misunderstandings, strong conflicts of opinion, and misinterpretations.
2. Restate ideas. Shape them differently to give another view point or insight.
3. Give students outlines. Attention spans are short; they cannot see the whole and its interrelated parts. Start with overall scheme of the course.
4. Leave room for spontaneity. Ad libs and unrehearsed arguments provide change of pace, creative ideas, and insights. Good teachers aim at catching a fresh idea now and then as it emerges and improvising on it.
5. Show vitality, drive, energy. These make for enthusiasm and are catching.
6. Vary the tone somewhat. Use some time for light discourse, comments on something relevant.

7. Cultivate a disciplined approach to study. Control behavior, reprove inattention, prod, weld, yet relax.
8. Teach principles of study and concentration. Students don't know how to study and have to be shown these matters in detail.
9. Carefully introduce each new concept. Define it, explain it, illustrate it, and apply it.

What students learn in the classroom must be transferred to the "real" world outside. This is not to say that the classroom is not real, but for maximum transfer of learning the tasks students perform should be identical to the real-world activities they are expected to carry out at the end of the instruction. And for communication theory to be meaningful, students must transfer what they learn about it to practical applications. One major difference between a college graduate in a management position and a counterpart who does not have the formalized education is the use of theoretical concepts and knowledge. The graduate has the theoretical framework with which to analyze and pinpoint problems and problem areas; the nongraduate bases an analysis on experiences which may have given just as many erroneous concepts as good ones to apply. The nongraduate is thus handicapped by not having the insight to deal creatively with problems.

Evaluation of the instructional program will let teachers know what has been learned and the degree of success reached. Teachers should plan to derive feedback for themselves at each learning step and to give feedback to students after each step. The level of success may motivate both student and teacher and will help both to improve effectiveness of learning. This can be done through questions and answers in face-to-face conferences, through testing, through problems, exercises, presentations, and use of checklists, and through evaluating to what degree objectives and goals were attained and with what results.

Communication Theory and Research

Yes, communication theory exists, and it is very much alive. Because it is interdisciplinary and integrating in nature, there is still an ongoing need for further study, analysis, and synthesis to form a meaningful body of communication theory. Thus, I would challenge you to become involved. Interaction of people and ideas needs to be observed and described to formulate theories of behavior on how people react and act, to what, in what way, with what effect or result. Theory may be further developed through empirical description and experimental research. Here again, studies of behavior can be done, for communication influences behavior and behavior patterns. How interpersonal relationships and attitudes are influenced within environmental conditions and organizational settings would be additional areas for study and analysis. Observing past communicative events and actions can take you into an analysis of political campaigns, sales promotions, public relations, and other areas from which theory can be further explored and formulated. Social structures within and outside particular organizations can be another basis for analysis. Likewise, attitudes, value systems, channels of communication, leadership characteristics and styles of management, and group behavior of persons interacting in small groups provide areas for investigation, observation, and analysis.

These are simply suggestions which would involve both instructors and students, especially on the graduate level, but you might be surprised what undergraduate students can do when given the opportunity.

Notes

1. Richard Hatch, "The Role of Communication Theory," *Business Education News* (Science Research Associates, fall 1976), p. 3.
2. Kenneth K. Sereno and C. David Mortensen, *Foundations of Communication Theory* (New York: Harper & Row, 1970), pp. 7, 8.
3. Leland Brown, *Communicating Facts and Ideas in Business,* 3d ed. (Englewood Cliffs, N.J.: Prentice-Hall, 1982); Lilian O. Feinberg, *Applied Business Communication* (Sherman Oaks, Calif.: Alfred Publishing Co., 1982); Richard C. Huseman, James M. Lahiff, and John D. Hatfield, *Business Communication: Strategies and Skills* (Hinsdale, Ill.: The Dryden Press, 1981); Dale A. Level, Jr., and William P. Galle, Jr., *Business Communications: Theory and Practice.* (New York: Business Publications, Inc., 1980); Bobbye Sorrels Persing, *Business Communication Dynamics* (Columbus, Ohio: Charles E. Merrill Publishing Co., 1982); Norman B. Sigband, *Communication for Management and Business,* 3d ed., (Glenview, Ill.: Scott, Foresman and Co., 1982).

Bibliography

Books That Explain or That Have Shaped Communication Theory

*Anderson, Kenneth E. *Introduction to Communication Theory and Practice.* Menlo Park, Calif.: Cummings Publishing Co., 1972.

Draws on research findings in rhetorical theory, linguistics, psychology, and sociology that have contributed to a broad perspective on communication theory. Divided into five sections: "Nature of Communication," "Human Elements," "Message Elements," "Settings and Forms," and "Perspectives on Communication." Theory and practice are integrated within the chapters. Suggested activities and readings at the end of each chapter.

BARNLUND, DEAN. *Interpersonal Communication*. Boston: Houghton Mifflin, 1968.

Surveys and studies compiled by Barnlund to bring together what the behavioral sciences have contributed to current knowledge about interaction in face-to-face, unstructured, communication situations. Among the research contributions dealt with are models, channels, verbal and nonverbal interaction, social contexts, etc.

*BERLO, DAVID K. *The Process of Communication*. New York: Holt, Rinehart and Winston, 1960.

A sound introduction to the communication process theory which examines the factors involved in the process and the role of language in human behavior. The core concepts are developed multidimensionally, using whatever disciplines and subject-matter specialties are relevant. Excellent treatment in chapters on interaction and interpersonal communication, meanings, and perception. His SMCR model has become classic and basic for later models.

*BLAKE, REED H., and EDWIN O. HAROLDSEN, *A Taxonomy of Concepts in Communication*. New York: Hastings House Publishers, 1975.

A useful and fruitful set of definitions and guides to resolve terminological confusions and to clarify the nature and function of the conceptual tools for both teachers and students of communication. Concepts are reinforced by terse explanations and appropriate illustrations. Chapters are sequenced under seven parts: "Basic Elements of Communication," "Forms of Communication," "What Is Communicated," "Process and Effects," "Mass Media Functions," "Social Environment," and "Investigative Approaches and Tools." Concepts are numbered, cross-referenced, alphabetically listed, and well indexed.

Encyclopaedia Britannica, vol. 6, pp. 203–205 and vol. 21, pp. 999, 1000. Chicago: Encyclopaedia Britannica, Inc., 1968.

Definitions and concepts of what is communication and what is theory.

FLESCH, RUDOLF. *The Art of Readable Writing*. New York: Harper & Brothers, 1949.

Complements Flesch's earlier work, *The Art of Plain Talk*. Both deal with scientific rhetoric, and Flesch's readability formulae have influenced writing clarity and interest for years. Clarity is basis for any effective communication.

GUNNING, ROBERT. *The Technique of Clear Writing*. Rev. ed. New York: McGraw-Hill Book Co., 1968.

Gunning's Fog Index is the easiest of the readability formulas to understand and apply. Its theory and practical concepts have contributed greatly to making written communication easily and quickly read and comprehended.

HANEY, WILLIAM V. *Communication and Organizational Behavior. Text and Cases.* 3d ed. Homewood, Ill.: Richard D. Irwin, 1973.

Considers communication in the organizational setting and in terms of a broad behavioral base for the communicative act. Focuses on what it is that happens *inside* communicators *before* and *as* they talk, write, and so forth, and *as* they listen, read, etc. This interrelates "thinking" and "communicating" aspects, such as perceiving, evaluating, visualizing, and interpreting, in the communication process. Part I treats communication and organizational behavior; Part II, behavioral bases; Part III, miscommunication patterns; and Part IV gives an overview.

HARRIS, THOMAS A. *I'm O.K.—You're O.K.* New York: Harper and Row, 1967.

Although a best-seller paperback for several years and not thought of as a communication text on theory, *I'm O.K.—You're O.K.* has had a great impact on interpersonal communication and relationships in the business field. First five chapters on transactional analysis concepts should be part of communication theory on interaction. Based on sound philosophy and common sense. Contains a lot of applied psychology and behavioral sciences views.

HAYAKAWA, S. I. *Language in Thought and Action.* 3d ed. New York: Harcourt Brace Jovanovich, 1972.

Hayakawa is one of the best-known semanticists in America. He has contributed much to communication theory from the semantics point of view. He defines semantics as "the study of human interaction through linguistic communication." Language symbols, perception, and meaning in encoding and decoding processes make us aware of meanings and behavior. Treats the role of language in human life through its uses: language to persuade and control behavior, to transmit information, to create and express social cohesion, and the language of poetry and the imagination.

JOHNSON, WENDELL. *People in Quandaries.* New York: Harper and Row, 1946.

Problems people have in trying to live with themselves and each other are discussed from the general semantics viewpoint. Communication is dealt with, then, as a means of personal adjustment to people and situations. His stage-by-stage process model is presented to set the stage for clarifying functions and disorders in various aspects of reading, writing, speaking, listening, etc. Johnson draws from psychiatry and clinical and abnormal psychology. His article dealing with how Mr. A communicates with Mr. B from *Harvard Business Review* has become a classic in itself, paramount to communication theory.

KORZYBSKI, ALFRED. *Science and Sanity: An Introduction to Non-Aristotelian Systems and General Semantics.* 4th ed. Lakeville, Conn.: Institute of General Semantics, 1958.

Provides a set of broad and informing principles on which other semanticists have built. An introduction to non-Aristotelian systems and general semantics. First published in 1933, it is the original source book of general semantics.

LEE, IRVING, J. *Language Habits in Human Affairs.* New York: Harper & Brothers, 1941.

An introduction to general semantics, founded on the premise that every human being is born into a *neuro*-linguistic and *neuro*-semantic environment from which there is no escape. The book has to do with words and their use in interaction. Significant chapters: "Language for the Living"; "Useful Use of Words"; "Acquaintance, Abstracting, Non-Allness"; "Indexing"; "Descriptions and Inferences"; and "Necessity for Application." Those who study this book should get a sense of the problems and difficulties involved in making accurate statements about themselves and the world in which they live as well as a sense of the maladjustments, personal and social, that have roots in improper evaluation and poor language habits.

*MORTENSEN, C. DAVID, comp. *Basic Readings in Communication Theory.* New York: Harper & Row, 1973.

Provides theoretical insights into basic understanding of process of human communication. Includes material from Dean Barnlund, Wilbur Schramm, Marshall McLuhan, etc. Topics include: perspectives, messages, channels, intrapersonal dimensions, interpersonal dimensions, and cultural dimensions.

*——. *Communication: The Study of Human Interaction*. New York: McGraw-Hill Book Co., 1972.

Provides broadly based introduction to study of human communication. Integrated treatment of communicative behavior across disciplinary lines of sociology, psychology, linguistics, speech, mass communication, and political science. Divided into four parts: "Foundations," "The Intrapersonal System," "The Interpersonal System," and "The Sociocultural System."

Osborn, Alex F. *Applied Imagination*. Rev. ed. New York: Charles Scribner's Sons, 1957.

Presents theories dealing with the creative process. Concepts have shaped creative problem solving, thinking of alternatives, and creation of ideas. His brainstorming techniques and creative problem-solving steps, both of which apply imagination, have been basis for further development of creativity in communication and relationships among persons. Although not a communication book or a book on communication theory, *Applied Imagination* has had a great impact on communication and human relations, especially throughout the 1960s and early 1970s.

Ruesch, Jurgen, and Gregory Bateson. *Communication, The Social Matrix of Psychiatry*. New York: W. W. Norton & Co., 1951.

The work of Ruesch and his co-workers in psychiatry has been to the front in development of theories in human communication. Later behavioral scientists in sociology and psychology have drawn from Ruesch.

*Sereno, Kenneth K., and C. David Mortensen. *Foundations of Communication Theory*. New York: Harper & Row, 1970.

Provides a framework of knowledge about the nature of human interaction, based largely on the fact that a core of communication does not exist. Accordingly, relates a core of theories for analysis, such as: a system of behavior, decoding-encoding behavior, interaction, and social context. These become the framework for discussing communicative processes which are the foundation for communication theory.

Shannon, Claude E., and Warren Weaver. *The Mathematical Theory of Communication*. Urbana: University of Illinois Press, 1949.

Starts with a schematic diagram of a general communication system. Classifies and explains various elements involved as mathematical entities. Deals with telegraph, radio, television as transmitters of speech. Provides mathematical formulas for such elements as capacity of the system, encoding bits of information into the system, noise, entropy, channels, decoding. This work became a base for much of the work involving computers and data processing systems today. Problems exist in capacity, coding, symbols, and noise at all levels. Shannon and Weaver in these last two aspects were forerunners of information theory today.

Thayer, Lee. *Communication and Communication Systems*. Homewood, Ill.: Richard D. Irwin, 1968.

One of the first and best references on the growing knowledge of communication systems. Author states in his preface that although the text is not a theoretical one, it presents tools for thinking about communication and systems. Many of his statements have been incorporated into a body of communication theory. Covers the dynamic nature of communication, qualities and characteristics of systems, functions of communication, technology, and theory and research problems and issues.

Representative Textbooks Surveyed

BOWMAN, JOEL, and BERNADINE P. BRANCHAW. *Understanding and Using Communication in Business.* San Francisco: Canfield Press, 1977.

CORNWELL, ROBERT C., and DARWIN W. MANSHIP. *Applied Business Communication.* Dubuque, Iowa: Wm. C. Brown Co., 1978.

GOLDHABER, GERALD M. *Organizational Communication.* Dubuque, Iowa: Wm. C. Brown Co., 1974.

HANEY, WILLIAM V. *Communication and Organizational Behavior.* 3d ed. Homewood, Ill.: Richard D. Irwin, 1973.

HATCH, RICHARD. *Communicating in Business.* Chicago: Science Research Associates, Inc., 1977.

HIMSTREET, WILLIAM, C., and WILLIAM M. BATY. *Business Communications.* 5th edition. Belmont, Calif.: Wadsworth Publishing Co., 1977.

HUSEMAN, RICHARD C., JAMES M. LAHIFF, and JOHN D. HATFIELD. *Interpersonal Communication in Organizations.* Boston: Holbrook Press, 1976.

LESIKAR, RAYMOND, U. *Business Communication Theory and Application.* 3d ed. Homewood, Ill.: Richard D. Irwin, 1976.

LEWIS, PHILLIP. *Organizational Communications: The Essence of Effective Management.* Columbus, Ohio: Grid, 1975.

LINDAUER, JOHN H. *Communicating in Business.* New York: Macmillan Publishing Co., 1974.

MENNING, J. H., C. W. WILKINSON, and PETER B. CLARKE. *Communicating Through Letters and Reports.* 6th ed. Homewood Ill.: Richard D. Irwin, 1976.

ROGERS, EVERETT M., and REPHA AGARWALA-ROGERS. *Communication in Organizations.* New York: The Free Press, 1976.

ROSENBLATT, S., T. BERNARD, RICHARD CHEATHAM, and JAMES T. WATT. *Communication in Business.* Englewood Cliffs, N.J.: Prentice-Hall, 1977.

SIGBAND, NORMAN B. *Communication for Management and Business.* 2d ed. Glenview, Ill.: Scott, Foresman and Co., 1976.

TREECE, MALRA. *Communication for Business and the Professions.* Boston: Allyn and Bacon, 1978.

VARDAMAN, GEORGE T., and PATRICIA B. VARDAMAN. *Communication in Modern Organizations.* New York: John Wiley & Sons, 1973.

WOLF, PHILIP M., and ROBERT R. AURNER. *Effective Communication in Business.* 6th ed. Cincinnati: South-Western Publishing Co., 1974.

Chapter 18

Precollegiate Business Communication

Doris D. Engerrand

THE BUSINESS COMMUNICATION COURSE taught on the high school level should include the development of reading, writing, listening, speaking, and interpersonal relations skills. With increasing competition for every job, the person with good communication skills will have a much better chance for success not only in getting a job but also in keeping it.

Textbooks available to the teacher include enough material for a one-year course in business communications; however, not all schools offer a one-year course. Schools on the semester system may offer a one-semester course instead of a two-semester course, and schools on the quarterly system may offer a one-quarter course or a two-quarter sequence instead of the three-quarter-sequence course. The teacher, therefore, must decide what materials to leave out of the shorter courses. In addition, the teacher faces the problem of finding and selecting material to supplement the textbook because no one textbook includes sufficient material in all the areas. The following pages will contain hints to help the business communication teacher decide what to include in the course and hints about helping the student acquire communication skills.

Developing Course Content

In the past, major emphasis in business communication courses has been placed on writing skills, and the textbooks reflect this emphasis. Although writing skills are very important, the other communication skills are also important for success in business. One suggestion for division of course content regardless of length would be allowing 15 percent for reading, 30 percent for writing, 20 percent for listening, 15 percent for speaking, and 20 percent for interpersonal relations. The actual division would depend upon teacher assessment of student competencies in each of these areas.

The first couple of days should be spent with pretesting in order to determine what the students need to bring them up to an employable level. The teacher may decide that the students need more time for the development of reading skills than 15 percent, for example. In such a situation, the teacher would make the necessary adjustment in the percentages of time to be devoted to the other areas. Regardless of the changes made, however, each course should contain some elements of each of the five areas.

Unless instruction is entirely individualized, a one-day laboratory should be held each week to provide for remedial work, enrichment work, or both on an individual basis. One student may need help with punctuation, another with giving directions, and yet another with proofreading. One or two students may be ready for materials not regularly included in the course, for example, the analysis of data or the preparation of special graphic aids for reports. This laboratory period should allow the students to work in areas of special need, be it remedial or enrichment exercises.

All five areas need not be included in each week's work. If, however, the teacher decides to include the five areas each week (if one assumes five 50-minute periods) and the same percentages given previously, the time spent with each area would be as follows: reading, 30 minutes; writing, 60 minutes; listening, 40 minutes; speaking, 30 minutes; interpersonal relations, 40 minutes; and laboratory, 50 minutes. Obviously, no one would be expected to plan activities so precisely, but the figures are given as possible guidelines.

Establishing Performance Goals

When establishing the goals for the course, the teacher should consider business requirements for entry-level jobs as well as student abilities. Broad area-performance goals should be first considered, then a series of competencies should be determined, which, when accomplished step by step, would result in the student's reaching the broad goal. An example follows:

GOAL

The student will correctly punctuate letters.

COMPETENCIES

1. The student will demonstrate the ability to correctly use the period, comma, semicolon, colon, question mark, and exclamation point by

successful completion of a series of exercises beginning with sentences and ending with letters.

2. The student will demonstrate the ability to correctly use the dash, hyphen, brackets, quotation marks, apostrophe, and parentheses by successful completion of a series of exercises beginning with sentences and ending with letters.

Obviously, using correct punctuation will be one of the early goals to reach in the course. For example, pretesting will determine which students need instruction in the use of the semicolon, apostrophe, or hyphen. Some students may have mastered the ability to punctuate before they enter the class and therefore will not be forced to do the exercises. These students will begin at a more advanced level, writing coherent paragraphs or writing with the "you" viewpoint.

Once pretesting in the five areas (reading, writing, listening, speaking, and human relations) has been completed, the teacher will assess the needs of each student. The student and the teacher together will establish the goals for the student to try to attain. Strategies will then be developed for achieving the goals.

Developing Strategies

In the event that a student needs improvement in the use of the semicolon, apostrophe, and hyphen, the teacher will give the student instruction in the use of the semicolon and then a series of exercises to complete until mastery in its use has been achieved. The student will then progress to the use of the apostrophe. This process will continue until the student has mastered the goal of correctly punctuated letters. It is important for the teacher to set in advance and for the student to know the standards used to determine the successful development of a competency.

Developing Means of Evaluation

Each competency must have a means of evaluation. The means of evaluation will, of course, vary depending upon the competency; however, with punctuation, an achievement level of ninety to ninety-five percent accuracy would be considered reasonable. A posttest including all forms of punctuation will be given upon successful attainment of the various competencies necessary to achieve a goal. The student who successfully completes the posttest will then be ready to move to the next goal. If the student is not successful, he or she must complete another series of exercises in the deficient area before taking another posttest.

Developing Reading Competencies

Reading speed and comprehension scores may be available from the students' permanent records; therefore, pretesting may not be necessary. If these scores are not available, the teacher may give one of the many published tests. The school counselor or the curriculum director will have information about these tests. Another possibility is a simple, teacher-made test consisting of directions the students will follow as they read. The test would have a time limit. Students with serious reading deficiencies will be referred to remedial reading classes if the latter are available.

Educational Developmental Laboratories has special equipment and materials which will help the students increase their speed, comprehension, and vocabulary. Through the use of a controlled reader, materials are flashed on a screen at preset speeds. Vocabulary-building materials are in the form of tapes and the students hear the new words used in context. Also, Science Research Associates has programmed materials which may be used on an individualized basis. These materials can easily be incorporated for use on laboratory days. In addition to these materials, the textbook *Business English and Communication* has a chapter devoted to "The Art of Reading."[1]

Following Written Instructions

Various sets of instructions can be compiled over a period of time to use in developing this competency. One group of students can write instructions for another group to read and follow step by step. The following are examples of what can be done in the classroom:

How to tie a shoelace
How to add a column of figures on a 10-key adding machine
How to multiply two figures on a 10-key adding machine
How to operate a mimeograph machine
How to plant a seed
How to set up a letter

The instructions must be clear and written in command form. A student may complete one or any number of exercises, beginning with the simple and ending with the complex, until both the teacher and the student are satisfied that the student can successfully follow written instructions.

Proofreading

Proofreading exercises will contribute to improved reading comprehension and to improved writing. The exercises may hinder reading speed, but they should improve spelling. Proofreading requires concentration. Ungraded practice letters done in typing classes make an excellent source of material for this exercise. In addition, the teacher may want to prepare materials with special problems not found elsewhere. Here are examples of proofreading exercises:

Proofread the work of other students
Proofread paragraphs with faulty spacing, or with characters inverted, missing, or added to words
Proofread paragraphs with words correctly spelled but incorrectly used, i.e., *is* for *if, as* for *is, their* for *there,* and *the* at the end of one line and also at the beginning of the next line

A student may complete one or any number of exercises until both the teacher and the student are satisfied that the student can proofread with a minimum of 95 percent accuracy.

Building Vocabulary

One way to build vocabulary is to use one or more of the many prepared materials available from publishers. Another means of building vocabularly is to have each student add one new word to his or her vocabularly each day. The student makes an effort to use the new word at least two or three times that day. In addition, students can make up simple crossword puzzles using their new words and exchange the puzzles with other students to solve.

Evaluation may be through observation (of students using the words they have on their lists) and through vocabularly tests. Vocabularly building should continue throughout an individual's lifetime.

Summary

The improving of reading is an individual effort. It involves a variety of approaches, and several problem-solving activities can be used in this area. Teaching aids, in addition to handouts, may include filmstrips, use of the overhead projector, use of the opaque projector, and bulletin board. The methods of evaluation include student self-analysis, teacher observation, and written tests. Encouragement of students' use of the library to obtain reading materials should not be overlooked.

Sometimes it is difficult to separate the skill areas because one may be dependent upon another. For example, the ability to write a correct letter may depend upon the students' ability to read the instructions and to proofread the letter when completed. However, it is possible to improve the students' reading and proofreading abilities to the point that their letter writing will be greatly enhanced.

Writing Competencies

Achieving the performance goal of writing effective business letters, memorandums, and reports requires that students be able to use correct English. The major portion of high school business communication textbooks is devoted to the development of writing skills, but not all students will have achieved the same level of competency before they enter the class. As a minimum, therefore, the following points should be covered on the pretest: punctuation, use of pronouns, agreement of subject and verb, troublesome words, parallelism, tense shifting, numbers, spelling, sentence fragments, and dangling modifiers. Students having already achieved an acceptable level of competency in all of these items should progress to the chapters concerning style. Students needing help with the items listed may use one of the many programmed sources on the market. Through the use of pretesting and programmed materials, the teacher can devote the major portion of class time to helping students develop competencies in areas they would not have been exposed to in other classes.

Pretest/Posttest Examples

Following are pretest and/or posttest examples the teacher may use to determine student competency in each of the items listed in the previous paragraph. (The teacher may omit all the punctuation in the examples if he or she would like to test more than one form at a time.)

PUNCTUATION

PERIOD

Dr Jones will give a speech this afternoon at 4:45 pm (*incorrect*)
Dr. Jones will give a speech this afternoon at 4:45 p.m. (*correct*)

Mr Ralph Smith PhD will begin working for the CIA in June (*incorrect*)
Mr. Ralph Smith, Ph.D., will begin working for the CIA in June. (*correct*)

COMMA

My first impulse was to run for the dog was showing his teeth. (*incorrect*)

My first impulse was to run, for the dog was showing his teeth. (*correct*)

Having arrived late he could not find a vacant seat. (*incorrect*)
Having arrived late, he could not find a vacant seat. (*correct*)

SEMICOLON

Mrs. Smith is the new manager she will begin work on Monday, July 1. (*incorrect*)
Mrs. Smith is the new manager; she will begin work on Monday, July 1. (*correct*)

Mr. Jones would like to buy a large house he has decided, however, that he does not have enough money. (*incorrect*)
Mr. Jones would like to buy a large house; he has decided, however, that he does not have enough money. (*correct*)

COLON

Students frequently misspell the following words receive, accommodate, bachelor, and convenience. (*incorrect*)
Students frequently misspell the following words: receive, accommodate, bachelor, and convenience. (*correct*)

There was only one thing to do, Resign now. (*incorrect*)
There was only one thing to do: Resign now. (*correct*)

QUESTION MARK

Are you coming home tonight. (*incorrect*)
Are you coming home tonight? (*correct*)

Answering the questions who what when where and how should be helpful when deciding upon a title for a report. (*incorrect*)
Answering the questions who? what? when? where? and how? should be helpful when deciding upon a title for a report. (*correct*)

EXCLAMATION POINT

Come now, tell the truth. (*incorrect*)
Come now, tell the truth! (*correct*)

Ouch. You are hurting me. (*incorrect*)
Ouch! You are hurting me. (*correct*)

DASH

"To be or not to be, that is the question." Shakespeare (*incorrect*)
"To be or not to be, that is the question."—Shakespeare (*correct*)

Harsh words I don't know how many were spoken by the teacher. (*incorrect*)
Harsh words—I don't know how many—were spoken by the teacher. (*correct*)

HYPHEN

You have too much self confidence, my friend. (*incorrect*)
You have too much self-confidence, my friend. (*correct*)

I bought a jack in the box toy for my son. (*incorrect*)
I bought a jack-in-the-box toy for my son. (*correct*)

BRACKETS

The title of the novel was *The Humen Factor The Human Factor* by Graham Greene. (*incorrect*)
The title of the novel was *The Humen Factor* [*The Human Factor*] by Graham Greene. (*correct*)

The school she attends (Baldwin High School the newest one in the county) now needs some minor repairs. (*incorrect*)
The school she attends (Baldwin High School [the newest one in the county]) now needs some minor repairs. (*correct*)

QUOTATION MARKS

I shall be happy to meet them, he said. (*incorrect*)
"I shall be happy to meet them," he said. (*correct*)

The Spirit of Saint Louis was the name of Lindbergh's plane. (*incorrect*)
"The Spirit of Saint Louis" was the name of Lindbergh's plane. (*correct*)

APOSTROPHE

You must have somebody elses book. (*incorrect*)
You must have somebody else's book. (*correct*)

The tree still has it's leaves. (*incorrect*)
The tree still has its leaves.(*correct*)

PARENTHESES

If you come, please bring your book, you have it in your room, haven't you? and meet me in the study. (*incorrect*)
If you come, please bring your book (you have it in your room, haven't you?) and meet me in the study. (*correct*)

I went to see John Brown, you know him, I believe, to ask him to go with me to buy a car. (*incorrect*)
I went to see John Brown (you know him, I believe) to ask him to go with me to buy a car. (*correct*)

SENTENCE FRAGMENT

(A fragment is not a complete sentence, but it is punctuated as one. It may be a phrase, a dependent clause, or just a word.)

I like to meet people. And to speak to them. (*incorrect*)
I like to meet people and to speak to them. (*correct*)

GRAMMAR

(Correct answer is italicized.)

CASE OF PRONOUNS

Jack, Jim, and __________ drove around all evening. (me, *I*)
The man __________ you saw is my brother. (who, *whom*)

REFERENCE OF PRONOUNS

Everybody wants __________ car repaired first. (their, *his or her*)
Neither John nor Jim brought __________ books. (*his,* their)

AGREEMENT OF SUBJECT AND VERB

Neither John nor his brothers __________ arrived. (has, *have*)
John's evaluation of his courses __________ good. (*is,* are)

TROUBLESOME WORDS

Is it __________ for us to play here? (*all right,* alright)
You don't have the correct __________ of exercises in your notebook. (amount, *number*)
There are __________ boys in the room. (less, *fewer*)
I shall study this matter __________. (*further,* farther)
__________ those two, there is no choice. (among, *between*)
Do this exercise __________ the teacher does. (like, *as*)
He likes to __________ on the grass. (lay, *lie*)
This action may __________ your position in the firm. (effect, *affect*)
This is all right __________ the last sentence. (accept, *except*)
Don't stand __________ the truck. (in back of, *behind*)
Do you know the __________ parts of this verb? (principle, *principal*)

TENSE SHIFTING AND INCORRECT TENSE SEQUENCE

He went home yesterday afternoon, and then he lies down on the bed and studied. (*incorrect*)
He went home yesterday afternoon, and then he lay down on the bed and studied. (*correct*)

They would have expected to have heard him. (*incorrect*)
They would have expected to hear him. (*correct*)

NUMBERS

The desk top measured 36 ________ 24 inches. (×, *by*)
________ days later he went to Europe. (33, *Thirty-three*)
John's sisters are ________, ________, and ________ years old. (*7, 11, and 15;* seven, eleven, and fifteen)
It is now ________ o'clock. (*twelve,* 12)
She spent ________ for a pair of shoes and ________ for candy. (thirty dollars, *$30*), (*fifty cents,* .50)
Please give me ________ of gas. (*8 gallons,* eight gallons, 8 gals.)
Every morning before breakfast, I jog ________ miles. (1½, *1.5,* one and one-half)

SPELLING

Words which illustrate the general rules of spelling as well as words frequently misspelled should be included on the pretest and posttest.

Use *ie* after any consonant except *c*.

achieve	relieve	hygiene
believe	siege	niece

Use *ei* after *c*.

receive	conceive	receipt
perceive	deceive	ceiling

In many instances, double the final consonant before adding the suffix.

occur	occurring	occurrence
drag	dragging	dragged

Drop the final *e* before a suffix beginning with a vowel, as shown:

arrange	arranging	
desire	desiring	desirable
force	forcing	

Retain final *e* before suffix beginning with a consonant.

arrange	arrangement
excite	excitement
fate	fateful

If the final *y* is preceded by a consonant, change *y* to *i* and add *es* to form the plural. (Exception: The plural of proper names, e.g., the Kennedys, the Germanys.)

ally	allies
mercy	merciful
busy	business

If the final *y* is preceded by a vowel, do not change the *y* to add a suffix or form the plural.

monkey	monkeys
alley	alleys
enjoy	enjoyable

When adding a suffix beginning with *i* to a word ending in *y*, keep the final *y*.

scurry	scurries	scurrying
hurry	hurries	hurrying
fly	flies	flying

Exceptions to final *y* rule include the following:

day	daily
pay	paid

The following words are frequently misspelled:

accommodate	familiar	proceed
accumulate	foreword	sergeant
bachelor	indispensable	sophomore
conscientious	irrelevant	stationary
council	marital	stationery
counsel	pastime	stature
consul	peculiar	strategy
convenience	precede	tragedy

Style

Good writing style involves not only the use of correct grammar and punctuation, but also an understanding and use of the seven C's of communication: clearness, completeness, conciseness, concreteness, correctness, consideration, and courtesy. Understanding and use of the seven C's may be developed first through analysis and then through the construction of sentences, paragraphs, letters, memorandums, and reports. Students find it helpful to work with paragraphs before they try writing letters. The next several paragraphs will contain hints about helping the student master the seven C's of communication.

Clearness

Writing in a clear manner makes it easier for the reader to understand the message. Clarity involves simplicity. Through the use of transparencies, handouts, analyses, and practice exercises, the students will be better able to write clearly.

Sentence Length. The fewer syllables in a word, the easier it is to read. The fewer words in a sentence, the easier it is to read. This does not mean that all sentences should be short. For example:

> John sees Mary. John gives Mary an apple. Mary eats the apple. John goes home.

A better construction would be

> When John sees Mary, he gives her an apple. After Mary eats the apple, John goes home.

or

> John gives Mary an apple when he sees her. He goes home after she eats it.

There are many examples the teacher can devise for practice work. Students should realize, however, that the average sentence length is seventeen to twenty words, and the average paragraph length is four or five lines. Reports may average up to eight or nine lines.

Difficult Words. Handouts can be prepared giving the simple word for the more difficult word (ascertain—find out, procrastinate—put off), and student papers marked with the difficult words underlined. The sentences with the underlined words would be simplified.

Ambiguous Sentences. Ambiguous sentences to be corrected can be compiled on a handout. A sentence such as the following would be excellent.

> Clean room for rent by a person with a big bay window. Apply after 6 at 749 Second Street. (*ambiguous*)
> Clean room with a big bay window for rent. Apply after 6 p.m. at 749 Second Street. (*corrected*)

Jargon. Another problem encountered in writing clearly is the use of jargon. Jargon is technical language and should be avoided when writing or speaking to someone not familiar with the trade. How many people outside the plumbing trade, for example, would be familiar with the phrase "to wipe a joint"? The accountant is familiar with language such as "deferred payments", "accounts receivable," and "capital accounts," but the average person is not; therefore, the accountant as well as the plumber puts these terms into language understandable by the layperson whenever he or she is speaking to someone outside the profession or trade.

Parallelism. The various elements in a sentence must be parallel in structure; for example, an infinitive must be matched with an infinitive, a gerund with a gerund.

She told me to go to school and that I should meet her later. (*incorrect*)
She told me to go to school and to meet her later. (*correct*)

I thought of reading the letter and to answer it right away. (*incorrect*)
I thought of reading the letter and answering it right away. (*correct*)

Dangling Modifiers. Modifiers must refer to the subject of the sentence, otherwise they are dangling.

Arriving late, the doors were closed. (*incorrect*)
Arriving late, he found the doors closed. (*correct*)

Being rare, he could not eat the steak. (*incorrect*)
The steak being rare, he could not eat it. (*correct*)

Writing clearly is not accomplished with a few exercises. It is a continuous process and, after the students complete a few exercises (unless some students are having difficulty), they should work with the other factors which make up style.

Completeness

A considerable amount of money and time could be saved if, before mailing a letter or report, people would answer the "journalist's 5 W's" plus "how." By answering the questions who? what? where? when? why? and how? before turning in papers, students could be reasonably sure that their work is complete. One student did not follow this advice and wrote the following to a travel agency: "My parents are giving me a trip to Europe this summer as a graduation present. Please send me all the information you have about Europe."

Conciseness

Conciseness can be achieved by carefully organizing ideas, sticking to the facts, and avoiding wordy expressions. Good organization involves making an outline first and then checking the outline against the questions: who? what? where? when? why? and how? When answering letters or memorandums, students do not have to make elaborate outlines—a few words written in the margin of the letter or memorandum or on a piece of paper will do. The problem will be to convince the students that this is a necessary prerequisite to writing. In order to get the students in the habit of making outlines, the teacher should require that the students submit the outlines before they begin to write. This requirement may be dropped once the habit has been established. Formal outlines should be written for reports unless the reports are very short.

Writers can easily lose goodwill and possibly confuse their readers by not sticking to the point of the message. By answering the journalist's 5 W's and the question "how," and by making an outline, the writer will be less likely to ramble. Students will find it easier to stick to the point when writing routine letters and reports. Special care, and perhaps additional instruction, should be given when the bad-news type of message is introduced. A good rule of thumb is to say what must be said and quit. Bad-news messages are usually longer than routine or good news because bad news usually requires some explanation before the reader is prepared to accept it.

Conciseness is also hindered through the use of wordy expressions. Here are two examples of wordy sentences and suggested revisions:

> John *received a letter from the bank stating that* he still owed them payments *in the amount of* $1,000 on his car. (*wordy*)
> The bank wrote John that he still owed $1,000 on his car. (*revision*)
>
> *Due to the fact that in the near future* this car *will cost the sum of* $15,000 dollars, *I would ask that* you buy it *at the present time.* (*wordy*)
> Because this car will soon cost $15,000, please buy it now. (*revision*)

Care must be taken that in striving for conciseness the message may become choppy and possibly cold. Include the necessary, eliminate the unnecessary, and use variety in sentence structure. Transparencies can be prepared for the initial instruction followed by exercises for the students to revise, and handouts can be prepared with many of the common wordy expressions the students should avoid. High school communication textbooks have examples of wordy sentences that the students may study.

Concreteness

The quality of concreteness is closely allied with clearness. By being specific, the writer may inadvertently make the writing more understandable.

> Laura is of medium height and weight, and she has dark hair. (*indefinite*)
> Laura is 5 feet 6 inches tall, weighs 120 pounds, and she has jet black hair. (*specific*)
>
> John is a superior student. (*indefinite*)
> John has a 4.5 grade point average on a scale of 5. (*specific*)

The teacher should help the student become aware of vague words which may hinder communication. Such words as *slow, fast, durable, tall, short, hard, soft, average, pleasure,* and *quality* may have one meaning for the writer and another meaning for the reader.

Choosing vivid, image-building words helps the reader form a mental picture, which is good. In business writing avoid the passive voice.

> It was felt that prices in New York were too high. (*passive*)
> Visitors to New York felt that prices there were too high. (*active*)
>
> The plate was put on the table. (*passive*)
> John put the plate on the table. (*active*)

Exercises should be prepared for students to change sentences from the abstract to the concrete and to change passive-voice sentences to the active voice.

Correctness

Letters and reports should be not only accurate regarding facts and figures but also mechanically correct. In addition, the language level should be appropriate or correct for the reader. Therefore, it is important for the writer to know the educational level of the reader. The writer who really wants to inform a cross section of the population of the bad weather in Maine would not write:

> The weather was tempestuous and the fog obfuscated the shore. The situation completely eradicated the good nature of the local population.

Instead, the following would probably be written:

> The weather was stormy, and the shoreline was hidden by the fog. The situation completely changed the good nature of the people.

If the purpose of the message is to communicate and the educational level of the reader is unknown, a good rule of thumb to follow is to keep the vocabulary simple. Generally, writing level does not cause high school students difficulty. Mechanics and accuracy do cause difficulty, and the students need to spend time in these areas.

Consideration and Courtesy

Consideration and courtesy are closely allied and will be discussed together. Courtesy and consideration are evident in writing which is done with the reader's point of view in mind. Just as it is difficult for persons to see both sides of an argument when they are emotionally involved, it is frequently difficult for a student to learn to write from the reader's point of view. The reader's point of view includes writing with the "you" viewpoint, using positive language, and avoiding disparaging language.

Introduction of the topic should be done with transparencies, showing sentences written with the "I" viewpoint or with negative or belittling language. After the students become familiar with the topic, the teacher should give them practice sentences to correct. With successful completion of the sentences, students can advance to correcting paragraphs. Once students have progressed through this step-by-step process, they should have no trouble writing with the reader's point of view in mind. Examples of sentences a teacher may use follow:

We received your order and it is being filled. (*"I" viewpoint*)
Your order will be shipped on Friday, April 2. (*"you" viewpoint*)

You failed to include your check for $25. (*negative language*)
Please send your check for $25. (*positive language*)

Mrs. Smith, your policy clearly states that you have a $150 deductible; therefore, we cannot honor your claim. (*belittling language*)
Mrs. Smith, because your policy has a $150 deductible, we will gladly pay you for any covered claim over this amount. (*tactful language*)

Writing with the reader's point of view also means avoiding worn-out phrases. It means that the writer must give some thought to the words and phrases used.

OPENINGS TO AVOID

We received your letter....
In reference to....
I have your letter....
Thank you for your letter....
In regard to....
Please be advised....

CLOSINGS TO AVOID

If I can be of further assistance, please do not hesitate to call.
Thank you in advance.
Thank you for your attention.

OTHER FORMS TO AVOID

I would like to take this opportunity....
May I take the liberty....
Permit me to say....

Students should be encouraged to write in simple, natural language, and the openings and closings should fit the situation.

Paragraphs

Each paragraph should contain one unit—that is one idea or thought.

Topic Sentence

The principal thought (topic sentence) may be placed first, last, or in the middle depending upon the purpose of the writer. Most business writing involves the use of the direct (topic-sentence-first) method because the major portion of business writing is routine—the asking or the giving of information. The teacher should first take the students through a series of examples. Start with several sentences, decide which one is the topic sentence, and then write a paragraph. The topic sentence may be the first sentence, in the middle of the paragraph, or the last sentence.

> John wants to buy a car. He will have to borrow money from a bank. He has a job. He has $1,000 in a savings account. John wants a compact car.
>
> *John wants to buy a compact car.* Although he has a steady job and $1,000 in a savings account, he will have to borrow money from a bank.
>
> John has a steady job and $1,000 in a savings account. *He wants to buy a compact car.* In order to buy the car, John must borrow money from a bank.
>
> John must borrow money from a bank even though he has a steady job and $1,000 in a savings account. *He wants to buy a compact car.*

After working through several examples, students are ready to try to compose paragraphs with just a topic given. They could be asked to describe a table, a shoe, a flower, a beach, a car, or a room; they could be asked to give directions, like how to get to the lunchroom or how to get to someone's house. Transitional devices may also be introduced at this point.

Transitions

Transitions are important to ensure the smooth flow from sentence to sentence, from paragraph to paragraph, and from section to section. A few examples of transitional words and phrases include *consequently, and, also, in addition, similarly, but, nevertheless, specifically, for example, following, not only . . . but also.* Complete lists may be found in English and communication textbooks.

Summary

Grammar and punctuation exercises in a communications course should be individualized. The students may engage in problem-solving activities using programmed materials and handouts. Teaching aids may include use of the chalkboard, the bulletin board, handouts, and programmed materials. Evaluation may be in the form of student self-analysis, teacher observation, and written tests. It is important that each student work in his or her greatest areas of need. The activities in the grammar and punctuation will be determined after pretesting.

Writing style includes the application of the seven C's of communication: clearness, completeness, conciseness, concreteness, correctness, consideration, and courtesy. Teaching methods include the use of transparencies, handouts, teacher-made exercises, and student-teacher analysis. The process begins with simple sentences, progresses to more complex sentences, and finally to short two- or three-sentence paragraphs. Methods of evaluation include student self-analysis and written tests. The seven C's are applied when writing letters, but the students should first be introduced to the principles of good paragraph construction and letter writing.

Students' abilities vary considerably; therefore, a sufficient number of exercises should be prepared to provide for the students who have difficulty mastering writing competencies so that they may work in this area on an individual basis.

Writing Letters, Memorandums, and Reports

The writing of letters, memorandums, and reports may be divided into three broad classifications: direct, indirect, and persuasive. *All* messages should be carefully checked for the following points:

Positive tone (free from the negative, belittling, "I" viewpoint)
Worn-out phrases (such as "I have received your letter.")
Correct grammar, punctuation, and spelling
Jargon (such as "wipe a joint")
Appearance (wide margins, and no strike-overs or faulty erasures)

Letters are primarily written to people outside the business firm, and memorandums to people inside the firm. Reports may be written for people inside the firm, but they may be written for people outside the firm as well. Students who have had typing already know how to type letters and memorandums and probably do not need additional instruction in how to set up either one. However, all students will need instruction in report writing. Those who have not had typing should be given a handout illustrating the format to follow when writing letters and memorandums.

The direct-form messages should be introduced first because they are the easiest to write. Several examples of good letters and memorandums and at least one poor one may be shown either on the overhead or the opaque projectors. Students should be encouraged to point out the good and the bad points, and the instructor can help the students discover why they are good or bad as the case may be. The first written assignments may be given for homework.

The regular class period does not provide sufficient time for the students to complete an assignment at this stage. The next day a few letters or memorandums can be randomly selected from the homework and shown on the opaque projector for critiquing purposes. Students, of course, place their names on the back of the homework so that no one will know who wrote the messages shown. After critiquing, the homework papers are returned to the students for rewriting. The revised letters or memorandums are graded. All other direct-form messages should be written in class. Students may be allowed to type the messages if typewriters are available, but those not typing can be required to set up the message in typewritten format. Work done in class may be accepted in rough draft form, but it should be correct in all aspects except neat appearance.

Grading standards vary from teacher to teacher, but, regardless of the standard used, students must know what it is. All writing should be graded for use of positive tone, worn-out phrases, grammar, punctuation, spelling, jargon, and appearance when mailable copy is desired. Specific points ought to be assigned for each type of error on test letters. However, for practice messages, students should be required to rewrite the messages until they are correct.

The same procedure for writing direct-form messages may be followed when teaching indirect form and persuasive messages and reports.

Letters

Since the format is different for direct and indirect letters, each one will be briefly discussed.

Direct Organizational Plan

Good news and routine letters are written using the direct form. In the direct-form organizational plan, the main idea is given in the first paragraph—frequently in the first sentence or in the form of a question. Sufficient explanation follows in the next paragraph or two for the receiver to answer the letter. The closing paragraph is courteous and sometimes contains an appreciation of goodwill, or a statement of the action desired. Usually these letters are simple and to the point; nevertheless, they have the qualities of the seven C's.

Depending upon the length of the course, the teacher may require that the students write one or more of some of the following letters:

- Request
- Order
- Acknowledgment
- Claim
- Public relations
    - Appreciation (thank you)
    - Congratulation
    - Invitation
    - Sympathy
- Favorable reply
    - Acceptance
    - Granting request
    - Granting adjustment

The students having no difficulty with the direct-form organization should write a minimum of three different letters; those having difficulty may have to write one or more of each type of letter before they become proficient. The students could, for example, write letters that do some of the following: request information concerning a class assignment, or information about insurance; order a stereo system, or automobile parts; acknowledge the orders previously written and tell when they will be shipped; register a claim concerning faulty stereo or automobile parts; show appreciation (thanks) to a class speaker; extend congratulations to classmates honored or to a businessperson who received a promotion; invite someone to a party or to a special meeting; offer sympathy to a friend whose parent or relative died; accept a speech invitation offer; respond to a request for the information concerning a class assignment, or information about insurance; or grant an adjustment concerning the faulty stereo parts, or automobile parts.

Indirect Organizational Plan

The indirect plan begins with a buffer statement. This statement is neutral; that is, it opens the letter but is noncommittal. It may be an appreciation of past business, a compliment, or any statement which is relevant but noncommittal. The buffer statement is followed with a carefully worded explanation of events. Here the writer is building his or her case, revealing the reasoning behind the decision. The explanation is followed by the decision not to do what has been asked. The decision is clearly but tactfully stated, and it should be positively stated if possible. The closing paragraph is friendly and positive.

Refusal letters of all types are usually written in the indirect plan, but they may also be written in the persuasive plan—refusing requests, claims, invitations, and credit. Since high school students will write few claim- and credit-refusal letters on an entry-level job, they should spend the major portion of their effort on refusing requests and invitations.

Previously written letters requesting information or adjustments (claims) may be answered. The teacher must use many examples to illustrate especially the buffer and decision sections because these areas are new to students. The seven C's should be observed, but special attention must be given to the you viewpoint and to negatives. Saying "no" without the use of negative language requires practice. It is also difficult to write while considering the receiver's point of view. The writer is usually concerned with his or her reasons for refusing but instead should be concerned with how the reader will accept the message. Refusal messages are closely allied to persuasive messages in that they both try to get the reader to either accept or do something.

Persuasive Organizational Plan

In persuasive messages, it is essential to get the reader's attention in the first paragraph. The statement or question should be closely allied with the message which follows. The succeeding paragraphs hold the reader's attention by developing interest in the subject. The closing paragraph suggests action (write today, complete and mail the postal card today). Students may write persuasive letters on the following subjects:

Request for cooperation
Request to speak to someone
Letter to solicit money
Persuasive adjustment request
Persuasive application for credit
Application for job
Sales
Credit refusal
Collection letters

High school students should spend the major portion of their time writing in the first six areas. Very few, if any, entry-level jobs require the writing of sales letters—most of these letters are written by professionals. However, there is some merit in spending time on credit refusals and collection letters, especially if students are getting jobs with small businesses. Many of the large firms have put their credit refusal letters and their collection series on a computer.

The number of letters written will depend upon the student's learning of the principles of persuasion; however, each student should write a letter of application unless he or she has already done this exercise in another class.

Memorandums

Memorandums are written to people inside the firm; nevertheless, they should contain the same seven C's used when writing to people outside the firm. The teaching procedure is the same as that used in letter writing; only the subject matter is different. Most memorandums concern the routine giving or asking for information and, therefore, are written in the direct form. A few may be persuasive especially if selling an idea or requesting that an anticipated unpopular action be taken. These should follow the indirect format. Memorandums which are short reports follow the report format (summary, purpose, scope, limitations, and discussion). Students will need practice in writing a summary, purpose, scope, and limitations before they write a memorandum report. Examples should be shown on the overhead or opaque projectors, and practice sessions should be held before a formal assignment is given. Examples of the kind of assignments which may be given using the three memorandum formats are:

DIRECT

Action taken concerning an employee who has been habitually late
Action taken to reduce accidents in the warehouse
Changes in government regulations
Routine changes in procedures

INDIRECT

Changes in work rules or break time which may meet employee resistance
Request to attend a meeting

MEMORANDUM-REPORT

Travel report
Equipment purchase
Selection of one person from several applicants

Although students will have practiced using the direct organizational form while writing letters, they frequently have difficulty when writing memorandums. Stating an action taken or a change already made in the first paragraph before the explanation seems to cause problems. Following the procedure given in the beginning of the section on letter writing should help to reduce the problem. Likewise, placing the summary in the beginning of a memorandum report is new to the student; therefore, the teacher should explain that this procedure saves much time to the reader who is usually a busy executive.

An excellent capstone activity for the letter- and memorandum-writing section is a series of short simulations. Students may change roles after each simulation. One suggestion for work flow and roles is as follows:

Customer to XYZ Company	Write letter placing an order
Sales manager to customer	Write acknowledgment letter
Sales manager to customer	Write letter explaining a delay in shipment

Sales manager to purchasing manager	Write memorandum asking why the delay
Purchasing manager to sales manager	Write memorandum telling when merchandise will be in warehouse
Sales manager to customer	Write letter telling when merchandise will be shipped
Customer to sales manager	Write claim letter (merchandise was damaged)
Sales manager to customer	Write letter either granting or refusing the claim
Credit manager to customer	Write three collection letters

Reports

Only the students successfully completing the letters, memorandums, and memorandum report section should attempt to write a report because report writing requires the application of all the skills previously learned.

In addition, the students must learn how to effectively use graphic aids in their reports. Teachers should prepare and show transparencies illustrating the various types of graphs, charts, and tables, and other illustrations commonly used in reports. Students may also need additional help when preparing graphic aids.

An outline of the proposed report must be approved by the teacher before the students begin the projects because students will frequently prepare an outline after they have actually completed the writing.

As a minimum, a report should contain the following parts:

Letter of transmittal
Title page
Table of contents
Summary or synopsis
Introduction
    Purpose
    Scope
    Limitations
Discussion
Conclusions and recommendations
Bibliography
Appendixes

Each part must be explained and exercises should be given for practice purposes before the students write their reports.

Report topics can be as varied as the teacher's imagination and the interest of the students. A few topics which may be considered are:

Changes in curriculum
Selection of a car
Selection of stereo equipment
Opportunities for employment in Milledgeville
Use of Lake View High School library

Summary

Direct-form messages should be introduced first because they are the easiest to write. The indirect organizational plan is next and the persuasive format last. After students have mastered letter writing, memorandums and report memorandums are introduced. Only the students successfully completing the letters, memorandums, and memorandum reports should attempt to write a report.

Activities include discussion, problem solving, demonstration, case study, and short simulations. Teaching aids frequently used are bulletin board, overhead and opaque projectors, and handouts. Grading standards will vary from teacher to teacher, but whatever standard is used, students must know what it is. Methods of evaluation may include student self-analysis, observation, case studies, and written tests.

Listening Competencies

Dr. Ralph G. Nichols said, "The average person spends 70 percent of his waking day in verbal communication, 45 percent of which is spent in listening. Yet unless he has had specific training in listening techniques, his efficiency in use of this skill is only 25 percent."[2]

Hearing is different from listening. Hearing is easy, listening is difficult. Listening requires effort, and therefore students must practice to improve their efficiency.

Activities

Listening may be practiced whenever someone is speaking. Here are a few activities which may be carried out in the classroom.

While giving instructions, a demonstration, or a lecture, stop talking and ask a student to repeat your last two sentences.

Pair off the students and ask each one to introduce the other. After four or five introductions, ask a student who was not involved in the previous introductions to repeat one of them.

The teacher identifies himself or herself by way of introduction. A student repeats the teacher's introduction and then does his or her own. The next student repeats what the first two people said, a third introduction, and so on. The process stops after five people and starts all over again until the entire class has participated. Each time this exercise is done, the teacher and the students say something different about themselves, and more people are added to the chain before it is stopped and started again.

One student may give a two-minute impromptu speech. The class writes a brief summary of the speech or one student may give an oral summary of what was said.

Select two students to discuss an issue—one for the issue, one against. As soon as one student finishes making a statement, the second student must repeat the essence of it before presenting another point of view. This procedure is followed throughout the discussion. When the two students are through discussing, all the students may write a brief statement of both arguments.

Evaluation

After the students have had time to improve their listening skills, some of the activities (for example, following oral instructions, summarizing speeches, repeating discussions) may be used for evaluation purposes. Evaluation may be oral or written; however, the written form is better. It is helpful if the teacher makes tapes of the activities, then the students as well as the teacher will be able to compare what they have written with what was actually said on the tapes. Grades may be assigned as a percentage of accuracy.

Summary

Listening must be learned. Activities to improve listening skills are varied and involve summarizing what was said. Evaluation may be included in the activities, but sufficient practice must be given before grades are assigned. Tapes should be made of the activities to assure an accurate record of what was said.

Speaking Competencies

Some of the same activities which were used to improve listening skills may also be used to improve speaking competencies. However, when emphasizing speaking, students would concentrate on this skill and the evaluation methods would be different. Speaking properly must be learned—we are not born with this skill. If videotape equipment is available, it should be used. Watching oneself on television is an excellent learning experience. If video equipment is not available, the activities may be tape-recorded for later analysis by the individuals.

Activities

The first activity should be a discussion of what is a good speech, and what individual characteristics make a good speaker. The class as a whole may do this or it may be divided into groups of five. In the former case, the teacher would put the items mentioned on the board as they are mentioned and discussed. In the latter case, the teacher would put the items on the board as the group spokesperson mentions them. As a minimum, the class should have the following items on the list. If any of the items are missing, the teacher may suggest them.

VOICE

Volume	Tempo or rate
Pitch	Enunciation
Attitude and feelings	

PERSONAL

Mannerisms	Dress and grooming
Facial expression and eye contact	Posture and carriage

CONTENT

Interest	Organization

When discussing the content division, the teacher must be certain that the following points are brought out:

How to analyze an audience—age, sex, occupation, interests, and education

How to develop ideas—quotations, analogies, anecdotes, comparison and contrast

How to adapt to the audience—vocabulary used

The first activity could involve committee oral reports; other committee oral reports could also be made. Any committee activity could be handled in this manner. Leaders could be appointed or they could be allowed to emerge. Likewise, spokespersons may be appointed or they could be allowed to emerge. In order to give everyone equal opportunity, however, it would be better to appoint leaders and spokespersons.

The two-minute impromptu speech on any topic a student may be expected to know about is an excellent activity. The topics may range from "My Mother" to "My Favorite Movie."

Biographies of actual or fictitious people may be prepared by the teacher, and the students would introduce these people.

Practice job interviewing is a practical activity. It is especially helpful if a person from industry does the interviewing.

Debates and panel dicussions may be held on current topics. Panel discussions require that the group coordinate its activities and therefore may be considered a group activity as well.

The more relevant the topics are to students' present lives, the more interested they will be. Once the students are interested, the topics may become more abstract. Also, Students with learning disabilities should also be given topics relevant to their present lives.

Evaluation

The list developed by the class during the first activity may be used for evaluation purposes. Each student participating could be evaluated by all other students and the teacher. The students' evaluation would not be seen by the teacher but used for student improvement only. The rating scale is excellent = 5, good = 4, average = 3, fair = 2, poor = 1, failing = 0. Total possible points are 55. When evaluating an outside speaker, the class may want to add four items: (1) extent to which the speaker was knowledgeable, qualified, and prepared; (2) ability to relate to the audience; (3) effective use of visual aids; and (4) effective use of notes (without obviously reading) and reference materials.

Summary

Good speaking habits must be learned. Before preparing a talk, the speaker must analyze the audience. The activities which may be used to learn good speech habits should be varied to provide for differences in students' abilities. Evaluation may be in the form of a check sheet developed by the class and used by both the students and the teacher.

Developing Interpersonal Competencies

Very few people view themselves as not being able to get along with others; yet more individuals are fired for interpersonal incompetence than for their skill deficiencies. Developing interpersonal competencies should be a very important part of the business communication course. Video equipment is a very important tool for teaching this skill and should be used whenever possible. The two techniques most frequently used in teaching interpersonal relations are role playing and analyzing case studies. Role playing is preferred because participants as well as nonparticipants are better able to see and understand how emotions affect interpersonal relations. Whether or not the role playing is being video-taped, a few of the students watching should make notes of the facial expressions and body movements of the participants. The remainder of the class may concentrate on the dialogue. Having students concentrate on different aspects of the interaction provides for interesting discussion later.

Activities

For role-playing activities, students may be divided into groups of various sizes, depending upon the situation, to act out a given interaction. Students should be allowed to portray the event as they see it—doing this will provide the basis for class discussion later. Situations which may be used for role playing are:

Telephone—giving information, handling an irate customer, transferring calls, or asking for information
Use of personal space
Handling an irate customer
How credibility affects believability
Differences in perception—football game, basketball game, an accident
Cultural differences—within the United States and customs of other countries
Reasoning with a brother or sister who borrows your car without telling you

Cases designed for the high school student to analyze are scarce. However, this fact need not deter the resourceful teacher. With a little imagination, any of the situations previously listed could be written in the form of a case. These cases would then be discussed as a class or in groups of five to seven students. Students may also be assigned to write cases to present to the class. Ideas for writing cases may also be obtained from office practice, communication theory, and interpersonal relations books.

Evaluation

The means of evaluation for this area of the course is more subjective. The role playing may be evaluated in terms of closeness to real situations. Students recording facial expressions and body movements can be graded according to the accuracy with which they observe, and the entire class on its participation in the discussions. Written tests covering the concepts presented may also be given. Student self-analysis is also an excellent means of evaluation.

Students presenting cases may be evaluated on the basis of whether they used the problem-solving approach in their analysis, whether they accurately defined the problem, and on the feasibility of their solutions. The class may be graded according to the participation in any discussions. Cases reviewing the concepts covered could be used for testing purposes.

Summary

Interpersonal relations activities can be fun as well as educational for students. Videotape equipment, while not essential, is a valuable teaching aid in these activities. Role playing is probably the best means of developing interpersonal competencies, although case discussion is beneficial. The situations to be portrayed or assigned as cases should be within the realm of student experience. These experiences may be the ones the students have had or have knowledge of through reading. Evaluation may be in the form of student self-analysis, teacher and student observation, and written tests.

Summary

The business communication course taught on the high school level should include the development of reading, writing, listening, speaking, and interpersonal relations skills. Pretesting is essential to determine where each student needs to devote his or her major effort. After pretesting, the student and the teacher together establish performance goals for the student to try to attain. Strategies will then be developed for achieving the goals. Each competency leading to the achievement of a goal must have a means of evaluation of which the student is aware.

The improving of reading is an individual effort and involves a variety of approaches. The methods of evaluation include student self-analysis, teacher observation, and written tests.

Grammar and punctuation exercises should be individualized and done on the day set aside for individual work (laboratory day). When teaching writing style, students begin with simple sentences and work up to paragraphs. The seven C's of communication, clearness, completeness, conciseness, concreteness, correctness, consideration, and courtesy, must be applied in all writing. Teaching methods are varied, and evaluation includes student self-analysis and written tests.

Letters, memorandums, and reports are written in either the direct, indirect, or persuasive format. The direct organizational plan is the easiest to write and therefore should be introduced first. After students have mastered letter writing, memorandums and report memorandums are introduced. Only the students successfully completing these areas should attempt to write a report. Activities include discussion, problem solving, demonstration, case study, and short simulations; and evaluation may include student self-analysis, observation, case studies, and written tests.

Students must practice to improve their listening efficiency. Some of the activities used for teaching may also be used for evaluation purposes—following oral instructions, summarizing speeches, and repeating discussions. Evaluation may be either oral or written; however, tapes should be made of the activities to insure an accurate record of what was said.

Good speaking habits must be learned. In teaching this skill, a variety of activities is provided to allow for differences in student ability, and a check sheet is used for evaluation.

Interpersonal relations activities have educational value for students and can be fun as well. Although not essential, videotape equipment can be very useful as an aid in teaching interpersonal skills. Role playing and case studies are the activities used most often, and evaluation may be in the form of student self-analysis, teacher and student observation, and written tests.

Notes

1. Marie M. Stewart et al., *Business English and Communication,* 5th ed. (New York: Gregg Division/McGraw-Hill Book Co., 1978).
2. Ralph G. Nichols, "Listening, What Price Inefficiency?" *Office Executive,* April 1959, p. 10.

Bibliography

ANDREWS, WILLIAM O., and DEBORAH C. ANDREWS. *Write for Results: How to Write Successful Memos, Letters, Summaries, Abstracts, Proposals, Reports, and Articles.* Boston: Little Brown and Co., 1982.

ARONOFF, CRAIG. *Getting Your Message Across: A Practical Guide to Business Communication.* St. Paul, Minn.: West Publishing Co., 1981.

BARR, DORIS W. *Communication for Business Professional and Technical Students.* 2d ed. Belmont, Calif.: Wadsworth Publishing Co., 1980.

BARRY, ROBERT E. *Business English for the Eighties, Grades 10–12.* Englewood Cliffs, N.J.: Prentice-Hall, 1980.

BASKIN, OTIS W., and CRAIG E. ARONOFF. *Interpersonal Communication in Organizations.* Santa Monica, Calif.: Goodyear Publishing Co., 1980.

BONNER, WILLIAM H., and JEAN VOYLES. *Communicating in Business: Key to Success.* Houston: Dame Publishing Co., 1980.

BRADLEY, PATRICIA H., and JOHN E. BAIRD, JR. *Communication for Business and the Professions.* Dubuque, Iowa: W. C. Brown Co., 1980.

BROWN, HARRY M. *Business Report Writing.* New York: Van Nostrand Reinhold Publishing Co., 1980.

BROWN, LELAND. *Communicating Facts and Ideas in Business.* 3d ed. Englewood Cliffs, N.J.: Prentice-Hall, 1982.

CAPPS, RANDALL, CARLEY H. DODD, and LARRY JAMES WINN. *Communication for the Business and Professional Speaker.* New York: Macmillan Publishing Co., 1981.

CHRISTEN, WILLIAM. *Strategies in Business Communications, Grades 10–12.* Englewood Cliffs, N.J.: Prentice-Hall, 1981.

FEINBERG, LILIAN. *Applied Business Communications.* Sherman Oaks, Calif.: Alfred Publishing Co., 1981.

FRANK, ALLAN D. *Communicating on the Job.* Glenview, Ill.: Scott, Foresman and Co., 1981.

GOOTNICK, DAVID. *Even You Can Give A Talk.* New York: David Gootnick Associates, 1975.

———. *Getting A Better Job.* New York: McGraw-Hill Book Co., 1978.

HAGGBLADE, BERLE. *Business Communication.* St. Paul, Minn.: West Publishing Co., 1982.

HAMILTON, CHERYL, CORDELL PARKER, and DOYLE D. SMITH. *Communicating for Results.* Belmont, Calif.: Wadsworth Publishing Co., 1982.

HAWKINS, BRIAN L., and PAUL PRESTON. Managerial Communication. Santa Monica, Calif.: Goodyear Publishing Co., 1981.

HENDERSON, GRETA L., and PRICE R. VOILES. *Business English Essentials.* 6th ed. New York: McGraw-Hill Book Co., 1980.

HILDEBRANDT, HERBERT W., ed. *International Business Communication: Theory, Practice, Teaching Throughout the World.* Ann Arbor: Graduate School of Business Administration, University of Michigan, 1981.

HILLMAN, HOWARD. *The Art of Writing Business Reports and Proposals.* New York: Vanguard Press, 1981.

HIMSTREET, WILLIAM C. *Business Communications, Grades 9–12.* Belmont, Calif.: Pitman Learning, 1982.

HIMSTREET, WILLIAM C., and WAYNE M. BATY. *Business Communications, Grades 7–12.* Boston: Kent Publishing Co., 1981.

HOLCOMBE, MARYA W., and JUDITH K. STEIN. *Writing for Decision Makers: Memos and Reports with a Competitive Edge.* Boston: CBI Publishing Co., 1980.

HOLLAND, G. PEPPER, and GEORGE H. DOUGLAS, eds. *Business Communication Casebook, No. 3.* Urbana, Ill.: American Business Communication Association, 1981.

HUMES, JAMES C. *Talk Your Way to the Top.* New York: McGraw-Hill Co., 1980.

HUSEMAN, RICHARD B. *Business Communication.* Hinsdale, Ill.: Dryden Press, 1981.

KISH, COLLEEN B. *Business English–30, Grades 9–12.* New York: McGraw-Hill Book Co., 1980.

KORNBLUH, ELAINE. *Business English, Grades 10–12.* Woodbury, N.Y.: Barron Publishing Co., 1980.

LEVEL, DALE A., JR., and WILLIAM P. GALLE, JR. *Business Communications: Theory and Practice.* Plano, N.Y.: Business Publications, 1980.

LODWIG, RICHARD R. *Career English.* Rochelle Park, N.J.: Hayden Book Co., 1981.

MAKAY, JOHN, and RONALD FETZER. *Business Communication Skills: A Career Focus.* New York: Van Nostrand Reinhold Publishing Co., 1980.

MORRIS, JOHN O. *Make Yourself Clear! Improving Business Communication.* New York: McGraw-Hill Book Co., 1980.

MURPHY, HERTA, and CHARLES PECK. *Effective Business Communications.* 3d ed. New York: McGraw-Hill Book Co., 1980.

PERSING, BOBBYE SORRELS. *Business Communication Dynamics.* Columbus, Ohio: Charles E. Merrill Publishing Co., 1981.

POE, ROY W. *How to Write Better Business Reports.* New York: McGraw-Hill Book Co., 1981.

REID, LOREN. *Speaking Well.* 4th ed. McGraw-Hill Book Co., 1982.

ROGERS, EDWARD J. *Getting Hired.* Englewood Cliffs, N.J.: Prentice-Hall, 1982.

RUFFINO, NORMA CARR. *Writing Short Business Reports.* New York: McGraw-Hill Book Co., 1980.

SAMOVAR, LARRY A. *Speech Communication in Business and the Professions.* Belmont, Calif.: Wadsworth Publishing Co., 1981.

SHEFF, DONALD A., and KEITH SLOCUM. *Business English, Grades 11 and Up.* Indianapolis, Ind.: Bobbs-Merrill Co., 1981.

SIGBAND, NORMAN B., and DAVID N. BATEMAN. *Communicating in Business.* Glenview, Ill.: Scott, Foresman, and Co., 1981.

TIMM, PAUL R. *Functional Business Presentations: Getting Across.* Englewood Cliffs, N.J.: Prentice-Hall, 1981.

TIMM, PAUL R., ELLIOTT A. POOD, and ETHEL C. GLENN. *Managerial Communication.* Englewood Cliffs, N.J.: Prentice-Hall, 1980.

VANHUSS, SUSIE H. *Basic Letter and Memo Writing.* Cincinnati: South-Western Publishing Co., 1980.

VARDAMAN, GEORGE T., and PATRICIA B. VARDAMAN. *Communication in Modern Organizations.* New York: John Wiley & Sons, 1981.

WEEKS, FRANCIS W., and KITTY O. LOCKER. *Business Writing Cases and Problems.* Champaign, Ill.: Stipes Publishing Co., 1980.

WELLS, WALTER. *Communications in Business.* 3d ed. Boston: Kent Publishing Co., 1981.

WILKERSON, C. W., and PETER B. CLARKE. *Communicating Through Letters and Reports.* 7th ed. Homewood, Ill.: Richard D. Irwin, 1980.

Chapter 19

Word Processing: A Vital Communication Tool

Cheryl M. Luke
Alfred B. Williams
Debra Jones

BUSINESS COMMUNICATION TEACHERS are familiar with what has become standard content used in their business communication classes and presented in business communication textbooks. Such topics as organizational communication, theory, writing styles, letters, memorandums, reports, interviewing techniques, resume preparation, listening, nonverbal communication, ad infinitum, are relatively standard. An area which lends itself to inclusion in a business communication class but which has received little emphasis is that of word processing.

Familiarizing students with word processing will help to bridge the gap in their educational training. Word processing is a means of facilitating the communication process albeit with automatic equipment. It is important that business communication students understand the relationship between the areas of written communication, dictated messages, and the completed document.

This chapter contains information which will be of help to a business communication teacher who wishes to bring word processing into the business communication course. Background information regarding word processing and its relationship to business communication is presented as well as such topics as word processing benefits, equipment, dictation skills, letter styles, and teaching approaches.

What Is Word Processing and How Does It Relate to Business Communications?

The term *word processing* has many definitions designed to communicate the unique concept of processing words. The meaning of the term originally was narrowly conceived as the product of automated equipment, particularly automatic typewriters. Credit is given to IBM for pioneering in the sixties an equipment revolution, the impact of which is still being felt.

In 1964, IBM introduced a typewriter with a memory which stored keystrokes on a magnetic tape. The Magnetic Tape Selectric Typewriter (MT/ST) enabled a typist to prepare a draft copy at high speed while storing the keystrokes on a magnetic tape. To correct errors the typist simply backspaced over the error and typed the correct material. The stored material could be played out in its entirety or sections could be added or deleted. Then, the playout was produced at high speeds. IBM's objective was the development of high-speed machinery capable of producing output economically and efficiently, thereby facilitating the business communication process and saving management time and money. Automatic equipment manufacturers agree that their equipment is designed to maximize high-quality office productivity and to minimize office inefficiency and waste.

IBM states that word processing is the transition of a written, verbal, or recorded idea to a typewritten form. This statement implies that there is a sender and a message, which are basic elements found in the most elementary of all communication models. IBM's statement could be taken a step further to include a receiver of the typewritten idea. This final output could be used internally or externally. Thus, the relationship between word processing and business communication is inextricable.

The Association of Information Systems Professionals (AISP) proposes this definition: "Word processing is the transformation of ideas and information into a readable form of communication through the management of procedures, equipment, and personnel."[1] AISP believes that the process of communication, which is basic to every business concern, necessitates the planning, actuating, and controlling of people and their work procedures in conjunction with automatic equipment to bring about a communication process and product indicative of today's ever increasing needs and demands.

How Does Management Perceive Word Processing?

Word processing implications are revolutionary inasmuch as they require reoriented thinking about the role of the traditional office, the duties of the secretary, and the responsibility of employers and management. Every person in a business organization is a word processor. This concept is not new. What is new is that word processing requires word processing equipment to speed up or mass produce copy in less time and with a minimum of wasted effort. Word processing technology and equipment gives management greater access to control and to coordinate work effort.

Management considers word processing as an administrative support function lending itself to a specialized area responsible for business communication within an organization. In examining word processing systems, Gerald Hershey believes that the word processing structure should follow these proven administrative principles:

1. Group (partially centralized) employees performing similar tasks.
2. Establish clearcut written procedures.
3. Establish explicit lines of authority and responsibility.
4. Have employees report to only one qualified supervisor.
5. Require users and providers of the service to follow standard procedures.
6. Recognize importance of employees by according appropriate status to support personnel and a support system manager.
7. Analyze costs benefits of services provided and procedures used.

These principles when applied to a word processing system should ensure the smooth functioning of word processing as an administrative support system of management.

What Is a Word Processing System?

Word processing is very much a systems approach to the processing of business communication. It is an orderly, logical progression from an originator to an individual responsible for processing the business communication. A word processing system approach is similar to a flowchart in which ideas are connected to show movement along and through the system from inception to completion. Such a flowchart depicting word processing was presented by Smith and Baker in *The Administrative Manager* and is shown in Figure 19–1.

Word processing systems have been made possible by such equipment as:

1. Automatic typewriters with internal or external memory
2. Text editing equipment
3. Dictation equipment
4. Automatic printing/copying equipment

The use of automatic typewriters with memory units for storage and retrieval expands the communication capability of any business. Being able to regulate work flow and to coordinate office productivity enhances time and motion studies as work feasibility projects.

The installation of word processing equipment will not automatically ensure efficient or economical word processing. A total word processing system

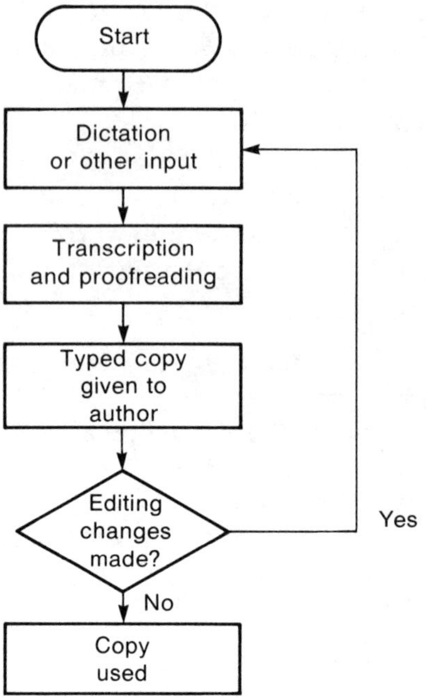

FIGURE 19–1 Word Processing Flowchart

From The Administrative Manager by Harold T. Smith and William H. Baker. © 1978, Science Research Associates, Inc. Reprinted by permission of the publisher.

must be designed to bring together the three key elements of (1) trained personnel, (2) automated equipment, and (3) specific procedures.

A word processing system begins with words from an originator and ends with printed communication (letter, memorandum, or report). A word processing system, however, is more detailed and intrinsic than the previous statement would lead you to believe. According to Keeling, Kallaus, and Neuner, a word processing system is a series of operations which combines input, processing, and output. Their illustration of this concept is presented as Figure 19–2.

In any communication process, the originator of a message has the options of writing in longhand, dictating to a secretary, or using a recording device. These are the media used to communicate input (the message) to another person who has the responsibility to convert the input into printed or typewritten form (output). In a traditionally structured office, the communication flow would be as shown in Figure 19–3, which appears on page 420. This is assuming there are no changes, deletions, errors, etc. Any special problems complicate the communication flow because of the necessity to keyboard the entire document again.

The word "throughput" is being used to represent the intermediary step

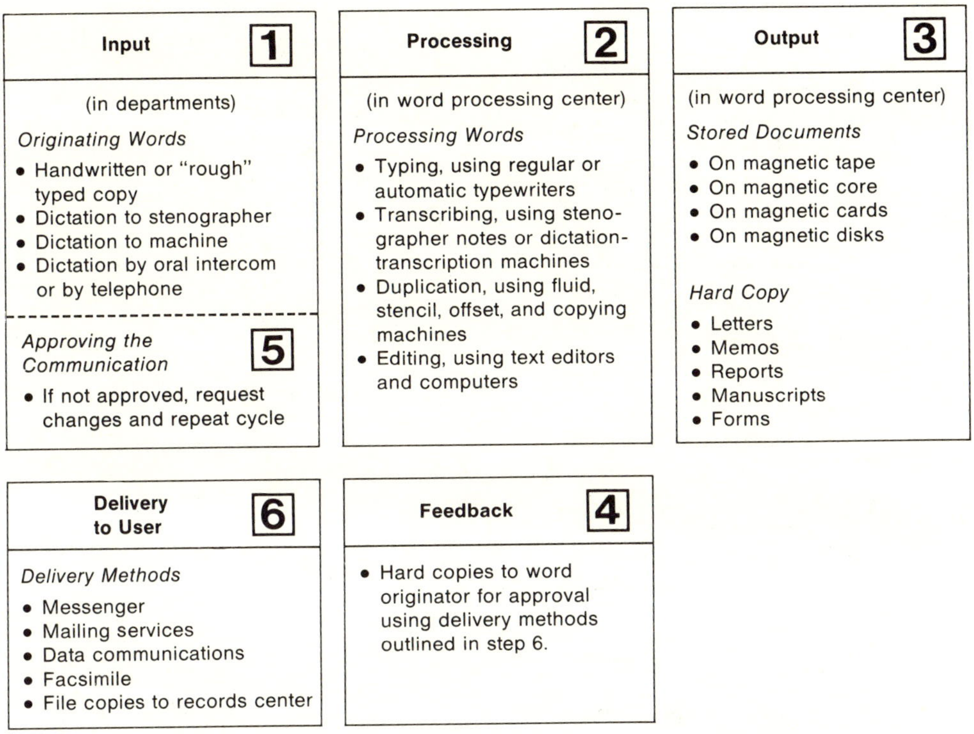

FIGURE 19–2 Elements of a Word Processing System

From B. Lewis Keeling, Norman F. Kallaus, and John J. W. Neuner, Administrative Office Management, 8th ed. (Cincinnati: South-Western Publishing Co., 1983), p. 393. Reprinted by permission of South-Western Publishing Co.

between input and output. In the throughput stage, the actual communication is being processed according to the nature of the document to be produced. Output is the end result. The objective of output is to present to the originator an error-free document in printed form. A byproduct is the retention of the document in magnetic form for immediate or future use.

Figure 19–4 (page 421) depicts a word processing system from origination to document completion.

What Are the Benefits of a Word Processing System?

There are numerous benefits to be derived from a word processing system. The following points were identified by Keeling, Kallaus, and Neuner in *Administrative Office Management,* 8th ed.:

1. Increased production of words by executives who use machines for originating communications. Many word originators are able to increase their

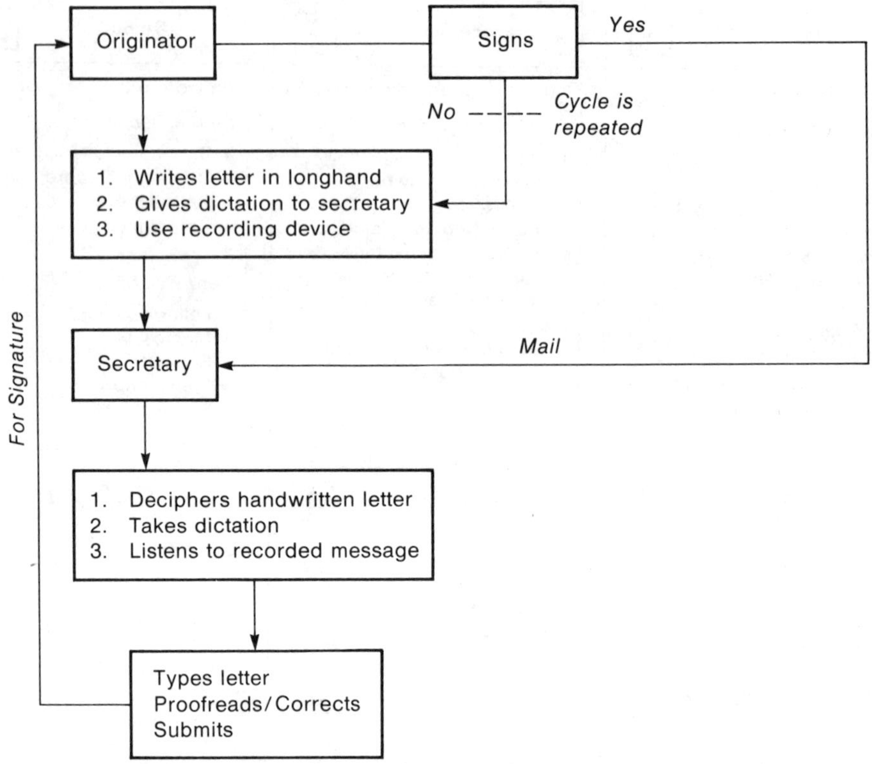

FIGURE 19–3 Processing a Business Letter in a Traditional Office

dictation speed from a range of 10 to 15 words per minute using the handwritten method to a range of 60 to 80 words per minute using dictating machines.

2. Higher productivity since the work is performed by expert operators. The retyping of copy is reduced, and error-free hard copy is obtained as completed paper documents. Much repetitive typing is eliminated. The amount of proofreading required is reduced, and documents may be revised much faster.
3. Better supervision of the work. The word processing operator is supervised by a specialist in the production of written communications rather than by an executive with more general management responsibilities.
4. More opportunities for measurement of the output, from simple tallies of documents completed to line counts per day, week, or month. Thus, an incentive system based upon work quantity and quality can be set up.
5. More consistent and more efficient service for management, such as faster turnaround time and lower unit costs as mentioned earlier. Further, there is better use of equipment and personnel by providing a system that keeps both the personnel and the equipment busy, thereby reducing the typical peak-and-valley periods in the work.

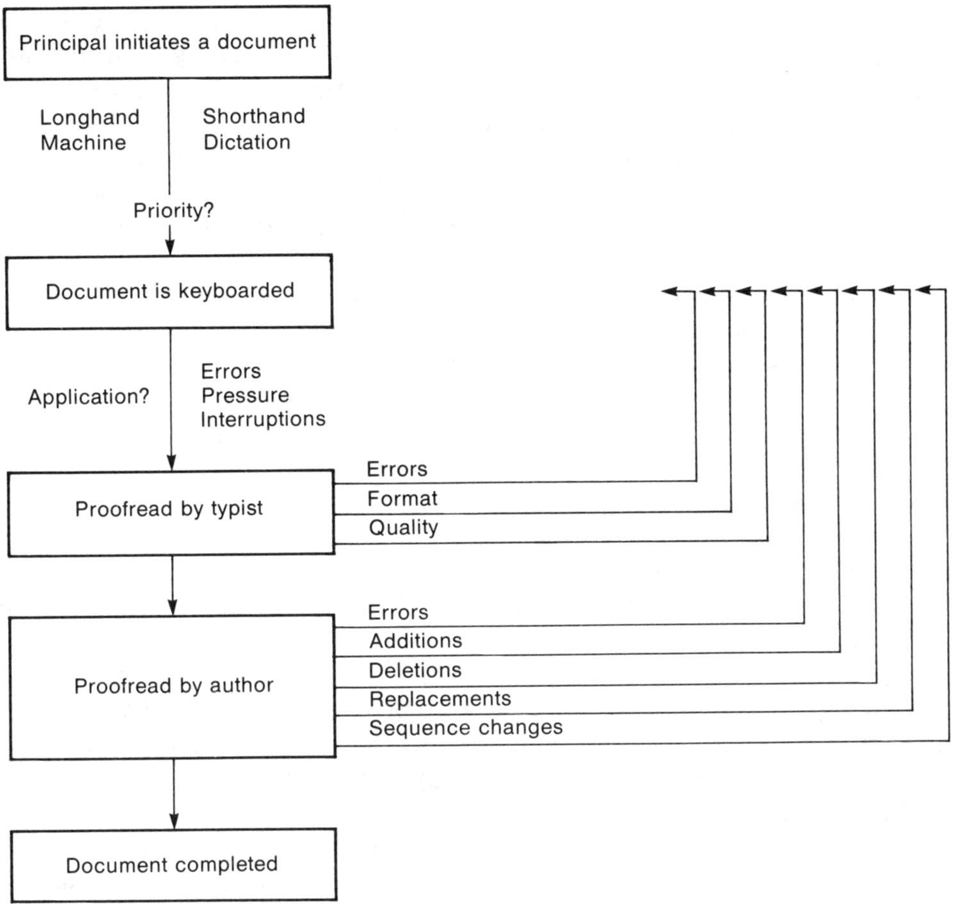

FIGURE 19–4 The Word Processing System

From "Technical Feature," Word Processing Report, vol. 8, no. 3 (February 1975). Reprinted with the permission of Information & Word Processing Report, Geyer-McAllister Publications, Inc., 51 Madison Ave., New York, NY 10010.

6. Closer ties between the company's word processing system and the data processing system. In more complex systems, the same hardware can be utilized for both types of systems.
7. Greater career opportunities in both the word processing and the administrative-support areas, with more management positions opening up for the secretarial personnel.

The advantages of word processing systems outweigh the disadvantages. As mentioned previously, there are numerous benefits derived from a word processing system being used in any size office. The one major disadvantage is people related. The psychological, emotional, and ego needs of the employee are factors management must consider whenever changing from a traditional work environment to the more fully automated word processing environment. Many office employees object to the dehumanization of their jobs. In actuality, word processing does not dehumanize but increases dependency upon high-powered technical machinery which cannot operate without trained personnel. To circumvent this problem, management must realize that a word processing system cannot function without a smooth flow of communication between all parties involved. The establishment of a word processing system necessitates added emphasis on oral communication within the work environment to ensure a cooperative, personalized, and understanding relationship between word originators and word processors.

How Important Are People to a Word Processing System?

The people aspect of word processing is crucial to the success of a word processing system. In order to use a secretary's time to the fullest and to reduce the amount of money lost through wasted time, proponents of word processing separated the secretarial duties into typing and nontyping (clerical and/or administrative) areas. To facilitate the word processing system, all dictation is directed to a centralized transcribing center where corresponding secretaries transcribed the dictation into printed copy. All other secretarial duties are handled by administrative secretaries.

Just as a secretary is instrumental to the success of any business, the importance of the role of the secretary is not diminished but is enhanced and expanded through conversion to a word processing system.

The advances in automated equipment require properly trained personnel to understand not only how the equipment functions but also the concepts behind the functions. Skilled personnel who have been highly trained are essential to a word processing center. Word processing brings another degree of specialization to the work environment thereby creating new and expanded positions. The following list identifies job titles and duties which may be found (all or in part) in a word processing center.

Administrative Secretary. Supports several individuals (managers or other personnel) by performing nontyping and administrative support functions such as filing, copying, compiling information, drafting, routine correspondence, scheduling meetings, arranging travel, and answering the phone.

Correspondence Secretary. Produces letters, reports, and other typewritten documents from dictation or "hard copy." Operates electronic transcription machines and automated typing equipment and handles a high volume of repetitive typing from recorded material.

Proofreader and/or Trainer. Possesses skill and capability to operate word processing equipment and also has good knowledge of work procedures. Responsible for final proofing and editing of correspondence. Conducts training on equipment and procedures. (Typically found only in large word processing centers.)

Center Coordinator or Scheduler. Is responsible for establishing priorities and assigning work. Prepares progress charts on word processing unit and may perform such duties as proofreading, filing, and training.

Operator. Is similar to correspondence secretary. Operates all word processing equipment—dictation/transcription, automated typewriter, copy machines, and telecommunications equipment.

Supervisor/Manager. Is responsible for planning, organizing, directing, and controlling work activities and personnel in the word processing center to ensure the attainment of the center's goals. Has specific responsibility for coordinating budgeting, training, selecting, personnel and equipment, and improving methods and procedures of operations. Usually reports to manager or vice president of administration services.[2]

What Word Processing Terminology Should a Business Communication Student Know?

An understanding of word processing, its concepts, strengths, and overall characteristics, would be incomplete without identifying and defining a few words and phrases commonly associated with word processing. This list is not intended to be exhaustive but is illustrative of the terminology associated with word processing.

1. *Word Originator* (*Author*). The person who dictates the business communication to be typed.
2. *Input.* Business communication sent to the word processing center.
3. *Output.* The finished product produced by the word processing center.
4. *Throughput.* The intermediate phase between input and output when the actual work is being performed.
5. *Operator.* The person responsible for performing work on the word processing equipment.
6. *Playback.* The repeating of the material which has been placed in the memory of word processing equipment.
7. *Principal.* The person who receives the material from the word processing center. It is usually the word originator.
8. *Editing.* The process of correcting errors or making changes in the copy.
9. *Text-Editing Machines.* Keyboard equipment which has the capability to store, retrieve, and play back material.

10. *Turnaround Time.* The amount of time it takes from receipt of the business communication to the final output.

These ten terms are a part of the specialized vocabulary used in word processing centers, and they are terms which should be understood and used by those who wish to exhibit a working knowledge of word processing. Words are an intrinsic part of business communication, thereby drawing the association of word processing and business communication even closer together.

How Does Cost of a Letter and Equipment Used Relate to Word Processing?

Since business has become so concerned over the increasing cost of office operations, there has been a very active search for procedures and equipment which would reduce, or at least minimize, the growth rate of office operating costs. The cost of a business letter has almost tripled in the last twenty years. Today the cost of a business letter is approximately $6.63; 24 percent of this, or $1.59, is the cost of the word originator's time. While business communication costs have been increasing, there has been a proliferation of sophisticated automated equipment designed to improve the efficiency of the word originator and the word processor. Such equipment includes automatic typewriters for repetitive typing, memory typewriters with storage capabilities, centralized dictation equipment (desk units, telephone hookups, or portable cassettes), editing typewriters with electronic memories, and typewriters that can communicate with other equipment (other typewriters and computers). However, the most sophisticated automated equipment is not being utilized effectively because little has been done to increase the proficiency of the word originator. For example, a dictation system is of little value to a person who cannot or will not use it to dictate communications.

How Does Longhand Compare with the Use of Dictation Equipment in a Word Processing System?

Longhand is still the most frequently used method of originating correspondence. In general, in offices where there is no word processing system, it is estimated that 75 percent of business correspondence is written in longhand by the executive before giving it to a secretary for typing. This is alarming in view of the cost of an executive's time. Certainly, longhand is convenient as it requires no set time, place, or specialized equipment; the writer can see the document developing; and revisions are easy to make.

In companies where word processing had been implemented, Lewis found that longhand was the most popular origination method before implementing a word processing system, and it ranked second afterwards. After the installation of a word processing system, dictation became the most popular origination method; it accounted for approximately 70 percent of all correspondence.[3] (See Table 19–1.)

Dictation, on the other hand, is a skill which must be learned through practice and application. Learning to dictate efficiently requires the ability to think, to organize, and to express ideas orally. The advantage of oral communications is in having a more rapid process of expressing oneself than in written communication. To be effective, however, one must develop dictation skill, which is an oral communication process.

The manufacturers of dictation equipment realized that it is necessary to acquaint the prospective user with the efficiency factors as well as to teach people how to dictate if they are to sell their products. Some companies saw the need to improve communications and provided training programs in dictation skills for their employees. Educational institutions have not taken advantage of a needed learning experience for their students; therefore, dictation skills have not been taught. However, business communication is an area that lends itself to the teaching of dictating skills.

What Are the Cost Factors of Dictation versus Longhand?

Let's look at the cost factor of dictation versus longhand. From the originator's point of view, the average writing speed of an individual is about

TABLE 19–1 Comparison of Business Letter Origination Methods Used Before and After Word Processing Implementation

Origination Method	Percent of Use Before WP*	Rank	Percent of Use After WP*	Rank
Personal handwriting	46	1	26	2
Personal typewriting	9	4	3	6
Dictation to a secretary writing shorthand	19	2	5	5
Dictation to a secretary using a shorthand machine	1	6	0	7
Desk-top dictation machine	16	3	14	3
Portable dictation machine	8	5	10	4
Direct telephone dictation to a word processing center	N/A	N/A	39	1

*Percentages are rounded.

Source: Stephen D. Lewis, "Word Processing's Impact on Business Letter Writing" (paper presented at American Business Communication Association Southeastern convention, Lafayette, La., March 31, 1979), p. 4.

ten words a minute. Dictation speeds vary depending on whether the dictation is being recorded by a shorthand writer or by using a dictation machine. Studies of the Dartnell Corporation cite 60 words a minute as the average dictation rate.

Consider the following example. Based on a thirty-five-hour work week for fifty-two weeks at varying annual salaries, you have the following breakdown:

Annual Salary	Cost Per Hour	Approximate Cost Per Minute
$20,000	$10.99	$.18
18,000	9.89	.16
16,000	8.80	.15
14,000	7.70	.13
12,000	6.60	.11

To illustrate, an average letter of 150 words could be dictated in about three minutes while the same letter would take fifteen minutes to write in longhand. Using the figures presented, it would cost approximately 33¢ to dictate the letter versus $1.65 to write the letter in longhand for an originator whose annual salary is $12,000. Logically enough, the higher the annual salary, the higher the cost. These figures do not reflect the total expense since the dictator's and typist's time must be considered, as well as equipment and materials cost. A comparison of rates indicates the need for communication originators to have dictation ability.

What Should a Word Originator Know about Letter Styles and Parts?

The ability to dictate effectively requires that the originator understand basic letter parts and placement. Typewriting courses stress letter styles, punctuation, placement of special notations, etc. Many business communication students may have had a typing course and will be familiar with basic letter styles and parts; however, there may be students who have not had typing and who need an understanding of a basic element in written communication, which is the business letter. Business communication students are prospective word originators and will be ultimately responsible for any document which bears their names.

When originators of business communications are not familiar with the letter styles, features, etc., they must depend on the ability and knowledge of the typist. Word originators are not equipped to set standards of quality for their own correspondence if they are not familiar with letter styles and parts.

What Are the Basic Parts and Placement of a Business Letter?

Business communication instructors stress the need for developing communications which convey an effective, accurate message in a concise manner while creating a favorable impression. In order to develop this ability during the learning phase, the business communication student should use longhand in order to evaluate the tone and organization of the message. The message or body is the most important part of a communication; however, the appearance and placement of special parts contribute significantly to the credibility given the message. These two areas must be harmonized.

Knowing the basic letter parts and placement enables people who dictate letters to become more effective word originators. By knowing about the basic process of producing a mailable letter, a dictator can give special instructions in proper sequence to alert the typist.

A review of the basic letter parts in the sequence as they would appear in a letter will help business communication students to develop dictation ability.

Date. Floats between lines 12 and 20 depending on the length of the letter *or* it is placed a double space below the letterhead.

Special Mailing Notations. Usually placed at the left margin a double space below the date. By placing the special mail service on the letter, the reader gets the impression that the letter is important, and a record of the mail service used appears on the file copy for future reference.

Inside Address. Usually placed four lines below the date when the floating date line is used; when the date appears a double space below the letterhead, between four and twelve lines are left before the inside address. When special mailing instructions appear on a letter, the inside address is usually a double space below the instructions.

Attention Line. Usually placed a double space below the inside address and at the left margin. The attention line is used when an individual or a special department should handle the correspondence.

Salutation. Usually placed a double space below the inside address or the attention line if used. (The appropriate salutation for a letter addressed to a company is "Gentlemen," "Ladies," or "Ladies and Gentlemen." When an attention line is used, these salutations are still appropriate. A person's name is used only when the letter is addressed to an individual.)

Subject Line. Usually placed a double space below the salutation, at the left margin.

Body. Usually single spaced with a double space between paragraphs.

Complimentary Close. Usually placed a double space below the body.

Writer's Name and Title. Usually placed four lines below the complimentary close; however, this space can be adjusted upwards or downwards to achieve a balanced appearance. The name and title can by typed on one or more lines to achieve balance.

Reference Initials. Usually placed a double space below the writer's name and title, at the left margin. It is appropriate to put only the typist's initials unless someone other than the person signing the letter dictated it. In the case of someone dictating the letter and another person signing it, the dictator's initials precede the typist's initials.

Enclosure Notation. Usually placed at the left margin a double space below the reference initials. The trend is to list the items being enclosed.

Copy Notation. Usually placed a double space below the enclosure notation, if used, or a double space below the reference initials.

Postscript. Usually placed a double space below the carbon copy notation, enclosure notation, or the reference initials, whichever appears last. Used mainly for emphasis.

What Are the Basic Letter Styles Used?

The most frequently used letter styles are the full block, modified block, and modified block with indented paragraphs. Research by Lewis indicates that these three styles account for over 95 percent of the letters used in word processing centers (Table 19–2).

TABLE 19–2 Percentage of Letters Typed in Word Processing Centers Using Various Business Letter Styles

Letter Style	Percentage of Use*
Full block	49
Modified block	30
Modified block—indented paragraphs	17
Simplified (AMS)†	3
Other	1

*Percentages are rounded.

†AMS = Administrative Management Society.

Source: Stephen D. Lewis, "Word Processing's Impact on Business Letter Writing" (paper presented at American Business Communication Association Southeastern convention, Lafayette, La., March 31, 1979), p. 7.

The basic difference between the full block and the modified block letter is the placement of the date, complimentary close, and writer's name and title. In the full block letter, every line begins at the left margin while in the modified block letter, the date, complimentary close, and writer's name and title usually begin at center. The modified block letter can have paragraphs blocked or indented. The letter styles are illustrated in Figure 19–5 through 19–8.

The full block style is the most efficient because there are fewer inden-

FIGURE 19–5 Block-Style Letter

```
DATE

SPECIAL MAILING NOTATIONS

INSIDE ADDRESS ----------
-------------------------
-------------------------
-------------------------


ATTENTION LINE

SALUTATION

SUBJECT LINE

BODY OF LETTER ---------------------------------------------------------------------
------------------------------------------------------------------------------------
------------------------------------------------------------------------------------
------------------------------------------------------------------------------------

------------------------------------------------------------------------------------
------------------------------------------------------------------------------------
------------------------------------------------------------------------------------
------------------------------------------------------------------------------------

------------------------------------------------------------------------------------
------------------------------------------------------------------------------------
------------------------------------------------------------------------------------
------------------------------------------------------------------------------------

COMPLIMENTARY CLOSE


TYPED NAME OF WRITER
TITLE OF WRITER

TYPIST'S INITIALS

ENCLOSURE NOTATION

CARBON COPY NOTATION

POSTSCRIPT
```

```
                                                DATE


SPECIAL MAILING NOTATIONS

INSIDE ADDRESS ----------
-------------------------
-------------------------
-------------------------

ATTENTION LINE

SALUTATION

SUBJECT LINE

     BODY OF LETTER ----------------------------------------------------------------
------------------------------------------------------------------------------------
------------------------------------------------------------------------------------

     -------------------------------------------------------------------------------
------------------------------------------------------------------------------------
------------------------------------------------------------------------------------
------------------------------------------------------------------------------------
------------------------------------------------------------------------------------

     -------------------------------------------------------------------------------
------------------------------------------------------------------------------------
------------------------------------------------------------------------------------
------------------------------------------------------------------------------------


                                                COMPLIMENTARY CLOSE



                                                TYPED NAME OF WRITER
                                                TITLE OF WRITER


TYPIST'S INITIALS

ENCLOSURE NOTATION

CARBON COPY NOTATION

POSTSCRIPT
```

FIGURE 19–6 Modified-Block-Style Letter

tions, and thus fewer strokes. It is suggested that a letter style be selected that makes an attractive appearance.

Once the student has learned to organize and express letter content and has become familiar with business-letter parts and placement, then he or she should be introduced to dictation techniques. The ability to dictate does not develop automatically as one learns to write. Dictation is a skill that must be

```
                                        DATE


SPECIAL MAILING NOTATIONS

INSIDE ADDRESS ----------
-------------------------
-------------------------
-------------------------


ATTENTION LINE

SALUTATION

SUBJECT LINE

BODY OF LETTER ----------------------------------------------------
-------------------------------------------------------------------
-------------------------------------------------------------------

-------------------------------------------------------------------
-------------------------------------------------------------------
-------------------------------------------------------------------
-------------------------------------------------------------------
-------------------------------------------------------------------

-------------------------------------------------------------------
-------------------------------------------------------------------
-------------------------------------------------------------------
-------------------------------------------------------------------


                                        COMPLIMENTARY CLOSE



                                        TYPED NAME OF WRITER
                                        TITLE OF WRITER


TYPIST'S INITIALS

ENCLOSURE NOTATION

CARBON COPY NOTATION

POSTSCRIPT
```

FIGURE 19–7 Modified-Block-Style Letter with Indented Paragraphs

learned and developed through practice. This practice should be included as a part of basic business communication courses.

Because of dependency upon longhand for word origination, the process has been relatively inefficient. Statistics from the Department of Labor show that one can dictate to a secretary two to three times as fast as he or she can write in longhand and that dictation to a machine is estimated to be six times

```
DATE

SPECIAL MAILING NOTATIONS

INSIDE ADDRESS ----------
-------------------------
-------------------------
-------------------------


SUBJECT LINE

BODY OF LETTER ------------------------------------------------------------------
--------------------------------------------------------------------------------
--------------------------------------------------------------------------------
--------------------------------------------------------------------------------

--------------------------------------------------------------------------------
--------------------------------------------------------------------------------
--------------------------------------------------------------------------------
--------------------------------------------------------------------------------

--------------------------------------------------------------------------------
--------------------------------------------------------------------------------
--------------------------------------------------------------------------------
--------------------------------------------------------------------------------



TYPED NAME OF WRITER
TITLE OF WRITER

TYPIST'S INITIALS

ENCLOSURE NOTATION

CARBON COPY NOTATION

POSTSCRIPT
```

FIGURE 19–8 AMS Simplified Letter

as fast as writing in longhand. Productivity for word originators can be increased significantly when the originator becomes efficient in the dictation process.

What Preparation Is Needed for Dictation?

Some basic steps a person can follow in order to become an efficient word originator are:

1. Determine the purpose for the correspondence.
2. Gather all necessary information. This simplifies the process of organizing facts and saves time when dictating.

3. Plan the letter. Jot down the key points, this enables a person to organize thoughts and thus dictate an effective letter.
4. Schedule daily dictation periods. Select a time for dictation and avoid interruptions if possible. Interruptions break the trend of thought and thus become costly because of time spent trying to get back in the same thinking process.

Business communication teachers have found that students need so much writing experience that there is not enough time to devote to teaching dictation techniques. Since people in business are concerned with controlling the costs of office work and more word originators will be required to use word processing systems, some attention must be given to the other factors which contribute to the efficiency and effectiveness of letter writing.

What Are Some Approaches to Teaching Dictation?

After students have had some experience in writing letters there should be a gradual transition to dictation of letters. For a person who is learning to dictate letters, it is advisable to have the letter written out and then read. As the person gains experience and confidence in the ability to dictate, the "written-out letter" should be reduced to a detailed outline. The need for details in the outline would be reduced further until the guide notes were sufficient for dictating a well-written letter.

For the teacher in a classroom setting with twenty-five to thirty students, devoting time to teaching dictation is a problem. However, the objective should be to help the student understand another aspect of communication, which is dictation of letters. At the same time, the student will understand the need to dictate as a cost-reduction technique and the student will gain some valuable experience dictating.

There are several approaches to providing dictation experience to students enrolled in business communication classes.

1. A cooperative learning project involving the office procedures and advanced shorthand classes with the business communication classes could be assigned. Toward the end of the semester, laboratory periods could be set up where students enrolled in either office procedures or advanced shorthand classes would take dictation from the students enrolled in business communication classes. Both sets of students from the different classes would gain valuable experience. The shorthand writers would gain experience by taking office-style dictation from someone other than an experienced teacher. The business communication students would have the opportunity to practice the skill of dictation.

2. Another approach to teaching dictation is through the use of dictation machines. A cooperative learning project could be developed whereby an office procedures or word processing class would transcribe the recorded dictation of the business communication students. This approach may be more practical because of word processing equipment and also because in many businesses, executives at lower levels use dictation equipment rather than shorthand writers for recording dictation. The dictated material would provide the students in office procedures and word processing with realistic dictated material while the students in business communication are learning to dictate.
3. A third approach would be to have the business communication students dictate to one another. While this approach may be easier to use, there could be some problems involved. The students recording the dictation may not possess the skill necessary to record dictation nor the skill necessary to type the dictated material. However, since the objective is to learn to dictate, the recording and typing skills may be overlooked.
4. A fourth approach would be to have the students dictate using dictation machines. Instead of having the material transcribed, the students would evaluate their own dictation skill using a checklist provided by the teacher. This approach enables students to analyze their own strengths and weaknesses. The instructor could also evaluate dictation skill by listening to the tapes. This seems like a very logical approach considering that the skill taught in business communication is dictation and not transcription.

Summary

The major topics of word processing, word processing's relationship to business communication, dictation skills, and dictation in the business communication class have been presented in this chapter. No attempt has been made to make this all-inclusive, as word processing and business communication are such broad areas. However, this chapter can serve as a guide to the teacher who wishes to incorporate word processing into the business communication class.

In any approach used, emphasis should be on dictation, that is, the oral development and expression of ideas into a well-written letter. Remember that to be good dictators, students should know the basic fundamentals of writing, typing, and dictating.

As more emphasis is being placed on using available time efficiently and reducing the cost of correspondence, the need for effective dictators of business communications becomes more evident. Together word processing and business communication will contribute to cost-efficient and effective communications.

Acknowledgments

First list on p. 417 reprinted by permission of the publisher from "Auditing Office and Word Processing Operations," by Gerald L. Hershey, *Management Review,* February 1979, © 1979 by AMACOM, a division of American Management Associations, pp. 50–51. All rights reserved.

List on pp. 419–421 from B. Lewis Keeling, Norman F. Kallaus, and John J. W. Neuner, *Administrative Office Management,* 8th ed. (Cincinnati: South-Western Publishing Co., 1983), p. 395. Reproduced by permission of South-Western Publishing Co.

Notes

1. International Word Processing Association, *IWP Packet Series: Part One, Selected Articles* (Willow Grove, Pa.: International Word Processing Association, February 1979), p. 1.
2. C. L. Littlefield, Frank M. Rachel, Donald L. Caruth, and Robert E. Holmes, *Management of Office Operations* (Englewood Cliffs, N.J.: Prentice-Hall, 1978), pp. 135–136.
3. Stephen D. Lewis, "Word Processing's Impact on Business Letter Writing" (paper presented at 1979 American Business Communication Association Southeastern convention, Lafayette, La., Mar. 31, 1979), p. 4.

Bibliography

Benton, L. Brent. How to Tailor Your WP Performance Guidelines." *Modern Office Procedures,* vol. 21, no. 9 (September 1976), pp. 76, 78, 80, 84.

Landi, Edith. "Word Processing and People." *The Office,* vol. 88, no. 6 (December 1978), pp. 62, 65.

Luke, Cheryl M. "Dictation: An Important Business Communication Skill." *Business Education Forum,* vol. 33 (October 1978), pp. 26–27.

Lutz, Carol. "Basic Skills in the Futuristic Office." *The Balance Sheet,* vol. 6, no. 7 (April 1979), pp. 303–306.

Naclerio, Nick. "The Automated Office." *VocED,* vol. 54, no. 2 (February 1979), pp. 40–42.

Nord, G. Daryl. "Interfacing Word Processing and Data Processing." *Business Education Forum,* vol. 33, no. 7 (April, 1979), pp. 21–22.

Chapter 20

Nonsexist Communication

Bobbye D. Sorrels

Sexist communication may be defined as communication that precasts people on the basis of sex. Because of the nature of the culture, however, sexist communication may better be defined as communication that assumes that anything male is inherently superior to anything female.

Why Nonsexist Communication?

The reasons for revision from sexist to nonsexist communication range from sheer idealism to practical legalism.

Idealism

Probably the best reason for making communication fair to both sexes is reflected in these words: "As a humanitarian, I view females and males as equal human beings. Therefore, a communication system that casts males as the norm and females as something other than the norm requires correction." As compelling as this reason is for many people, it falls short for others.

Impact of Words

Many people perceive themselves as humanitarians, but just do not view communication symbols as important to the recognition of human equality. The old adage "Sticks and stones may break my bones, but words can never hurt me" perhaps summarizes this belief. However, careful reasoning leads to rejection of the adage. The symbols of human social interaction—particularly communication—*do* hurt or help in the development and maintenance of the self.

We are largely what was and is communicated to us that we are. Perhaps we can never fully grasp the depth of the human impact of that truth. However, neither can we deny that the sexist communication system creates within females a reduced self- and other-centered image and often a self-fulfilling prophecy of second-ratedness. How can the female mature to full capacity when the communication that shapes her methodically instructs her that she is inferior to the male?

Just ask those who argue against nonsexist communication on the basis of "words aren't that important" to create for a moment the pain felt by people when called such derogatory words as *old maid, fatso, retardo, beanpole, tramp, broad, cow, horseface, egghead, witch, bitch, bastard, sissy, jock, nigger, honky, dago,* and *gook*. If they counter that sexist words do not hurt as much as the types of words just cited, remind them that many of these words (*old maid, tramp, broad, cow, witch, bitch, bastard, sissy*) *are* sexist. In addition, call to their attention that the communication system includes a much more extensive set of explicit sex-derogatory terms for females than for males.

Most important, though, establish that the male-as-generic forms (for example, male pronouns and "-man" nouns for both females and males) probably do more sweeping, permanent damage to the female than the outright sex-discriminatory forms do—primarily because they do seem so innocent. The guise of innocence allows them to continue as the "sentence in, sentence out" reminders to both females and males that females just are not as important as males.

A return to the sticks-and-stones imagery brings up another old saying: "Actions speak louder than words." And they probably do. However, communication involves the full range of symbols, including both actions *and* words, both nonverbal and verbal communication. Thus, indeed, as part of the communication system, sexist actions probably "speak" more loudly than sexist words, though, as established, sexist words speak quite loudly all by themselves.

The continuing debate over which comes first—change in behavior or change in attitude—also relates to this discussion. Some people believe that attitudes must change before introducing and practicing nonsexist communication. However, with the knowledge that a culture both shapes and is shaped by its communication, the communicator knows that a merry-go-round results: Communication influences attitudes, but attitudes influence communication. Therefore, the question of where to jump onto the sexist merry-go-round is moot.

Agreed, revising the symbols from sexist to nonsexist forms will not alone change the attitudes that underlie those symbols. Such revision will not automatically create within women the self-confidence to accomplish their potential and within men the acceptance of women as equals. However, communication is behavior, and because we can change behavior, the positive results that come with even the surface appearance of nonsexism improve the system. Once behaviors change, attitudinal modifications usually follow.

The concept of behavior modification frightens some people. However, if they would merely give careful thought to the simple, noninjurious, nonthreatening behavior change necessary for nonsexist communication, their fears would dissipate. Fortunately, the conversion to patterns of communication that are fair to everyone does not hurt anyone; it requires no significant trade-offs for its accomplishment. It does require the learning necessary to change some habits. However, with awareness and commitment, the change comes rather easily.

Granted, people resist change from the familiar, particularly if they view the familiar as the secure. Thus, another key to this level of reasoning rests with the understanding that each culture creates its own communication system and continually revises it to reflect changes in the culture. Just because we learned to use masculine pronouns as the generic forms, that does not mean that the "rule" came from "on high" as an immutable truth not subject to change.

Exclusion of Females

A third tier of persuasion toward nonsexist communication calls for understanding that sexist communication forms do exclude females—or at the least reduce their status. Research shows that people do not usually perceive male words as including females. For example, Schneider and Hacker randomly divided three hundred college students into two groups and asked them to find pictures to illustrate chapter titles for a hypothetical sociology book. The students thought they were searching for illustrations for an actual book yet to be published. One group found illustrations for such titles as *Social Man, Political Man,* and *Industrial Man.* The other group found pictures for such titles as *Society, Political Behavior,* and *Industrial Life.* Statistical analysis showed that both men and women collected a significantly larger proportion of pictures showing only men to illustrate the *man* titles than to illustrate the sex-neutral ones.[1]

The sexist exclusion of females in both reality and symbolism excludes humans who could help solve the myriad of problems that beset the world. Research can never reveal the countless numbers of female minds and creative abilities sacrificed because of a sex-role-stereotyped communication system that exemplifies the culture that created it. The culture systematically "tells" females that they cannot or should not be physicians, scientists, engineers, mathematicians, political leaders, inventors, managers, business*men,* police*men,* fire*men,* and crafts*men.* It also "tells" males that they should not be tender, emotional, sensitive, and gentle beings. As an end result, both females and males suffer from sexist communication.

Human Relations

Human relations form a fourth level at which reasoning operates in favor of nonsexist communication. Even if communicators discount all of the more idealistic arguments, they usually understand the contribution of a "you"-centered attitude—the human relations approach to interaction. Treating the female portion of the "you" as just as important as the male portion of the "you" cannot help but please and elevate the females, and it would not injure the males. Therefore, human relations communicators understand that their audiences—the "you" receiving their message—include females. They communicate in a nonsexist way to recognize that fact, and thus establish a higher probability of attaining their objectives than sexist communicators do.

Reality

Evolving naturally from human relations reasoning, a fifth level lies with the practical acknowledgment that females now participate in every aspect of life. Granted, at one time, all who drew blueprints were drafts*men,* all who carried mail were mail*men,* all who sold goods were sales*men,* and all who chaired committees were chair*men.* Now that many who engage in these activities are women, the language must adjust to that reality. To cling to an outdated system that no longer accurately portrays life as it actually exists denies that reality.

Unfortunately, those in the academic realm too often ignore reality and treat symbols as if they are inscribed in stone—as if they are permanent truth. Teachers must instead recognize the dynamic nature of language and convey that concept to their students. New expressions may seem strange when first introduced, but what in nature dictates that *flagman* is an inherently better word than *flagger?*

Keeping Current

A sixth position recognizes the communicator's need to keep up to date. If communicators or instructors of communicators ignore contemporary patterns, they run the risk of losing credibility. Some people who have adopted the nonsexist style may not genuinely embrace the concepts associated with the fairness of the process, but simply stay current and do what a progressive style dictates they do.

Profit

The profit motive forms a seventh basis for nonsexist communication. The shrewd business communicator does careful audience analysis and meets the expectation of the audience in order to "sell" the message and ultimately make a profit. A number of audiences now demand a nonsexist communication approach. The thinking, profit-minded business communicator will meet that demand.

Legality

Legality forms the eighth and final category of logic for adopting nonsexist business communication methods. Equal employment opportunity and affirmative action guidelines exist as established elements in business and organizational life. Discrimination cases based upon the use of sexist language have been filed and won in the courts. Therefore, the prudent business communicator simply takes care not to allow discriminatory communication to occur.

The federal government has reaffirmed the importance of the language in establishing an affirmative action commitment by revising the job titles in the *Dictionary of Occupational Titles.* This excerpt summarizes the importance of the revision:

> This publication brings job titles listed in the *Dictionary of Occupational Titles, Third Edition,* into conformance with equal employment legislation such as the Civil Rights Act of 1964 and the Age Discrimination in Employment Act of 1967, and with recent administration policy statements and instructions on the same subject. Included in the legislation, policy statements, and instructions is language which prohibits the use of sex- and/or age-referent language by the public employment service. As a result of these prohibitions, it is necessary to provide the employment service and other public and private users of the *Dictionary of Occupational Titles* with revised job titles to replace existing *Dictionary* job titles now considered to be potentially sex and/or age discriminatory.[2]

It may be more meaningful to change because it is just and logical than to change at the request or order of the government. Whatever the level of justification, though, nondiscriminatory communication represents the tide of the future.

Guidelines for Nonsexist Communication

Awareness of sexism and the resolution to change from sexist to nonsexist communication carry within them the keys for making the transition. Once awareness and resolution exist, commonsense alternatives to sexist forms become evident. However, a review of some of the alternatives already developed by others can facilitate the transition. The bibliography contains a listing of publications to aid in the review. In addition, because nonsexist communication has been introduced so recently, this chapter contains a brief review of some of the guidelines.

Nouns

The predominant sexism in nouns occurs in so-called generic words that include "man." However, other male words also appear in sexist nouns. Another type of sexism in nouns tacks "ess," "ette," and "ix" on already generic words to make them "feminine."

SEXIST	NONSEXIST
Chairman	Chairperson
Fireman	Fire fighter
Postman	Mail carrier
Workman	Worker
Brotherhood of man	Bond of humanity
Mankind	Humankind
Aviatrix	Aviator
Stewardess	Flight attendant
Usherette	Usher

Pronouns

Probably the most pervasive type of sexism in verbal communication occurs in the use of male pronouns as generic pronouns.

SEXIST	NONSEXIST
Each executive must include his. . . .	All executives must include their. . . .
	Each executive must include the. . . .
	Each executive must include her or his. . . . (sparingly)
	Each executive must include his/her. . . . (sparingly)
	Each executive must include their. . . . (if grammar does not matter to the audience)
Each engineer . . . he . . . himself. . . .	(Adjustments similar to those illustrated for "his")

Adjectives

Though sexism can occur in adjectives through words containing *man* and through other such forms, the most-common sexist modification occurs in conjunction with stereotypes about the roles of females and males.

SEXIST	NONSEXIST
Lady attorney	Attorney
Woman doctor	Doctor
Male nurse	Nurse
Male menopause	Climacteric

Courtesy Titles

In traditional courtesy titles, women are required to state marital status while men are not. Because men probably will never adopt marital-status courtesy titles, the ultimate solution lies in the use of *Ms.* (pronounced "miz") by all women. Until the universal adoption of *Ms.,* however, retain the sexist courtesy titles for those women who insist upon them.

SEXIST	NONSEXIST
Miss	Ms.
Mrs.	Ms.

Salutations and Complimentary Closes

Salutations and complimentary closes often contain the same kinds of sexism found in other forms of communication.

SEXIST	NONSEXIST
Acme Co. . . . . Gentlemen:	Acme Co. . . . . Ladies and Gentlemen: (or omit salutation)
Vice-President of Production . . . . Dear Sir:	Vice-President of Production . . . . Dear Vice President (or omit salutation)
Sincerely yours, *Joan Oaks* (Miss) Joan Oaks	Sincerely yours, *Joan Oaks* Joan Oaks
Cordially, *Mrs. Jim Rogers* Mrs. Jim Rogers	Cordially, *Ellen Rogers* Ellen Rogers

Nonparallelism and Order

Many pairings and orderings of female and male names diminish females. The journalistic style of reporting contributes significantly to such sexism.

SEXIST	NONSEXIST
Man [for male 18 years old or older] and girl [for female 18 years old or older]	Man and woman Woman and man Boy and girl
Saleslady and salesman	Saleswoman and salesman Salespersons
Male listed before female all the time: Boys and girls Men and women	Female listed before male half the time: Girls and boys Women and men

SEXIST	NONSEXIST
Males and females	Females and males
Bob and Mary	Mary and Bob
Elkins and Miss Harris. . . .	Elkins and Harris. . . .
Klein and Nell	Klein and Corrigan Nell and Bill

Religious and Royal Expressions

Expressions from religion and royalty contribute to sexism.

SEXIST	NONSEXIST
Lord and King	God
Our Father. . . .	Our Creator. . . .
King of the hill	Conqueror
Little princess	Little girl (for female about 6 years old or younger)

Stereotypes

Female and male stereotypes contribute to sexism in communication.

SEXIST	NONSEXIST
The nurse . . . she . . . and the doctor . . . he. . . . [generic usage]	The nurses . . . they . . . and the doctors . . . they. . . .
What do you expect from a woman driver?	That woman was involved in an automobile accident
What a dumb blonde.	That woman didn't know the answer to the question.
The farmer and his wife. . . .	The farmers. . . .
The housewife . . . she. . . . [generic usage]	The homemaker . . . he or she. . . .

Oral Communication

Oral communication allows for more crass and overt sexism than written communication. Overcoming oral sexism calls for concentration and immediate revision.

SEXIST	NONSEXIST
Just look at that stacked broad.	I think that woman is beautiful.
Now, girls, don't get emotional.	Would you members of the committee explain your concerns about. . . .
Did you hear the one about the mother-in-law who. . . .	Did you hear the one about the father-in-law (man, woman) who. . . .
[Woman speaker]: "This probably isn't a good idea, but I think. . . ."	"I think that we should. . . ."

Nonverbal Communication

Wordless communication contributes more than half of the social meaning in human interchanges. Therefore, sexism occurs through the use of touch, territory and space, voice, face, postures and movements, silence, time, environment, and dress and appearance.

SEXIST	NONSEXIST
Women smile more than men as a basic indication of servility.	Women smile less and men smile more.
Women use a high-pitched, little-girl voice with a questioning lift at the end of a sentence.	Women speak at moderate pitch with a resolute volume and speed.
Men dominate conversations by interrupting more and speaking longer than women.	Men share equally with women in time allocations during conversations.
Women stand, sit, walk, and gesture with minimal use of space and power.	Women stand, sit, walk, and gesture, making comfortable use of space and power.
Women dress to communicate powerlessness and sexuality.	Women dress to communicate power and non-sex-related confidence.
Men touch women to signal domination.	Men do not touch women to signal domination.

Citations from Secondary Sources

Citations from secondary sources require adjustment by the nonsexist communicator. Use nonsexist paraphrases and summaries, omissions and ellipses, insertions and brackets, and [*sic*], with an obvious preference for paraphrases and summaries.

SEXIST	NONSEXIST
"Every foreman should tell each member of his task force that he has the responsibility to contribute ideas for best use of manpower."	Every supervisor should tell each member of the task force of the responsibility to contribute ideas for best use of the workforce. "Every [supervisor] should tell each member of [the] task force that he [or she] has the responsibility to contribute ideas for best use of manpower [*sic*]."

Nonhuman References

Sexism carries into communication about animals and other nonhumans. Solutions parallel those for preceding examples.

SEXIST	NONSEXIST
Filly, chick, fox, tomato (for woman)	Woman
Tigress	Tiger
Mr. Calculator (for children's calculator)	My Own Calculator
Mother Nature wreaked havoc last night.	The storm wreaked havoc last night.

Methods and Materials for Teaching Nonsexist Communication

This section gives suggestions for teaching nonsexist communication.

Instructor

An age-old teaching device calls for the instructor (professor, teacher, leader, coordinator) to act as a role model. This device proves particularly appropriate for nonsexist learning. Thus, the instructor must first become a complete nonsexist communicator in every context, not just the one including the subject of nonsexist communication. If the instructor does not commit to nonsexism, or practices it only when teaching it, the students have every right to question the sincerity of the instructor and even the importance of the topic itself.

A role model for students will also serve as a role model for colleagues. However, the instructor should try to move beyond that stage to enlisting the support of colleagues to act as role models and instructors of nonsexist communication themselves. As for all communication, nonsexism cannot be the responsibility of just those who work with courses including "English," "writing," "speaking," or "communication" in the titles. Everyone dealing with the curriculum needs to share the responsibility for communication learning.

Settings

As suggested, every component of the curriculum represents an appropriate setting for learning nonsexist communication. However, certain courses lend themselves particularly well to specialized units on the subject. Examples include high school and college courses in business communication, business English, English, human relations, management, women's studies, psychology, marketing, sociology, public speaking, and secretarial training. In addition, nonsexist communication belongs in in-service-training courses in business, industry, and government.

The possibilities for the study of nonsexist communication emerge from every quarter of the academic and business worlds. The placement awaits only the energy of vital, committed people.

Library

Because of the relatively recent introduction of the topic of nonsexist communication, institutional and public libraries may need to purchase publications on the topic. The bibliography at the end of this chapter can serve as a beginning list for that purpose.

Publications and Handout Materials

To establish shared responsibility for nonsexist communication, make nonsexist language and illustrations two of the criteria for selection of textbooks for all fields of study. If forced to use a sexist textbook, point out to students the sexism in the first few pages, and suggest that they watch for, and even mark, sexist words and illustrations as they encounter them in their reading. Call attention to the textbook's sexist passages throughout the term of study.

For special units on nonsexist communication, use guidelines that introduce genuine nonsexism. For example, some "guidelines" still support the male-as-generic pronouns and nouns if a preliminary notice indicates that they also refer to females. Such a guideline does not eliminate sexism. Again, the bibliography includes publications with an extension of the guidelines introduced in this chapter. My book *The Nonsexist Communicator* probably provides the most comprehensive practical coverage for use as a handbook or as a supplement for classroom or training settings.

Exercises can take several forms. One involves writing sexist sentences and asking students to mark the sexist passages and write nonsexist forms for them. Another has the students collect examples of actual sexist messages, analyze them for sexism, and correct them. Other suggestions appear in other sections.

Audiovisual Aids

Visuals and tapes of examples and corrections of sexist messages contribute to learning. For identification and correction of nonverbal sexism, use photographs, slides, videotapes, role playing, and films of staged sexism or of randomly chosen groups of people for analysis. Henley and Thorne's *She Said/He Said* provides a particularly good summary of research findings on the subject.

Approaches to Learning

The integrated and blocked methods define the two logical approaches to the teaching of nonsexist communication.

Integrated Approach

The integrated approach uses several important devices already introduced: the instructor as model, selection and development of nonsexist books and materials, and expansion of nonsexist library holdings. In addition, several others have been implied.

Another device calls for discussing any sexism traditionally associated with the major topic of a given session. For example, in a lecture about an advertising or consumer problem, avoid stereotypes about the "housewife," and use the word "homemaker" instead. Cite some statistics about the decrease in the number of traditional homemakers, the increase in the number of women who work outside the home, and the dramatic changes in the composition of families. In addition, point out that many consumers are not married and that large numbers of those who do marry consider homemaking, careers, finances, parenting, shopping, and other such activities to be joint responsibilities of males and females—not sex-differentiated roles.

In similar fashion, if a film shows all managers as men and all secretaries and receptionists as women, lead the group into a discussion of the stereotyped communication in the portrayals.

Another tactic calls for routine identification and correction of sexist errors in the written and oral presentations of the participants. A sexist word or phrase is at least as serious an error as one involving incorrect grammar, pronunciation, spelling, or punctuation—and certainly must receive at least as much attention. Thus, mark the sexism in written work and take account of the marks in the grade.

As one way to handle sexism in an oral presentation, have all participants jot down errors as they occur, and discuss them soon after the speaker is finished. When using evaluation forms for rating formal oral presentations, note sexist errors and consider them in the grading.

Still another integrative device has the participants use sexism as the topic for some assignments associated with the primary subject matter. For example, if an assignment requires students to write a paper on office politics, have them include a subtopic on sex-role stereotyping in office politics.

Blocked Approach

The blocked unit can bring nonsexist communication into focus as a topic in its own right. With the blocked unit the sessions and the associated readings, exercises, assignments, and direct evaluations may be compressed into successive meetings or interspersed with the other units of the overriding subject matter.

Allow at least one hour for the blocked unit or expand it into a five- or six-hour program—whether offered in successive, spaced sessions or in a one-day workshop—in either a traditional academic setting or in training programs for public and private organizations.

Activities

Activities that can make a nonsexist unit productive include:

Pretest and posttest
Reading
Lectures
Illustrations and examples
Large-group discussions

Small-group discussions
In-session exercises and assignments
Homework exercises and assignments
Written performances
Oral performances
Nonverbal performances
Role playing
Cases
Collecting, analyzing, and correcting written examples
Taping, listening to, viewing, and criticizing oral and nonverbal presentations of self and others
Viewing, listening to, and discussing audiovisual presentations on the subject of sexism and nonsexism
Talking with or writing to those who produce sexist messages to ask them to change
Research into sexism
Term papers on the subject
Evaluation over all of the material

Evaluation

Evaluation methods for the nonsexist unit and the integration of nonsexist principles into the work of the entire term should follow the regular pattern for other aspects of the course. Otherwise, the students will consider the material unimportant. Thus, assign points for such work as exercises, assignments, cases, and class participation in the nonsexist unit just as for the core subject. Test over the nonsexist until just as for each of the core subject units.

An excellent device for a basic business communication course gives bonus credit for letters written to such creators of sexist messages as advertisers, publishers, authors, and speakers. The letters should call attention to their sexist errors and tactfully call for their correction. Use the same criteria for assigning points as for similar activities in other parts of the course.

In addition to the direct points for the nonsexist unit and the evaluation associated with it, give points for the indirect nonsexist coverage. On any evaluated work, whether written, oral, or nonverbal, and on every topic covered in the core course, count off for sexist usage. For example, include in the evaluation form for grading term papers a certain number of points for nonsexist style. For a paper worth two hundred points, perhaps allocate ten to fifteen points to nonsexism.

An essay or short-answer question on an examination could require the student to identify sexism associated with a situation you have posed. In addition, deduct points for sexist references or language included in answers to all questions—even if the questions have nothing directly to do with sexism. Treat sexist errors as other stylistic or mechanical errors. For example, on a one hundred-point, one-hour examination, in addition to the independent scoring for content of the answer, check all errors related to such things as grammar, spelling, punctuation, capitalization, paragraphing, usage of numbers, and sexism for all questions. Then count the checkmarks for the entire paper and use the following scale:

No. of Checkmarks	No. of Penalty Points
0–2	0
3–5	1
6–8	2
9–11	3
12–14	4
15 or more	5

When assigning points to the various parts of the examination, assign the five (or whatever number) points for the style, mechanics, and sexism. Notify the students ahead of time that you have assigned points in that fashion.

Include points for nonsexist style on evaluative instruments used in conjunction with oral presentations. For example, for an oral presentation form with ten equally weighted parts to it, include one which relates to grammar, pronunciation, and sexism.

Some sample examination questions—which could also serve well as exercises—complete this section on evaluation:

1. For these sentences (a) underline the sexist words and (b) write nonsexist versions above the underlined words.
   (1) John Q. Public denounces the government for spending his taxes on such projects. He tires of manning the stations in the work force just to have his money wasted on activities that do not further the cause of mankind.
2. Name and briefly discuss at least three reasons for becoming a nonsexist communicator.
3. Name, briefly describe, and give examples for at least four devices for correcting the sexism in the use of the male pronouns as the generic pronouns.

Sample Nonsexist Unit

A sample unit can help summarize some of the recommendations for nonsexist learning. If the unit forms only one element of an overriding course, complete it as early in the term as possible.

Item No.	Minimum No. of Minutes	Components of Unit in Order of Presentation
*1	2	Include nonsexist communication in all appropriate sections (objectives, book list, topics, testing schedule, etc.) of course outline or syllabus. Distribute in printed form and discuss—along with other units or components—on first or second day of term.
*2	15	Administer pretest. Ask each person to check her or his own paper, record number correct, and check against predetermined scale. Discuss nonsexist alternatives briefly. Collect pretests and file, but do not record scores.
*3	10	Distribute materials and discuss specific objectives for unit. Make first assignment, covering sexism in nouns, pronouns, adjectives, and courtesy titles.
4	45	Use a consciousness-raising activity such as a discussion of the role reversal in "A Tale of Two Sexes" in The Nonsexist Communicator. In the discussion include treatment of definitions, reasons for using nonsexist communication, some role reversal, and a call to commitment. Discuss sexist nouns, pronouns, adjectives, and courtesy titles.
5	5	Make second assignment, covering salutations and complimentary closes, nonparallelism and order, religious and royal expressions, and stereotypes.
6	45	Use audiovisuals, lecture, or large- and small-group discussion over the material and exercises associated with salutations and complimentary closes, nonparallelism and order, religious and royal expressions, and stereotypes.
7	5	Make third assignment, covering oral communication, nonverbal communication, citations from secondary sources, and nonhuman references.
8	45	Use audiovisuals, lecture, or large- and small-group discussion over the material and exercises associated with oral communication, nonverbal communication, citations from secondary sources, and nonhuman references.
9	5	Preview evaluation procedures and types of questions over nonsexist unit.
*10	20	Administer posttest and other unit evaluation instruments and/or component parts of combined-unit hour examinations.
*11	5	Return and review scored evaluation instruments.

*Items 1, 2, 3, 10, and 11 should be considered parts of the core course time schedule.

Acknowledgments

For a complete discussion of the subject of nonsexist communication, the interested reader should see Bobbye D. Sorrels, *The Nonsexist Communicator* (Englewood Cliffs, N.J.: Prentice-Hall, 1983).

Notes

1. Joseph W. Schneider and Sally L. Hacker, "Sex Role Imagery and Use of Generic 'Man' in Introductory Texts: A Case in the Sociology of Sociology," *American Sociologist,* vol. 8 (February 1973), pp. 12–18.
2. U. S. Department of Labor, Manpower [*sic*] Administration, *Job Title Revisions to Eliminate Sex- and Age-Referent Language from the Dictionary of Occupational Titles, Third Edition* (Washington, D.C.: Government Printing Office, 1975), p. iii.

Bibliography

"Addendum to Style Guide for Authors: Academy of Management Review." *Academy of Management Review,* July 1976, pp. 150–52.

American Psychological Association Task Force on Issues of Sexual Bias in Graduate Education. "Guidelines for Nonsexist Use of Language." *American Psychologist,* June 1975, pp. 682–84.

Burr, Elizabeth, Susan Dunn, and Norma Farquhar. *Guidelines for Equal Treatment of the Sexes in Social Studies Textbooks.* Los Angeles: Westside Women's Committee, 1973.

"Desexing the Language." *Managementips,* Special Edition.

Dolecheck, Carolyn Crawford. "Are You Teaching Affirmative Action Writing?" *ABCA Bulletin,* vol. 41 (December 1978), pp. 20–21.

Editorial and Graphics Criteria for Art and Design. Lexington, Mass.: Ginn and Co., 1975.

Fair and Balanced Treatment of Minorities and Women. Cincinnati: South-Western Publishing Co., 1976.

Graham, Alma. *Non-Sexist Language Guidelines.* New York: Alma Graham, n.d.

Guidelines for Creating Positive Sexual and Racial Images in Educational Materials. New York: Macmillan Publishing Co., 1975.

Guidelines for Equal Treatment of the Sexes. New York: McGraw-Hill Book Co., 1972.

Guidelines for Improving the Image of Women in Textbooks. Glenview, Ill.: Scott, Foresman and Co., 1972.

Guidelines for Multi-Ethnic/Nonsexist Survey. New York: Random House.

Guidelines for Richard D. Irwin Authors and Copy Editors for Equal Treatment of Men and Women. Homewood, Ill.: Richard D. Irwin, n.d.

"He" Is Not "She." Los Angeles: Westside Women's Committee, n.d.

HEADQUARTERS STAFF OF NATIONAL COUNCIL OF TEACHERS OF ENGLISH. "Guidelines for Nonsexist Use of Language in NCTE Publications." *NCTE,* March 1976, pp. 23–26.

HECHT, MARIE B., JOAN D. BERBRICH, SALLEY A. HEALEY, and CLAIRE M. COOPER. *The Women, Yes!* New York: Holt, Rinehart and Winston/Rinehart Press, 1973.

HENLEY, NANCY M. *Body Politics: Power, Sex, and Nonverbal Communication.* Englewood Cliffs, N.J.: Prentice-Hall, 1977.

HENLEY, NANCY, and BARRIE THORNE, comps. *She Said/He Said: An Annotated Bibliography of Sex Differences in Language, Speech, and Nonverbal Communication.* Pittsburgh: Know, Inc., 1975.

LAKOFF, ROBIN. *Language and Women's Place.* New York: Harper & Row, 1975.

MARTIN, LOIS A. "How to Reduce Sex-Role Stereotyping." *Today's Education,* November-December 1978, pp. 59–61.

MILLER, CASEY, and KATE SWIFT. *Words and Women.* Garden City, N.Y.: Anchor Press/Doubleday, 1976.

MOTLEY, ROBERT J. "'Sexism' and Modern Business Communications." *Business Education Forum,* November 1978, pp. 28–29.

ONE, VARDA. *Manglish.* Venice, Calif.: Everywoman Publishing Co., 1971.

OROVAN, MARY. *Humanizing English,* 1972.

PERSING, BOBBYE. "Sticks and Stones *and* Words: Women in the Language." *Journal of Business Communication,* vol. 14 (winter 1977), pp. 11–19.

PERSING, BOBBYE SORRELS. *Business Communication Dynamics.* Columbus, Ohio: Charles E. Merrill Publishing Co., 1981.

PICKENS, JUDY E., PATRICIA WALSH RAO, and LINDA COOK ROBERTS. *Without Bias: A Guidebook for Nondiscriminatory Communication.* San Francisco: International Association of Business Communicators, 1977.

RUSSELL, LETTY M., ed. *The Liberating Word: A Guide to Nonsexist Interpretation of the Bible.* Philadelphia: The Westminister Press, 1976.

SCHNEIDER, JOSEPH W., and SALLY L. HACKER. "Sex Role Imagery and Use of Generic 'Man' in Introductory Texts: A Case in the Sociology of Sociology." *American Sociologist,* vol. 8 (February 1973), pp. 12–18.

SORRELS, BOBBYE D. *The Nonsexist Communicator.* Englewood Cliffs, N.J.: Prentice-Hall, 1983.

STEAD, BETTY ANN. "The Semantics of Sex Discrimination." *Oklahoma New Woman,* vol. 24 (April 1976), pp. 4–5. Reprinted from *Business Horizons.*

——, ed., *Women in Management.* Englewood Cliffs, N.J.: Prentice-Hall, 1978.

Treatment of Minority Groups and Women. Lexington, Mass.: Ginn and Co., n.d.

U.S. DEPARTMENT OF LABOR, EMPLOYMENT AND TRAINING ADMINISTRATION. *Dictionary of Occupational Titles,* 4th ed. Washington, D.C.: Government Printing Office, 1977.

U.S. Department of Labor, Manpower [*sic*] Administration. *Job Title Revisions to Eliminate Sex- and Age-Referent Language from Dictionary of Occupational Titles, Third Edition.* Washington, D.C.: Government Printing Office, 1975.

Wendlinger, Robert M., and Lucille Matthews. "How to Eliminate Sexist Language from Your Organization's Writing: Some Guidelines for the Manager and Supervisor." In *Affirmative Action for Women: A Practical Guide,* edited by Dorothy Jongeward, Dru Scott, and Contributors. Reading, Mass.: Addison-Wesley Publishing Co., 1973, pp. 309–320.

Chapter 21

Intercultural and International Communication

Larry D. Hartman
Tika Nath Sharma

INTERCULTURAL COMMUNICATION is the process of exchanging thoughts and meanings between people of differing cultures.[1] Behind each individual is a vast accumulation of history, environmental values, and education supporting cultural attitudes of his or her society. Because there is a large measure of common experience in the history of humanity, there are fortunately many similarities, but there are also many differences.[2]

Hildebrandt states, "By cultural we mean the total system of values and habits stored up implicitly by foreign nationals which they bring along to the host country."[3] Haneda indicates, "The use of a common language is no guarantee for complete understanding between people with different cultural backgrounds. Differences arise in the way of thinking, value systems, belief systems, customs and manners."[4]

Reasons for Intercultural Concern

Several factors are responsible for our concern with intercultural and international communication. First, teachers involving international students in their classes react according to their own cultural values. Yet, many cultural values are involved.

The participative method of teaching communication encourages a communication instructor to accept and empathize with international differences even if they are beyond his or her total comprehension. A teacher should have the desire and the capability to interpret international students' perceptions, apply the perceptions and resulting human action to the educational concept involved, and then relate the perceptions to the students' own understanding of the educational concept.

Encouraging international students to function outside of the security of their language, their food, their personal values, and their families requires time and direction. Native students form norm groups because of their physical appearance, their language, their religious and other customs—so that the international student fears to deviate from the norm group, fears the host nationals, fears their classrooms, communicates less—yet wants desperately to succeed, to learn, and to be accepted. Therefore, the teacher needs to reconcile both the recognizable and the unknown conflicts between groups and between values.

Numerous international students study in the United States. Every year immigrants, refugees, and exchange visitors seek educational experiences. The vast number of students from one or two cultures (such as Spanish or Japanese) may generate bilingual programs—but in large part, international students integrate and are assimiliated directly into existing educational programs without an intermediate step.

This extends the scope of multicultural and multilingual understanding to the nation's own ethnic and subethnic populations as well, so that the need expands to the non-American foreign born as well as to the multicultural American born. Therefore, an instructor in the United States needs to understand intercultural communication not only as a value identification experience but also as a language-meshing skill.

An additional need for instructors of business communication is to expand the number of short-term training programs for employees of national and multinational corporations. These firms employ foreign-born workers and technicians in the United States and American-born individuals in offices in other countries. To enhance good employee and customer relations, managers must be sensitive to intercultural and international communication needs.

Technological developments, and their facilitating global exchange and communication capabilities, are an important third area for instructors to understand. Developments in telecommunication and computer adaptations permit nearly worldwide involvement. These technological changes encourage and permit people-to-people exchange and intercultural educational experiences never thought possible before.

To relate and to instruct under these circumstances, instructors should modify the content of their business communication courses, expanding subject and case studies beyond American business situations into the international sphere. Such modification and expansion will prevent alienation among international students. American-born individuals also need to be able to understand the values of other societies.

As a result, classroom subject matter becomes more timely and relevant, and this enables the international student to relate to a degree.[5] This also "enables the professor to lead the student to an understanding of the value system, belief systems, social change, and humanistic and social concepts which are dependent upon communication."[6]

The exchange of faculty members between universities and the exchange of personnel among multinational corporations identify another concern for the communication instructor. Universities are exchanging "visiting professors" with universities of other countries. Professors in the United States go to other countries and deal with students of completely different cultural backgrounds. Similarly, professors of other countries travel to the United States and experience similar cultural adjustments. In business, managers and technicians are also exchanged so that technical know-how can be transferred.[7] Corporations have jointly developed cultural, multicultural, international, and technical communication systems and systems hardware. American businesses, as well as those of other nations, have heavily funded institutions and have developed company languages that are not only translatable but also mesh into computer languages.

Additionally, students trained in a technologically advanced country return to their technologically developing countries, where they want to apply their knowledge. The techniques, typical of a mechanized society, do not apply to their home cultural system or to the technological capacity. The "trained" graduates experience cultural shock in the home setting. Students' failure to apply the fundamental techniques in their own systems proves that their instructors did not teach them from a conceptual perspective—but rather they have been taught to duplicate the rudiments of the programs or the systems of the host country. A slightly more participative variation in the educational concepts or perceptions of the host country would provide international study with adaptable or even creative solutions rather than rote duplication. As students solve problems from their country's point of view, they do apply the technological capacities where mechanization permits; but, from their viewpoint, they can begin to introduce change through conceptual planning and developing.

Teaching Considerations

In order to teach intercultural and international communication effectively, a communication teacher should consider the following: similarities in human communication capabilities, differences in business and management approaches, methods of adapting techniques and activities in the classroom, and evidence of empirical research in communicating in second- or third-language circumstances.

Similarities in Human Capabilities

Innate intelligence and motor abilities are enhanced by diet, environment, and educational opportunities. If proper conditions are provided, people learn equally well. Basic emotions and feelings are different in cultures, yet they remain equally strong and valid. People must satisfy their most critical needs. Piaget's concept of stages of intellectual development,[8] Bruner's concept of growth,[9] and operant conditioning of learning[10] apply to students regardless of their nationality. The psychology of motivating workers and of managing people and materials are similar in theory regardless of their national origin. Differences are evident, however, when cultural acceptance or rejection is based both on perceived and suggested values. Nepalese and Dutch advertisements seek to persuade their customers just as American advertising does. However, the visuals, language, and delivery will differ vastly in each country.

Labor strikes may be discussed in classrooms, but in cultures where strikes are not permitted, application is limited.

Differences in Management and Business Approaches

In spite of the similarities, there are also many differences in business managing styles and in motivation styles. Educational psychologists have recognized individual life styles and unique actions of people and believe they are caused by environmental and ethnic "settings."[11] The settings or "customs" become evident through studies of real business situations. Hildebrandt conducted an intensive study interviewing and visiting parent and "daughter" companies located in Germany and the United States.[12] The study showed that such personal problems as social adjustment of spouse, language problems involved in shopping, school problems for the children—all had to be solved before the German expatriate could work with assurance and forget about the distractions and unhappiness of home.[13] The same study revealed a major difference in oral and written communication between Americans and Germans. In oral discussions, the Germans were, by cultural heritage, well organized and well prepared. In written reports, Germans were also thorough.

Differences, however, were encountered. The formality of people to people exchange was important. Germans did not like being called by first names by American counterparts because in their country, titles were added to the last name as a status symbol, but more importantly as a sign of respect.[14] Job mobility was another important difference. Among American business representatives, mobility and flexibility are regarded as a source of experience, but in Germany, as well as in other cultures, mobility from one job to another shows a thin loyalty to an organization and a lack of dedication or commitment.

A study reviewing differences between Japanese and American companies indicated that the Japanese were less reliant on written communication. Yet face-to-face interactions initiated by peers was not as important as originally believed.[15] Japanese firms used written communication less often for routine matters, thereby significantly lowering the overall use of written communication. Abegglen, Yoshina, and Johnson and Ouchi all supported the same findings indicating that Japanese managers have the ability to communicate quickly and easily up and down the hierarchy.[16, 17, 18]

Other interesting European cultural differences illustrate further the need for a more flexible and relevant classroom content and instructional procedures. Dual signatures are common business procedures—yet in the United States it may be considered an affront or a sign of lack of delegation or trust. Inordinate and lengthy details are required in written reports, whereas in the United States less detailed data—geared to final decision making and performance are valued. Status distance, subordination, and position appear more important to the European than to the American—though each needs reinforcement for security and for authorization. Other examples are available, but these illustrate well how value judgments may differ and how the accompanying communication messages and delivery styles will likewise differ.

Methods of Adapting Techniques and Activities in the Classroom

The concern for teaching intercultural and international communication is not limited to a teacher of communication; it is a concern of all teachers dealing with intercultural topics and international students. Of the teaching methods that have evolved through many decades, the influence of behaviorism dominates communication pedagogy today, but a mix of methodologies have had an effect as well.[19] Such methods as teaching students to organize their ideas and facts (idealism); teaching rules of grammar and punctuation (classic realism); using objectives, testing, programmed learning (scientific realism); learning by doing rather than thinking, experimenting with accepted theories, and incorporating problem-solving techniques rather than logical inquiry (pragmatism); and teaching students that they will be held responsible by the business world for their acts (existentialism)[20] are evidence of educational philosophies. Current philosophies might be characterized as a "ragbag with B. F. Skinner holding the bag."[21]

Today, involving participative curricular patterns is more suitable because it involves flexible teaching methods and approaches, uses materials as reinforcement, and adapts educational equipment.[22] As is true in education, combining approaches in teaching multicultural communication is also appropriate. Effective teaching involves varying techniques and methods to meet the immediate learning needs of the moment.

The conference method, laboratory method, language-structure method, message-processing method, and message-channeling method permit technical specialities to be utilized in any communication training.[23]

Providing other learning experiences both in and out of the classroom is essential for students of writing and communication. Frequently, English is the second or third language; therefore, students from other countries have additional learning needs. Difficulties with listening, meanings, and rhythm styles are evident. To meet both the initial input or instruction needs and then to provide supplemental facts or reinforcement, instructors should also consider styles of organization as well as facilities and self-help programs for language review and remedial learning. Reinforcement and additional grading options will also be necessary in order to secure an acceptable "version" of a written assignment.

Large-group instruction is typically not appropriate for international students. Although grouping styles vary from the traditional 25 students per section to large lecture sessions with 250 students, international students become intimidated in these too large and too formal sessions and need time to meet on a one-to-one basis with the teacher. Not only must the students have access to an instructor in order to ask questions or to ask for semantic interpretation, they must be involved in peer growth and small-group growth sessions to develop their oral and conversational abilities.

Small-group instruction can be supplemented with a learning laboratory or a communication clinic. International students are diligent workers and will complete both prescribed as well as individualized concept reviews or programmed grammar reviews designed to improve their basic skills. Students need to have time to sit with a proctor out of class and to write and rewrite their assignments. Graduate students studying in the United States have sound education backgrounds which are generally based on British or other European systems. Academically promising students are selected from a number of applicants. They generally have high abilities—both verbal and mathematical. These students pass English proficiency tests, but their knowledge of the language is based on the "grammar approach." More than likely they are very good in grammar usage but have difficulty with meanings. They translate their thoughts from their language to English. Articles, connectives, plurals are occasionally misused.

Because international students understand concepts well but remain tied by an interpretation difference or by a sentence-structure problem, they respond well to sound-on-slide presentations, they see and can conceptualize the sound-on-page illustrations also. Small-group discussions also permit them to have an input and help them overcome their shyness at speaking or asking questions.

Reinforcement techniques and learning techniques assist international students in undergraduate writing and communication courses. Modeling permits students to compare gradients of style and a series of finished models. They must be encouraged not to mimic or paraphrase the models. Be certain too that they know which models are not appropriate and why. Too frequently the negative concept is stressed to the extent that it is overlearned. Mapping is an additional technique that is important to in-class development. Frequently an instructor or student can provide well-selected, well-written topic sentences, and then other students provide appropriate second or third sentences and action ending paragraphs.

International students must be permitted to rewrite. They are sensitive to their mistakes and will correct concepts or fundamentals as soon as they understand the rule or concept.

Research Summarizing Language Teaching

An understanding of second or third languages and their teaching considerations helps an instructor. Lee suggests that grammar, situations, and motions are starting points in the teaching of foreign language, but they should be within the framework given by knowledge about the learners.[24] Ghadessy suggested that error analysis of compositions written by the students with the same background can be a good technique of teaching a foreign language at the collegiate freshman level.[25] Haneda points out that the source or base language also makes a difference. He says that most languages in America and Europe belong to the same Indo-European family with their Greco-Roman and Judeo-Christian influences, and so language should not pose as great a problem to multinational companies based in American and European environments as it does to companies based in Japan and other Oriental countries.[26] Hildebrandt also stated that language problems between American and European companies exist less at upper levels (board of directors or executive committees) than at lower levels.[27]

Communications for international business contain more legal and technical elements than the psychological strategy as found in American-style business communications.[28] The International Chamber of Commerce and other organizations of lawyers or businesspeople have made some efforts toward unification of trade terms and practice.[29] But the rules are getting out of date and further efforts are required for the worldwide unification of business practice and terminology.

In a study conducted with Mexican participants, Eure concluded that principles such as planned presentations, positive emphases, conversational tone, adaptation, and reader concern have validity when used in cross-cultural situations.[30] These students formed a positive mental image of the company by reading letters using "accepted principles" and a negative image of the company when not using them.[31]

The implication of the studies concerning second- or third-language instruction and the use of languages in business shows that all bilingual students have language differences. Communication instructors should recognize these differences when possible.

Conclusions

International and multicultural students in classrooms and at work in the United States are numerous. A concern for in-class instruction and for multicultural understanding and communication indicates a need for effective teaching, the transfer of meaning in messages, the use of a variety of content in classrooms and a selection of methods and approaches. Classroom teachers, especially those at colleges and universities, should be mediators between students from other countries and their American students. Teachers need to understand and empathize with their language and their value differences.

Teachers of multicultural communication should consider the similarities and differences between their students' cultures. Other countries have developed business and administrative practices and will always be unique. Other countries have also developed their own management styles, communication styles and decision-making styles. They are likely to be different from those practiced in the United States.

Consequently, communication teachers should recognize these factors and help international students learn conceptually so that they are able to make their own decisions when they return to their countries. This lessens cultural shock and permits a problem-solving approach to management.

Flexible and participative classroom approaches, methods, and techniques are suggested. Activities, including small-group work, individual guidance, reinforcement centers, and adaptations of learning principles to teaching machines, are helpful to students with more than one language base. Instructors should be encouraged to study research and to accept and adapt pertinent learning discoveries. These permit a caring and involved teaching and learning experience.

Notes

1. Jack D. Eure, Jr., Applicability of American Written Business Communication Principles Across Cultural Boundaries in Mexico,'' *Journal of Business Communication,* vol. 14, no. 1 (fall 1976), p. 51.
2. Ibid.
3. Herbert W. Hildebrandt, "Cultural Communication Problems of Foreign Business Personnel in the United States,'' *Journal of Business Communication,* vol. 13, no. 1 (fall 1975), p. 13.
4. Saburo Haneda, "On International Cooperation for Business Communication Studies,'' *Journal of Business Communication,* vol. 13, no. 3 (spring 1976), p. 26.
5. William P. Boyd and Thomas H. Inman, ''A Historical Development of Business Communication,'' *NBEA Yearbook,* no. 14 (Washington, D.C.: National Business Education Association, 1976), p. 136.
6. Ibid.
7. Hildebrandt, p. 13.
8. Jean Piaget, *The Origins of Intelligence in Children,* translated by Margaret Cook (New York: International Universities Press, 1952).
9. J. S. Bruner, *Toward a Theory of Instruction* (Cambridge: Harvard University Press, 1966).
10. N. L. Gage and David C. Berliner, *Educational Psychology* (Chicago: Rand McNally College Publishing Co., 1965), p. 7.
11. Ibid., p. 8.
12. Hildebrandt, p. 13.
13. Ibid.
14. Ibid., p. 16.
15. Richard Tanner Pascale, "Communication and Decision-making Across Cultures: Japanese and American Comparisons.'' *Administrative Science Quarterly,* vol. 23 (March 1978), p. 108.
16. James C. Abegglen, *The Japanese Factory* (Glencoe, Ill.: Free Press, 1959).
17. Michael Yoshino, *Japan's Managerial System: Tradition and Innovation* (Cambridge: MIT Press, 1968).
18. R. Johnson and W. Ouchi, ''Made in America: Under Japanese Management,'' *Harvard Business Review,* vol. 5 (1974), pp. 61–69.
19. Jeremiah J. Sullivan, "The Importance of a Philosophical Mix in Teaching Business Communication,'' *Journal of Business Communication* (1978), p. 30.
20. Ibid., pp. 30–33.
21. Ibid., p. 33.
22. Homer Cox and Larry D. Hartman, "Issues in Teaching Business Communication,'' *NBEA Yearbook,* National Business Education Association, no. 14, (Washington, D.C., 1976), p. 217.

23. Ibid., p. 221.
24. W. R. Lee, "What Type of Syllabus for the Teaching of English as a Foreign or Second Language?" *International Review of Applied Linguistics,* vol. 15, no. 3 (1977), p. 246.
25. Mohsen Ghadessy, "An Error Analysis of the Writings of Iranian Freshmen Students Learning English—A Pilot Study," *IRAL,* vol. 14 (1976), p. 81.
26. Haneda, p. 29.
27. Hildebrandt, p. 20.
28. Haneda, p. 25.
29. Ibid., p. 28.
30. Eure, p. 62.
31. Ibid., p. 51.

Bibliography

ABEGGLEN, JAMES. C. *The Japanese Factory*. Glencoe, Ill.: Free Press, 1959.

BRUNER, J. S. *Toward a Theory of Instruction*. Cambridge: Harvard University Press, 1966.

HANEDA, SABURO, and HIROSHUKE SHIMA. "Japanese Communication Behavior as Reflected in Letter Writing." *Journal of Business Communication,* vol. 29, no. 1 (winter 1982), pp. 20–32.

HILDEBRANDT, HERBERT W. "Cultural Communication Problems of Foreign Business Personnel in the United States." *Journal of Business Communication,* vol. 13, no. 1 (fall 1975), pp. 13–24.

HILDEBRANDT, HERBERT W., et al. *International Business Communication: Theory, Practice, Teaching, Throughout the World.* (Champaign, Ill.: University of Michigan and American Business Communication Assn., 1981).

JOHNSON, R., and OUCHI, W. "Made in America: Under Japanese Management." *Harvard Business Review,* vol. 5 (1974), pp. 61–69.

MURRAY, ROBERT STUART. "Interpersonal Communication Skills in Task-Oriented and Relationship-Oriented Leaders." Dissertation completed at University of Georgia, 1977.

PIAGET, JEAN. *The Origins of Intelligence in Children*. Translated by Margaret Cook. New York: International Universities Press, 1952.

SULLIVAN, JEREMIAH J., and NAOKI KAMEDA. "The Concept of Profit and Japanese-American Business Communication Problems." *Journal of Business Communication,* vol. 29, no. 1 (winter 1982), pp. 33–39.

TIMM, PAUL R., and BRENT D. PETERSON. *People at Work: Human Relations in Organizations*. St. Paul, Minn.: West Publishing Co., 1981.

YOSHINO, MICHAEL. *Japan's Managerial System: Tradition and Innovation*. Cambridge, Mass.: MIT Press, 1968.

Index

Index of Contributors